GNOSTIC TRUTH
AND CHRISTIAN HERESY

In memory of my father
John Black Logan
1904–1987
who first kindled in me
a love of theology

GNOSTIC TRUTH
AND CHRISTIAN HERESY

A Study in the History of Gnosticism

ALASTAIR H. B. LOGAN

Published in Great Britain by
T&T Clark Ltd
59 George Street
Edinburgh EH2 2LQ
Scotland

This edition published under license from T&T Clark Ltd by
Hendrickson Publishers, Inc.
P.O. Box 3473
Peabody, Massachusetts 01961-3473

First published 1996

Library of Congress Cataloging-in-Publication Data
Logan, Alastair H. B.
    Gnostic truth and Christian heresy : a study in the history of
Gnosticism /
    Alastair H. B. Logan.
        p.   cm.
    Includes bibliographical references and index.
    ISBN 1-56563-243-5
    1. Gnosticism.   2. Apocryphon of John—Criticism, interpretation,
etc. I. Title.
    BT1390.L64 1996
    273'.1—dc20   95-52625
                                                                CIP

Typeset by Waverley Typesetters, Galashiels
Printed and bound in Great Britain by Bell & Bain Ltd, Glasgow

Contents

Acknowledgements

This book is the result of many years' labour and of the encouragement of a few key people. It began life in the late 1960s as a doctoral thesis at St Andrews University under the genial fatherly eye of R. McL. Wilson, to whom I owe a great debt. Not only was he a demon for detail and a stickler for accuracy, but he was one of the team, based at Claremont and led by James M. Robinson, responsible for the English translation of the Nag Hammadi Library, and thus had draft translations of all my key texts, to which he kindly allowed me access. I had first come across the Nag Hammadi Library in a formative year at Harvard Divinity School, 1968–9, an *annus mirabilis* for me as for so many. There I was privileged to participate in the extremely high-powered postgraduate Seminar on the Nag Hammadi texts led by Helmut Koester and George MacRae. Several present luminaries of the Gnostic and New Testament scene were members and, like them, I owe an incalculable debt to George MacRae in particular, who showed great courtesy and tolerance despite my lack of background and expertise, and inspired me to tackle as a research topic the *Apocryphon of John*.

The work of relating the various versions of the *Apocryphon* proved a mammoth task in a field littered with abortive and incomplete attempts, but despite the demands of a full-time teaching post and the arrival of twin daughters, it was completed in 1980. Then it lay dormant, to me an enormous and shapeless mass, until the arrival in Exeter of a new colleague, Ian Markham, an expert in a very different field, who bravely asked to read it and encouraged me to take it up again, since he felt it contained something important. Fired by his enthusiasm, I looked at it afresh, and began to rewrite, discovering in the process the germ of this book, a new way of looking at the phenomenon which kept opening up fresh vistas and proved enormously exciting. Thanks to the award of a Small Personal Research Grant from the British

Academy, which I here most gratefully acknowledge, and the support of my colleagues in the Theology Department, I was able to spend the summer term of 1992 in Oxford doing the major research required. There I must acknowledge the help and kindness shown by the Principal and Bursar of Mansfield College in arranging accommodation and making me a Visiting Fellow of the College. There too I enjoyed the stimulating company of a group of ordinands of the United Reformed Church, Pauline, Janet, David and Peter, who cheered me in my more solitary moments.

On return to Exeter progress proved much slower, but the book was eventually completed with financial help from the Research Fund of Exeter University, enabling me to purchase a word-processor and speed up the process considerably, and by continued cheerful pressure from Professor David Catchpole, my most understanding Head of Department, my colleagues and not least my long-suffering wife Kathryn and children, Jacqueline, Sarah and Roderick, who have lived under the shadow of this topic for so long. Finally I must acknowledge the generous interest of Dr Michael M. Waldstein of the University of Notre Dame, Indiana, in sending me a draft copy of a synopsis of the versions of the *Apocryphon of John* which has proved a godsend.

ALASTAIR H. B. LOGAN
Exeter
Advent 1994

Abbreviations

AA	*Apocalypse of Adam*
AAA	*Acta Apostolorum Apocrypha*
ADAIK	Abhandlungen des Deutschen Archäologischen Instituts Kairo
AG	Analecta Gregoriana
AGSU	Arbeiten zur Geschichte des späterer Judentums und des Urchristentums
AJ	*Apocryphon of John*
AJP	*American Journal of Philology*
APS	Acta Philologica Suecana
ATD	Acta Theologica Danica
B	Berlin Coptic Papyrus 8502
BA	*Biblical Archaeologist*
BBA	Berliner Byzantinische Arbeiten
BCNH	Bibilothèque copte de Nag Hammadi
BO	*Bibliotheca Orientalis*
BWANT	Beiträge zur Wissenschaft vom Alten und Neuen Testament
BZNW	Beihefte zur *ZNW*
C	Cairo Nag Hammadi Codex
CBQ	*Catholic Biblical Quarterly*
CCSL	Corpus Christianorum: Series Latina
CH	*Church History*
CH	Corpus Hermeticum
CHSB	Corpus Scriptorum Historiae Byzantinae
CSCO	Corpus Scriptorum Christianorum Orientalium
CSEL	Corpus Scriptorum Ecclesiasticorum Latinorum

EPRO	Études préliminaires aux religions orientales dans l'Empire romain
ET	English Translation
Eug	*Eugnostos*
FRLANT	Forschungen zur Religion und Literatur des Alten und Neuen Testaments
GCS	Die griechischen christlichen Schriftsteller der ersten Jahrhunderte
GE	*Gospel of the Egyptians*
HA	*Hypostasis of the Archons*
HTR	*Harvard Theological Review*
JA	*Journal Asiatique*
JbAC	Jahrbuch für Antike und Christentum
JEH	*Journal of Ecclesiastical History*
JETS	*Journal of the Evangelical Theological Society*
JNES	*Journal of Near Eastern Studies*
JSNT	*Journal for the Study of the New Testament*
JSOT	*Journal for the Study of the Old Testament*
JTS	*Journal of Theological Studies*
LR	Long recension of the *Apocryphon of John*
LTP	*Laval théologique et philosophique*
MPG	Migne, Patrologia Graeca
MPL	Migne, Patrologia Latina
MGWJ	*Monatschrift für Geschichte und Wissenschaft des Judentums*
NedTTs	*Nederlands theologisch tijdschrift*
NHLE	*The Nag Hammadi Library in English*
NHS	Nag Hammadi Studies
NorTT	*Norsk Teologisk Tidsskrift*
NovT	*Novum Testamentum*
NTA	*New Testament Apocrypha*
NTS	*New Testament Studies*
OC	*Oriens Christianus*
OW	*On the Origin of the World*
PGL	A *Patristic Greek Lexicon*, ed. G. W. H. Lampe

PGM	Papyri Graecae Magicae, ed. K. Preisendanz
PP	*La Parola del Passato*
PS	*Pistis Sophia*
PTS	Patristische Texte und Studien
RAC	Reallexikon für Antike und Christentum
RE	*Realencyklopädie der klassischen Altertumswissenschaft,* ed. A. Pauly, G. Wissowa et al.
REA	*Revue des études augustiniennes*
RevScRel	*Revue des sciences religieuses*
RGG	Die Religion in Geschichte und Gegenwart
RMM	*Revue de metaphysique et de morale*
RSR	*Recherches de science religieuse*
RSPT	*Revue des sciences philosophiques et théologiques*
RThPh	*Revue de théologie et de philosophie*
SAC	Studies in Antiquity and Christianity
SBT	Studies in Biblical Theology
SC	Sources chrétiennes
SGM	Sources gnostiques et manichéennes
SHR	Studies in the History of Religions
SJC	*Sophia of Jesus Christ*
SJLA	Studies in Judaism in Late Antiquity
SPAW	Sitzungsberichte der kgl. preussischen Akademie der Wissenschaften zu Berlin
SR	Short recension of the *Apocryphon of John*
ST	*Studia Theologica*
TLZ	*Theologische Literaturzeitung*
TP	*Trimorphic Protennoia*
Tru	*Theologische Rundschau*
TU	Texte und Untersuchungen zur Geschichte der altchristlichen Literatur
TZ	*Theologische Zeitschrift*
VC	*Vigiliae Christianae*
WMANT	Wissenschaftliche Monographien zum Alten und Neuen Testaments
WUNT	Wissenschaftliche Untersuchungen zum Neuen Testament

WZKM	*Wiener Zeitschrift für die Kunde des Morgenlandes*
ZNW	*Zeitschrift für die neutestamentliche Wissenschaft*
ZPE	*Zeitschrift für Papyrologie und Epigraphik*
ZRGG	*Zeitschrift für Religions- und Geistesgeschichte*
ZTK	*Zeitschrift für Theologie und Kirche*

Introduction

The discovery in 1945–6 of the Nag Hammadi Library of Coptic Gnostic texts[1] has revolutionized our traditional understanding of Gnosticism, which had seen it as in essence a Christian heresy. This interpretation goes back to the first Christian heresiologists, the early Christian Fathers, particularly Irenaeus, Bishop of Lyons (*c.* 140–200 CE), writing around 180,[2] but was made intellectually respectable by the great German church historian Adolf von Harnack (1851–1930), who saw Gnosticism as the 'thorough-going (*akute*) Hellenisation of Christianity'.[3] Such a judgement depended, of course, on the evidence then available, which consisted almost entirely of the accounts of the Christian heresiologists such as, in addition to Irenaeus (and his predecessor Justin Martyr (*ob.* 166), the first to write a work against heresies, since alas lost), Hippolytus of Rome (*c.* 160–235), Tertullian of Carthage (*c.* 150–223), Clement of Alexandria (140/150–211/215), Epiphanius of Salamis in Cyprus (315–403) and Theodoret of Cyrrhus (395–466).[4] But they, in their turn, appear to have been largely dependent on Irenaeus (and Justin) and to have developed particular stereotyped lines of argument, seeing Gnosticism as a plethora of distinct sects, each with its own system, inspired by the Devil and Greek philosophy and deriving from the mysterious figure of Simon Magus of Acts 8.[5] What direct evidence did survive was either in the fragments preserved by the Fathers (and thus suspect as subject to their heresiological concerns and tendentious interpretations) or in a few late works in Coptic such as the *Pistis Sophia* of the Askew Codex in the British Library and the two *Books of Jeu* and *Untitled Treatise* from the Bruce Codex in the Bodleian.[6] Both codexes have been known to the scholarly world since 1778, but the treatises in them appear to represent a rather late and decadent form of Gnosticism, and so did not seem to offer much help in the matter of the origins of the phenomenon.

Tomb inscription of Flavia Sophe, Rome, third century. *Courtesy of the Museo Nazionale Romano.*

More promising might have been the discovery of the Berlin Coptic Codex (Papyrus Berolinensis 8502 = B) reported by Carl Schmidt in 1896.[7] It contained the *Gospel of Mary*, the *Apocryphon of John* (whose first, theogonic part represents a striking parallel to – or according to Schmidt the actual original of – the 'Gnostic' system summarized by Irenaeus in his *Adversus haereses* 1.29), the *Sophia of Jesus Christ* and the *Acts of Peter* (the last not a Gnostic work at all). (Plate 1.) But because of a chapter of accidents this most significant collection was not to appear in print until 1955.[8] However, this did mean that the editor, Walter Till, was able to have access to one of the Nag Hammadi codices (Cairensis Gnosticus (= C) III), which contained versions of the *Apocryphon* and the *Sophia of Jesus Christ*.

Thus it was only with the final publication, after another even more tortuous saga, of the complete Nag Hammadi Library, first in the Facsimile Edition[9] and then in the English translation under the editorship of J. M. Robinson, that scholars could begin to assimilate the new primary evidence and attempt to evaluate the claims of the Christian heresiologists, independently of their interpretative framework. In fact the first attempt to do this and to demonstrate the lack of correlation between the Nag Hammadi Gnostic texts and the accounts of the heresiologists had been Frederik Wisse's 1971 article.[10] Wisse effectively undermined attempts to continue to use the traditional categories of inter-pretation and of identification in terms of particular sects, suggesting that the only factor that appeared to unify the Nag Hammadi texts was a developed asceticism.[11] But nevertheless the attempt was made by Hans-Martin Schenke in 1974 to identify a number of tractates as 'Sethian' in terms of their content, as representing in varying degrees 'one and the same gnostic system' (the *Apocryphon of John*, Irenaeus *Adv. haer.* 1.29, the *Hypostasis of the Archons* (C II,*4*), the *Gospel of the Egyptians* (C III,*2*; IV,*2*), the *Apocalypse of Adam* (C V,*5*), the *Three Steles of Seth* (C VII,*5*), *Zostrianos* (C VIII,*1*), *Melchisedek* (C IX,*1*), the *Thought of Norea* (C IX,*2*), and *Trimorphic Protennoia* (C XIII,*1*)).[12] The fundamental dogma of Sethianism, according to Schenke, was the self-understanding of these Gnostics as the seed of heavenly Seth.[13]

Now one of the implications of such an analysis was that the Sethian system, as far as it could be treated as a single phenomenon, represented a non- and indeed pre-Christian form of Gnosticism, but one profoundly influenced by Jewish motifs, in fact, a form of heterodox Judaism or Jewish sectarianism of the

first centuries BCE and CE. This thesis of the likely Jewish origins of
Gnosticism had been developed particularly by Gilles Quispel who,
in a seminal article in 1954, argued for the Jewish origins of the
Gnostic figure of the heavenly Anthropos (and thus of Gnosticism
as a Jewish phenomenon), over against the claims of Bousset and
Reitzenstein that the heavenly Anthropos/Redeemer was of
Iranian provenance (and thus that Gnosticism was a non-Christian
religion deriving from the Orient).[14] Other scholars took up this
theme, such as R. McL. Wilson, R. M. Grant, Jean Daniélou,
George MacRae, Kurt Rudolph and Birger Pearson,[15] although it
was criticized by some, including Hans Jonas who had
revolutionized the study of Gnosticism as a serious religious and
philosophical phenomenon by his existential analysis of it.[16] But
such was the emerging consensus, buttressed by the careful
exploratory work of Martin Krause who had provisionally
distinguished three types of texts in the Nag Hammadi Library:
(1) non-, perhaps indeed pre-Christian works; (2) non-Christian
works later Christianized; and (3) purely Christian Gnostic works,[17]
that a major international conference on Gnosticism could be
held (in Yale in 1978) divided into two sections, one dealing with
Valentinianism (i.e. Christian Gnostics, Krause's third category),
the other with Schenke's 'Sethians' (i.e. groups included in
Krause's first and second categories), despite Wisse's protests
about their 'elusiveness'.[18] In all this the general view of the
Apocryphon of John (and thus of Irenaeus' account in *Adv. haer.*
1.29, which was taken to be a summary of a version of it) was that
it represented a Christianization of a previous Jewish–Gnostic
'Sethian' treatise.[19]

More recent contributions such as articles by Pearson and J. D.
Turner have attempted to confirm the Jewish origins of the
'Sethian' sect and its leading ideas, and in the case of the latter,
suggest a literary history of 'Sethian' Gnosticism from its origins
in a non-Christian baptismal sect of the first centuries BCE and CE
by way of increasing Christianization (the 'Sethian–Ophite' system
described by Irenaeus in *Adv. haer.* 1.30 is taken as an early
example, combined with the *Apocryphon* and *Adv. haer.* 1.29) and
Platonization, as found in the late forms of 'Sethian' Gnosticism
(e.g. *Zostrianos, Marsanes, Allogenes,* etc.).[20] This general approach
seems to have been widely accepted, as has Gedaliahu Stroumsa's
particular attempt to derive its characteristic mythology from
speculations on Gen 6:1–4 as answers to the question of the origin
of evil.[21]

But such a scenario has recently been radically questioned by Simone Pétrement, one of the few scholars who has held out from the beginning for understanding Gnosticism as a Christian phenomenon.[22] She has argued at great length and in detail that Gnosticism cannot be understood in its essence apart from the idea of God as entirely unknown up to the coming of Christ as the Pauline and Johannine Son who reveals the Father; that its essential features and key ideas derive primarily from Pauline and Johannine concepts (and from the enigmatic figure of Apollos); that the heretics from Simon Magus on were Christians, the Gnostics proper appearing from Saturninus onward; that the Gnostics (or Sethians) of Irenaeus *Adv. haer.* 1.29 and the *Apocryphon* (this she considers a trump card) derive from the Valentinians and not vice versa as Irenaeus was thought to indicate, and that the Nag Hammadi and other texts claimed to be non- and pre-Christian (as well as other non-Christian forms of Gnosis, e.g. Hermetism and Mandaeism) are in fact, on closer analysis, later than and influenced by Christianity.[23]

Finally, from the perspective not of doctrine and mythology but of ritual and liturgy, J.-M. Sevrin has examined those 'Sethian' texts of Schenke which seem to display evidence of an initiatory rite of baptism, whether spiritual or actual (*Apocryphon of John, Trimorphic Protennoia, Gospel of the Egyptians, Apocalypse of Adam, Zostrianos, Untitled Treatise* of the Bruce Codex, and *Melchisedek*) and argued (*a*) that such an actual baptismal rite as the reception of the saving *gnosis* did exist if always understood as both an actual and a spiritual rite, with a later tendency to spiritualize it; (*b*) that it was of Jewish origin and inspiration but was later superficially Christianized; (*c*) that it combined two independent mythological characteristics: the Barbeliote triad (Father, Mother, Son) and the Sethian vision of history (the origin of Seth and his seed and his triple parousias to save it); and (*d*) that a genealogy of this family of texts presupposing such a rite can be suggested, with the *Apocryphon* as the oldest, the *Apocalypse of Adam* the earliest Sethian document, the *Trimorphic Protennoia* as influenced by the *Apocryphon,* and the *Gospel of the Egyptians* as a syncretistic anthology of all these traditions, containing a baptismal dossier as its final section.[24]

The striking thing that emerges from all this is the central role played by the *Apocryphon of John* and the related texts from Irenaeus (*Adv. haer.* 1.29 and 30). They have played a key part in the various debates and attempts to trace the origins and development of

Gnosticism. Irenaeus' catalogue of heresies culminating in the 'Gnostics' of 1.29 and 30 still forms the basis, if treated with some scepticism and reserve, for attempts to reconstruct Gnostic origins, sects and developments,[25] and the facts that there are no less than four versions (two in a long recension (= LR): C II,*1* and IV,*1*, and two in a short (= SR): B 8502,*2* and C III,*1*) of the *Apocryphon*, that it appears to be echoed in other texts from Nag Hammadi and elsewhere,[26] and that it is perhaps the only uncontested example of a Nag Hammadi Gnostic text known to the Church Fathers,[27] and one which seems to be so comparatively early, all go to confirm the significance of this particular constellation of documents and the myth or myths they contain. Although as great an expert as Bentley Layton has admitted that no single telling of what he dubs 'the classic gnostic myth' has survived, he thinks one may be reflected in the *Apocryphon* and the *Gospel of the Egyptians* (and Irenaeus' account of Saturninus), and his own reconstruction depends largely on the *Apocryphon*.[28]

Thus it would seem that a careful examination of the myth or myths, system or systems underlying the *Apocryphon*, Irenaeus *Adv. haer.* 1.29 and 30 and the related 'Sethian' texts from Nag Hammadi as identified by Schenke, Pearson and Turner,[29] and in the light of Sevrin's valuable perspective, by means of all the main techniques developed to deal with the Gnostic phenomenon, literary-critical, existential, *motivgeschichtlich*, theological and *religionsgeschichtlich*, might help to answer the fundamental questions regarding the origins and development of Gnosticism, in particular of its so-called 'Sethian' form, which is central to the issues of Gnosticism as a non- and pre-Christian phenomenon, and of the derivation of the Gnostics (i.e. the 'Sethians') from the Valentinians or vice versa.

In this enquiry my basic presuppositions, which can only be justified by the success of the analysis and reconstruction offered by the work as a whole, are, *first, that the form or forms of Gnosticism found in the so-called 'Sethian' texts cannot be understood apart from Christianity,* and that the attempts to derive the phenomenon from Jewish sectarianism break down both because of the lack of evidence of the existence of the Jewish sects and heterodox opinions that require to be posited, and because of the lack of any coherent rationale for the revolutionary position adopted by these Gnostics. Many scholars have demonstrated the undoubted existence of Jewish ideas in the Gnostic, particularly the 'Sethian', texts, but none, in my opinion, have been able to derive Gnosticism directly from Judaism with any degree of plausibility. Jonas is surely correct here in his criticism of Quispel,[30] and Pétrement has made a strong case for understanding the heart of Gnosticism as the revelation by Jesus Christ of the God who was previously entirely unknown, which makes the claim of revelation or revealer figures prior to, or apart from, Christ redundant.

Now if one is justified in seeing 'Sethian' Gnosticism as a basically Christian phenomenon, but one that has a claim to being a religion in its own right, with its distinctive understandings of God, the world, humanity and salvation, and its cultus and forms of communal life, *my second presupposition is that one is justified in seeking both a central core of ideas, a myth or myths based on and concretely expressed in a rite of initiation as a projection of Gnostic experience,* which holds it together, *and in treating it as a valid form (or forms) of interpreting Christianity.* Thus even those Gnostic texts which seem most remote from that (Christian) myth (e.g. *Zostrianos* and *Allogenes*) can only be understood in the light of some presupposed form of it, and as a corollary, examination of features of the contemporary Christianity of the 'Great Church' in its varied forms, including fringe figures and the apocryphal and pseudepigraphical literature, may well cast considerable light on Gnostic texts and features. Some reference will thus be made to such material where apposite.

It follows from this that I do not find helpful the distinction, proposed by the Messina Colloquium and accepted by some, between elements and concepts which can be seen as either pre- or proto-Gnostic, which have not yet developed into the full-blown form.[31] Nor do I find helpful the distinction between Gnosis as a more general religious phenomenon prevalent in the Near East from around the second century BCE (a term and understanding preferred by German scholars and by many Americans influenced by them) and Gnosticism as the developed form or forms of the second century CE onwards (a concept more acceptable to British scholars). On my understanding there must be at the heart of the Gnostic phenomenon some form of myth or myths, some unified way of seeing the world, arising from genuine experience, often visionary, on the part of a religious genius or geniuses (such as e.g. Basilides, Valentinus, Marcion, Elchasai, Mani) and in relation to an existing rite of initiation. It will be my contention that behind the myths and systems of the 'Gnostics' of Irenaeus 1.29 and 30, as developed by the *Apocryphon of John* and dependent texts and variants, we can identify a basic pattern of theogony, cosmogony, anthropogony, soteriology and eschatology, unified by its relation to a rite of initiation, which is the work of such a religious genius or geniuses, and that, against Pétrement, it was they who inspired perhaps the greatest of the Christian Gnostics, Valentinus and his school. Unlike Pétrement, too, I am not claiming to explain the whole variegated phenomenon of Gnosticism in terms of Christianity; my more modest proposal is that this most striking and significant myth and its dependents and variants cannot be understood without such a premise.

My final presupposition is to assume that Irenaeus' summary in Adv. haer. *1.29 is closest to the original form of the Christian Gnostic myth of Father, Mother and Son, and that it underwent progressive development including 'Sethianization',* until it emerged in the latest form of the *Apocryphon,* the long recension. Such a hypothesis not only makes more sense of Schenke's claimed 'Sethian' constellation of texts by showing, for example, how texts which make no mention of heavenly Seth still belong in it, and explains the persistence and true Christian significance of recurring heavenly figures and ritual elements, but reveals the secondary character of key texts in the argument for a non- and even pre-Christian Gnosticism (e.g. the *Apocalypse of Adam* and the *Paraphrase of Shem*), and relates Gnostic developments and concerns to contemporary 'orthodox' Christian ones. The 'classic' Gnostic myth underlying Irenaeus 1.29 and the *Apocryphon* could not but develop differently from the 'orthodox' version by its downgrading of the Old Testament, its Creator God and his prophets, its preference of the heavenly Son/Christ of Paul, John and Hebrews to the earthly Jesus of the Synoptics, and its focus on baptism and chrismation rather than on the eucharist as the climax of illumination and salvation, but its claim to be a valid interpretation of the Gnostic's ecstatic experience of and identification with the heavenly Revealer/Redeemer, i.e. Christ, should not be doubted.

In my first chapter I shall attempt to identify those who created and propagated the myth underlying the *Apocryphon,* the Gnostics of Irenaeus, as Platonically-influenced Christians constructing their own myth of origins in reaction to contemporary Jewish persecution, a myth which in its several variants was influenced by Johannine and Valentinian ideas and then underwent a 'Sethian' reinterpretation, largely as a response to 'orthodox' Christian criticism. My second chapter will first analyse the character of the myth as Christian and Platonic, a projection of the Gnostic experience of salvation in terms of the key figures of Christ and Sophia, articulated and held together by its basis in the initiation rite of baptism and chrismation (the five seals), and then attempt to suggest how it may have developed by way of a number of redactions, and how it is related to a whole series of Gnostic texts and systems from the late first to the late third century CE.

The remaining chapters will then constitute the proof of my claims by a detailed analysis of the Gnostic myth as expressed in the *Apocryphon*, Irenaeus *Adv. haer.* 1.29–30 and related texts and systems. Chapters three and four will deal with Gnostic theogony and cosmogony, chapter five with Gnostic anthropogony and anthropology, chapters six and seven with Gnostic soteriology and chapter eight with Gnostic eschatology. The basis of this analysis of a – if not the – 'classic' Gnostic myth will be my reconstruction of the redactional history of our present *Apocryphon* (i.e. the relation between the versions, which is the earliest and what factors might account for the differences between them).

Notes

[1] See J. M. Robinson, *The Nag Hammadi Library in English*[3] (Leiden: Brill, 1988), Introduction; 'The discovery of the Nag Hammadi codices', *BA* 42 (1979), 206–24; 'From Cliff to Cairo' in B. Barc ed., *Colloque international sur les textes de Nag Hammadi* (Québec: Université Laval/ Louvain: Peeters, 1981), 21–58. For the earliest account, see J. Doresse, *The Secret Books of the Egyptian Gnostics* (London: Hollis & Carter, 1960).

[2] In his *Adversus haereses* 1–5, esp. 1 (critical edition in Sources chrétiennes series vols 263–4 by A. Rousseau and L. Doutreleau, *Irénée de Lyon. Contre les hérésies* (Paris: Editions du Cerf, 1979); see also W. W. Harvey, *Sancti Irenaei Libros quinque adversus Haereses* (2 vols, Cambridge, 1857)).

[3] *Lehrbuch der Dogmengeschichte*[3] 1 (Freiburg–Leipzig, 1894), 211ff. (ET *History of Dogma*, tr. N. Buchanan, London: Williams and Norgate, 1905, 1.253).

[4] Justin mentions his *Syntagma* in *1 Apol.* 26. For a proposed reconstruction, see P. Prigent, *Justin et l'Ancien Testament* (Paris: Gabalda, 1964); Hippolytus wrote both an early, lost work, the *Syntagma*, which Adolf Hilgenfeld attempted to recontruct with the aid of Pseudo-Tertullian, *Adversus omnes haereses* (= *Adv. omn. haer.*, ed. A. Kroymann, CSEL 47) and Epiphanius, *Panarion* (= *Pan.*, ed. K. Holl, GCS 25, 31, 37, rev. ed. of 31 by J. Dümmer), in *Die Ketzergeschichte des Urchristentums*

(Leipzig: Fues, 1884), and the later *Refutatio omnium haeresium* or *Philosophoumena* (= *Ref.*, ed. P. Wendland, GCS 26); Tertullian, who may have been responsible for *Adv. omn. haer.* (see above) also wrote *Adversus Valentinianos* and *Adversus Marcionem* (ed. CCSL 1–2); Epiphanius (see above); Theodoret, *Haereticarum fabularum compendium* (= *Haer.*, MPG 83).

[5] Cf. Iren. *Adv. haer.* 1.22.2–31.4; 2.praef.; Hipp. *Ref.* 6.2f.; Tert. *Praescr.* 7; Eusebius of Caesarea *Hist. eccl.* 4.7, etc.

[6] For the *Pistis Sophia* (= *PS*), see C. Schmidt and V. MacDermot, *Pistis Sophia* (NHS 9) (Leiden: Brill, 1978); for the Bruce Codex, see id., *The Books of Jeu and the Untitled Text in the Bruce Codex* (NHS 13) (Leiden: Brill, 1978).

[7] 'Ein vorirenäisches gnostisches Originalwerk in koptischen Sprache', SPAW (Berlin, 1896), 839–47.

[8] Edited (apart from the *Acts of Peter*) by W. C. Till, *Die gnostischen Schriften des koptischen Papyrus Berolinensis 8502* (TU 60), rev. ed. H.-M. Schenke (Berlin: Akademie, 1972).

[9] In 13 volumes (Leiden: Brill, 1972–8). A critical edition in English, *The Coptic Gnostic Library*, is being published in the Nag Hammadi Studies (= NHS) monograph series (1975ff.). For a full bibliography, see D. M. Scholer, *Nag Hammadi Bibliography 1948–1969* (NHS 1) (Leiden: Brill, 1971) and annual issues of *NovT* from vol. 13 (1971).

[10] 'The Nag Hammadi Library and the Heresiologists', *VC* 25 (1971), 205–23.

[11] 'Heresiologists', 220f.

[12] 'Das sethianische System nach Nag-Hammadi Schriften', in P. Nagel ed., *Studia Coptica* (Berlin: Akademie, 1974), 165–73. In a follow-up paper in 1978, 'The Phenomenon and Significance of Gnostic Sethianism', in B. Layton ed., *The Rediscovery of Gnosticism: Proceedings of the International Conference on Gnosticism at Yale, New Haven, Connecticut March 28–31, 1978* (Leiden: Brill, 1980–1), 2.588f., he added *Marsanes* (C X,*1*), *Allogenes* (C XI,*3*) and the *Untitled Treatise* (= *AnonBru*) of the Bruce Codex as well as the Gnostics, Sethians and Archontics of Epiphanius.

[13] 'System', 166.

[14] 'Der gnostische Anthropos und die jüdische Tradition', *Eranos Jahrbuch* 22 (1954), 195–234 (= *Gnostic Studies* 1 (Istanbul, 1974), 173–95).

[15] See Wilson, *The Gnostic Problem* (London: Mowbray, 1958, 1964²) and frequently since; Grant, *Gnosticism and Early Christianity* (New York: Columbia, 1959, 1966²); Daniélou, *RSR* 48 (1960), 603ff.; *Théologie du judéochristianisme* (Tournai: Desclée, 1958; ET *The Theology of Jewish Christianity* (London: Darton, Longman & Todd, 1964)); MacRae, 'The Jewish Background of the Gnostic Sophia Myth', *NovT* 12 (1970), 86–101; Rudolph, 'Gnosis und Gnostizismus, ein Forschungsbericht' *TRu* 36 (1971), 89–119; *Die Gnosis* (Leipzig: Koehler & Amelang, 1977, 1980²;

ET *Gnosis. The Nature and History of Gnosticism* (Edinburgh: T & T Clark, 1984), 276–82, etc.); Pearson, *Gnosticism, Judaism, and Egyptian Christianity* (SAC 5) (Minneapolis: Fortress, 1990), essays 1–9.

[16] See *Gnosis und spätantike Geist*, 2 vols (Göttingen: Vandenhoeck & Ruprecht, 1993); *The Gnostic Religion* (Boston: Beacon, 1958, 1970³); and his 'Response to G. Quispel's *Gnosticism and the New Testament*' in J. P. Hyatt ed., *The Bible in Modern Scholarship* (Nashville, 1965), 279–95.

[17] See W. Foerster ed., *Die Gnosis 2* (Zürich: Artemis, 1971; ET *Gnosis 2* ed. R. McL. Wilson (Oxford: Clarendon, 1974)).

[18] Layton, *Rediscovery*, vol. 1, *The School of Valentinus* (1980); vol. 2, *Sethian Gnosticism* (1981). See Wisse, 'Stalking those elusive Sethians' in 2.563–76.

[19] See on this e.g. Quispel, *Gnosis als Weltreligion* (Zürich, 1951), 5; Wilson, *Gnosis and the New Testament* (Oxford, 1968); Rudolph *TRu* 37 (1972), 311f., etc.

[20] J. D. Turner, 'Sethian Gnosticism: A Literary History' in C. W. Hedrick and R. Hodgson eds, *Nag Hammadi, Gnosticism, and Early Christianity* (Peabody, Mass.: Hendrickson, 1986), 55–86. Pearson's three stages of Sethian Gnosticism, 'Gnosticism as Platonism', *Gnosticism* 152, n. 20, are (1) origins in a Jewish milieu; (2A) Christianization; (2B) Platonization in a pagan milieu.

[21] G. A. G. Stroumsa, *Another Seed: Studies in Gnostic Mythology* (NHS 24) (Leiden: Brill, 1984). Cf. P. Perkins, *Gnosticism and the New Testament* (Minneapolis: Fortress, 1993). But R. van den Broek, 'The Present State of Gnostic Studies', *VC* 37 (1983), 41–71, while accepting the distinct Jewish (and Platonic) elements in Gnosticism, argues that it cannot be explained exclusively from either (71).

[22] *Le Dualisme chez Platon, les gnostiques et les manichéens* (Paris, 1947); *RMM* 60 (1965), 385–421; *RMM* 85 (1980), 145–77. Cf. also the criticisms of the pre-Christian hypothesis by E. M. Yamauchi, *Pre-Christian Gnosticism* (London: Tyndale, 1973); 'Some Alleged Evidences for Pre-Christian Gnosticism' in R. N. Longenecker and M. C. Tenney eds, *New Dimensions in New Testament Study* (Grand Rapids: Eerdmans, 1974), 46–70; 'PreChristian Gnosticism in the Nag Hammadi Texts?' *CH* 48 (1979), 129–41.

[23] *A Separate God. The Christian Origins of Gnosticism* (London: Darton, Longman & Todd, 1991; ET of *Le Dieu séparé: les origines du gnosticisme* (Paris: Editions du Cerf, 1984)). However, van den Broek, 'Present State' 67–71, would reject such a derivation and Perkins, *Gnosticism* 206, n. 2, dismisses the book as 'simply outdated in its analysis of the tradition history of the Nag Hammadi materials'.

[24] *Le Dossier baptismal séthien: études sur la sacramentale gnostique* (BCNH Section 'Études' 2) (Québec: Université Laval, 1986).

[25] E.g. Rudolph, *Gnosis* 294–300, 308–25; Pétrement, *Separate* Part 2; G. Filoramo, *A History of Gnosticism* (Oxford: Blackwell, 1990), chs 9–10, etc.

[26] Cf. the very similar system in *Trimorphic Protennoia*, the similarities in the *Gospel of the Egyptians*, the exactly parallel passages in Allogenes (62.27–63.23) and *AJ* (B 24.7–25.13), and the transmission of the *melothesia* of Adam's psychic body (*AJ* B 49.9–50.14 and par) traced by M. Tardieu in his edition (SGM 1 (Paris: Editions du Cerf, 1984) = *Écrits*) to Syriac Christian (Audi), Manichaean and Arabic (Ismaili) sources down to the ninth century CE (ib. 43–6, 300–8).

[27] The *Paraphrase of Shem* (C VII,*1*) seems related to Hippolytus' 'Paraphrase of Seth' (*Ref.* 5.22.1), but opinion is divided about precisely how. See Pétrement, *Separate* 441–6 and 96.

[28] See *The Gnostic Scriptures* (Garden City: Doubleday, 1987), 5–21. Even Perkins, while insisting that myths only exist as collections of variants (*Gnosticism* 13), notes the acceptance by many scholars of a sequence of characteristic Sethian mythemes, while insisting that the character of myth makes it impossible to establish a chronological ordering of the variants. We shall attempt to demonstrate that such can be done in the case of the *Apocryphon* in terms of the appearance of certain mythologoumena and similar developments in 'orthodox' Christianity.

[29] See n. 12, Pearson, 'The Figure of Seth in Gnostic Literature', *Gnosticism* 55–8; Turner, 'Sethian Gnosticism' 56.

[30] See n. 16 above. Perkins' attempt, *Gnosticism* chs 2 and 4, to appeal to Jewish traditions as the source of Gnostic mythemes (Wisdom's fall, Adam and Eve, etc.), to Semitic word-play and to the supposedly superficial Christianization, are heavily dependent on the theses of Schenke, Pearson and Stroumsa, and will be answered in detail in what follows.

[31] See on this U. Bianchi ed., *Le origini dello gnosticismo: Colloquio di Messina 13–18 Aprile 1966* (SHR/Supplements to *Numen* 12) (Leiden: Brill, 1967, 1970²), xx–xxxii; Rudolph *TRu* 36 (1971), 13–23.

1

◆━◆◆◆━◆

The Myth and Its Makers

1 Irenaeus 1.29 and the *Gnōstikoi*

As we have seen, the myth which appears to underlie Irenaeus *Adv. haer.* 1.29 and 30 and the *Apocryphon of John* seems to have played a central and fundamental role in the recent debate about the origins and development of Gnosticism. So our first task is to attempt to establish the origin and nature of that myth, who were responsible for it and how it developed. As is well known, the starting point of any such investigation is paramount, since it will have an inevitable and profound influence on any conclusions reached. Thus some justification is required for starting where I intend to start, with Irenaeus' summary of the views of certain *gnōstikoi* in *Adv. haer.* 1.29 rather than with the *Apocryphon* and its version of the myth. The correctness of such a procedure can only be established by the success of my investigation as a whole, but my provisional defence would be (*a*) that Irenaeus seems to have had access to original sources, Valentinian and otherwise, which he must have obtained from Gnostics; (*b*) that his procedure in Book 1 is to lay out the views of such Gnostics in as clear and unbiased a manner as possible, since he thinks such exposure should constitute refutation enough:[1] any blatant misrepresentation would surely have triggered Gnostic protests; and (*c*) that he was in a better position to know and judge the situation than we can ever be.[2] And, as we shall attempt to demonstrate in what follows, his account would often appear to be a more original version of the myth than that in the *Apocryphon* as we have it.

What then can we learn from Irenaeus about the Gnostics, particularly from 1.29? It is generally accepted that chapters 29 and 30 of Book 1 of *Adversus haereses* form a unit distinct from the earlier heresiological catalogue of chapters 23 to 27 and its concluding summary, chapter 28.[3] Irenaeus appears to make a

1

fresh start with chapter 29, which deals with a mushroom-like growth of 'Gnostics' whom he does nevertheless link with the previous catalogue originating with Simon Magus, the 'source and root' of all heretics:[4] they have arisen from the aforementioned Simonians, he says.[5] Chapter 29 then goes on to deal with the principal opinions of some of them. However, the term 'Barbelo' used to describe them appears to be the gloss of a later editor based on the name of the supreme female entity and not due to Irenaeus himself, although for convenience modern scholars often refer to the group and its characteristic opinions as Barbelognostic.[6]

Chapter 29 only deals with the theogony and cosmogony of the myth, stopping short with the Pro(t)archon or Demiurge creating the earthly realm and boasting that he is the only true God in the exclusivist language of the God of the Old Testament (Exod 20:5; Isa 45:5f.; 46:9). The account in chapter 30, on the other hand, attributed to certain others, i.e. other 'Gnostics', continues (after a similar blasphemous claim by the Demiurge, here called Ialdabaoth) with the rest of the myth involving anthropogony, soteriology and eschatology. Since the *Apocryphon* has a similar continuation after Ialdabaoth's blasphemy, the question arises whether Irenaeus' source only contained the first half of the myth or whether it had the rest but he decided to omit it, preferring the version in chapter 30 as perhaps more akin to the Valentinian systems whose prototypes were, he claimed, those of chapters 29 and 30.

We shall have to deal with this question in detail later. Suffice it to note that the Demiurge's blasphemy, which occurs in a number of related texts from Nag Hammadi and elsewhere,[7] does form a natural point of transition from cosmogony to anthropogony and the obvious introduction to the Gnostic interpretation of the opening chapters of Genesis dealing with the creation and fall of humanity.[8] And there are, in fact, examples of Gnostic works dealing only with theogony and cosmogony, such as *Eugnostos* (C III,*3*; V,*1*) limited to the heavenly world, and its offshoot the *Sophia of Jesus Christ* (B; C III,*4*) alluding to how the rest of the mythological scheme would develop. More importantly, as Greer has persuasively argued, since Irenaeus' fundamental argument in Books 1 and 2 is to defend his view of God as 'containing – not contained', he simply selected from the *Apocryphon* the theological section that best suited his interests and laid the groundwork for his polemic.[9]

At the end of chapter 30 Irenaeus concludes his summary of the principal opinions of two groups of 'Gnostics', suggesting (although, as we shall see, the interpretation of the Latin translation is disputed) that from them was born that many-headed wild beast, like the Lernaean hydra, of the school of Valentinus (30.15). That serpentine allusion leads him naturally to mention the views of others about Sophia and the snake (30.15), and others still (31.1) who glorify Cain and other biblical villains such as Judas. He even mentions a writing of theirs, a 'Gospel of Judas', whose contents, however, he does not seem to know. But more intriguingly he also refers to other writings of theirs he had collected, which urged the destruction of the works of the Womb, i.e. the creator of heaven and earth; from these he appears to quote an invocatory formula addressed to an evil angel (31.2). Mention of such writings in the case of the various 'Gnostics' surely confirms the hypothesis that Irenaeus had written sources for chapters 29 and 30,[10] which he chose from among a selection of Gnostic works he knew and had obtained from various groups including Valentinians, his chief targets, as most relevant to demonstrate their literary and spiritual ancestry. Surely this is the most natural reading of the opening sentences of 31.3 where, summing up the first book and its catalogue of heresies, he speaks of the disciples of Valentinus as issuing from such mothers, fathers and ancestors.

Who are these 'Gnostics' of chapters 29 to 31?[11] In a recent detailed discussion of this question, Pétrement considers that R. A. Lipsius still presents the best treatment of Irenaeus' use of the term *gnosticus/gnōstikos*.[12] According to Lipsius, Irenaeus often uses the term as a collective description of all the heresies he is opposing, but that even when he does so, one can usually deduce from the context which sects he particularly has in mind. These are sometimes the Valentinians or both the Valentinians and the Gnostics of 1.29–31 together. But he argues that in most cases it is the latter he is thinking of.[13] That is, Lipsius appears to be suggesting that, over against the claim of Catholic Christians like Irenaeus to have the true *gnōsis*, there are the whole mass of heretics who falsely claim that knowledge (cf. 1 Tim 6:20: 'Gnostics' in the more general sense), among whom one can distinguish a group (those of 1.29–31) who make a special claim ('Gnostics' in the more restricted or strict sense). However, Lipsius does admit that Irenaeus only calls them that because he does not know what other name to give them (i.e. the name may not be their own self-designation).[14]

As Pétrement points out in her comment on Lipsius' claim and Irenaeus' usage, the heretics of 1.29–31 do not appear to form a number of distinct sects, 'Barbelo' seems a later gloss, and furthermore calling the whole group 'Gnostics' would agree with Irenaeus' usual practice elsewhere.[15] Moreover the later heresiologists like Epiphanius and Filaster call the heretics of 1.29 Gnostics as the name of a particular sect: the names of Ophites and Cainites were applied by them to the groups of 1.30 and 31 respectively from the mistaken deduction that they were or ought to be separate sects.[16]

Such an interpretation as offered by Lipsius, suggesting the existence of a sect of 'Gnostics' in the strict sense, and also Irenaeus' further claim to see in them the spiritual ancestors of the Valentinians, were generally accepted by later scholars such as Adolf Hilgenfeld, who claimed Justin must have known them and mentioned them in his lost *Syntagma* as the link between Simon Magus and Valentinus.[17] Wilhelm Bousset saw the name as originally belonging to many small groups of the larger movement of Gnosticism which had not yet developed into the later distinctive schools under named individuals, and as forming the oldest level of the Gnostic movement.[18] R. P. Casey, whom Pétrement does not mention in her discussion, argued that both orthodox and heretic claimed *gnōsis* and the title 'Gnostic' in good faith, and agreed with Lipsius that in a number of cases Irenaeus is clearly referring to the Gnostics in the strict sense (Casey calls them Ophites) of 1.29–31; it is out of sheer irritation at the assumption by the heretics of the honourable title *gnōstikos* that Irenaeus applied it carelessly and in an ironical sense to sects who never employed it of themselves.[19]

More recently Norbert Brox has re-examined the term *gnōstikoi* in Irenaeus and other heresiologists. On the basis of his analysis of the heresiologists' usage, he agrees with Bousset that originally the Gnostics were a number of sects from a relatively early phase of the movement, and argues that this term always applied in the heresiologists before and after Irenaeus to particular groups and not to the whole phenomenon.[20] It was Irenaeus, Brox thinks, who expanded the term to apply as a special designation to the whole phenomenon.[21] Brox agrees with Lipsius that Irenaeus does sometimes use the term in a restricted sense, especially or even exclusively to apply to the heretics of 1.29–31. But as Pétrement points out, whereas Brox sees Irenaeus as *expanding* the term from the more restricted usage, for Lipsius Irenaeus implies the more general sense and sometimes restricts it to one particular group, that of 1.29–31.[22] What is, of course, new and significant for our purposes is that Brox is aware of the *Apocryphon of John* and claims that Irenaeus used the first part of it to describe the Gnostics of 1.29.[23]

In Pétrement's critical comments, devoted, as we shall see, to arguing in support of her main thesis of the Christian origins of Gnosticism that there is no evidence in the heresiologists for the existence of the Gnostics of 1.29–31 as a distinct sect prior to and the spiritual ancestors of the Valentinians – that in fact the latter inspired the systems of 1.29 and the *Apocryphon*, she casts doubt on Irenaeus' assertions about the relationship between the Gnostics and the Valentinians; Irenaeus' claims are primarily based on the doctrinal resemblances and are expressed in a deliberately ambiguous way. Further, they are not even accepted unanimously by later heresiologists despite their dependence on him. Thus Pétrement finds Lipsius more correct than Brox as regards the priority in Irenaeus of the more general over the more restricted sense of the term.[24] She can also point out, with some justification, to the lack of evidence for a particular sect of Gnostics with the ideas found in 1.29–31 prior to Irenaeus and the dependence of the later heresiologists (Pseudo-Tertullian, Epiphanius, Filaster), for whom the Gnostics were generally seen as a particular sect or group of sects associated with Nicolaus and the Nicolaitans, on Hippolytus and his interpretation of Irenaeus in his lost *Syntagma* (which Lipsius attempted to reconstruct via the three aforementioned heresiologists) and *Refutatio*.[25]

Finally Pétrement discusses the research paper of Morton Smith at the 1978 Yale Conference on Gnosticism,[26] in which he investigates the original meaning of the term *gnōstikos* and its use by Christians and non-Christians. He traces its probable origin to Plato, noting its restriction prior to the second century to Platonic, Aristotelian and Pythagorean philosophers, with the meanings 'leading to knowledge, resulting in knowledge, capable of knowing'.[27] But it is strikingly absent from the Septuagint, from Jewish works in Greek and from the New Testament, and Smith concludes from his analysis, first, that the *gnōstikoi* of the second century probably got their claim to be such (and also their doctrines) from the Platonic–Pythagorean tradition,[28] and, second, that the claim to be a *gnōstikos* was rather to be *capable of knowing* than to possess particular items of information.[29]

Pétrement in criticism rightly points to the differences between the use of *gnōstikos* by the Gnostics and by the philosophical schools: the former used it of *persons* not of techniques or skills; they meant by it not the capacity for knowledge but divine revelation brought by a saviour, and their doctrines, despite the undoubted debt to Platonism in particular, are too distinctive in structure and style to be derivable wholly or chiefly from Platonic traditions. She also rightly draws attention to the use of *gnōsis* in the New Testament, which differs as much from the classical meaning as does the Gnostic term *gnōstikos* from the philosophical, in having an absolute sense, one found almost exclusively in Jewish and Christian texts.[30] But she agrees with Smith's conclusions that the term 'Gnostic', as applied by some groups to themselves, according to the heresiologists does not necessarily designate a sect; that the heretics may have used the term as Clement of Alexandria does, and that Irenaeus sometimes implies certain things without daring to state them clearly for fear of contradiction by his enemies.[31]

More recently, without reference to Pétrement, M. J. Edwards, in an article dedicated to distinguishing the Valentinians from the Gnostics, has rejected Smith's claims that Irenaeus' usage is deliberately confusing and designed to blacken his opponents and that the Western Fathers followed him in applying the term indifferently to all opponents of orthodoxy.[32] In successfully demonstrating the likelihood that the Valentinians were never called or called themselves 'Gnostics', and the major differences between the two groups, Edwards does make a good case for linking together the 'Gnostics' of Irenaeus, the Naassenes (who called themselves *gnōstikoi*) and the opponents of Plotinus as a group of related sects. In a later article Edwards goes further and claims to be able to demonstrate that Plotinus, his disciples, the Christian Fathers and the Greek alchemists all agree in their portrayal of 'this well-defined and extraordinary sect'.[33] If one is thus led to discount Smith's general and debatable conclusions about the Platonic and non-Christian origin of the term *gnōstikos* and Irenaeus' supposed deliberate confusion (accepting Edwards' robust defence of the latter), what is interesting is both Smith's limitation of the title to those few groups, Christian and non-Christian, whom he thinks actually used it (Prodicus and his followers, Naassenes and Ophites, Clement, the 'gnostics' of Porphyry and Plotinus – here he and Edwards agree), and his allowance of the first record of Christian usage as Celsus' report (in Origen *C. Cels.* 5.61f.) that some among the different sorts of Christians called themselves 'gnostics'. This contemporary non-Christian evidence surely offers some support to Irenaeus' understanding and claims. But in the end the possibility of establishing the existence of a Christian group calling themselves 'Gnostics', the 'Gnostics in the narrower sense' of Irenaeus 1.29–31 and Lipsius, and their precise relation to the *Apocryphon of John* and Valentinianism comes down to assessing the validity and coherence of what Irenaeus himself says, to which we now turn.[34]

Pétrement points to the apparent ambiguity and ambivalence of the two crucial passages in Irenaeus, 1.30.15 and 31.3, crucial because she claims that without them no one would dream of identifying the 'so-called Gnostic heresy' of 1.11.1, supposed to have inspired Valentinus, with the doctrines described in 1.29–31.[35] Both, unfortunately, survive only in the Latin translation and, as she points out, have been paraphrased or corrected by the editors in their attempts to understand them.[36]

1.30.15 reads: 'Tales quidem secundum eos sententiae sunt: a quibus velut Lernaea hydra multiplex capitibus fera de Valentini schola generata est' ('Such are their opinions; from which, like the Lernaean hydra, was born the many-headed wild beast of the school of Valentinus'). Pétrement points to the lack of clarity about the wild beast; it is derived from the school of Valentinus, but there is nothing in the text as it stands, she claims, to make us think the wild beast is that school.[37] The editors of the *Sources chrétiennes* edition see the difficulty of the double derivation of both doctrines and school, but convinced, following Irenaeus' hint in 1.11.1, that the many-headed Valentinian school is derived from the Gnostics, they delete the 'de' in their Greek retroversion, equating the many-headed beast with the school of Valentinus.[38] They are surely correct to take 'multiplex capitibus' with 'fera' and not, as Pétrement does, with 'Lernaea hydra'. But the 'de' does not need to be excised: it could well represent a Greek genitive as elsewhere in the Latin translation[39] and thus one could reconstruct the Greek original as 'to polykephalaion thērion tēs tou Oualentinou scholēs' ('many-headed wild beast of the school of Valentinus') and eliminate much of the ambiguity claimed by Pétrement. Such a link of the Lernaean hydra and many-headed with the school of Valentinus rather than with the Gnostics would make better sense of Irenaeus' statement than Pétrement's interpretations, which are hard to follow in the English translation but seem to relate the wild beast to offspring of the Gnostics of 1.29–31, themselves derived from the Valentinians.

Further, the links with 1.11–12, where Irenaeus illustrates the variety of views of Valentinus and his followers, are clear and do not, as Pétrement avers, simply boil down to the mention of Valentinus adapting the basic principles of the so-called 'Gnostic' sect to his own school style. The Gnostics may have been recent mushroom growths (1.29.1), but it is the Valentinians who are the hydra! Further, Irenaeus' following reference to the similarity between the left-hand ruler of Valentinus and that of those he will later mention, the 'falsely so-called Gnostics', overlooked by Pétrement, although not exactly corresponding to what he says of the serpentine son of Ialdabaoth in 1.30.6, seems close enough to establish the connection and relationship of dependence he sees between Valentinus and the Gnostics of 1.29–31.[40]

Careful analysis of his usage of the term *gnosticus/gnōstikos* does indeed reveal a more general meaning denoting all the heretics from Simon Magus,[41] as well as a reference, which Irenaeus probably took from his heresiological catalogue, to the Carpocratians as calling themselves 'Gnostics' (1.25.6). But it also reveals a considerable number of references specifically to the *Gnostici* of 1.29–31.[42] Indeed in a number of other passages in Book 1, where Irenaeus' mention of certain Valentinians claiming to be more perfect than the perfect and more gnostic than the 'Gnostics' (e.g. 1.11.3; 11.5) has been interpreted by Pétrement and others as referring to a general quality rather than a particular sect,[43] it can be shown that Irenaeus had precisely the Gnostics of 1.29–31 in mind.

The key texts in this regard are 2.13.8 and 10, where Irenaeus, in rebutting the ideas of emanation of divine intelligible entities from God, claims his arguments should suffice to refute the followers of Basilides (a reference to 1.24.3) and the rest of the Gnostics from whom the Valentinians were convicted in the first book of having taken the beginnings of their emissions ('adversus reliquos Gnosticos, a quibus et hi initia emissionum accipientes, convicti sunt in primo libro'). In 2.13.10 Irenaeus confirms this by reference to the internal wrangles among the fathers (*patres*) of the Valentinians, 'the falsely so-called Gnostics (falso cognominati Gnostici)', about the order of emission of the aeons Man and Church, an unmistakable allusion to 1.30.1 and 1.29.1 and 3 as well as to

1.12.4. Indeed the term 'fathers' obviously picks up the second of Pétrement's crucial passages, 1.31.3:

> A talibus matribus et *patribus* et proavis eos qui a Valentino sint, sicut ipsae sententiae et regulae ostendunt eos, necessarium fuit manifesto arguere et in medium adferre dogmata ipsorum, si qui forte ex his paenitentiam agentes et convertentes ad unum solum Conditorem Deum et Factorem universitatis salvari possint.

The reference in 1.11.3 and 5 and elsewhere to Valentinian claims to be 'more gnostic than the Gnostics' must be seen in this context of primal emanations: the Gnostics, Irenaeus is claiming, were the first to develop the concept of the emission of mental states or attributes of the Father like intelligence (*nous*) and reason (*logos*) as hypostases. The various Valentinian attempts to posit prior emissions and entities to these is to try to outdo these Gnostics, their spiritual ancestors! But what about Pétrement's appeal to the absence of any allusion to the Gnostics of 1.29–31 and their characteristic doctrines in any heresiologist prior to Irenaeus, and the tendency of those after him not to follow or even to reverse his understanding of the relation between Gnostics and Valentinians? Or what of her claim that it was the attempts of Hippolytus and his successors to systematize the hints thrown out by Irenaeus that led to the later heresiological identifications of the Gnostics as a particular sect?[44] She does concede that Irenaeus himself honestly believed that the Gnostics had influenced the Valentinians: in the end the only way to decide the matter, as she points out, is to examine the doctrines of both and see which interpretation is more justified, to explain the Gnostic myth from Valentinianism or vice versa. This will be undertaken in detail in what follows, but in the meantime it might be advisable to suggest some preliminary conclusions about the existence and identity of the Gnostics of Irenaeus.

(*a*) Although the evidence of Irenaeus, his predecessors (Ignatius, Justin, Hegesippus, also the pagan Celsus) and successors does not point unequivocally to the existence of an identifiable sect, it is clear that Irenaeus himself knew and was in touch with certain groups related by mythological systems whom for want of a better term and from certain characteristics of their doctrines he dubbed 'Gnostics'.

(*b*) More importantly they had a varied collection of books dealing with an all-embracing mythology involving theogony, cosmogony, anthropogony, soteriology and eschatology of which he summarized those parts which seemed to him to cast light on the origins of Valentinianism. What is striking is that they appear to have been quite happy to let him have such books: it might even be that he got his copies of the treatises underlying 1.29 and 30 from the Valentinians he was acquainted with along with their own 'commentaries'.[45] Whether the treatise underlying 1.29 in particular closely resembled our present *Apocryphon*, as Pétrement and the other commentators usually assume, remains to be determined.

(*c*) Even if Irenaeus, as Pétrement argues, already saw the Christians of the Great Church as possessing the true *gnōsis* and thus considered the heretics 'Gnostics falsely so-called', those who wrote and/or had copies of the treatise underlying 1.29 had very good claim to be called 'Gnostics' and to be fundamentally concerned with the ontological implications of knowledge and ignorance, such as were to be made much more explicit by the Valentinians.[46] Thus not only did they count Foreknowledge (*Prognosis*) as one of the first Aeons to come forth from the supreme Father and the consort of Intelligence (*Nous*),[47] they dubbed the consort of the perfect heavenly Man Adamas, Perfect Knowledge. Not only does the union of these two, the archetypes of Adam and Eve, thus give Adamas knowledge of the supreme God, it also leads to their producing a son called both 'Tree' and 'Knowledge', evidently the archetype of the tree of knowledge in Paradise,[48] thereby forming the prelude for a Gnostic reinterpretation of Genesis such as follows in the *Apocryphon of John*. But in it both the consort of Adamas and their son have disappeared, to be replaced by heavenly Seth in what I shall argue is a later process of Sethianization.

(*d*) As we shall see, most if not all of those who Smith thinks actually used the title 'Gnostics' after Irenaeus (Prodicus, the Naassenes and Ophites and the 'Gnostics' of Plotinus and Porphyry), will turn out to be Christian Gnostics related to those who created, reinterpreted and were influenced by the myths underlying Irenaeus 1.29 and 30 and the *Apocryphon*.[49] Thus it may well be that there is some truth in Irenaeus' allusion to 'Gnostics' in the strict sense, as an identifiable group or groups, united by their allegiance to the doctrine and ritual practice of this 'classic' myth. In the end the particular sect names do not matter; it is the myth and the ritual which are decisive.[50]

For whatever the truth about the existence or non-existence of a 'Gnostic' (or 'Barbelognostic') sect such as can be gleaned from the literary evidence, what does exist and has had a fundamental influence upon a whole range of Gnostic texts from Nag Hammadi and beyond, not limited to Schenke's 'Sethian' corpus, is the central mythological scheme and figures underlying Irenaeus 1.29 and 30 and the *Apocryphon of John*. The triad of Father, Mother and Son which I will argue is central and fundamentally Christian; the figures of Barbelo and her Son anointed and perfected as Christ, the Autogenes and Adamas, aspects of Christ; the syzygies of male and female Aeons, hypostases of divine attributes; the four illuminators; Sophia, her archetypal fall and repentance; her abortive offspring Ialdabaoth/Saklas, unwitting vehicle of the saving divine light-power with his six (or seven) creator archons, and the pattern of a *Heilsgeschichte* reinterpreting the Old Testament accounts of Genesis and the prophets and Jewish apocalyptic eschatology in terms of the repeated descents of the Saviour (Christ/Seth) to impart revelation and finally to save the elect seed: these are all to varying degrees reflected and reinterpreted in other Gnostic texts.

Despite the efforts of Wisse and others to argue that there was, indeed there could be, no single, universal Gnostic myth, Schenke has posed a valid question by his identification of recurring figures, patterns, mythologoumena, doxologies, all the more surprising given the endless variety of Gnostic imagination and the plasticity of Gnostic myth. It may be that we have to posit some unifying factor not always obvious from the texts, such as the kind of initiation ritual as both actual and spiritual reality which Sevrin has identified so painstakingly behind texts like Irenaeus 1.29 and the *Apocryphon*, if we are to make sense of the phenomenon Schenke has identified. If the 'Gnostic' and 'Sethian' texts do not have the remarkable unity and continuity of the great Valentinian or Manichaean systems, deriving as they do from two individual religious geniuses and visionaries, they still reflect the pervading influence of a basic mythological scheme (and I will argue, following Sevrin, a basic rite of initiation into saving *gnōsis*), which can best be understood as equally the work of a hitherto unknown visionary or visionaries, which led to the interrelated mythological systems underlying Irenaeus 1.29 and 30 and the *Apocryphon of John*. And as Valentinus and Mani can only be understood against the background of a Christian community with its characteristic doctrines and experiences projected in myth and ritual, so too with the 'classic Gnostic myth'.

We shall have to leave detailed discussion of Pétrement's thesis deriving the Gnostics from the Valentinians to later chapters; suffice it to say at this point that far from being only explicable in terms of Valentinian ideas, the Gnostics would appear to have contributed certain fundamental concepts to the former, such as the ontological role of the concretion of divine thoughts and emotions into the substances of the universe, the application of biological metaphors of sexual union and generation, of syzygies and emanations, above all the evolution of the Sophia myth absent in predecessors and contemporaries like Saturninus and Basilides. As for the absence of references to the Gnostics prior to Irenaeus (and Celsus!) and their downgrading by later heresiologists to a minor libertine sect associated with the Nicolaitans, this is to overlook the importance of *texts* to the Gnostics. They are literary creatures, exegetes of texts, scriptural and other, whose myths feed on existing ones, and who do not seem to see the need for fixed interpretations and set groupings. They possess libraries of very varied and eclectic content. If we can query the independent existence of many of the heresiologists' sects, we cannot query the existence of fundamental Gnostic texts.

Further, it would seem that it was the Gnostics, along with Saturninus, Basilides and Valentinus, who were the first Christians to develop a thoroughgoing Platonic understanding of the world in terms of a hierarchy of being on two levels, the transcendent, spiritual level emanating from God the Unknown Father, and the terrestrial, material level, a poor travesty or imitation of it, the work of the Demiurge of the *Timaeus* and his archons, with Sophia as the mediating World Soul. With this they combine the Platonic myth of the fall of the divine spark or soul into the material body as a tomb and its re-ascent. But against Pétrement it is they, not Valentinus, who pioneer the Sophia myth and anticipate what she calls 'the Valentinian turning point'[51] in their modification of the flagrant anti-Judaism of Saturninus and Basilides by a certain rehabilitation of the Creator God as a vehicle of the divine power and, in the system of Irenaeus 1.30, of the Old Testament as a partial instrument of Sophia's revelations.[52] However, Pétrement is surely correct to see behind this unique combination and perspective the Pauline and Johannine theology of the cross as the revelation of the hitherto unknown Father, and hence of the ignorance and folly of the Creator/Demiurge of this world and his rulers/archons, and even more so, as I will stress, the theology of Hebrews with its pre-existent Wisdom/Son Christology and blend of Jewish concepts and popular contemporary (Middle) Platonism.

2 The *Apocryphon of John* and the 'Sethians'

If Irenaeus claims that groups of 'Gnostics' were responsible for the systems he summarizes in 1.29 and 30, what of the *Apocryphon of John* and the claim of Schenke and others that it and Irenaeus 1.29 are the products of pre- and non-Christian Sethianism? One of Pétrement's arguments for the late character of the Gnostic system in 1.29, and hence of the likelihood of its having been influenced by Valentinianism, is to appeal to the *Apocryphon* as evidence, implying that Irenaeus' version corresponded to the first section of it, and therefore that at least that section existed when Irenaeus wrote *Adversus haereses*, around 185 CE.[53] But what if both represent a secondary Christianization of a Jewish Sethian–Gnostic original? We shall have to consider this and the precise relation between the *Apocryphon* and Irenaeus 1.29, but before we do it might be helpful to examine the *Apocryphon* itself, to determine its background, character and purpose. As is well known, it exists in four Coptic texts (B; C II,*1*; III,*1*; IV,*1*), representing two distinct traditions, a short version (SR) found independently in B and III, and a long version (LR) found in the similar but not identical II and IV.[54] All evidently derive from Coptic translations of a Greek original or originals. III and IV are more fragmentary than II and B, which is the best preserved and probably the most recent of all. The two versions thus differ both internally (but II is much more similar to IV than B is to III) and externally, and although, as will be argued below, the latter may overall represent an earlier redaction, the former sometimes preserves more original readings, so that, as Sevrin points out, one must consider all the texts when seeking the original version.[55]

As it stands, the work represents a post-resurrection revelation discourse of the Saviour, Christ, to John the son of Zebedee, about the past, present and future. Tardieu, in his recent valuable analysis,[56] identifies three principal parts apart from the frame story with its prologue (in which Jesus appears to John in the style usual to such apocalyptic works and proclaims himself the Father, the Mother and the Son) and epilogue. The first part (B 22.16–36.15; II 2.25–9.24) is an exposition of the Saviour's opening proclamation, a theogony dealing successively with Father, Mother or Barbelo, and Son, Christ, and the entities issuing from them and him, culminating in heavenly Adam, Seth and his seed and their aeonic abodes. The second part (B 36.16–64.13; II 9.25–25.16) is an exegesis of the first four chapters of Genesis, i.e. a cosmogony and anthropogony, punctuated by three questions by John and concluding with the birth of earthly Seth. The long version adds a long *melothesia* to the account of the creation of Adam's psychic body (II 15.29–19.2).

The third part (B 64.13–75.10; II 25.16–30.11) contains John's seven remaining questions about the fates of various souls, i.e. soteriology, allowing a further section of biblical commentary on the Flood and the giants (Genesis 5–9) and the origin of the counterfeit spirit and human bondage to Fate. The long version then has a hymnic passage in which the heavenly figure of Pronoia (i.e. Barbelo) recounts in the first person her three saving descents into this world, in the final one of which she illuminates and frees the imprisoned Gnostic soul, seals it with the five seals (i.e. an initiatory rite of baptism/chrismation?) and re-ascends. Tardieu has shown convincingly that the short version actually knew this hymn, but has omitted all but its first and last words.[57]

The value of Tardieu's analysis is that it treats the work as a literary unity which has undergone several redactions. However, he does not begin from Irenaeus' summary as a possible precursor of the *Apocryphon*, but argues that the latter is based on and reflects the structure of the concluding Pronoia hymn, an ancient source deriving from a dissident member of the Johannine circle. This was developed by a later theologian of the same tendency in a commentary on the hymn employing the Fourth Gospel and revelation treatises of Platonizing Chaldaeans, which formed the basis of Irenaeus' entirely independent account (Tardieu's source π). This first redaction (n), dated by him around 170, was followed by a second (n¹) adding the detailed *melothesia* and the Pronoia hymn: abbreviation of this (o) led to the short version, and further redaction of it (n²) led to the long version.[58] Thus for Tardieu the work, which is essentially Christian, exhibits five essential characteristics: a methodically elaborated construction (brilliantly demonstrated by him); a Gospel scenario; a revelation with a ternary rhythm; a form of argument both scriptural and dialectical; and a basically anti-Jewish thrust and intention. The treatise is thus for him essentially a matter of exegesis: the first part of Jesus' words in the opening vision: 'I am the Father, I am the Mother, I am the Son'; the second of Genesis 1–4; the third a kind of catechesis on the destiny of the soul after death.[59] Moreover the whole plan for Tardieu is focused on Seth and a midrashic interpretation of Gen 4:25: the first part is a systematic evocation of the transcendent God known by Adam, Seth and the original Sethites (and present-day Gnostics); the second supplies the analytic proof of the first, by explaining how the first four chapters of Genesis are to be understood; the third part maps out the final status of Seth's descendants, i.e. the Gnostics, in the last days. As Tardieu puts it: 'Seth constitutes the essential articulation, which achieves the transition from one world to another, one part to another.'[60]

Tardieu's analysis of the structure of the *Apocryphon* is undoubtedly illuminating and suggestive, but, as we shall attempt to argue, his reconstruction of the stages of development needs to be amended and his rejection of the possibility of Irenaeus' version having directly influenced the *Apocryphon* and his characterization of the source of that version as 'Platonizing Chaldaean' will be strongly contested. But his remark above about the role of Seth is more apropos.

Indeed it recalls the claim by Schenke noted in the Introduction that the *Apocryphon* and Irenaeus 1.29 and a number of texts from Nag Hammadi and elsewhere and the systems of Epiphanius' Gnostics, Sethians and Archontics represent a 'Sethian system', built on the fundamental dogma of the self-understanding of those involved as being 'the seed of Seth'.[61] Other fundamental characteristics for Schenke include the four illuminators of the *Apocryphon* (and related texts) who constitute the heavenly abodes of respectively Adamas, Seth, his offspring and later repentant souls; the figure of Autogenes; the triad of Father, Mother and Son, etc.[62] Despite criticisms of his methodology and language Schenke has stuck to his thesis, if modifying it in some ways in his second article to add certain common literary features, doxologies, etc. and emphasizing the liturgical aspect, insisting on the great value of a synoptic treatment of the texts.[63]

Of course Schehnke would argue in both his contributions that Sethian Gnosticism is originally and essentially non- and even pre-Christian, and that the *Apocryphon* represents the most Christianized version of it.[64] He points to what he sees as the artificiality of the Christian frame story of the *Apocryphon* and its absence in Irenaeus' excerpt, which itself he claims has only a faint contact with Christianity, namely and simply its endowing the typically Sethian figure of the Son with the name 'Christ'.[65] But he does accept in the later article that, as Klijn's monograph conclusively demonstrated, Jewish sources are indifferent to Seth and thus are an unlikely source for Sethianism,[66] and that the appeal to a possible origin in Samaritanism is inconclusive.[67]

3 Irenaeus *Adversus haereses* 1.29 and the *Apocryphon*

So are we to assume that the makers of the myth were really Sethians? Certainly Schenke's thesis has found widespread support, particularly as buttressed by Sevrin's findings on the presence of a kind of initiatory ritual, actualized and/or spiritualized to varying degrees, in a group of Schenke's 'Sethian' texts. Once again it would seem that the crucial issue lies in the character and relationship of Irenaeus' summary of a Gnostic system in 1.29 and the so-called 'Sethian' *Apocryphon of John*. How exactly are they related? Do they represent a non- and pre-Christian form of Sethian Gnosticism, as Schenke argues? Or is the *Apocryphon* essentially a Christian work, as Pétrement and Tardieu argue from different perspectives, directly related to Irenaeus' summary and developed from Christian Valentinianism as Pétrement holds, or arising from the Johannine circle and simply making use of a common Chaldaean Platonizing source independently of Irenaeus, as Tardieu claims?

In both cases the figure of Seth is crucial: Schenke counts Irenaeus' summary in 1.29 as Sethian and Seth's relation to the four illuminators in the *Apocryphon* as fundamental to his case; Tardieu points to the pivotal role of Seth in the *Apocryphon*. But any reference to Seth and his seed is strikingly absent from Irenaeus' summary in 1.29 of the views of those he dubs 'Gnostics' (although earthly Seth does occur in 1.30, but as ancestor with Norea of the entire human race); instead, as we have noted, there is the figure of the Tree of Knowledge. Further differences between Irenaeus' account and the *Apocryphon* are noted by Krause,[68] although he argues in the light of the many resemblances that Irenaeus' source was similar to the cosmogony and fall of Sophia in the *Apocryphon*. This more guarded view of the relation, which still assumes, if implicitly, the priority or superiority of the *Apocryphon*, has tended to prevail over the original view of Schmidt that Irenaeus had borrowed directly from our *Apocryphon* itself.[69]

My contention, which will be argued in detail in what follows, is that Irenaeus' version in 1.29 represents an excerpt from the classic Christian Gnostic myth as far as the cosmogony and blasphemy of the Demiurge, complemented by the full account of the related myth in 1.30, more relevant to his purpose of demonstrating the spiritual ancestors of the Valentinians, and that that classic Gnostic theogony and cosmogony of Father, Mother and Son (and the omitted anthropogony and soteriology), after being presented as a revelation dialogue about past, present and future between John and Christ, has undergone a process of Sethianization. This process would seem to reflect the parallel interest in Seth of Christians of the Great Church around the beginning of the third century CE, and was prompted by the need to demonstrate a Gnostic genealogy and a continuing revelation in human history versus critical 'orthodox' Christian charges of novelty, and the development of a speculative exegesis based on Gen 4:25f. and the idea of a race or seed of Seth, to give this scriptural grounding. The Valentinian concept of Seth as representing the spiritual race or element may well have had considerable influence on this process. Thus R. Bergmeier, in an article on the characteristic Sethian self-designation 'kingless (*abasileutos*)', has argued both for it, as meaningful only in the light of Valentinianism, and for Valentinian ideas on the three generations having been reabsorbed into the Sethian reworking of the Barbelognostic system of the four illuminators.[70]

Klijn's detailed investigation has not only shown the lack of interest in Seth in Jewish and mainstream Christian circles (apart from the late Byzantine chronographers), it has also focused on the Gnostic interest in Seth as attested by the Christian heresiologists on the one hand and by the original Gnostic texts, in particular the *Apocalypse of Adam*, the *Apocryphon of John* and the *Gospel of the Egyptians*, on the other. Further it has shown how the heresiologists' picture goes back to Pseudo-Tertullian's cryptic comments (*Adv. omn. haer.* 2) and Epiphanius' attempt to clarify them (*Pan.* 39.1.3–3.5), and stresses the role of *earthly* Seth in the former as the originator of a particular human generation or pure seed deriving from the Highest God or Mother, and continuously assailed by hostile angelic and human (unnamed but presumably Cainite or mixed Cainite and Abelite) forces.[71]

It is only therefore in the Nag Hammadi 'Sethian' tractates that we hear of a rather different understanding of Seth as primarily a *heavenly* being, son of heavenly Adamas and saviour of his seed, race or generation, somehow linked with earthly Seth. Here the chief opponent is the Creator God of the Old Testament and there is no mention of Cainites, although in the *Apocalypse of Adam* we do find a distinction between Noah, Ham and Japheth and those of their offspring who remain loyal to the Creator, a group of the descendants of Ham and Japheth who join the Sethites and are saved from the wrath of the Creator, and the Sethites proper, the seed of (heavenly) Seth.[72] The Archontics of Epiphanius perhaps come closest to the views of the 'Sethians' of the Nag Hammadi tractates in that they represent the higher power descending with the ministering angels of the good God[73] and carrying Seth (called 'the Allogenes') above, returning him later as spiritual, as superior to the Creator God, Sabaoth and his powers, and the source of divine revelation.[74]

Now the view of earthly Seth as the progenitor of the virtuous Sethites (identified with the 'sons of God' of Gen 6:1), their battle with the Cainites and survival until the time of the Saviour, which underlies the heresiological accounts, does not occur in Western Greek and Latin sources before Julius Africanus (and Pseudo-Tertullian) in the early third century,[75] and the appearance of groups called Sethians with a clearly developed system centring on Seth and his seed does not seem attested any earlier. The significance of the Sethians of Hippolytus and his 'Paraphrase of Seth', which does not seem on the surface to have much to do with the biblical Seth, may thus well be that they attest that growing interest in Seth and represent a system akin to that of the Gnostics at the time the latter was in process of Sethianization.[76]

On the other hand the evidence of Epiphanius about the Gnostics, Sethians and Archontics with their collections of books in the name of Seth and his seven sons, the 'Allogeneis',[77] and of Theodoret giving the title 'Sethian' (along with 'Ophian' and 'Ophite') to the system in Irenaeus 1.30 (despite the fact that Seth's role in it is the very un-Gnostic one of being the ancestor of the entire human race after Cain),[78] does suggest that by their time Seth was considered a significant figure by various Gnostic groups. Equally it suggests that Sethian texts with recognizable and related systems were well-known and were in use by various circles, not all of whom could be designated 'Sethian'. What is most significant is that, as Klijn notes, 'Seth was clearly introduced *into an already existing system*'.[79] And once again, as we saw in dealing with the 'Gnostics', it is a matter of *texts* and their influence on various groups not slavishly tied to and identified exclusively with certain texts.

Finally, we must not overlook the evidence of Sevrin for the existence of an initiatory baptismal rite both actual and spiritualized, with its corresponding doctrine, in a family of 'Sethian' texts he identifies following Schenke. Despite his claim that this rite and its mythology go back to pre-Christian Jewish baptismal circles, which we would question, he makes the significant observations not only (*a*) that the doctrine combines a Barbeliote triad with a Sethian vision of history,[80] but more importantly, (*b*) that the combination of the water of life imagery with the Barbeliote triad and the five seals in the *Apocryphon* and *Trimorphic Protennoia* might suggest that this (Barbeliote?) baptism was not Sethian in origin but was only progressively integrated into a properly Sethian mythology.[81] As we shall argue, Sevrin has not seen the full significance of the prototypical Christian imagery of the anointing and perfection of the heavenly Son in Irenaeus 1.29.1, the *Apocryphon* and *Trimorphic Protennoia*, and is too ready to dismiss the Christian trinitarian character of the Barbeliote triad.[82] We will argue that, ironically, it was the 'Gnostics' of Irenaeus who, by their myth of the primal anointing and perfection of the heavenly Son, were the first to claim to be Christians precisely because of that chrism, and who may even have been responsible for the introduction of postbaptismal anointing into 'orthodox' Christianity![83]

Conclusion: Gnostics, Sethians and Valentinians

What then are we to make of the various candidates proposed as makers of the myth underlying Irenaeus 1.29 (and 30) and the *Apocryphon*: Gnostics, Sethians, even Valentinians? We have already discussed in a preliminary way Pétrement's thesis that the 'Gnostics' of Irenaeus and the *Apocryphon* can best be understood as deriving their ideas from the Valentinians rather than vice versa, as Irenaeus seemed to believe. Her trump card is her explanation of the origin of the theme of the four illuminators, seen by Schenke and other defenders of the pre-Christian origins of Gnosticism as essentially Sethian and inexplicable from Christianity, in terms of the figure and character of the Jesus of Ptolemy's version of Valentinianism, the star, fruit and flower of the Pleroma.[84] Indeed, the key to the original makers of the myth would appear to lie here, as Pétrement surmises. So how convincing are the various explanations of the origin of these key figures?

Schenke argues in his original article that the four illuminators or aeons represent the heavenly resting places for respectively Adam, Seth, the primal Sethians ('*Ur Sethianer*'), and the historical Sethians. The enigmatic references of the *Apocryphon* are solved for Schenke by synoptic comparison with the *Gospel of the Egyptians*, the *Apocalypse of Adam*, and the *Hypostasis of the Archons*. This suggests that the four aeons correspond to four different world periods, originally the four stars or planets of the (Iranian) world year, ranked alongside rather than beneath one another, as he thinks the 'Sethian' speculation presents it.[85] But Pétrement demonstrates some of the problems and inconsistencies in Schenke's scheme, the confusion of transcendent and historical, and the difficulties of distinguishing the eras of Adam and Seth, or of the sons of Seth and the souls late in repenting.[86]

Tardieu, in a joint article with P.-H. Poirier, criticizes Schenke's method but echoes his conclusion about the illuminators with appeal to Colpe's attempt to demonstrate Zoroastrian influence: the four illuminators undoubtedly represent an angelization of the Zervanite tetrad articulating the days of the month. Thus Harmozel derives from *Ohrmazd-el* (= first day); Oroiael from *Xwar* (= light/eleventh day); Daueithe from *Day* (= creator/twenty-third day), Eleleth from the Aramaic '*illith*, corresponding to the female Zervanite *Den*, *Xrad*, Wisdom personified.[87] Consequently Tardieu is led to dismiss Pétrement's hypothesis without discussion,[88] but like Pétrement he is unable to fit Eleleth very convincingly into his explanation, which is entirely dependent on his assumption that the mythologoumena of Irenaeus 1.29 and the *Apocryphon*, such as the four illuminators as abodes of Adamas, etc. derive from pre-Christian Platonizing Chaldaeans. And like Schenke he uneasily combines the heavenly archetypes, Adamas and Seth, with the earthly, heavenly mythology with earthly history. Furthermore his general appeal to Iranian influences is not on the face of it more plausible than Pétrement's Valentinian hypothesis, and is greatly weakened if the crucial passage in the *Apocryphon* on the four aeons as abodes of Seth, etc. is a later insert, as I and Bergmeier would argue.[89]

If one assumes that Irenaeus' summary is prior and that the *Apocryphon* represents a Sethianization of that more original scheme, then closer examination reveals that in Irenaeus' excerpt Adamas and Christ do not rest in but are removed from the illuminator Armoges (= Harmozel), i.e. elevated above the realm of the angels (1.29.3, cf. Heb 2:7 and Ps 8:4–6); that the four are originally and primarily angelic figures, perhaps based on the archangels of *1 Enoch* 9, etc. and not places/aeons, and that, as their later activity in Irenaeus, the *Apocryphon*, the *Hypostasis of the Archons* and *Trimorphic Protennoia* suggest, they were originally of equal rank, with the primary function of revealer/redeemer figures, attendants of the Autogenes.[90] Their soteriological role is also evident in the fact that it was they who were somehow responsible for the appearance of Sophia, and thus for the existence of the Gnostics in this world, and it is in all probability they who with the Autogenes preside over the Gnostic initiatory ceremony of chrismation (the five seals) to which Sevrin has drawn attention.[91]

It was only in the Sethianization process that they were linked with and transformed into aeons and a clumsy attempt, echoing the Valentinian distinction of pneumatics (corresponding to Seth) and psychics (corresponding to Abel), was made to fit the figure of heavenly Seth and his seed on the one hand, and the rest of humanity on the other, into the scheme. This will be demonstrated in detail when we come to discuss the cosmogony of the myth. The one remaining issue is therefore Pétrement's ingenious attempt to derive the four illuminators from the Valentinian Jesus. Despite her efforts she cannot plausibly derive all the names from Greek and/or Hebrew or Aramaic from characteristics of the Saviour; Eleleth defeats her, and the fact that the Valentinian Saviour is *already* accompanied by angels akin to him, might weaken any claim that the Gnostics were led to invent four from his characteristics.[92] The four illuminators seem too deeply rooted in Gnostic mythology and liturgical practice to be borrowed from the Valentinians, and once we discount their function as aeonic abodes for heavenly Adam, Seth and his seed, etc. as a later Sethianizing interpretation and insertion, then Pétrement's speculations about their links with the Valentinian aeons Man and Church, however plausible, become irrelevant.[93] She may be justified in detecting Valentinian influence on the *Apocryphon* as we have it, but if my analysis is correct, the Gnostics of Irenaeus 1.29 and 30 antedate both it and the Valentinians, probably even Valentinus himself.

In conclusion, if neither Tardieu's Platonizing Chaldaean nor Pétrement's Valentinian hypothesis seems entirely convincing, the latter is surely correct to relate the Gnostics of Irenaeus to the great creative figures of the early second century, Saturninus and Basilides associated with Antioch, and Valentinus of Alexandria, in all likelihood influenced by the Gnostic ideas (and texts?) Basilides brought there from Antioch. But while Pétrement has plausibly traced the development of Gnosticism in the strict sense from Saturninus and Basilides, and pointed to the way Basilides seems to have opened the door to Greek philosophy, particularly Platonic and Pythagorean, her hypothesis of Valentinian origins in the case of Irenaeus' Gnostics has led her to omit the vital missing link. As we have suggested already, these Gnostics are the innovators here by their introduction and development of both the Sophia myth missing in Saturninus and Basilides and the concepts of the emanation of male and female aeons in syzygy, and above all by their application of biological and psychological processes and metaphors to theology and cosmology as well as to anthropology. That Sophia's emotions concretize into the elements of the visible universe and her experiences form the archetype of those of the Gnostic elect is a fundamental Gnostic tenet shared with or, as I would argue, copied by the Valentinians.

The world-view of these Gnostics, as with Saturninus, Basilides and Valentinus, is undoubtedly Platonic. It reflects the attempt to derive the Many from the One, and to explain the visible universe as the work of a lower god, the Demiurge, emanated from the transcendent One beyond being, in terms of the inexplicable self-revelation and unfolding of the supreme God as Father, Mother and Son. Thus it is not far removed from the ideas of Syrian Middle Platonists of the second century like Numenius of Apamea, but as the fundamental concept of the self-revelation of the divine triad suggests, it is essentially a *Christian* scheme. It reflects Christian ideas and ways of interpreting the Old Testament in the light of the message of Paul and John, which see the God of the Old Testament as a blind, ignorant and arrogant Demiurge, and thus seek to discover the hitherto unknown God beyond God, first revealed by Christ and his proclamation. And it builds its theogony not on the basis of Genesis and the prophets, reflecting the work of and inspired by that Demiurge, but on the basis of Christian speculation on Christ and Wisdom such as is found in Hebrews, derived from the Psalms and Wisdom books but interpreted in the light of contemporary Platonic ideas. Above all it reflects the experience of salvation through a Christian Gnostic initiation ritual based on baptism in the name of the Gnostic triad, and unction (or sealing) patterned on the primal chrismation and perfection of the heavenly Son and promising the eschatological descent of the Spirit.

Notes

[1] Cf. *Adv. haer.* 1.31.3–4; 2.praef.2.

[2] Cf. Pétrement, *Separate* 15–18; R. McL. Wilson, 'Twenty years after' in Barc, *Colloque* 61; P. Perkins, 'Ireneus and the Gnostics', *VC* 30 (1976), 193–200; R. A. Greer, 'The dog and the mushrooms: Irenaeus' view of the Valentinians assessed' in Layton, *Rediscovery* 1.146ff. and discussion.

[3] Cf. Wisse, 'Library' 213–15, who although recognizing the unity of 1.29–31.2, ascribes it to Irenaeus' heresiological source, and not to him.

[4] Cf. 1.22.2.

[5] 1.29.1. That Irenaeus is the author of 1.29–32, against Wisse, has been convincingly demonstrated by Perkins, 'Ireneus'.

[6] See Rousseau–Doutreleau on 1.29.1 (SC 264 358 n. 1) in SC 263, 296–9. For the term 'Barbeliote' to describe them, cf. Sevrin, *Dossier* 11f. Even Turner, despite his focus on Sethianism, speaks of the 'Barbeliote' system of Irenaeus 1.29, 'Sethian Gnosticism' 71f. I will follow this convention, but see below.

[7] Cf. *AJ* B 44.14 and par; *HA* 86.30f.; 94.21f.; *On the Origin of the World* (C II,*5* = *OW*) 103.11–13; 107.30f.; *GE* III 58.25f.; *TP* 43.33–44.2; *Second Treatise of the Great Seth* (C VII,*2*) 53.27–31; 64.17–26; Iren. *Adv. haer.* 1.5.4 (cf. Hipp. *Ref.* 6.33 – Valentinians); Epiph. *Pan.* 25.2.3 (Gnostics); Theodore bar Konai *Schol.* 11 (Ophites).

[8] Schenke, 'Nag Hamadi Studien I: Das literarische Problem des Apokryphon Johannis' *ZRGG* 14 (1962), 60ff., detects a literary seam at this point in the *Apocryphon*. Cf. Krause in Foerster, *Gnosis 1* 100ff.; A. Werner, 'Bemerkungen zu einer Synopse der vier Versionen des Apokryphon des Johannes' in Nagel, *Studia Coptica* 137–46.

[9] 'Dog' 170.

[10] Cf. Perkins, 'Ireneus', esp. 200, where she suggests Irenaeus came across them among works he got from Valentinians.

[11] The *tabula capitulorum* of the Mss have Gnostics in 30 and Ophites and Cainites in 31 (Rousseau–Doutreleau 2 17).

[12] *Die Quellen der aeltesten Ketzergeschichte neu untersucht* (Leipzig, 1875), 191–219.

[13] *Quellen* 219.

[14] 219–20.

[15] *Separate* 352.

[16] Cf. Epiph. *Pan.* 25.2.1 (Gnostics from Nicolaus who revere Barbelo); 26.1.1f. (libertine Gnostics); 37.1.1f. (Ophites); 38.1.1–2 (Cainites).

[17] *Die Ketzergeschichte des Urchristentums* (Leipzig: Fues, 1884).

[18] In his article 'Gnostiker' RE VII/2 1534.

[19] 'The Study of Gnosticism', *JTS* 36 (1935), 48–51.

[20] '*Gnōstikoi* als häresiologischer Terminus', *ZNW* 57 (1966), 105–14, esp. 106f.

[21] 'Terminus' 109f.

[22] *Separate* 358.

[23] 'Terminus' 111.

[24] *Separate* 358.

[25] *Zur Quellenkritik des Epiphanios* (Vienna, 1865).

[26] 'The History of the Term Gnostikos' in Layton, *Rediscovery* 2.796–807.

[27] 'History' 799f.

[28] 800.

[29] 801.

[30] *Separate* 360f.

[31] 361.

[32] 'Gnostics and Valentinians in the Church Fathers', *JTS* n.s. 40 (1989), 26–47, esp. 26–34.

[33] 'Neglected Texts in the Study of Gnosticism', *JTS* n.s. 41 (1990), 26–50. He would even include the *Poimandres*, on the basis of the original non-Christian character of the sect's beliefs as a 'diverse amalgam of older faiths' (48).

[34] For a helpful survey of the uses of *gnōstikos*, see M. Tardieu and J.-D Dubois, *Introduction à la littérature gnostique 1* (Paris: Editions du Cerf/ Editions du CNRS, 1986), 21–9.

[35] *Separate* 361.

[36] 361, cf. Rousseau–Doutreleau 1, 311 note on 2, 384 n. 2, dropping *de.*

[37] 362.

[38] See n. 36.

[39] Cf. e.g. 1.8.3 (SC 264 120.69 *de mediis* = 121.841 *tōn mesōn*).

[40] Could Irenaeus' allusion imply that he knew more of the system in 1.29 than he summarizes, and that like the Gnostics of Epiph. *Pan.* 25.2.2, 3.4; 26.10.3–11 and the systems of *HA* (94.34–96.14) and *OW* (101.9–107.1), it too distinguished between an arrogant chief Archon or Demiurge (usually Ialdabaoth) and a disobedient or ambiguous rival Archon (Sabaoth or the 'left hand ruler')?

[41] E.g. in 1.23.4; 2.31.1; 3.4.2, 11.2, 12.12; 4.6.4, 33.3.

[42] E.g. in 1.11.1; 2.praef.1 where he distinguishes the Gnostics of 1.29–31 from the heresiological catalogue of the predecessors of Valentinus (1.23–28); 2.13.10, 35.2f.; 3.10.4, 11.1; 4.35.1; 5.26.2.

[43] Cf. *Separate* 357. Casey, 'Study' 49, denies the claim of Lipsius (and Pétrement) that 'Gnostics' in these contexts can be interpreted as Valentinians.

[44] *Separate* 363f.

[45] Cf. 1.praef.2 and Perkins, 'Ireneus' 200.

[46] Cf. e.g. Iren. 1.21.4; *Gospel of Truth* (C I,*3*) 18.1–11.

[47] 1.29.1.

[48] 1.29.3. This passage may reflect an Aramaic word-play on Eve (*hawwah*/Eve–*hawwa*/life:*hawwah*/Eve–*hawja*/instructor) who awakens and instructs earthly Adam as in *HA* 89.11–90.18 and *AA* 64.6–19. Cf. M. A. Williams, 'Variety in Gnostic Perspectives on Gender', in K. L. King ed., *Images of the Feminine in Gnosticism* (SAC 4) (Philadelphia: Fortress, 1988), 9f.

[49] Edwards, 'Neglected' 32ff., while clearly recognizing the Christian character of the 'Gnostics' of Plotinus and Porphyry, yet asserts the originally non- and pre-Christian nature of *AJ*, the Naassene Preaching, etc. (48).

[50] Purely for convenience, in what follows I will designate the successive versions of the text and the mythologoumena characteristic of them in terms of the traditional sect names; Barbelognostic, 'Ophite' and 'Sethian'.

[51] *Separate* 370ff.

[52] Cf. 1.30.10–11.

[53] *Separate* 387f., 406.

[54] Coptic text of B collated with C III with German translation in W. C. Till, *Die gnostischen Schriften des koptischen Papyrus Berolinensis 8502* (TU 60) (Berlin: Akademie, 1955, 2nd ed. rev. H.-M. Schenke, 1972); Coptic text of C II, III and IV with German translation in M. Krause and P. Labib, *Die drei Versionen des Apokryphon des Johannis im koptischen Museum zu Alt-Kairo* (ADAIK, Kopt. Reihe 1) (Wiesbaden: Harrassowitz, 1962); Coptic text, English translation and commentary on II in S. Giversen, *Apocryphon Johannis* (ATD 5) (Copenhagen: Munksgaard, 1963); French translation and commentary on B, II and III in M. Tardieu, *Écrits Gnostiques. Codex de Berlin* (SGM 1) (Paris: Editions du Cerf, 1984). See also Tardieu and Dubois, *Introduction* 107–23.

[55] *Dossier* 10.

[56] *Écrits* 26–45. For earlier, less satisfactory analyses, see Giversen's commentary; A. Kragerud, 'Apocryphon Johannis. En formanalyse', *NorTT* 65 (1966), 15–38.; M. Krause in Foerster, *Gnosis 1* 100f.

[57] *Écrits* 42, 163, 339–40.

[58] 38–43.

[59] 35.

[60] 33.

[61] 'System' 165f. See Introduction p. xv and n.12 for the list.

[62] 'System' 166.

[63] 'Phenomenon' esp. 593–7, 602–7. For a critique, see R. van den Broek, 'Present State' 55f.

[64] 'System' 169; 'Phenomenon' 607, 611f.

[65] 'Phenomenon' 612.

[66] A. F. J. Klijn, *Seth in Jewish, Christian and Gnostic Literature* (Supplements to *NovT* 16) (Leiden: Brill, 1977), 28, 117.

[67] 'Phenomenon' 592f. Cf. Stroumsa, *Seed* 11–13; Perkins, *Gnosticism* 21, n. 7.

[68] In Foerster, *Gnosis 1* 100–3.
[69] C. Schmidt, 'Irenäus und seine Quelle in *adv. haer.* I,29' in *Philotesia. Paul Kleinert zum 70 Geburtstag dargebracht* ed. A Harnack et al. (Berlin: Trowzisch, 1907), 335.
[70] 'Königlosigkeit als nachvalentinianisches Heilsprädikat' *NovT* 24 (1982), 316–39, esp. 316–28. See also his *Glaube als Gabe nach Johannes* (BWANT 112) (Stuttgart/Berlin/Köln/Mainz, 1980).
[71] Cf. Klijn, *Seth* 81–8.
[72] Cf. *AA* 69.4–76.7. This distinction appears to represent a Sethian version of the Valentinian threefold division of humanity. Cf. Bergmeier, 'Königlosigkeit' 323; *Glaube* 186ff.
[73] Cf. the role of Autogenes and the four illuminators in *AJ* B 51.9–14 par, of the illuminator Eleleth in *HA* 92.32–93.13, and the ascent of Allogenes in *Allogenes* 58.7–60.12.
[74] *Epiph. Pan.* 40.7.1–3.
[75] Cf. Klijn, *Seth* 61f. On Julius Africanus and Seth, see George Syncellus, *Chronographia* ed. G. Dindorf (Corpus Scriptorum Historiae Byzantinae) (Bonn: Weber, 1829), 16–18, 34.
[76] The scheme of light, darkness and intermediate spirit reflects the Gnostic systems of Iren. 1.29 and particularly 30; the concept of the 'unclean womb' (Hipp. *Ref.* 5.19.11–22) recalls the Gnostic ('Cainite') demiurgic Womb (Iren. 1.31.2; cf. Epiph. *Pan.* 25.5.1–3); Seth occurs as representing the supreme light (*Ref.* 5.20.2); and there may even be some trace of an initiatory baptismal rite (cf. the references to baptism, cup of living water, and robing in 5.19.22). On the much-vexed issue of the relation between Hippolytus' 'Paraphrase of Seth' and the Nag Hammadi *Paraphrase of Seem* (*sic*, C VII,2: Seem is usually identified as Shem), see Pétrement, *Separate* 441–6. She points to similarities between the figure of Seem/Shem in VII,2 and Seth and to the consensus that the two works are related, as well as the recognition, even among those arguing for a pre- and non-Christian origin of *Paraph. Shem*, that behind the revealer figure Derdekeas lies Christ. Although the claimed influence of Valentinianism may seem exaggerated, the suggestion that the work is late and a critical 'correction' and deliberate camouflaging of an earlier, more Christian Sethian source shared by Hippolytus' 'Paraphrase', polemicizing against Sethians and their baptismal practice, provides a more plausible explanation of the relationship than the alternative, which would see Hippolytus' 'Paraphrase' as a later Christianization of *Paraph. Shem*.
[77] Cf. *Pan.* 26.8.1; 39.5.1f.; 40.2.1–2, 7.1–5.
[78] *Haer.* 1.14.
[79] *Seth* 115 (my italics).
[80] *Dossier* 12, 276–9, 292.
[81] 275f.
[82] 276.

[83] See G. W. H. Lampe, *The Seal of the Spirit* (London: SPCK, 1967²), 120–32. Cf. the crucial evidence of the Naassene Gnostics in Hipp. *Ref.* 5.7.19; 9.21f. The Valentinian rite of chrism (cf. Iren. 1.21.3–5; *Gospel of Philip* (C II,*3* 74.12–24; 67.19–30)) may have been adopted from the Gnostics for whom chrism was crucial.

[84] Cf. Iren. 1.2.6., Pétrement, *Separate* 388–96. She would derive Harmozel from the *harmodios/zō* of 1.2.6; Oroiael from the beauty (*hōraios,* in season?) of 1.2.6; Daueithe from David, i.e. the 'beloved' of Valentinus frag. 6, *Gos. Truth* 30.31; 40.24f., and *Tripartite Tractate* (= *Tri. Trac.* C I,*5*) 87.8, and Eleleth from *El* in some form, or 'Paraclete' in *Tri. Trac.* 87.8f. as 'he who is called to help', as in *HA* 92.33–93.13, or, only too aware of the unsatisfactory character of all the above, from the pluperfect of *lanthanō* meaning 'he had been hidden', as an off-chance hypothesis (*Separate* 487)!

[85] 'System' 166–9.

[86] *Separate* 397ff.

[87] 'Catégories du temps dans les écrits gnostiques non valentiniens', *LTP* 37 (1981), 3–13.

[88] *Écrits* 272f.

[89] 'Königlosigkeit' 328.

[90] Cf. *AJ* B 51.1–52.1 and par; *HA* 92.27–94.2; *TP* 39.13–40.4 and the Archontics of Epiph. *Pan.* 40.7.1–2.

[91] On the origin of Sophia, cf. Iren. 1.29.4 (Sophia emitted from the First Angel standing beside Monogenes, i.e. Harmozel/Armoges), *GE* III 56.22–57.21 and par (Eleleth apparently responsible for 'hylic Sophia' and Saklas), and *TP* 39.13–32 (Eleleth responsible for the appearance of Saklas/Ialdabaoth, the offspring of Sophia); on the Autogenes and the four as linked with the five seals, cf. *GE* IV 74.9–78.10 and par; *TP* 47.28–48.35; 49.20–50.20; *Zost.* 6.7–7.22. On the significance of the five as on my conjecture related to the sealing with chrism of eyes, ears and mouth of the initiate, see ch. 2, section 2 and ch. 7, section 3.

[92] On the Valentinian angels escorting Jesus, cf. Iren. 1.4.5; Clem. Alex. *Exc. ex Theod.* 44.1, etc.

[93] *Separate* 397–406.

2

The Character and History of the Myth

1 The character of the Gnostic myth underlying Irenaeus 1.29 and 30 and the *Apocryphon of John*

We may know little about the original makers of the two related myths of Irenaeus *Adv. haer.* 1.29 and 30 apart from the fact that Irenaeus appropriately terms them Gnostics and that their ideas profoundly influenced Valentinianism and supplied the basis for the present *Apocryphon of John*. We have suggested that the most likely location and date for their literary activities is Syrian Antioch around the second and third decades of the second century CE. The first thing to note, as we have already remarked, is the Christian and specifically Christian Platonist character of the myth. If we dismiss the Schenke thesis of a hypothetical Jewish–Gnostic 'Sethianism' and/or sect responsible for it, perhaps related to Samaritanism, for the reasons outlined above, what of Tardieu's suggestion that the original author of the *Apocryphon* was a Christian related to, if critical of, the Johannine school, who rejected Christian use of the Jewish Torah as either rule and text (Judaeo-Christians) or text only (other Christians), and employed two types of sources to achieve this: the Fourth Gospel and material Tardieu terms 'Chaldean'?[1] The latter, he suggests, without spelling it out in detail, are revelations written in Greek by Syrians claiming to be simultaneously disciples of Berossus and Plato, and uniting Chaldaean astrology and Platonically-inspired philosophy.[2]

He may be correct in putting forward this kind of influence for e.g. the addition in the long version of the *melothesia* describing the creation of Adam's psychic body, purportedly taken from a 'Book of Zoroaster',[3] and the astrological details, zodiac, etc.[4] But as argued above, his suggestion of a similar source for the cosmogony shared by Irenaeus 1.29.1–4 and the *Apocryphon* does not seem entirely plausible or necessary. Why should Christians in Antioch influenced by the Johannine school and hostile to

Judaism appeal to that brand of Jewish–Platonic speculation? It is the Christian Platonists Saturninus and Basilides of Antioch, with their virulent anti-Judaism, who develop the kind of theogonical and cosmogonical speculations which most resemble those of our Gnostics. However, Tardieu's allusion to the Fourth Gospel does seem more convincing. Further comparison with Saturninus and Basilides brings out both the common Antiochene milieu and the developing influence of the Gospel of John and the Johannine community with their hostility to Judaism and concern for their Christian identity. Yet it is worth pointing out that the former's influence is indirect both in the case of Basilides and the Gnostics of Irenaeus 1.29 and of the *Apocryphon*: both subordinate Logos to Nous in their account of the heavenly world, and the secondary character of the influence of the Johannine Prologue is even more obvious in the exegesis of it supplied by the Valentinian Ptolemy.[5]

On the other hand, the continuing influence of John's Gospel on the myth underlying Irenaeus 1.29 in particular seems to illustrate both certain features of it (e.g. the role of Logos destroying the original ternary scheme, the descriptions of Christ and Autogenes, the light motif) and of the *Apocryphon* and related and dependent treatises from Nag Hammadi such as *Trimorphic Protennoia*.[6] And the concern of the author of the Johannine epistles with the themes of Christian identity, of chrism and knowledge, of Christ and counterchrists (i.e. the Antichrist), of the true and the false spirit,[7] uncannily mirrors that of our Gnostics, while Ignatius of Antioch may be including them among those who claim to be Christian but abstain from Catholic rites and believe in Jewish-type fables.[8] Finally, comparison with the christological and soteriological interests of another Syrian Christian, Tatian, around the mid second century, and his use and exegesis of John's Gospel, proves instructive. Again central are the problems of cosmology and soteriology: (*a*) how to understand the relation of God to the world in terms of prevailing mediatory models (e.g. Sophia, Logos, Holy Spirit); and (*b*) how to understand the problem of salvation – was it by natural endowment or by divine gift?

As I have argued elsewhere,[9] the basic Christian character of the myth underlying Irenaeus 1.29 and the *Apocryphon* appears first in its understanding of the supreme triad of Father, Mother and Son, a theme generally admitted to be fundamental.[10] Like the Fourth Gospel it identifies God as Spirit, but develops its myth in terms of the progressive emanation and diversifying descent of

Spirit understood in different ways on the various levels, on the analogy of Being in Platonism. Thus the Father is the great Invisible Spirit, entirely transcendent;[11] the Mother is the virginal Spirit who gives birth to the Son;[12] from the first of the four illuminator angels who surround him is derived the Holy Spirit (or Sophia, Wisdom),[13] whose saving activity finds its demonic counterpart in the final events of world history in the work of a counterfeit spirit.[14] It also develops the parallel Johannine theme of light: the Father the supreme Light, the Son the product of the Mother's bedazzlement by the Father, a light like him;[15] the Son emitting via an emanation of the Father, Light, the four illuminators to surround him, the first of these being responsible for the Holy Spirit or Wisdom.[16] Her power of light is transmitted to her abortive offspring, the Protarchon or Jewish Creator God, by his theft, and thus via him into this lower created world.[17] The other main theme, besides those of Spirit and light, involves the ontological character of the basic antithesis between knowledge and obedience and ignorance and recklessness, reflected in the contrasts between the archetypal patterns of male initiative combined with female action over against female initiative without male permission, and of divine revelation, emanation and appropriate doxological response over against demiurgical ignorance and hubris.[18]

The Christian character of the myth is equally evident in the, at first sight, peculiar episode of the anointing, perfection, and elevation of the heavenly Son, who thus becomes Christ. This features in several of the texts related to the *Apocryphon*,[19] but only Sevrin has glimpsed its importance. Unfortunately, however, he has limited his discussion to the possible liturgical implications; he sees the long version as having adapted a purely spiritual unction to fit the baptismal five seals rite.[20] And far from being a sign of later Christianization, this episode, which appears to have no precise parallel in pagan or Jewish theology, is central to the Gnostic's self-understanding: the experience of Christ is the archetype of that of the Gnostic, and the various heavenly entities (Christ, Autogenes, Adamas) are both hypostatizations of the one figure of the Son, as Pétrement has rightly pointed out,[21] and of the Gnostic, who, after initiation into *gnōsis* through baptism in the name of the triad Father, Mother, Son, is then anointed (the five seals of the Autogenes and illuminators) and perfected (Christ), becoming free from all deficiency and a true image of the Perfect Man (Adamas).[22] We should not forget that it was in Antioch that the name 'Christian' first emerged (Acts 11:26), and that second-century 'orthodox' Christians like Justin and Theophilus (of *Antioch!*) derived the titles 'Christ' and 'Christian' from their being anointed.[23]

In a manner strikingly reminiscent of Hebrews 1 and 2 with its similar idiosyncratic combination of Jewish–Christian and Platonic ideas, these Christian Gnostics have constructed a myth of primal Father, Mother and Son as an alternative myth of origins to Genesis 1–5, which for them applied to the later creation of the visible universe and humanity, the work of an ignorant and arrogant Demiurge, the God of the Old Testament, and his archons.[24] Again, rather than presuming a borrowing from supposed 'Chaldaean' sources for this original theogony and cosmogony, we should recognize the creative character of the myth and its makers, who are certainly influenced by Jewish Wisdom speculation like the Prologue of the Fourth Gospel, but who use that speculation more cosmologically than christologically. Thus they distinguish Christ from Barbelo/Sophia and from the Logos, a later addition.[25] The Sophia myth, *pace* Stead, MacRae, and Pétrement,[26] I would see as *the* contribution of the Gnostics of Irenaeus 1.29 and 30 to Valentinus and Christian theology. One significant task of second-century Christian theology could be said to be to determine the role and identity of Sophia, Wisdom, in relation to the Father, Son and Holy Spirit.[27] And although MacRae has clearly illustrated elements of the Gnostic Sophia myth from Jewish Wisdom and other materials, he has not to my mind convincingly demonstrated the existence of such a myth in Judaism. It was the Gnostics who created it.[28]

Furthermore, these Gnostics, along with those of 1.30, may with justice be seen as the pioneers in developing an understanding of God as triadic or trinitarian, perhaps even in immanent as well as economic terms. What unites the two systems of 29 and 30, besides the light theme and the Sophia myth, is that both develop alternative trinitarian schemes. Thus the system in 1.29, probably mainly under the influence of the female figures of Holy Spirit and Wisdom of Jewish Christianity,[29] but also aware of the speculations of contemporary Middle Platonists and Neopythagoreans on the divine hierarchy,[30] develops a triad of Father, Mother and Son, splitting the Mother into a higher and a lower Sophia, the latter of whom it identifies with the Holy Spirit.

The system in 1.30, on the other hand, whose idiosyncratic treatment of the figures of First Man and Son of Man (or Ennoia) uniting with First Woman or Holy Spirit to produce Christ as Third

Male has baffled commentators,[31] can best be interpreted as an attempt to develop a triad of (male) Father, (male/female) Son and (female) Spirit, generating Christ as the Only-Begotten Son. The Father can only reveal himself by self-projection or emanation as his Thought (Ennoia) and thus his Son: by an intellectual process of illumination, Father and Son generate Christ by the Holy Spirit of Gen 1:2. Whereas the system of 1.29 splits the second person into higher and lower Sophia and identifies the latter with Holy Spirit and Wisdom, the system of 1.30 splits the third person and identifies the higher as Spirit, the lower as Wisdom, and whereas the system of 1.29 identifies Christ as the Son within the Trinity, the system of 1.30 has Christ as fourth outside the Trinity, ascending to it.[32]

This reference to emanation indicates another major characteristic of the underlying Gnostic myth to which I have already drawn attention more than once: the pervading influence of Platonic/Pythagorean ideas, hinted at in Basilides, even more obvious in Valentinus.[33] All three share, according to Irenaeus' account, a concern with the ineffable, nameless, unoriginate Father, his self-revelation by a process of emanations, of which the first or supreme male is Nous and a later is Logos.[34] In all, but most obviously in Valentinus, Neopythagorean speculations about the monad, dyad, tetrad and ogdoad seem to play some part.[35] All three also share the concept of a progressive descent from being and perfection until we reach the visible cosmos and humanity, the work of a lower god, a cross between the Demiurge of Plato's *Timaeus* and the Jewish Creator, and his subordinates, copying the heavenly world in some fashion.[36] But the Gnostics, and even more so Valentinus, present a much more orderly scheme of emanations in terms of male–female syzygies and multiples of two than the Basilides of Irenaeus' account, which I, with Pétrement, would see as closer to the original than that of Hippolytus.[37] Again it would seem – against Pétrement – that the Gnostics were the creative thinkers here, developing beyond the pioneering efforts of Basilides and stimulating the more sophisticated and abstract speculations of Valentinus and his followers. And it is surely significant that, as Turner has so ably shown, it was from the Sethian reworking of the Barbelognostic system, and *not* from the Valentinian tradition, that the *Zostrianos* group of tractates emerged which so profoundly affected Plotinus, Porphyry and the later Neoplatonists.[38]

Indeed it could be suggested that the Gnostics were among the first Christians to be influenced by Platonism, and thus that the claim of scholars like Schenke, Turner and Pearson to detect a Platonization of the later Sethian writings like *Allogenes, Zostrianos*, the *Three Steles of Seth* and *Marsanes* is slightly misleading: the Gnostics were Platonists from the first! They developed their Platonism in dialogue with the evolving Platonic tradition, perhaps even anticipating Neoplatonism in some respects.[39]

Finally, although the myths of Irenaeus 1.29 and 30 and the *Apocryphon* are, as Schenke, Tardieu and Stroumsa argue, essentially literary and exegetical, developing the proper Gnostic understanding of the Old Testament and Genesis 1–9 in particular,[40] they cannot be explained purely and simply as *originating* from such a process: they are creative, original works deriving from specific Christian groups with particular rituals. Schenke and others are right to stress the importance of that aspect, reflected in the recurring mention in certain texts of the mysterious 'five seals'.[41] But rather than see such as a ritual deriving from a supposed Jewish Sethian baptist sect, of which we have no firm evidence apart from interpretations of the 'Sethian' texts, it is surely more plausible to understand it as emerging out of the *Christian* ritual of initiation. The heart of the Gnostic myth would seem to be the archetypal experience of Christ and of Sophia – the reception, in one's alienated state of exile (*paroikēsis*) or oblivion, of the saving revelation or *gnōsis* through a vision or experience of the Saviour and his attendant angels. This leads to repentance (*metanoia*), illumination (*phōtismos?*) and exaltation to the status of or to union with Christ, the Autogenes or Self-Begotten, one's heavenly consort, symbolized by the three stages of *Zostrianos* (*paroikēsis, metanoia, autogenēs*)[42] and the processes of purification (robing, baptism, enthronement, glorification, final rapture) leading to the 'five seals' (i.e. symbols used in chrismation) outlined in *Trimorphic Protennoia*.[43]

Just as in the case of Valentinus, Elchasai and Mani, whose distinctive mythologies arose from visionary experiences within a Christian community setting,[44] so we might also conjecture with regard to the author(s) of the Gnostic systems, particularly of Irenaeus 1.29 and the *Apocryphon*. The constant character of the basic mythologoumena of Father, Mother Barbelo, and Son; of Christ, Autogenes, and Adamas; of the four illuminators; of Sophia and her offspring Ialdabaoth/Saklas, and the recurring doxological pattern of request for revelation, resulting emanation and thanksgiving, usually accompanied by references to living water and the five seals in a liturgical/initiatory context, despite the variety of interpretations and the different literary genres involved, surely point to a unified underlying phenomenon, a community or communities with its appropriate ritual and myth of origins. For this last we should not so much look to the continuing influence of hypothetical Platonizing Chaldaean treatises borrowed from outside, as to inspired internal creation corresponding to the existential and soteriological experiences, desires, and needs of the community which originally produced it, and the communities which continued to use, adapt, and develop it, including Gnostics, Valentinians and Sethians.

The text of the *Apocryphon* and of those works most closely related to it, such as *Trimorphic Protennoia* and the *Gospel of the Egyptians*, suggest a mythology that has evolved over a considerable period of time, that is used in different ways for different purposes, apologetic, liturgical, catechetic, but nevertheless one that retains a certain inner core and coherence, remarkable in the light of the evidence, both external and internal, of the variety and plasticity of Gnostic mythology. Schenke's appeal, in the face of Wisse's criticisms of the 'Sethian unicorn', to the evidence of a central concern with an initiatory rite of baptism in these texts, confirmed by Sevrin's researches, is surely justified. How else is one to explain the tendency in evidently later texts not to replace such figures but to reduplicate them and add to them; they are fundamental, not just as individuals but as part of a central 'classic' myth.

2 The history of the Gnostic myth

That last point brings us to the final and perhaps most speculative section in our discussion of the myth, its makers, and character: namely an attempt to suggest how the myth underlying Irenaeus 1.29 and the *Apocryphon*, as well as the closely related one in Irenaeus 1.30, might have evolved.[45] We have attempted to highlight the influence of Christian ideas such as those found in Paul and the Pauline tradition, John and his community, and especially Hebrews, a theme that will be developed further in what follows. We have also noted the importance of exegesis, especially of Genesis 1–9 and of Hellenistic Jewish and early Christian speculation about Wisdom, Spirit, and Logos. We have also suggested evidence of a process of 'Sethianization', in some way related to Valentinian ideas and probably reflecting the Gnostic response to 'orthodox' criticism of the novelty of their beliefs, and have drawn attention to the continuing influence of and dialogue with the Platonic tradition as it evolves from Middle to Neoplatonism. Finally we have noted the significance of ritual liturgical elements and practices, apparently centring around initiation into *gnōsis* (baptism and five seals), which are only hinted at in the *Apocryphon* but which are more marked and more spiritualized in certain (most likely later) texts such as the *Gospel of the Egyptians* and *Zostrianos*.

Perhaps the boldest and most detailed attempt to sketch how the 'Sethian' Gnosticism of Schenke's group of texts might have developed is Turner's recent essay.[46] In it he first draws attention to the same major factors I have outlined above (Hellenistic–Jewish speculation on Sophia; midrashic interpretation of Genesis 1–6; doctrine and practice of baptism; the developing Christology of the early Church; religiously orientated Neopythagoreanism and Middle Platonism).[47] But he presupposes and begins with the Schenke thesis of Sethianism as a pre-Christian religious phenomenon, the product of a Jewish baptismal sect of the first centuries BCE and CE, encapsulating the sacred history of the seed of (heavenly) Seth and deriving from a peculiar exegesis of Genesis 1–6. This sect was then successively Christianized and Platonized.[48]

Turner sees Sethianism as having interacted with Christianity in five phases: (1) as a non-Christian baptismal sect given primordial divine wisdom via Adam and Seth and expecting a final saving visitation of Seth; (2) as gradually Christianized from the later first century on by the identification of pre-existent Christ with Seth or Adam; (3) as increasingly estranged from a Christianity becoming more orthodox towards the end of the second century; (4) as rejected by the Great Church but increasingly attracted to the individualistic contemplative practices of third-century Platonism; and (5) as estranged from orthodox Platonists of the late third century, and increasingly fragmented into derivative and other sectarian and gnostic groups.[49]

I can accept Turner's stages (3) to (5), but, as regards (1) and (2), as Klijn has demonstrated and I have already argued, not only is there almost no evidence of interest in Seth as an earthly, let alone heavenly, figure in Jewish circles in the relevant period (including what little we know of contemporary baptist groups) and nothing much in 'orthodox' Christian groups before the third century, but Turner's ingenious reconstruction does not explain why *Seth* should be the heavenly redeemer; why not simply Adam? Further, it elides the vital distinction between heavenly and earthly Seth, and fails to do justice to the texts which Schenke and others want to claim as Sethian, but which unfortunately do not actually mention Seth and his seed at all (e.g. *Hypostasis of the Archons, Trimorphic Protennoia* and even *Apocalypse of Adam*), or in which, as I and others argue, Seth and his seed are a later addition which cuts across the underlying pattern of revelation and salvation.[50] Why, too, should the non-Christian Sethians, if they existed, have wished to Christianize their beliefs? Why not, like the Mandaeans, reject Christianity, its doctrines and practices, in particular its baptismal practices? As Pétrement has argued, it seems much simpler to account for the anti-Judaism, the hostility to the Old Testament Demiurge and his archons as ignorant world creators, the interest in heavenly Man and Son of Man, Adamas and Seth, and the centrality of Christ as heavenly figure obviously identified with the Illuminator and persecuted on his third parousia, despite efforts to suggest otherwise, by presupposing Christian influence.[51]

From the perspective of the likely existence of a Sethian baptismal rite of initiation (the five seals) Sevrin, too, while accepting the centrality of both Sethian and Barbeliote elements in the *Apocryphon*, but seeing the former as progressively integrating the latter's rite and doctrine of baptism into its later scheme, still refuses to accept that the rite and doctrine could be of Christian origin. He insists that this Barbeliote and Sethian baptism cannot be considered Christian in its stock elements or origin, but he does allow it might have come into being after Christianity.[52] On the basis of his analysis he finds that the *Apocryphon* represents the oldest tradition, and the *Apocalypse of Adam* the oldest Sethian document. *Trimorphic Protennoia* he sees as developing from the data of the *Apocryphon*, particularly its Pronoia hymn, and echoing a liturgical formula from the latter. This process culminates in the *Gospel of the Egyptians* on the Sethian side; it also integrates the baptismal traditions of *Zostrianos*. The latter must be considered a late form (although it contains baptismal traditions prior to the *Gospel of the Egyptians*). The only direct dependence he finds is that of the *Untitled Treatise* in the Bruce Codex on *Zostrianos*. *Melchisedek* appears to be a Christian work employing a hymnic/liturgical tradition combining the Barbeliote and Sethian elements.[53]

This sketch of course only applies to the liturgical material and not to the doctrinal relationships which are our primary concern, but it does once again confirm the priority of the *Apocryphon* and from a different perspective, offering a most promising insight into the character and unity of the 'Sethian' text group. It does help to explain the way certain mythologoumena and liturgical patterns keep on recurring, and may thus assist in any proposed reconstruction of the underlying myth and its evolution. The unity in diversity may be found more in practice than in doctrine, just as conversely the differences between texts which appear to be close doctrinally (e.g. *On the Origin of the World, Hypostasis of the Archons* and *Apocalypse of Adam*) may derive from differences in practice.[54]

Finally we might note a most significant suggestion made by Sevrin in a footnote which would tend to confirm my claim that the myth underlying the doctrine and practice of the Gnostics of Irenaeus 1.29 and the *Apocryphon* represents an increasingly elaborate development and reduplication of the experiences of the Gnostic elect as expressed archetypically in those of Christ (his heavenly virgin birth, anointing, perfection and elevation) and Sophia (her exile, repentance, affusion and elevation). His suggestion is that the formula applied in the *Apocryphon* to those who persisted and finally repented and are placed in the fourth aeon of Eleleth might indicate the origin of the stages of *paroikēsis* and *metanoia* in *Zostrianos*.[55]

Sevrin's analysis is undoubtedly penetrating and suggestive but he may be too hasty in rejecting a possible Christian origin for the baptismal rite of his 'Barbeliote/Sethian' texts. He has seen and demonstrated the secondary character of the Sethian material, but is still too much under the spell of Schenke, Tardieu and Poirier and their explanation of the four illuminators/aeons as four stages of Sethian salvation history, and has been unable to grasp the full significance of the unction of the Son in the *Apocryphon, Trimorphic Protennoia* and the *Gospel of the Egyptians,* and the link of the Autogenes and the four illuminators with the initiation rite of the five seals.

Sevrin argues that the five seals rite probably involved a five-fold affusion (in the name of the Autogenes),[56] rather than unction, but an alternative interpretation of the evidence based on the similar phenomenon among the Marcosians and Naassene (and Ophite) Gnostics would seem more satisfactory. G. W. H. Lampe has argued that it was Christian Gnostics such as the Marcosians who first attest post-baptismal unction with chrism and that it is to this that the term 'seal' is mostly attached.[57] Quispel too has plausibly interpreted the enigmatic epitaph of Flavia Sophe with its mention of Sophe 'anointed (*chrio*), with incorruptible holy ointment (*myron*) from the baths (*loutron*) of Christ' (see plate 2) as deriving from the Italian Heracleonite school of Valentinus, who Quispel claims derived his theology of baptism from the 'Ophite' Gnostics.[58] If we then ask *why* this practice should have developed, I would point to the centrality of the heavenly anointing/ perfection of Christ motif among the Barbeloite (including Naassene) Gnostics.[59] The evidence suggests that they practised a threefold baptismal affusion in the name of Father, Mother and Son followed by chrismation (of eyes, ears and mouth using some mystic sign = the five seals?) in the name of the Autogenes and four illuminators.[60] The last hypothesis reflects the fundamental role of Christ/chrism and the illuminators in the myth, offers some explanation of the number and nature of seals, and perhaps even finds some support in the – admittedly – exceedingly obscure language of the hymnic passage at the end of the *Gospel of the Egyptians* and the ending of the *Apocalypse of Adam*. The former seemingly has the baptized initiate refer to sight, understanding and proclamation of the Father, Mother and Son, as well as to chrism mixed with water,[61] while the latter refers to Adam's hidden knowledge as the holy baptism of those who have eternal knowledge through those born of the Word (*Logos*) and the illuminators.[62]

How then did the Christian Gnostic myth underlying Irenaeus 1.29 (and 30) and the *Apocryphon*, as reflected in both doctrine and ritual practice, develop? In attempting to answer this question we shall have to consider where, when and how the major elements, theologoumena and factors came together: the triad of Father, Mother and Son and the Son's anointing as Christ; the emanation of the Father's attributes in male/female syzygies; the appearance of the four illuminators, of Autogenes and Adamas, and finally the origin of Sophia and her fall, which gave rise to the ignorant and arrogant Demiurge, Ialdabaoth, the Creator God of the Old Testament and Judaism, as unwitting vehicle of the divine light-power present in the Gnostics and requiring to be awakened and rescued by divine revelation and sacramental initiation. Where can we find such a combination of revolutionary – if modified – anti-Judaism and anti-cosmicism; a Sophia myth involving theogony and cosmogony rather than Christology; a Platonically-inspired understanding of the hierarchical levels of being and of the descent

Apocryphon of John, Berlin Coptic Codex (Papyrus Berolinensis 8502 = B).
Courtesy of Staatliche Museen zu Berllin-Preussischer Kulturbesitz Agyptisches Museum und Papyrussammlung, Budestr. 1-3, 10178 Berlin.

and ascent of the divine soul or spark; a soteriology which centres in the revelation to the elect of a hitherto Unknown God through his Son, identified as the pre-existent Christ; and a sacramental initiation apparently involving baptism and chrismation?

There may be elements of this in the fragmentary and possibly distorted picture given by Irenaeus' heresiological catalogue of the figures of Simon Magus and Menander (anti-Judaism; anti-cosmicism; Ennoia figure analogous to Barbelo/Sophia; revelation of Unknown God), but Pétrement is surely right to derive the beginnings of this kind of Gnosticism from the figures of Saturninus and Basilides.[63] Both are associated with the cosmopolitan city of Antioch where contemporary Christians were struggling to define their identity in the face of powerful Jewish and pagan currents.[64] And as Layton points out, Saturninus gives perhaps the nearest approximation to a full telling of the Christian Gnostic myth besides the *Apocryphon* and the *Gospel of the Egyptians*.[65] In Saturninus we find, apparently for the first time, such Gnostic elements as a marked anti-Judaism and anti-cosmicism (hostility to the God of the Jews as one of the seven angels who created the world and humanity; ascetic rejection of procreation, etc.); the descent/ascent of a divine spark in the context of a Platonic cosmology and anthropology fused with reinterpretation of Genesis 1–9 (the human body made by the seven angels in the divine image, animated by a heavenly spark attracted down into it, the various elements finally restored to their original states); a docetic Christology (Christ sent by the Father to destroy the Jewish God and the evil section of humanity, appearing like a man to save those who believe in him); a critical reading or reverse exegesis of the Jewish scriptures (Gen 1:26f. applied to the creator angels; the Old Testament prophecies divided between them and Satan).[66]

What is missing (possibly because of the compression of the heresiological account)[67] is any explanation of how everything originated, i.e. the characteristic speculations of the *Apocryphon* on the One and his emergence, and above all of anything corresponding to the Sophia myth of the Gnostics and Valentinians. What is striking about their use of it is that it both derives the Demiurge and the visible cosmos from the emotions and passions of the lower Sophia, and gives the Demiurge a more positive role as transmitter of the divine and creator of the visible universe as the necessary theatre for the salvation of the elect. In

Saturninus the basic mythology appears to involve a heavenly figure (whether male or female is unclear) being spied and copied by the seven angels.[68]

On the other hand, although we find reference in the Basilides of Irenaeus to Sophia as one of a series of hypostatized attributes of the Father, responsible with Dynamis for the ensuing emanated worlds,[69] there is no logical scheme of progression echoing philosophical ideas or developed Sophia myth as with the Gnostics and Valentinians. So I would argue that it is with the Gnostics of Irenaeus that we must begin, as a Christian group reacting to Jewish (and 'orthodox' Christian?) rejection of them and their claims, with a characteristic form of initiation based on their own experiences or (more likely) those of the creative genius responsible for their myth. Despite the lack of evidence we could plausibly infer the existence of similar initiatory rites for the Saturninians and Basilidians as visible sectarian groups identified by the heresiologists from Justin onwards.[70]

I have attempted to sketch the original form of the Gnostic myth elsewhere,[71] and have noted the major elements above: the supreme triad of Father, Mother and Son and the last's heavenly chrismation; the characteristic development of the themes of Spirit and light in terms of two levels, the celestial and terrestrial, linked by a descending series of emanations; the use of the figure of Sophia as split into a higher (Barbelo) and lower (Holy Spirit), like the Numenian Demiurge or two aspects of the Platonic World Soul, and developed cosmologically (as in Proverbs 8 and Wisdom of Solomon 7) rather than christologically (as in Hebrews 1 and the Prologue of the Fourth Gospel); the fundamental similarity with and likely influence of Hebrews 1–2 and its proof texts from the Psalms and Wisdom literature, its understanding of the Son in relation to the angels, as well as the growing influence of the Fourth Gospel and the Prologue in particular, which has led to a distortion of the original ternary structure of the myth by the introduction of the Logos and Autogenes figures. Thus the original myth must probably be dated as roughly contemporary with those of Saturninus and Basilides and just prior to that of Valentinus, who echoes its view of Adam as the creation of angels,[72] and who, as I have argued above, was very probably influenced by it.

In all likelihood this myth must have included more than the summary in Irenaeus 1.29. If on the basis of the prototypical experiences of Christ and Sophia we presume a form of initiation involving invocation of the Son, Christ (with Father and Mother and with Adamas as the prototype heavenly Man), and the imparting of the saving *gnōsis* to the initiates who have seen the light, repented of their blindness, renounced the world and undergone baptism and chrismation, then this presupposes and requires a developed myth which could account for past, present and future. Such a myth would include an account of origins, an explanation of the present paradox of the Gnostic as possessing divine power yet needing illumination and salvation from the ignorant and evil rulers of this world (i.e. a Gnostic history of salvation involving reinterpretation of Genesis), as saved by initiation yet still awaiting future perfection (i.e a realized but also futurist eschatology).

Now there are hints even in Irenaeus' condensed summary in 1.29 of further developments beyond cosmogony. Thus there is the blasphemy of the Demiurge as the natural transition to a likely response from heaven; creation of earthly Adam and hence Genesis reinterpretation as in 1.30 and the *Apocryphon*, etc.; the title 'Soter' for Armoges (Harmozel); the elevation of Christ/Light and Adamas from the angelic realm of Armoges; the mysterious and neglected figure of Tree/Knowledge; as well as the underlying soteriological structure I have isolated (the prototypical experiences of Christ and Sophia). All these point to a further necessary development of anthropogony, soteriology and eschatology, probably along the lines suggested by the continuation in the allied myth in 1.30, and in the *Apocryphon*. Certainly the Autogenes and the four illuminators do have a significant saving role in the *Apocryphon* in persuading Ialdabaoth to breathe his stolen light-power into the inert Adam.[73] It may be that the lack of a clear consort for the Sophia of the more original form of the *Apocryphon*, as compared to the version in 1.30, much more like the Valentinian Achamoth as sister of Christ, might have persuaded Irenaeus to take only the theogony and cosmogony of his version of the *Apocryphon* in 1.29 (a[1]), and use 1.30 for the remaining composite material. Thus while the theogony and cosmogony of 1.29 is much more akin to the Valentinian system Irenaeus is attempting to refute, in the case of anthropogony and soteriology the myth of 1.30 is more germane. He probably included the theogony and cosmogony of 1.30 because of the relevance of the speculations about Man, Son of Man, and Church, and Sophia split into higher and lower, with Christ the son of the higher and brother of the lower being caught up into heaven.[74]

But our hypothetical (a¹) redaction of the *Apocryphon* probably did not yet possess its present frame story or its developed negative theology, and certainly not the Pronoia–Epinoia scheme, Pronoia hymn of the long recension or Sethian material. On the other hand it almost certainly had its triple ternary structure, as analysed by Tardieu, as a revelation treatise expounding the triad of Father, Mother and Son in terms of past (myth of origins), present (Genesis reinterpretation and history of salvation as in Irenaeus 1.30), and future (destiny of souls). Our hypothetical document would thus contain the whole myth and resemble the source from which Irenaeus took his excerpt, probably developing the roles of the Tree/Knowledge, of Harmozel as Saviour and of the Son, Christ, and presenting Sophia as an active revealer/redeemer.[75] Again this redaction may not yet have had the mythologoumenon of Ialdabaoth and the seven creator archons.[76] It would certainly not have contained the passage on the four aeons as abodes of Adamas, Seth and his seed,[77] nor that on the dispatch of the Epinoia of light as helper which Tardieu includes in his original redaction (n).[78]

Since it would only make sense for Gnostics claiming to be Christians and evidently influenced by the Fourth Gospel and its community to compose a pseudepigraphical work in the name of John, son of Zebedee, when that Gospel had come to be accepted in the Great Church, i.e. by the time of Irenaeus and Theophilus, the next stage (a²) of adding the frame story, expanding the negative theology section, developing the Pronoia–Epinoia scheme with its final Pronoia hymn, and converting the revelation treatise into a dialogue between the risen Saviour and John, must date from that period (last quarter of the second century). The Naassene Psalm, with its reference to the Saviour's revelatory descent with seals to impart awaking *gnōsis*, in all likelihood reflects that Pronoia hymn, as Tardieu claims.[79] Sophia becomes downgraded and relieved of her soteriological functions, and we can also probably ascribe to this redaction the development of the Ialdabaoth–Saklas–Samael material, the seven archons and twelve powers, which appears to combine traditions from the system of Irenaeus 1.30 which are developed in the *Hypostasis of the Archons*. The latter seems to presuppose a Barbelognostic theogony and cosmogony but concentrates on and develops other traditions about its main subject, the archons.[80] That its interpretation of Genesis 2–6 is closer to the Septuagint and betrays the influence of Jewish midrashic material and Aramaic wordplays might suggest a date in the mid second century and acquaintance with Jewish or Jewish–Christian circles and concerns. But it ultimately seems dependent on the scheme underlying the *Apocryphon*, as it in turn preserves material further developed by *On the Origin of the World*.[81]

The latter, as Perkins has so ably demonstrated, is best seen as a coherent reinterpretation of the Gnostic cosmological traditions of the *Apocryphon*, the *Hypostasis* and the 'Ophites' in terms of the philosophical terminology and debates of the time, in order to defend the author's views against popular Middle Platonic and Stoic alternatives.[82] Thus Perkins is led to date the work to somewhere around 175 CE.[83]

Despite its fragmentary nature, the very brief untitled piece (C IX,2) dubbed *The Thought of Norea* by the American editors, reveals enough similarity with the figures and themes of Barbelognostic theogony, cosmogony and anthropology to link it both with the *Apocryphon* and the *Hypostasis* (Norea herself representing both higher and lower Sophia as Turner acutely observes;[84] Father of the All, Adamas, Nous, Light, Logos, Autogenes, Epinoia, the four holy helpers (i.e. the four illuminators)). The prominence of Norea in the latter may even have inspired the work, as Turner suggests,[85] and the experience of Norea/Sophia (cry to heaven, response, rest in the Autogenes as self-generated, help from the four) echoes the prototypical soteriological pattern I have identified in the *Apocryphon* and related texts.[86] A date from around the end of the second century seems likely.[87]

It is only at this stage (beginning of the third century) that one can envisage the reworking of (a^2) (= Tardieu's (n^1)) into (a^3), a 'Sethian' reinterpretation of the myth provoked by 'orthodox' Christian criticism of novelty: the Gnostics appealed to and developed the myth of the Seth of Gen 4:25f. as 'another seed' (*sperma*), the son of Man/Adamas and heavenly progenitor of their race, the 'kingless' or 'immovable race'.[88] This would account for salvation in the past and suggest a continuity of revelation. To accommodate this, the four illuminator figures were transformed into spatial aeons and the history of salvation was partitioned (not very successfully!) into four periods. This rather predestinationist approach, as we shall see, cuts across or ignores the earlier scheme of salvation for various souls of redaction (a^2) and reflects the Valentinian concept of the 'seed' and distinction between the pneumatics and the psychics.[89] The redactor of (a^3) also probably added the further Genesis reinterpretation (chs 5–9) which reflects Sethian themes[90] and perhaps an excerpt on the creation of psychic Adam from a certain 'Book of Zoroaster'.[91] We can perhaps place the short recension (s) at this point. Its redactor may not have had the material from the 'Book of Zoroaster' and omitted the Pronoia hymn because of its length or because it was difficult to reconcile it with the roles of the Saviour or the Mother.[92]

But the *Apocryphon* with the Pronoia hymn undoubtedly under-lies and structures *Trimorphic Protennoia*,[93] which may be roughly contemporary with the (a³) recension of the *Apocryphon* but which, intriguingly, seems unaware of the Sethian material. Thus it seems to mark a fascinating moment of transition in that it presupposes and develops the Barbelognostic theogony, cosmogony and soteriology (the triad Father, Mother and Son; Christ identified with Autogenes; the four illuminators and servants, baptizers, etc.; and the five seals), identifies Sophia with the Epinoia of light as a passive figure,[94] assigns aeons to the four illuminators but does not structure them hierarchically or temporally as abodes of Adamas, Seth and his seed:[95] all these are conspicuously absent from this supposedly 'Sethian' work. Turner's detailed literary analysis, although sophisticated and ingenious,[96] is vitiated by his assumptions that this work is Sethian, that the Sethians were a pre-Christian breakaway Jewish sect, and that one of their fundamental ideas was a tripartition of history involving the triple descent scheme of a saviour figure.[97]

It seems simpler to assume that the redactor(s) of *Trimorphic Protennoia* knew the (a²) version of the *Apocryphon* with the Pronoia hymn, and developed the pattern of the three inter-ventions/rebukes/descents of the female saviour figure as respectively Voice (Father), Sound (Mother) and Word (Son).[98] The glosses we find added to Barbelo in the (a²) version (e.g. 'primordial Man', 'triple male', 'with three powers, three names', etc.)[99] form the basis of an expansion of the former's doctrine into the three main sections of the work and conclud-ing revelation. That the redactors developed an already existing myth involving cosmogony, eschatology and soteriology, adding aretalogies, etc., seems more likely than Turner's supposition that they expanded the original Pronoia hymn by aretalogies and added doctrinal passages to them.[1] The revealer figure Protennoia is obviously an extrapolation of Barbelo/Pronoia. For similar, related aretalogies one could compare passages in *On the Origin of the World*,[2] the 'Gospel of Eve' of Epiphanius' Gnostics,[3] and *Thunder: Perfect Mind*.[4]

One might find Turner's redaction theory of the *Protennoia* overelaborate and flawed by its Sethian presuppositions, and be led to reject his claim of secondary Christianization, but his interpretation of the third subtractate as a polemic, in the light of John's Gospel and the Prologue in particular, against certain non-Gnostic understandings of Christ is attractive and persuasive.[5] Yet here again one must reject his claim that this was part of an explicit Christianization: the mythology underlying the work is, as I have argued, at bottom of Christian origin.[6] The echoes of the Fourth Gospel derive from some awareness of it and reinterpretation of it in a Gnostic context.[7] Such a reinterpretation might well have been suggested by the reworking of the *Apocryphon* as a dialogue between the risen Christ (who appears in three forms!) and John about past, present and future. The final reference to the Protennoia placing her seed in the holy light in silence may mark the beginnings of Sethianization.[8]

For it is precisely in this period early in the third century that we find emerging an interest in Seth as Christ and his pure seed in the Sethoites of Pseudo-Tertullian,[9] and an identification by Julius Africanus of the 'sons of God' of Gen 6:1 as the righteous descended from him (*genealogoumenoi*) until the time of the Saviour.[10] Further, around the middle of the century Mani knows and quotes from an 'Apocalypse of Sethel' (i.e. Seth), in which Seth is transformed into an angelic being, transported to heaven and receives revelations of the greatest mysteries.[11] The middle of the third century also seems a likely date for the long recension of the *Apocryphon* (1), the work of a harmonizer, Tardieu's (n^2).[12]

Despite the efforts of the original editors and others to date it earlier,[13] the *Apocalypse of Adam* also seems to derive from early in the third century. For although Sevrin considers it the earliest of the Sethian tractates proper because of its lapidary formulae and somewhat oblique association of the baptized with the seed of Seth,[14] it does presuppose a developed version of the cosmogony of the *Apocryphon*, and introduces mythologoumena without explanation precisely as already known traditional material.[15] But there seems no need to posit two sources in the way Hedrick does, one (A) a Jewish–Gnostic apocalypse marking the transition from Judaism to Gnosticism, the other (B) more clearly Gnostic, non-Christian, less Jewish, both redacted before 150.[16] Besides the criticisms of Perkins and Sevrin which suggest that Hedrick's analysis separates elements which belong together,[17] there is the fact that *both* sources presuppose the same Sethian form of the

Gnostic myth.[18] What Hedrick's analysis does bring out is the –
not entirely successful – attempt to combine a soteriological
scheme of archontic move and angelic countermove (A) with a
triple descent of the Phoster/Illuminator scheme (B).[19]

Further, Sevrin's arguments for seeing the figure of the Phoster/
Illuminator in its context as a Christian feature, and for the work
as a post-Christian, Christian–Gnostic text, seem more persuasive
than the attempts to deny that the *Apocalypse* has undergone any
Christian influence.[20] But I part company from Sevrin over his
interpretation of the Phoster as Seth as being non-Christian, and
of the *Apocalypse* as superficially Christianized, on the basis of my
analysis of the Barbeloite–Sethian myth. Perkins has rightly drawn
attention to the literary character of the work as not a Gnostic
Shorter Catechism (against Beltz)[21] or as imparting any dogma at
all (against Schottroff),[22] but an ironic polemic using existing
Jewish literary models (testament and apocalypse) to attack the
Creator God of Jews (and Christians!) and reinforce the solidarity
and identity of the Gnostic community.[23]

Here surely lies the key to understanding the work. Under the
growing influence of Seth traditions in Christianity at this period,
the *Apocalypse* has used the figures of Adam and Seth, the traditions
surrounding them and the literary forms of apocalypse and
testament familiar to both Jews and Christians, to defend and justify
the particular mythology and baptismal doctrine propounded by
its *Christian* Sethian Gnostic group. Thus Christ, the Phoster, has
continually preserved that Sethian group throughout history
against the continual attacks of the Jewish (and Christian) Creator
God and his powers (triple descent scheme), and brought the
saving knowledge and the true understanding and practice of water
baptism, defiled by non-Gnostic Christians, whose belief and
practice remain under the tyrannous sway of Saklas and his
subordinates.[24] The utilization of old Jewish haggadic traditions
and the conventions of pseudepigraphical authorship (Adam's
knowledge should not be too accurate!) have combined to conceal
the true Christian Gnostic character and late dating of what is a
sophisticated piece.[25]

Finally, as regards the dating, there is also some evidence to
suggest the work is post-Valentinian. That the descendants of Ham
and Japheth can participate in a kind of salvation alongside the
elect seed of Seth surely recalls the Valentinian distinction between
the psychics (the seed of Abel) and the pneumatics (the seed of
Seth).[26] And Bergmeier would argue for the actual dependence

of the *Apocalypse* on Valentinian ideas on the basis of the former's designation of the elect seed as the 'kingless race'.[27] This designation, he argues, only makes sense in the light of Valentinian soteriology and eschatology: the Valentinians entitle the Demiurge 'King',[28] and 'kinglessness', meaning perfect salvation in the Pleroma as transcendence over the sphere of the Demiurge, is only possible and comprehensible in the post-Valentinian period, as among the Naassenes[29] and in *On the Origin of the World*.[30] Indeed, on the basis of his analysis Bergmeier would link together as equally influenced by Valentinianism the Naassene Preaching, the *Gospel of the Egyptians*, the *Apocryphon* and the *Paraphrase of Shem*.[31]

Of these the Naassene Preaching and Psalm very probably represents a learned commentary on some of the basic themes of the Barbelognostic scheme (e.g. the designation 'Gnostic'; heavenly Adamas; Man and Son of Man; threefold division of reality; the fiery Demiurge, framer of the material creation; the inner man fallen into 'the creature of oblivion'; the animation of inert Adam made in the image of Adamas but created by several powers; the soul as a fetter; the seed; the 'kingless race'; salvation by baptism and chrism; Jesus' descent with the seals to impart saving *gnōsis*, etc.).[32] The same might be said of *On the Origin of the World* (heavenly image/Man and earthly copy ('seduction of the archons'); role of Pistis Sophia; Ialdabaoth and the seven; Adam and Eve episode, etc.).[33] But the *Paraphrase of Shem*, if related in some way to Hippolytus' 'Paraphrase of Seth', probably as a later 'corrective', and another contemporary piece of anti-baptismal polemic like the *Apocalypse of Adam*,[34] seems too lacking in characteristic features, doctrinal and liturgical, to locate with any degree of certainty in relation to the 'classic myth'.[35]

Then there is the *Gospel of the Egyptians*. The editors of the critical edition suggest a date of composition in the second or third century,[36] while Turner places it in the second half of the second century since it seems to presuppose the existence of the extant versions of the *Apocryphon* and *Protennoia* which he sets before 150.[37] This work is clearly and unambiguously Sethian, a 'mythological history of the salvation of the Sethians' according to Sevrin.[38] The first part (III 40.12–55.16/IV 50.1–67.1) expounds the Barbeloite–Sethian theogony and cosmogony in detail with many new figures as well as some merely alluded to in the *Apocalypse of Adam* and the *Protennoia*.[39] The second (III 55.16–64.9/IV 67.2–75.24) relates the work of heavenly Seth in producing, protecting and saving his race, while the third section (III 64.9–68.1/IV 75.24–80.15)

develops liturgical material pertaining to baptism. There is a final
conclusion (III 68.1–69.5/IV 80.15–81.2).[40]

Turner in his illuminating discussion develops Schenke's claim
that the third part marks the climax and that the whole work has
thus to be understood as the mythological justification of a well-
defined baptismal ritual.[41] Turner sees the first part as built almost
entirely on the five doxologies which enumerate the origins of
the principal figures (Invisible Spirit, Barbelo, Triple male child,
Youel (a double of Barbelo), Esephech (a double of the Triple
male child), the Doxomedon aeon containing the last three), and
suggests that the redactor has here combined the Barbelognostic
triad with the Sethian baptismal pentad.[42] The redactor also
appears to be dependent on the version of the Sophia myth found
in the *Protennoia*, which seems to make Eleleth responsible for
Sophia and the created order. Further, the three parousias of Seth
in the treatise seem to show awareness of the scheme in the
Apocalypse of Adam.[43]

In his equally valuable and detailed analysis of the liturgical
elements, Sevrin also sees the work as a key text uniting traditional
Barbeloite and Sethian mythological and liturgical material in a
syncretistic and harmonizing manner, which thereby betrays its
late date.[44] From his examination of a list of saving powers,
including the four illuminators now explicitly the abodes of
Adamas, etc.,[45] Sevrin deduces that it is a baptismal list reworked
to harmonize the vocabulary and doctrine of the *Gospel of the
Egyptians* with the Sethian myth, and that it represents a kind of
profession of *gnōsis* as a first stage of the rite of the five seals.[46]
Moreover he draws attention to the apparent parallels with
Christian baptismal practice and terminology particularly evident
in Codex III,[47] only in the end to deny that this rite owes much to
Christianity at all![48]

But this is perhaps because Sevrin has failed to understand the
symbolic significance of the primal unction of the Son, Christ,
baptism in the name of the Autogenes, etc. and the fivefold chrismation of the five seals as originating in the Christian sect of the
Barbelognostics. Parallels with, indeed, as Lampe has argued,
influences on, developing 'orthodox' baptismal terminology, belief
and practice should be easily understandable.[49] The complex rite
of 'orthodox' Christian initiation as we know it in the early third
century (instruction, exorcism, renunciation of Satan and his
forces, disrobing, triple immersion, profession of faith, robing,
anointing, insignation/sealing),[50] surely forms the closest parallel

to the mysterious five seals ceremony as cautiously reconstructed by Sevrin and by myself, apart of course from the kindred baptismal, anointing and redemption rituals of the Christian Gnostic Marcosians of Irenaeus.[51] One must also not overlook the ancient Christian belief in the central role of guardian angels in baptism, orthodox equivalents to the angelic illuminators of the Barbelo-gnostic–Sethian rite.[52] In the light of these parallels we could perhaps assign the *Gospel of the Egyptians* to early in the third century.

The final stage of the history and development of the myth underlying Irenaeus 1.29 and 30 and the *Apocryphon,* and one where we seem at last to be able to assign a date with some confidence, is the encounter of a Gnostic group championing a collection of Barbelognostic–Sethian tractates with the nascent Neoplatonism of Plotinus and his circle in Rome in the mid third century. Both Schenke and Turner, along with others, have developed the suggestion of Puech and Doresse that the Nag Hammadi treatises *Zostrianos* and *Allogenes* were identical with those apocalypses of the same name mentioned by Porphyry in his *Life of Plotinus* as produced or used by Gnostic attenders at Plotinus' lectures and refuted by him and his pupils in the period between 244 and 269 CE.[53] Thus Schenke and Turner would identify the Nag Hammadi tractates *Zostrianos, Allogenes,* the *Three Steles of Seth* and *Marsanes* (Turner also includes the *Untitled Treatise* in the Bruce Codex)[54] as belonging to the Sethian Gnostic group as it became increasingly attracted and assimilated to the monistic metaphysics and individualistic contemplative practices of the Neoplatonism of Plotinus after rejection by the Great Church.[55] But as Porphyry suggests and I (and Edwards) would argue, this Sethian Gnostic group was still Christian – at least in its own eyes!

Here it seems best to follow the generally plausible analysis, ordering and dating of these tractates offered by Turner. Of the group listed above he puts *Allogenes* first at the beginning of the third century. This treatise is the spiritual autobiography of a seer in which the eponymous subject first receives divine revelations, then undergoes an inward 'ascent' of the soul culminating in a primary revelation and its interpretation in a philosophical treatise, all recorded in a book for his son Messos. The reference to the name 'Allogenes' and his book recalls the traditions about Seth, the Allogenes, among the Gnostics, Sethians and Archontics of Epiphanius,[56] and the mention of Messos recalls Porphyry's allusion to an apocalypse by that name among his Gnostics.[57] The first part (45.1–57.23) appears to recount five revelations of Youel (in all likelihood the male virgin of the supreme aeon of the *Gospel of the Egyptians*)[58] concerning the heavenly cosmology. This is ultimately based on the Barbeloite triad of Father/Invisible Spirit, Mother/Barbelo and her aeon divided into three, the Son/Autogenes as lowest of the three. But the Father, representing the supreme ontological level, is mediated as the Triple Powered One with three modalities, Being, Vitality, Mentality,[59] and the Mother or Aeon of Barbelo, the next level, is the self-knowledge of the Unknown God also existing in three aspects or hypostases, the Kalyptos (Concealed), the Protophanes (First Manifest) and the Autogenes.[60] This characteristic tripartitioning of Father and Barbelo recurs in the other treatises in the group.

The second part (57.24–69.19) recounts Allogenes' inward spiritual ascent through the Aeon of Barbelo and the modalities of the Triple Power to the point where he experiences a primary revelation of the Unknown One. This is then interpreted by the powers of the illuminators (!) in a philosophical piece of negative theology which reproduces virtually word for word a passage from the negative theology section at the beginning of the *Apocryphon*.[61] Turner is surely justified in suggesting that *Allogenes*, as well as *Trimorphic Protennoia*, is 'documentarily dependent on some version of the *Apocryphon of John*'.[62]

The work is very hard to interpret accurately, but Turner is probably right to see in it the combination of nascent Neoplatonic metaphysics (the Neopythagorean ontological or 'stoicheological' tripartition of the monad or One into Existence, Life, Intelligence which emerges with Porphyry, alongside a Middle Platonic 'noological' tripartition of the second hypostasis, Intellect, into inert, contemplative and planning intellects) with Sethian mythology, the latter perhaps suggesting some of the concepts of the former.[63] His other main thesis is that while the *Allogenes* and related treatises (*Zostrianos, Three Steles of Seth*) are more philosophical and tripartitioned structurally in terms of an *ascent* through the three ontological levels, the *Apocryphon* and the *Protennoia* are more mythological and are structured narratively in terms of a threefold *descent* scheme.[64]

His derivation of the 'stoicheological' triad from the three female divine attributes of the Father in the original Barbeliote scheme may be far-fetched,[65] but his analysis of the ontological and psychological implications of the Barbeloite–Sethian myth and the convertibility from myth to philosophy evident in *Allogenes* and related treatises tends to confirm my contentions about the structure and durability of that 'classic Gnostic myth': it arises directly from Christian experience of salvation expressed in the objectifying symbolism of myth, ritual, and philosophy. Thus the ever more complex and abstract ramifications are very much the reduplications and further projections of the original and continuing saving experiences, always seen in terms of the reception of divine revelation.

This is obvious in *Zostrianos*, the very long and fragmentary treatise from Codex VIII, which seems to depend both on the structure of the heavenly world and the ascent scheme developed in *Allogenes* (which it adopts in a confused fashion, interpreting the ascent in terms of the older Sethian baptist tradition) and on the figures of the *Gospel of the Egyptians*, while apparently inventing more of its own.[66] What is significant is the way the new elements or aeons in the treatise, those of exile/sojourn (*paroikēsis*) and repentance (*metanoia*) as well as self-originate (*autogenēs*), in all probability represent, as I have already suggested,[67] further projections of the archetypal experience of Sophia (i.e. of the Gnostics themselves).[68] Thus Sevrin sees the principal characteristic of the work as the close association of baptismal concepts with the mythological system, reflecting an actual baptismal practice where repeated baptisms marked the stages of a progressive initiation/ascent.[69]

Like *Allogenes* the work is the spiritual autobiography of an ancient seer, Zostrianos, associated with the Persian sage Zoroaster, in which he receives a series of revelations from various angelic figures as he progressively ascends to the supreme God through the interlinked heavenly spheres, being baptized in each, and then descends. Because the work, unlike *Allogenes*, is not simply concerned with the supreme heavenly realms, we find a more detailed picture of the lower aeons and the familiar entities of the Barbeloite–Sethian pantheon, the Great Invisible Spirit, Barbelo, the Autogenes, the four illuminators and their hierarchically ranked aeons, the triple male child, Ephesech, (Ger)adamas, Seth and his seed, the baptizers Michar and Micheus, Sophia, etc.[70] However, the apparent lack of Christian features does not make the work necessarily non-Christian: the basic mythological and ritual structure I have argued derive from Christianity, and Porphyry's testimony suggests that the work, like *Allogenes* (and the *Three Steles of Seth*?), was the product of Christian Gnostic groups. The date of its composition might be around the 220s to 230s.

Of the remaining Sethian works (*Three Steles of Seth*, *Marsanes*, the *Untitled Treatise* in the Bruce Codex), we may note their kinship with *Allogenes* and *Zostrianos* as regards their meta-physical structures and mythological cast lists. The first of these appears to be a Gnostic hymnal of three doxologies of the heavenly Seth to, respectively, Adamas, Barbelo and the Father, used in a communal practice of a three-stage ascent and descent, and containing a prayer tradition common to both *Allogenes* and *Zostrianos*.[71] *Marsanes* is another apocalypse (surviving in an extremely fragmentary state) which relates the visionary experiences of a Gnostic seer whose name is already known, and expands the divine hierarchy of *Allogenes* into thirteen levels. It has a totally transcendent supreme One reminiscent of Iamblichus and a numerological speculation recalling the Marcosians. Turner associates *Marsanes* with Syria and the late third century.[72] Finally, the *Untitled Treatise* of the Bruce Codex has affinities with the *Gospel of the Egyptians* and is clearly dependent on *Zostrianos*.[73] But its syncretistic, prolix character and casual use of traditional Barbeloite–Sethian material from *Zostrianos* or a source very like it suggest a date in the late third century at the earliest: Turner suggests around 350.[74] Yet even in it traces of the Barbeloite–Sethian baptismal initiation rite have not entirely disappeared, despite the fact that it appears to employ baptism simply as a metaphor for salvation.[75]

Conclusion

We have attempted to describe the character of the myth underlying Irenaeus 1.29 and 30 and the *Apocryphon*, drawing attention to its original Christian and Platonic colouring, its dependence on Christian speculations about Wisdom, Spirit and Logos, its projection of Christian soteriological experience and its ritual expression parallel to and even influencing contemporary Christian liturgy and belief. We have also tried to suggest how the myth may have developed as the basis of a wide variety of related treatises, marked by influences from John in particular, then undergoing a process of Sethianization in the early third century, developed polemically in debate with the beliefs and practices of the Great Church, while at the same time being assimilated to and even perhaps influencing the developing Neoplatonism of Plotinus and his school, finally ending in the syncretism and fantastic speculations of the *Untitled Treatise* of the Bruce Codex. The following stemma and table illustrate that history and the sources and redactions of the myth.

Stemma and influence of the Gnostic myth

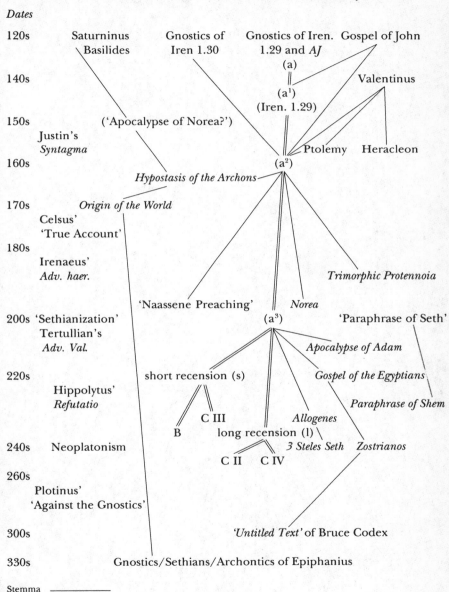

Dates

120s Saturninus   Gnostics of   Gnostics of Iren.   Gospel of John
            Basilides   Iren 1.30   1.29 and *AJ*
                                                      (a)

140s   Valentinus
                                                      (a¹)
                                                 (Iren. 1.29)

150s   ('Apocalypse of Norea?')
        Justin's
        Syntagma   Ptolemy   Heracleon
160s   (a²)

        Hypostasis of the Archons

170s   *Origin of the World*
        Celsus'
        'True Account'

180s
        Irenaeus'
        Adv. haer.   *Trimorphic Protennoia*

              'Naassene Preaching'   *Norea*
200s 'Sethianization'   (a³)   'Paraphrase of Seth'
        Tertullian's
        Adv. Val.   *Apocalypse of Adam*

220s   short recension (s)   *Gospel of the Egyptians*
        Hippolytus'
        Refutatio   *Paraphrase of Shem*
                              C III   *Allogenes*
                    B   long recension (l)
240s Neoplatonism   *3 Steles Seth*   *Zostrianos*
                        C II   C IV

260s
        Plotinus'
        'Against the Gnostics'

300s   *'Untitled Text'* of Bruce Codex

330s   Gnostics/Sethians/Archontics of Epiphanius

Stemma ========
Influence ————

Analysis of the Redactions

(a) original myth	(a¹) Irenaeus 1.29	(a²) Influence of Iren. 1.30, John and Valentinianism	(a³) Sethian interpretation
Father/Mother/Son		+ John framework (prologue epilogue)	
Female/male triads	+ Ennoia & Logos (tetrads)	+ 3 names, etc. of Barbelo	
	Son = Light (Will lost)	+ Pronoia/Epinoia scheme	
4 illuminators			Four illuminators become aeons
4 ministers	+ Autogenes/Truth	Autogenes = Christ	
Adamas & consort	(Prognosis & Nous lost)		Pigeradamas
'Tree'			+ Seth & seed / 'immovable race'
Sophia from Harmozel		(consort & 'Tree' disappear)	
Protarchon		Sophia 12th from Eleleth + consort	
[Continuation	(continuation omitted)	+ Ialdabaoth & 6	
Left-hand ruler		= Samael/Saklas	+ Zodiac (7/5 powers)
Adam & Eve		+ 'Man & Son of Man' formula	+ creation of psychic body
Seth & Norea			+ material from Book of Zoroaster
Sophia as Saviour		Sophia relieved of saving role	+ Gen 5–9 reinterpretation
Counterfeit spirit			
Destiny of souls		Dialogue on souls	
5 seals rite]		+ Pronoia hymn	

Notes

[1] *Écrits* 38–40.

[2] 39.

[3] Cf. II 15.29–19.10, and Zosimus, *On the Letter Omega* 10–12 (Scott–Ferguson, *Hermetica* 4.106.17–107.15).

[4] Cf. B 39.10–44.9 and par. But Basilides already shows an interest in astrology according to Iren. 1.24.3, 5–7.

[5] Cf. Iren. 1.8.5. On this secondary character, see P. Perkins, 'Logos Christologies in the Nag Hammadi Codices', *VC* 35 (1981), 379–96, esp. 379f.

[6] See on this my article 'John and the Gnostics: The Significance of the *Apocryphon of John* for the Debate about the Origins of the Johannine Literature' *JSNT* 43 (1991), 41–69.

[7] Cf. 1 John 2:18–27; 4:1–6.

[8] Cf. e.g. *Magn.* 4–10; *Smyrn.* 5–7.

[9] 'John' 54–5.

[10] Cf. Iren. 1.29.3; *AJ* B 21.19f. and par; *GE* III 42.3f. and par; IV 51.20f.; *TP* 37.20f.; Schenke, 'System' 166; Poirier-Tardieu, 'Catégories' 3; Tardieu, *Écrits* 27, 31, 245 (he derives the triad from three modalities of Jesus in John 14:16–17); A. Böhlig, 'Triade und Trinität in den Schriften von Nag Hammadi', in Layton, *Rediscovery* 2.618 (although Böhlig denies that the Gnostic triad is of Christian provenance); Sevrin, *Dossier* 275f. (agreeing with Böhlig); Turner 'Sethian Gnosticism' 57, etc.

[11] Cf. *AJ* B 22.18–23.5; 31.2–5 and par; *GE* III 44.10f. and *passim*; *Zost.* 17.11f.; 128.20f.; 129.8f.; *Allogenes* 47.7–38; *TP* 38.10f. Cf. also *HA* 93.21f.

[12] Cf. Iren. 1.29.1; *AJ* B 27.20f. and par; *GE* III 42.12f. (= male virgin Barbelo); *TP* 37.3–38.16; Gnostics of Epiph. *Pan.* 26.10.4. One source of these ideas would seem to be Wis 7:22ff.

[13] Cf. Iren. 1.29.4. The later texts, as we shall see, associate Sophia's origin with Eleleth, the lowest of the four illuminators in the Sethian reworking, the abode of those who, like Sophia, only repent late (*AJ* B 36.7–15 and par). Thus, clearly under the influence of Valentinian ideas, she is the last or twelfth aeon (*AJ* B 34.2–7 and par). This association with Eleleth seems to underlie the obscure passages about Sophia and her offspring Ialdabaoth in *TP* 39.13–40.4 and *GE* III 56.22–57.5.

[14] Cf. *AJ* B 67.14–18; 71.2ff.; 74.6–75.10 and par. Cf. *PS* Book 1, ch. 39 (Schmidt–MacDermot 63.21f.); Book 3, ch. 131 (Schmidt–MacDermot 333.14), etc.; Zos. *Omega* 16–18 (Scott–Ferguson, *Hermetica* 4.109f.).

[15] Cf. Iren. 1.29.1–2. Note the comment that the Mother thus marks the beginning of the illumination and generation of the universe ('Hanc initium et luminationis et generationis omnium dicunt'). Again Wis 7:22ff. would seem to be a source.

[16] Cf. Iren. 1.29.1–4. On the confusion caused to the original scheme which distinguished the Son/Christ from the emanation Light, the consort of Incorruptibility, see my article 'John' 51–4.

[17] Cf. Iren. 1.29.3–4 and 1.30.1–6; *AJ* B 37.6–39.18; 42.9–43.6; 51.1–52.15 and par; *TP* 39.13–40.29 and the parallel (and dependent?) Valentinian concept, Iren. 1.5.6; *Exc. ex Theod.* 49–53; *Tri. Trac.* 100.19–105.35; *Valentinian Exposition* (C XI,2) 37.20–38.

[18] Cf. Iren. 1.29.1–4; *AJ* B 26.19–35.20 and par and 36.16–47.14; *TP* 37.3–40.29; *GE passim.* Cf. King, 'Sophia' 162f.: the proper pattern of salvation requires the combination of male permission or instigation (the Father) and female action (the Mother/Sophia).

[19] Cf. e.g. *GE* III 44.22–24 and par; *TP* 37.30–34. The attempt of C. W. Hedrick, 'Christian Motifs in the *Gospel of the Egyptians*: Method and Motive', *NovT* 23 (1981), 242–60, to demonstrate that all the references to Christ in *GE* are Christianizing interpolations, although it does establish the secondary character of some of the passages, fails to do justice to his central role as anointed Son, which underlies *GE*, a Sethian reworking of the Barbelognostic myth of *AJ* (see below).

[20] *Dossier* 38–48. He notes, but unfortunately does not feel able to follow the interpretation of A. Orbe (*La Unción del Verbo: Estudios Valentinianos 3* (AG 113) (Rome, 1961), 100), that the transcendent unction of the Son may represent the basis of the salvation of the gnostics, perfecting them, removing their deficiency. King, 'Sophia' 162f., is also aware of the theme but does not develop it, accepting the prevailing view of the text as secondarily Christianized.

[21] *Separate* 391, 412–18.

[22] Cf. *AJ* B 64.3–13 and par; *TP* 49.28–50.9; *HA* 96.31–97.9; *GE* III 62.24–64.9 and par; 65.26–66.8; 66.22–68.1 and par. The Naassenes, who call themselves 'gnostics' (Hipp. *Ref.* 5.6.4) seem to hint at a similar combination of initiatory motifs: reverence of Adamas as bisexual Perfect Man and Son of Man, of whom the reborn spiritual men are images (5.6.4f.; 8.10), initiatory baptism and anointing as regeneration (5.7.19; 5.8.21, 24, 37–8, 44; 5.9.21–2; 5.10.2: Jesus descending with the seals!). The Ophite diagram of Celsus (Orig. *C. Cels.* 6.27), has the initiate, called 'newborn' and 'son', sealed with white chrism from the tree of life transmitted by attendant angels of light, and the Valentinians have rites of redemption (baptism, bridal chamber, anointing), one involving anointing first with a mixture of oil and water then with chrism (Iren. 1.21.4, cf. *GE* III 67.22–4) and another involving anointing the dying (Iren. 1.21.5). Cf. also *Gos. Phil.* 74.12–21 on the superiority of chrism to baptism, and the allusive language of the epitaph of the Valentinian Flavia Sophe (Plate 2) which associates being anointed (*chrio*) with ointments (*myron*) with the baths of Christ. See on this, G. Quispel, 'L'inscription de Flavia Sophe' in *Mélanges Joseph Ghellinck, S.J.* (Museum Lessianum–Section Historique 13), 201–14 (= *Gnostic Studies* 1, 58–69).

[23] Cf. Justin, *1 Apol.* 12.9; *2 Apol.* 6.3; *Dial.* 63 (quoting Ps 45:7–12); Theoph. *Autol.* 1.1,12. Post-baptismal chrism *may* already have been practised by Antiochene Christians and the resulting composite initiation

rite have influenced the originators of the myth. Conversely, the Gnostic order might have influenced later Syrian Christians to put anointing before baptism. Cf. D. H. Tripp, 'The "Sacramental System" of the Gospel of Philip', *Studia Patristica* 17/1 ed. E. A. Livingstone (Oxford: Pergamon, 1982), 258; P. Bradshaw, *The Search for the Origins of Christian Worship* (London: SPCK, 1992), 163–71.

[24] See n. 9 above.

[25] See n. 6 above.

[26] G. C. Stead, 'The Valentinian Myth of Sophia', *JTS* n.s. 20 (1969), 75–104 (origins in Philonic currents); MacRae, 'The Jewish Background of the Gnostic Sophia Myth', *NovT* 12 (1970), 86–101 (origins in Jewish concepts); Pétrement, *Separate* 378ff. (origins in Paul).

[27] For various solutions, see Justin, *1 Apol.* 33, etc.; Tatian, *Or. ad Graec.* 5; Athenag. *Leg.* 10; Theoph. *Autol.* 2.10, 22.

[28] The same criticism holds good for the efforts of Stroumsa, *Another Seed*, to derive a supposed Sethian Gnostic myth of origins from Jewish speculations on Gen 6:1–4, and for Perkins' assertions, *Gnosticism* ch. 1, about characteristic Sethian Gnostic mythemes; they may include 'distinctive versions of first century Jewish material' (19), but only as included in a new overarching anti-Jewish myth of Sophia which downgrades her and demonizes the Old Testament Creator God and his angels. Culianu's attempt, 'Feminine versus Masculine. The Sophia Myth and the Origins of Feminism: Struggles of the Gods', *Papers of the Groningen Work Group for the Study of the History of Religions* ed. H. G. Kippenberg and H. J. W. Drijvers (Berlin/New York/Amsterdam: Y. Kuiper, 1984), 65–98, to derive the myth from a widespread pagan belief, seems too general.

[29] Despite the value of his analysis, MacRae, 'Jewish Background', is unable, like other defenders of the thesis of a Jewish origin of Gnosticism, to account for its revolutionary character. Wisdom could be appropriated by the Christian Gnostics from Jewish Christians precisely because it was not authoritative or influential in contemporary Judaism: David (Psalms) and Solomon (Proverbs, Wisdom) are *not* included in the prophets inspired by Ialdabaoth in Iren. 1.30.11! N. A. Dahl, 'The Arrogant Archon and the Lewd Sophia' in Layton, *Rediscovery* 2.689–712, appeals to Philo and his view of Sophia as the mother of the Logos, but Philo was appropriated by Christians, not by Jews. On the possible influence of Philo on the Valentinian myth of Sophia, see Stead, 'Valentinian Myth' 90–101. He merely mentions the 'Barbeliote' system of *AJ* and Iren. 1.29, and the less closely related 1.30 as the nearest parallel.

[30] Cf. e.g. J. D. Turner, 'The Gnostic Threefold Path to Enlightenment: The Ascent of Mind and the Descent of Wisdom', *NovT* 22 (1980), 332–41; 'Sethian Gnosticism' 59, 71.

[31] Cf. Pétrement, *Separate* 94.

[32] Marcellus of Ancyra, on the basis of a work of Valentinus entitled *On the Three Natures*, claimed that the latter was the first to conceive of a trinity of three hypostases of Father, Son and Holy Spirit (Ps. Anthimus, *De sancta ecclesia* 9 = Valentinus frag. 9). Cf. Stead, 'Valentinian Myth' 103f. The systems of Iren. 1.29 and 30 are much more explicitly trinitarian than those of the Valentinians, apart from the more 'orthodox' *Tri. Trac.* (cf. 127.25–128.19: Father, Son, Holy Spirit, but cf. also 56.31–57.35: Father, Son, Church).

[33] Cf. Pétrement, *Separate* 186f., 343ff. On Valentinus, cf. Iren. 2.14.3; Tert. *Adv. Val.* 5; Hipp. *Ref.* 6.37.6–8; Edwards, 'Gnostics' 34–47. On the theme of Platonism and Gnosticism, see Rudolph, *TRu* 38 (1973), 12–25; Pearson, 'Gnosticism as Platonism' in *Gnosticism* 148f.

[34] Cf. Iren. 1.1.1 (Ptolemy); 1.11.1 (Valentinus); 1.24.3f. (Basilides); 1.29.1 (Gnostics).

[35] Cf. Iren. 1.1.1–3; Hipp. *Ref.* 6.21.1–30.3 (Pythagorean/Platonic roots of Valentinianism). Note Basilides' order of three male followed by three female divine entities, the last pair responsible for everything else (Iren. 1.24.3), and even more the structure of the Gnostic myth as reconstructed by me: Father revealing self to Mother as three female emanations; then to Son as three male; their syzygies responsible for two tetrads of ministering angels, etc. (Iren. 1.29.1–2, 'John' 52f., 68).

[36] Cf. Iren. 1.2.1–4; 4.1–5.3; 11.1; *Exc. ex Theod.* 47 (Valentinians); Iren. 1.24.3 (Basilides); 1.29.1–4; *AJ* B 36.16–44.9 and par (Gnostics).

[37] Pétrement, *Separate* 336ff. versus W. Foerster, 'Das System des Basilides' *NTS* 9 (1962/63), 233–55, etc. See on this Rudolph, *TRu* 38, 2–5; *Gnosis* 309–12, who thinks neither account reproduces the whole original system.

[38] Cf. Turner, 'Threefold Path' 328–51; 'Sethian Gnosticism' 59, 79–85; Schenke, 'Phenomenon' 613–5; Pearson, 'Gnosticism as Platonism' 148–64, esp. 152; Edwards, 'Neglected' esp. 42ff.

[39] Cf. Turner, 'Threefold Path' 332–9; Pétrement, *Separate* 423–31. Edwards, 'Gnostics' 34ff. may be justified in interpreting Valentinus as a genuine Platonist, but not in entirely distinguishing him from the supposedly superficially Platonized Gnostics on the basis of more Platonic interpretations of matter and the Demiurge: he takes the Naassene Preaching's negative view of the Demiurge as his exemplar, not the Gnostics of Iren. 1.29 and 30 who portray the Demiurge as a vehicle of the divine, partly rehabilitating him and distinguishing him from the cause of evil, the left-hand ruler.

[40] Cf. Schenke, *Der Gott 'Mensch' in der Gnosis: Ein religionsgeschichtlicher Beitrag zur Diskussion über die paulinische Anschauung von der Kirche als Leib Christi* (Göttingen: Vandenhoeck & Ruprecht, 1962); Tardieu, *Écrits* 35–7; Stroumsa, *Seed* 1–4.

[41] Schenke, 'Phenomenon' 602–7; Turner, 'History' 58f.,67–9; Sevrin, *Dossier* esp. ch. 8. Cf. *AJ* II 31.23–5 and par; *GE* IV 58.6; III 55.12; 63.3; IV 74.16; III 66.3; *TP* 48.30f.; 49.26ff.; 50.9f.

[42] Cf. *Zost.* 3.23–7.22: *AnonBru* ch. 20 (Schmidt–MacDermot 263.13–264.6).

[43] 48.12–35.

[44] On Valentinus as visionary, cf. Hipp. *Ref.* 6.37.6–8, 42.2; on Elchasai, cf. Hipp. *Ref.* 9.13–15; on Mani, cf. Cologne Mani Codex p. 64 (A. Henrichs/L. Koenen *ZPE* 5 (1970), 108; 19 (1975), 65; L. Koenen/ C. Römer eds, *Der Kölner Mani Codex* (Papyrologica Coloniensia 14) (Opladen: Westdeutscher, 1988)).

[45] On the need to take this question seriously, cf. Stroumsa, *Seed* 2.

[46] 'Sethian Gnosticism'.

[47] 'Sethian Gnosticism' 55–9.

[48] Ibid. Cf. Pearson, 'Gnosticism as Platonism' in *Gnosticism* 152, n. 20.

[49] 56.

[50] See p. 20, n. 86.

[51] See for the debate Rudolph, *TRu* 34 (1969), 161–9; E. M. Yamauchi, 'Pre-Christian Gnosticism in the Nag Hammadi texts', *CH* 48 (1979), 130–5. For arguments for *AA* as pre-Christian or non-Christian, see e.g. Böhlig's edition, 95; G. W. MacRae, 'The Coptic Gnostic Apocalypse of Adam', *Heythrop Journal* 6 (1965), 27–35; 'The Apocalypse of Adam Reconsidered', *SBL 1972 Proceedings: Seminar Papers* (Missoula, Mont.: Scholars, 1972), 573–7; P. Perkins, 'Apocalypse of Adam: The Genre and Function of a Gnostic Apocalypse', *CBQ* 39 (1977), 382–95; L. Schottroff, '"Animae naturaliter salvandae" Zum Problem der himmlischen Herkunft des Gnostikers' in W. Eltester ed., *Christentum und Gnosis* (BZNW 37) (Berlin: Töpelmann, 1969), 65–97, esp. 65–83. For arguments for its Christian character, see e.g. J. Daniélou, *RSR* 54 (1966), 31–4; R. McL. Wilson, *Gnosis and the New Testament* (Oxford, 1968), 233–9; G. M. Shellrude, 'The Apocalypse of Adam, Evidence for a Christian Gnostic Provenance' in M. Krause ed., *Gnosis and Gnosticism* (NHS 17) (Leiden: Brill, 1981), 82–91.

[52] *Dossier* 275–9. He does allow possible later Christian influence in some texts, and a likely post-Christian origin.

[53] 292.

[54] Cf. Sevrin, *Dossier* 293.

[55] 278. The same would apply to the Autogenes stage in *Zost.* Cf. also the references in Plotinus (*Enn.* 2.9.6) to the three stages (*paroikēsis, antitypos, metanoia*).

[56] Cf. *Zost.* 6.7f.; *GE* III 66.22–68.1 and par (a five-strophe hymn, as the editors Böhlig and Wisse have shown, *Gospel* 198–205, reflecting baptismal initiation and the threefold name, Father (as Autogenes), Mother and Son). See Sevrin, *Dossier* 126–44. Cf. the Valentinian baptismal formulae

in the names of Father, Mother and Christ (Iren. 1.21.3) and the role of the Valentinian Saviour and his angels in forming Achamoth according to knowledge (Iren. 1.4.5; *Exc. ex Theod.* 44–5).

[57] *The Seal of the Spirit* (London: SPCK, 1967²), 120–30. Cf. the allusions to chrism and knowledge (and the Antichrist!) in the Johannine community (1 John 2:20, 27), a possible context for such Christian Gnostic developments.

[58] 'L'inscription' 66–9.

[59] Cf. esp. the revealing Naassene formula in Hipp. *Ref.* 5.9.22: 'we alone are the true Christians (*Christianoi*) . . . anointed (*chriomenoi*) with an unutterable ointment (*chrisma*) . . .' Note also the rite implied in Celsus' Ophite diagram in Origen, *C. Cels* 6.27: the initiate as 'newborn' and 'son', sealed/anointed by a figure called 'father', responding 'I have been anointed (*chrio*) with white chrism (*chrisma*) from the tree of life', with attendant angels of light who transmit the seal to the soul of the redeemed body.

[60] Cf. the practices of the Marcosians (Iren. 1.21.3–5), the Naassenes (Hipp. *Ref.* 5.7.19; 9.22; 10.2: Jesus and seals) and Celsus' Ophites (Orig. *C. Cels.* 6.27); *Gos. Phil.* 74.12–21; *HA* 96.33–97.9; *PS* Book 2, ch. 86 (Schmidt–MacDermot 197.16ff.). Sealing of the organs of sense and speech would protect against archontic influence. *Zost.* 7.7–17 may reflect a later echo: it has Zostrianos baptized in the name of the Autogenes and sealed by five (!) heavenly figures to elevate him to the fourth (Eleleth?) aeon.

[61] *GE* III 66.22–68.1/IV 79.3–80.15. Cf. Iren. 1.21.5 on the mixture idea.

[62] *AA* 85.22–9.

[63] *Separate* 330, etc.

[64] Antioch is associated with the first use of the term *christianos* (Acts 11:26) for a follower of Christ (or anointed one?). Cf. Ignatius' attack on those who call themselves Christians but who appear to be holding independent rites and to have views resembling those of Saturninus (cf. *Magn.* 4.1; 8–10), and Theophilus' defence of the title (*Autol.* 1.1, 12).

[65] *Scriptures* 14. Grant's claim, 'The Earliest Christian Gnosticism', *CH* 22 (1953), 88–90, that Saturninus was the author of *AJ*, while implausible on our evidence (e.g. no Sophia myth), still points in the right direction.

[66] Iren. 1.24.1–2. See Pétrement, *Separate* ch. 8.

[67] So Layton, *Scriptures* 161 n.b.

[68] Iren. 1.24.1. The Genesis text (1.26) might imply a heavenly Anthropos figure. On the interpretation of Gen 1.26 and the 'seduction of the archons' motif, see Schenke, *Gott 'Mensch'*; J. Jervell, *Imago Dei: Gen. 1.26f. im Spätjudentum, in der Gnosis und in den paulinischen Briefen* (FRLANT n.f. 58) (Vandenhoeck & Ruprecht: Göttingen, 1960), 122–70; Y. Janssens, 'Le thème de la fornication des anges' in Bianchi, *Origini* 488–94, etc.

[69] 1.24.3.

[70] Cf. Justin, *Dial.* 35 and his *Syntagma* (Hilgenfeld, *Ketzergeschichte* 29f.); Hegesippus in Eus. *H.E.* 4.22.5, etc. Note the pregnant assertion of the Basilidians that they were no longer Jews but not yet Christians (Iren. 1.24.6; Epiph. *Pan.* 24.5.5).

[71] 'John', *JSNT* 43 (1991), 41–69.

[72] Cf. fragment 1 in Clem. Alex. *Strom.* 2.8.36.2–4. See my review of C. Markschies, *Valentinus Gnosticus?* (WMANT 65) (Tübingen: J. C. B. Mohr (Paul Siebeck), 1992), in *JTS* n.s. 45 (1994), 310–13.

[73] B 51.1–52.1 and par. Cf. the similar role of the Valentinian Saviour and his angels in Iren. 1.4.5; 5.6.

[74] 1.30.1–2. 'Depth' (*Bythos*) is also mentioned. Cf. the system of Ptolemy in Irenaeus' 'Great Notice' (1.1.1; 2.2–6), but also Valentinus himself (1.11.1; 12.3).

[75] Cf. e.g. the traces of speculation about the tree of knowledge in *AJ* B 57.8–58.1 and par; 60.16–61.7 where the episode of Gen 2:16f. and 3 has been reinterpreted, but not so as to exclude the tree, in terms of the Epinoia of light figure. Cf. also the parallel treatment in *OW* 115.30–116.32. The derivation of the white chrism of Celsus' Ophites (Orig. *C. Cels.* 6.27) from the tree of life might suggest another aspect of the figure in 1.29.3.

[76] Thus Iren. 1.29.4 merely speaks of the Protarchon – as *AJ* still does frequently (cf. B 38.14f.; 39.1f.; II 14.15f., 25, 31; II 19.16f.; III 24.11f.; II 20.12; B 55.19; II 22.18, 29f.; II 24.9, 16, 27; II 25.8; B 71.15). On the background, see B. Barc, 'Samaël, Saklas, Yaldabaôth. Recherche sur l'origine d'un mythe gnostique' in Barc, *Colloque* 123–50.

[77] B 35.20–36.15 and par.

[78] B 52.17–54.4 and par.

[79] *Écrits* 44, re Hipp. *Ref.* 5.10.2. Cf. Turner, 'Sethian Gnosticism' 62. However, against Tardieu, who argues for the antiquity and independence of the Pronoia hymn, the Naassene Psalm implies awareness of our *AJ* (a²); the female Pronoia in her third mode is the Saviour, the Jesus of the Psalm.

[80] Cf. *HA* 86.27–87.23; 92.4–end, and Layton, *Scriptures* 65f. Note the three supreme entities, Father of the All, Incorruptibility (= Barbelo), Son; the four illuminators and saving role of Eleleth; the figure of Pistis Sophia; Ialdabaoth's boast, the heavenly voice and image and the seduction of the archons; the concern with Man and with the providential character of the whole sequence of events; the reference to anointing, etc.

[81] For editions of *HA* and discussion, see B. Barc, *L'Hypostase des Archontes* (BCNH Section 'Textes' 5) (Québec: Université Laval, 1980); R. A. Bullard, *The Hypostasis of the Archons* (PTS 10) (Berlin: De Gruyter, 1970); B. Layton, 'The Hypostasis of the Archons or the Reality of the

Rulers', *HTR* 67 (1974), 351–425; P. Nagel, *Das Wesen der Archonten aus Codex II der gnostischen Bibliothek von Nag Hammadi* (Wiss. Beiträge der Martin-Luther-Universität Halle-Wittenberg) (Halle, 1970); F. T. Fallon, *The Enthronement of Sabaoth: Jewish Elements in Gnostic Creation Myths* (NHS 10) (Leiden: Brill, 1978). For *OW*, see the Böhlig–Labib edition. Turner ('Sethian Gnosticism' 76) also suggests a date in the middle of the second century for *HA*, and accepts Schenke's hypothesized 'Apocalypse of Norea' ('Phenomenon' 596) as the source common to *HA* and *OW*.

[82] 'On the Origin of the World (CG II.5): A Gnostic Physics' *VC* 34 (1980), 36–46, esp. 44.

[83] 'Physics' 45.

[84] 'Sethian Gnosticism' 76.

[85] 76.

[86] See p. 67f. Cf. B. A. Pearson, 'Revisiting Norea', in King, *Images* 272–5. Pétrement, *Separate* 437–41, notes the similarities with Iren. 1.29 and 30 and *AJ*, but finds greater kinship with Valentinianism.

[87] *NHLE* 404.

[88] Cf. F. T. Fallon, 'The Gnostics: The Undominated Race', *NovT* 21 (1979), 271–88; Bergmeier, 'Königlosigkeit'; M. A. Williams, *The Immovable Race, A Gnostic Designation and the Theme of Stability in Late Antiquity* (NHS 29) (Leiden: Brill, 1985), etc.

[89] Cf. B 64.13–71.2 and par; Bergmeier, *Glaube* 147f.; 'Königlosigkeit' 323–8; Pétrement, *Separate* 398ff.

[90] B 71.2–75.10 and par. Note the references to the 'seed' (71.10) and the 'immovable race' (73.9f.). Thus the parallels with *1 Enoch* 6–8 detected here would not particularly assist claims for Jewish origins (see Perkins, *Gnosticism* 24f.).

[91] II 15.29–19.15; Tardieu, *Écrits* 300–16. Edwards' attempt, 'Neglected' 41–6, to derive the myth underlying *AJ* from a 'Book of Zoroaster' found in Proclus, etc. seems rather speculative: Porphyry, *Vit. Plot.* 16, unmasks it as a recent forgery.

[92] Cf. the cryptic comment in B 76.1–5/III 39.18–21, omitted in the long version, about the Mother's saving activity in the world prior to the Saviour's coming. See ch. 7, section 3.

[93] See Turner, 'Sethian Gnosticism' 62; 'Threefold Path' 326f; Sevrin, *Dossier* 50f., 292.

[94] Cf. 39.13–40.4.

[95] 38.30–39.13. The allusive mention of the seed of the Protennoia figure at 50.17ff. does not in itself imply knowledge of the Sethian theme.

[96] 'Sethian Gnosticism' 63–7.

[97] 57ff.

[98] See ch. 7, section 3.

[99] B 27.21–28.4 and par.

[1] 63f.

[2] *OW* 114.8–15.

[3] *Pan.* 26.2.6–3.5.
[4] C VI, 2 13.15–14.9.
[5] 64–7.
[6] 64ff. See my 'John' esp. 55–8.
[7] Sevrin, *Dossier* 51 n. 13, suggests 'dechristianizing' rather than Wilson's 'dechristianized'. Perkins, *Gnosticism* 115, 117, argues that neither depends directly on the other.
[8] 50.17–20.
[9] *Adv. omn. haer.* 2.
[10] Cf. George Syncellus, *Chronographia*, ed. G. Dindorf (CSHB) (Bonn: Weber, 1829), 34. Syncellus also refers to revelations about the flood and incarnation to Adam and to Seth when transported to heaven (16–18). Unfortunately he does not reveal his source.
[11] Cologne Mani Codex 50.7–52.7. Could Syncellus' information on Seth (see previous note) have come from such a work?
[12] *Écrits* 42, 45.
[13] Cf. Böhlig and Labib, *Koptisch-gnostisch Apokalypsen* 95; 'Die Adamapokalypse aus Codex V von Nag Hammadi als Zeugnis jüdisch-iranischen Gnosis', *OC* 48 (1964), 47 (pre-Christian, but cf. his modification in W. Eltester ed., *Christentum und Gnosis* (BZNW 37) (Berlin: Topelmann, 1969), 2, n. 5); J. M. Robinson, 'The Johannine Trajectory' in J. M. Robinson and H. Koester, *Trajectories through Early Christianity* (Philadelphia: Fortress, 1971), 234, n. 4; G. W. MacRae, in *NHLE* 256; H. Goedicke, 'An Unexpected Allusion to the Vesuvius Eruption in 79 AD', *AJP* 90 (1969), 340 (not later than the first decade of the second century); R. Kasser, 'Bibliothèque gnostique V: Apocalypse d'Adam' *RThPh* 16 (1967), 317–18 (end of first, beginning of second century); Schenke, 'Phenomenon' 607 (pre-Christian), etc. On the debate about its character and date, see E. M. Yamauchi, 'Pre-Christian Gnosticism in the Nag Hammadi Texts' *CH* 48 (1979), 130–5.
[14] *Dossier* 292. Cf. *AA* 66.4–8.
[15] E.g. it refers to Adam and Eve's heavenly origin (64.9–12), Eve as instructing Adam in heavenly knowledge (64.12f., cf. *HA* 89.11–17, etc.), the figure of heavenly Seth and his seed (65.5–9), Saklas as the ignorant creator god of the Shemites (74.3–75.16, etc.), Abrasax, Samblo, and Gamaliel (cf. *GE* III 52.19–53.10 and par), a third saving descent of the Phoster (76.8ff., cf. *GE* III 62.24–63.9), the thirteen kingdoms and their god over against the fourteenth, 'kingless' (77.27–84.3, cf. *GE* III 63.4–64.9 and par), the baptizers Micheu, Michar, and Mnesinous (84.5–8, cf. *GE* III 64.14–20 and par), etc. Cf. Bergmeier, *Glaube* 185f.; Pétrement, *Separate* 435f., and W. Beltz, 'Bemerkungen zur Adamapokalypse aus Nag-Hammadi Codex V' in Nagel, *Studia Coptica* 159–63, who argue for the dependence of *AA* on both *AJ* and *GE*. However, MacRae, 'The Apocalypse of Adam Reconsidered', *SBL 1972 Proceedings* 2.575f., versus W. Beltz in his 'Habilitation' (204–5, 215), rejects this presupposition

argument, finding *AA* 'typologically prior' to *GE*, and primitive. Scott T. Carroll, 'The *Apocalypse of Adam* and Pre-Christian Gnosticism' *VC* 44 (1990), 263–79, dates it to between the late second and fourth century from an analysis of its representation of Solomonic lore.

[16] 'The Apocalypse of Adam: A Literary and Source Analysis', *SBL 1972 Proceedings* 2.581–90.

[17] Perkins, 'Apocalypse' 383 n. 5; Sevrin, *Dossier* 149–51.

[18] Thus e.g. both have the *spora* and the Sethites (cf. 65.3–9 (A) and 66.3–8 (B)) and (A), the supposed Jewish–Gnostic source, has Sethian jargon like 'alien' (65.18f.; 69.17f.).

[19] Cf. the similar phenomenon in redaction (a²) of *AJ*. See ch. 1, p. 17f. That the saviour figure is unambiguously male and an incarnation of Seth as Christ is further evidence of the Sethianization of the Barbeloite Pronoia/Protennoia, and of the likely dependence of *AA* on the (a³) redaction of *AJ*.

[20] *Dossier* 155–7. Cf. Pétrement, *Separate* 433–5, Yamauchi, 'Pre-Christian' 131f. For an allowance of a Christian element, see even Perkins, 'Apocalypse' 395, and MacRae, 'Reconsidered' 573f.; 'Seth in Gnostic Texts and Traditions', P. J. Achtemeier ed., *SBL 1977 Seminar Papers* (Missoula, Mont.: Scholars, 1977), 21.

[21] 'Bemerkungen' 161, 163.

[22] 'Animae' 68–83.

[23] 'Apocalypse' 383–95. To be fair, Schottroff, 'Animae' 68, does classify *AA* as a Gnostic polemic against the adulterated anthropology of other Gnostic groups.

[24] Stroumsa, *Seed* 98, has an inkling of this in seeing *AA* as a restoration of the primary Sethian myth to counteract the growing influence of Christianity, as does F. Morard, 'L'*Apocalypse d'Adam* de Nag Hammadi et sa polemique antibaptismale', *RevScRel* 51 (1977), 214–33, in her tying the anti-baptismal polemic and lack of obvious Christian allusions to a possible Archontic provenance or redaction. The latter (part of our Gnostic tradition) were opposed to the traditional 'orthodox' water baptism in the name of the God of the Law, but valued *gnōsis* whereby the redeemed soul ascended through the archontic spheres with appropriate defences/passwords (cf. Epiph. *Pan.* 40.2.6–8).

[25] Cf. Pétrement, *Separate* 434.

[26] Cf. *AA* 73.13–27; 74.8–26; 75.17–76.24 and Iren. 1.7.5; *Exc. ex Theod.* 54.1–3; Bergmeier, *Glaube* 186.

[27] 82.19f. Bergmeier, 'Königlosigkeit' 319–27.

[28] Cf. Iren. 1.5.1; *Tri. Trac.* 100.19–30.

[29] Hipp. *Ref.* 5.8.2, 30.

[30] 125.4–7.

[31] 'Königlosigkeit' 327f.

[32] Cf. Hipp. *Ref.* 5.6.4–7; 7.6–9, 16–19, 25, 30–3, 35–6, 40–8.2, 14–21, 26–9, 40–5; 9.1–4, 21–10.2. Note the striking similarities with *Norea*

(Father of the All, bisexual Adamas: cf. *Ref.* 5.6.5; 9.1 and *Norea* 27.11; 28.29–29.5; the titles Logos, Voice, Nous: cf. *Ref.* 5.7.32–3 (Logos); 8.14 (Voice); 10.1 (Nous) and *Norea* 27.11–19; the state of self-generation/Autogenes figure: cf. *Ref.* 5.7.9; 8.10, 21 and *Norea* 28.5–11), etc. On its Gnostic provenance, see Edwards, 'Gnostics' 31f. (mistaking the adoptionist Theodotus for the Valentinian!), 36f.; 'Neglected' 40–2.

[33] Cf. relevant passages in *OW*; Tardieu, *Trois mythes gnostiques: Adam, Eros et les animaux d'Egypte dans un écrit de Nag Hammadi (II,5)* (Paris: Études Augustiniennes, 1974).

[34] See p. 18, n. 76; Morard, 'polemique' 226f.

[35] Bergmeier, 'Königlosigkeit' 323f., 328, would, however, place it among the late Sethian texts, pointing to its post-Valentinian division of the stages of salvation, etc. Cf. also Pétrement, *Separate* 441–6.

[36] Böhlig–Wisse, *Gospel* 38, cf. Sevrin, *Dossier* 82.

[37] 'Sethian Gnosticism' 77.

[38] *Dossier* 81.

[39] E.g. new entities like Domedon Doxomedon, Youel, Esephech, Mirothoe, Plesithea, Metanoia, Hormos, Edokla and many angelic figures. Already known figures include the angelic rescuers Abrasax, Samblo, Gamaliel (*AA* 75.21–3; *TP* 48.27ff.), the baptizers Micheus, Michar, Mnesinous (*AA* 84.5f.; *TP* 48.18–20) and Yesseus Mazareus Yessedekeus (*AA* 85.30f.).

[40] So Sevrin, *Dossier* 82–4. The editors (p. 26) end the second section at III 66.8.

[41] 'Phenomenon' 600.

[42] 'Sethian Gnosticism' 77f.

[43] Ibid. 78. On Eleleth and Sophia, cf. *GE* III 56.22–60.2 and par.

[44] *Dossier* 81ff., 108.

[45] III 64.9–65.26/IV 75.24–77.20. Cf. *AJ* B 35.20–36.15 and par.

[46] 106–9.

[47] Cf. 65.26–66.8: *epiklēsis, apotaxis, sphragis, baptisma, pēgē*.

[48] 143f. Schenke, 'Phenomenon' 604f., had already stressed the centrality and soteriological significance of Sethian baptism in both *TP* and *GE*, and noted the striking parallelism between *GE* III 63.9–64.9 and Col 2:11–15, involving the Gnostic imitation of the Saviour's putting off the body of the flesh, etc. But he too is unable to accept any possible influence of Colossians on *GE* because of his presuppositions.

[49] Cf. Lampe, *Seal* 120–32.

[50] Cf. Hipp. *Apost. Trad.* 19–22; Lampe, *Seal* 132–42.

[51] 1.21.1–5; cf. *Gos. Phil* 67.23–30; 74.12–21. As suggested above, the Valentinians may well have borrowed chrism from the Barbelognostics for whom it was fundamental. On a similar phenomenon, the likely responsibility of Valentinus for pre-baptismal exorcism, reflecting *his*

particular theology, see Elizabeth A. Leeper, 'From Alexandria to Rome: The Valentinian Connection to the Incorporation of Exorcism as a Prebaptismal Rite' *VC* 44 (1990), 6–24.

[52] Cf. Tert. *De bapt.* 5f. and the attendant angels in Celsus' Ophite diagram (Orig. *C. Cels.* 6.27).

[53] Porphyry, *Vita Plot.* 16. These appear, despite the ambiguity of Porphyry's Greek, to have been Christians. Porphyry describes them as 'members of a sect (*hairetikoi*)' and students of Greek philosophy. He mentions Plotinus *Ennead* 2.9 'Against the Gnostics', which was the last of four consecutive works (3.8, 5.5, 5.8, 2.9 – 30–3 in the chronological list). See H.-C. Puech, 'Les nouveaux écrits gnostiques découverts en Haute Egypte' in *Coptic Studies in Honor of W. E. Crum* (Boston, 1950), 91–154, esp. 106 and 126–32; J. Doresse, 'Les Apocalypses de Zoroastre, de Zostrien, de Nicothée . . . (Porphyre, Vie de Plotin, 16)' in *Coptic Studies* 255–63; *Secret Books* 155–9; J. M. Robinson, 'The Three Steles of Seth and the Gnostics of Plotinus', in G. Widengren ed., *Proceedings of the International Colloquium on Gnosticism, Stockholm, August 20–25, 1973* (Stockholm: Almqvist & Wiksell, 1977), 132–42; J. H. Sieber, 'An Introduction to the Tractate Zostrianos from Nag Hammmadi', *NovT* 15 (1973), 232–40; H.-M. Schenke, 'Phenomenon' 613–6; Turner, 'Threefold Path' 324–51; Pearson, 'Gnosticism as Platonism' in *Gnosticism* 148–64; Edwards, 'Neglected' *passim*.

[54] 'Threefold Path' 325; 'Sethian Gnosticism' 85.

[55] Schenke, 'Phenomenon' 614–16; Turner, 'Sethian Gnosticism' 56, 59. C. Schmidt, *Plotins Stellung zum Gnostizismus und kirchlichen Christentum* (TU 20) (Leipzig: Hinrichs, 1901), esp. 50–83, as Schenke 'Phenomenon' 614, notes, had already suggested this identification of Plotinus' Gnostics as Sethians, and included among them the Gnostics of Epiphanius *Pan.* 39 and 40, Iren. 1.29, the *Apocryphon* and *AnonBru*.

[56] *Pan.* 40.7.2–6.

[57] *Vit. Plot.* 16.

[58] See p. 50 and *GE* III 44.26f.; IV 59.22f.; III 50.1f.; 53.24f.; 61.5f., etc.

[59] This may be a further development of the Barbelo figure and aeon as first the triple power of the (a^2) redaction of *AJ* B 27.20–28.4 and par, and then as the triad Father/Mother/Son as three powers in *TP* 37.20–30 and *GE* III 41.7–12 and par.

[60] Turner, 'Threefold Path' 328f.; 'Sethian Gnosticism' 79f. For a different analysis, see Layton, *Scriptures* 141f.

[61] *Allogenes* 62.28–63.23; cf. *AJ* B 24.9–25.19; II 3.18–35. See Turner in Hedrick, *Nag Hammadi Codices XI, XII, XIII* 263ff.

[62] 'Threefold Path' 330. Schenke, 'Phenomenon' 599, assumes that 'the illuminators' of 61.24 are the four Barbeloite–Sethian figures.

[63] 'Threefold Path' 328–41. But cf. the different interpretation of Edwards, 'Neglected' 49f.: the earlier Numenian order Being–Mind–

Life of the Gnostics is displaced in *Zost.* and *Allogenes*, adapting to contemporary trends in Neoplatonism.

[64] 'Threefold Path' 330–2.

[65] 'Threefold Path' 336–41.

[66] On the structure, cf. Turner, 'Sethian Gnosticism' 79, 83. On the likely dependence on *GE*, cf. Pétrement, *Separate* 423f. It was in all probability the excessive multiplication of hypostases in *Zost.* which Plotinus attacks in *Enn.* 2.9.1,6.

[67] See p. 34.

[68] Cf. Plot. *Enn.* 2.9.6.

[68] *Dossier* 201–3.

[70] Cf. *Zost.* 6.7–7.22; 9.1–11.9; 13.1–14.14; 29.1–30.14; 127.15–129.16.

[71] Cf. Turner, 'Sethian Gnosticism' 83f.; *Steles Seth* 125.23–126.17; *Allogenes* 54.11–37; *Zost.* 51.24–52.24; 86.13–bottom. See Robinson 'Three Steles'; M. Tardieu, 'Les Trois Stèles de Seth' *RSPT* 57 (1973), 545–75; Schenke, 'Phenomenon' 593, 600–2. For a different analysis, see Layton, *Scriptures* 148f.

[72] 'Sethian Gnosticism' 84. Cf. Pearson, *Nag Hammadi Codices IX and X* (NHS 15) (Leiden: Brill, 1981); 'The Tractate Marsanes (NHC X) and the Platonic Tradition' in B. Aland ed., *GNOSIS: Festschrift für Hans Jonas* (Göttingen: Vandenhoeck & Ruprecht, 1978), 373–84; 'Gnosticism as Platonism' (which seems to suggest a later date than the 'early third century' of his introduction in *NHLE* 417).

[73] Cf. Turner, 'Sethian Gnosticism' 85; Sevrin, *Dossier* 204–22, esp. 213ff.

[74] 'Sethian Gnosticism' 85; Sevrin, *Dossier* 207 for the earlier dating.

[75] Sevrin, *Dossier* 220.

3

Gnostic Theogony and Cosmogony 1: The Heavenly World

We have seen the centrality of the Gnostic myth underlying Irenaeus *Adv. haer.* 1.29 and the *Apocryphon*, the problems over the relation between the two and indeed between the various versions of the latter, and the questions of the relation with Valentinianism and the Christian or non-Christian character of the original myth. We have suggested that Irenaeus' version is nearer to that essentially Christian original, and sketched in the character and development of the myth and its influence on various related texts, mainly those of Schenke's 'Sethian' corpus. Now we must put flesh on the bare bones of our thesis and justify our presuppositions. Despite the warnings of Tardieu in particular about the impossibility of establishing a history of the text of the *Apocryphon* and getting back to the hypothetical original,[1] that is precisely what needs to be attempted, including establishing the relationship between the long and short recensions.

Helmbold, in a slightly tongue-in-cheek article, has drawn attention to the inconclusive and indeed contradictory results arrived at by means of literary analysis of the *Apocryphon*, although he does note that most scholars see three main subjects discussed within the revelational frame story, namely cosmogony (description of the supreme Being, the world of light, the fall of Sophia and the creation of this world by her offspring Ialdabaoth leading to her repentance), anthropology (including the creation of human beings and the contest between light and darkness for control of them), and soteriology (including the dialogue on the destiny of souls and the Pronoia hymn).[2] This doctrinal or theological analysis of the myth as a whole in terms of its own logic may help us to avoid or overcome some of the problems caused by the literary–critical impasse and the shortcomings of our texts.

Thus we shall structure our attempt to answer the questions about the original form of the Gnostic myth and how it developed, the relations between Irenaeus *Adv. haer.* 1.29 and 30 and the *Apocryphon*, the truth of the Sethian hypothesis of Schenke and the Valentinian hypothesis of Pétrement as ways of explaining the origin of the texts, and of the claim that the myth was originally non-Christian and later Christianized, within the framework of the major theological divisions of the myth. The attempt begun by the likes of Schenke and Schottroff to discover the theological stance and purpose behind each text and version, or even the various theological tendencies within a text or version, may well offer the best key to unravelling the mysteries of the many-headed hydra of the Gnostic myth. In this and the following chapter we shall analyse the Gnostic theogony and cosmogony, look at Gnostic anthropology in chapter five, soteriology (including Christology) in chapters six and seven and eschatology in chapter eight.

1 The frame story

The *Apocryphon* begins with a frame story with features typical of apocalyptic revelatory treatises and of the Gnostic dialogue in particular,[3] which sets the scene and encapsulates, as Tardieu has so well demonstrated, the ternary structure of the whole work.[4] It also establishes its Christian Gnostic character and is evidently permeated with echoes of the Fourth Gospel, not all of which Tardieu has noted. Thus it relates how, as John the brother of James and son of Zebedee (cf. John 21:2) is going up to the Temple, he encounters a Pharisee named Arimanios who asks him where his master is. John replies that he has returned to where he originally came from (cf. John 8:14; 16:28; 20:17). The Pharisee then claims that this Nazorean (*Nazōraios*; cf. John 18:5) led them astray (*plana*; cf. John 7:12), closed their hearts and turned them away from the traditions of their ancestors (cf. John 12:37–42).[5] The slanders of the Pharisee (who Giversen suggests is given the symbolical name of the evil spirit of Zoroastrianism in its Greek form)[6] both stimulate John's doubts and questions and find their refutation in the appearance of the Saviour to John and his revelation of the truth. Further, it will appear at the conclusion of the exposition that it was not the Saviour who led people astray and closed their hearts but the counterfeit spirit, the creation of the ignorant, arrogant, and exclusive Creator God of the Jews and his powers.[7] The frame story thus fits neatly into the main narrative,[8] but is it part of the original, as Tardieu claims, or of a later Christianization, as Schenke, Krause and others argue?

John turns from the Temple to the mountain, a desert place, the antithesis of the Temple and the Jewish Law and the traditional place for apocalyptic revelations, as Tardieu notes.[9] In great grief he is led to ask how the Saviour was chosen and why he was sent into the world, who his father is who sent him, and what the nature of the aeon (i.e. heavenly location) to which the elect will go. The Saviour had said that the present aeon had assumed the form of the imperishable aeon but had not given any information about the latter.[10] Clearly any ensuing revelation is going to have to deal with the nature of God (theology) and the heavenly aeon (cosmology), the nature of the Saviour and his work (soteriology) and the final goal of the elect (eschatology).

And in fact when the Saviour does then appear in a vision in the stereotyped manner of the apocryphal Acts of the Apostles or the *Pistis Sophia*,[11] but in a threefold form (echoing the ternary pattern?) as infant, old man and youth,[12] he identifies himself as the one who is with them for all time, the Father, the Mother and the Son, the eternally existent, who will teach John about what exists, what has come to be, and what is to be.[13] His purpose is summed up as to teach John about the invisible and the visible, and about the perfect (*teleios*) Man, and John is bidden to pass on this teaching to his fellow spirits of the immovable race of the perfect Man, a theme echoed in the epilogue.[14] Now the concepts of the perfect Man and his immovable race do occur in the main body of the *Apocryphon*: the perfect Man is almost certainly the heavenly Man Adamas,[15] and his 'immovable race' designates the Gnostics themselves.[16] But since in the later Sethian texts Seth rather than Adamas is the real father of the immovable race,[17] the latter designation would appear to be part of our Sethian reinterpretation (a^3).

Further, the description of the Revealer as appearing in three forms and his *ego eimi* self-predication, although reflecting the ternary scheme of the *Apocryphon*, strikingly recall the portrayal of both Barbelo herself in the cosmogony (triple male, triple powered, triple named) and of the triple descending Revealer/Redeemer of the concluding Pronoia hymn of the long recension (as well as the Protennoia of *Trimorphic Protennoia*) and thus I would argue belongs to redaction (a^2).[18] Therefore neither of these links between the frame story and the main text necessarily supports Tardieu's case for the originality of the former. As further possible evidence of its secondary character, the frame story with its Johannine colouring would only make sense in a Christian document (such as I claim the source underlying Irenaeus 1.29 and the *Apocryphon* was from the outset),[19] when the Fourth Gospel was generally accepted in the Great Church. The redactor has cleverly picked up and further exploited the Johannine connection, one already evident in the earlier redactions, but not original to the myth.

Thus it seems very likely that, as Schenke and Krause argue, Irenaeus' source (a[1]) did not contain the frame story, but on the other hand he evidently considers it a Christian document and may indeed have obtained a copy of it from the Valentinians, who he believed derived their ideas from it.[20]

2 The Supreme Being: Father, Mother and Son

(a) The Father

The description of the theogony and higher cosmogony of the myth now commences in the *Apocryphon* with explication of the Supreme Being as Father, Mother and Son; the Saviour's self-identification: 'I am the Father, I am the Mother, I am the Son', is evidently secondary, based on the reinterpretation of the Mother, Barbelo in redaction (a[2]).[21] However, the assertion that the Monad is a monarchy to which nothing is superior[22] could represent an appropriate start for an esoteric, Gnostic treatise on God, the world and humanity.[23] The supreme Being, the Father of the All, is described first as Spirit and Light, not only major Johannine themes but the two key categories, as I have already suggested, for understanding the structure of the myth.[24] Then follows a classic if stereotyped passage of philosophical apophatic theology in three sections,[25] the middle section of which has, as already remarked, an almost word-for-word parallel in *Allogenes*, which Turner and I would see as borrowed from the *Apocryphon*, although Tardieu may be right to suggest that both are utilizing a common piece of tradition.[26]

At first sight it might seem that Irenaeus' extremely brief and elliptical description of the supreme Being in 1.29.1 did not contain such a passage. However, we have already suggested that he knew more than he says and that his source not only continued with cosmological, anthropological and soteriological themes,[27] but that it had a more developed theogony.[28] Thus we find that when Irenaeus mocks certain Valentinian epigones for trying to be 'more gnostic than the Gnostics'[29] in positing an ogdoad of negative hypostases, no less than four correspond to those in the *Apocryphon* at this point.[30] And to build on R. A. Greer's persuasive argument: precisely because Irenaeus' overriding theological concern in Books 1 and 2 was to insist on the orthodox Christian view of God over against the Gnostics as 'containing, not contained',[31] he would be only too anxious to omit any Gnostic negative theology which echoed such a theme.[32]

Certainly it seems to have been a favourite device of Gnostic tractates dealing with cosmogonical matters to begin with such a passage of negative theology. It occurs at some length at the beginning of the *Tripartite Tractate*,[33] in Hippolytus' description of the system of Basilides,[34] and in *Eugnostos*,[35] a treatise on theogony and the higher cosmogony. Even more relevant is the *Sophia of Jesus Christ*, which I would argue is a more explicitly Christian version of *Eugnostos*, recasting it into a dialogue between Christ and his disciples, so similar in its frame story and many points of detail to the *Apocryphon* that it seems undoubtedly dependent on it.[36] Furthermore, just such a concern with the absolute transcendence of the supreme deity seems to have been characteristic of second-century philosophy and theology, pagan and Christian.[37]

As regards the relation between the recensions in this section, despite the fragmentary state of all the texts with the partial exception of B, there do not appear to be significant differences, apart from the omission in LR, probably through homoeoteleuton, of a brief reference to the Father as neither boundless (*apeiros*) nor bounded but something far superior.[38] The parallel in *Allogenes* clearly confirms the correctness of SR at this point.[39] And SR would again appear to be more original in the catalogue of the Father's positive functions as eternal, life and life-giving,[40] where although LR apparently agrees with SR in describing him as 'immeasurable light',[41] it does not mention that he is light and light-giving as SR does.[42] The redactor of LR may again have been guilty of homoeoteleuton, like Tardieu![43]

Tardieu is probably correct to see the following interjection as redactional,[44] but his explanation of it as further expansion by the redactor of SR (o) of the single Johannine-influenced exclamation of the original (n),[45] the only addition to the entire text by the former, seems unconvincing. Its undoubted Johannine colouring makes it a prime candidate for my redaction (a²), the addition of the Johannine framework and dialogue. Despite the slight differences within SR at this point, both versions seem to suggest the inability of the speaker to comprehend the inexpressible

Father.[46] But that point is then repeated in the next section which relates the emergence of the second divine being, the Father's Aeon (i.e. the Mother, Barbelo), in a way which does not quite fit the context. Thus there is a jump from mention of the Father as head of all the aeons, 'if there is anyone with him' (SR) or 'who gives them strength' (LR) to the assertion that 'none of us knows the Immeasurable except whoever has dwelt in him (LR adds: namely the Father); he it was who has told us'.[47] The unmistakable allusion to John 1:18 surely suggests that this passage is equally part of the Johannine redaction. The redactor of LR has removed the bulk of the earlier Johannine material because of its theological implications, but failed to spot the later allusion, adding the clumsy gloss.[48]

(b) The Mother

The whole problem of how the diversity and plurality of the heavenly world, and hence of our visible world, arose from the perfect unity of the Monad is one which exercised the minds of the Gnostics as it did those of orthodox Christians and pagan philosophers. But over against the tendency of the latter two to develop a single answer, the Gnostics characteristically present a variety of views reflecting various kinds of imagery. Thus the *Apocryphon*, after stressing the untroubled rest and silence of the supreme Being's Aeon (whether in its hypostatic rather than spatio-temporal sense is not clear),[49] suggests, as Layton points out,[50] three symbolic models whereby the Father comes to be responsible for the aeons (in the hypostatic sense) and the worlds which emanate from him. These models are, first, a solitary *intellect* (*nous*) which in thinking about itself objectifies itself; second, a solitary *eye* surrounded by reflective luminous water in which it sees itself reflected, i.e. objectified; and third, a *spring* (*pēgē*) *of living water* endlessly flowing (cf. John 4:10, 14) and thus objectifying itself.[51] The last two images recall, of course, two of the characteristics of Wisdom in Wis 7:25–6 (mirror and effluence), and Tardieu's analysis of this whole section on the Mother as a mythological exegesis of personified Jewish Wisdom with parallels in John 1 and Colossians 1:15–17 is surely justified.[52] SR gives a clearer picture of these three processes than LR and alone preserves the allusion to John 4:10 and 14 (the spring of the spirit (*pneuma*) flowing from the living water of the light and supplying (*chorēgein/epichorē[gei]*) all the aeons and their worlds).

Janssens has drawn attention to the use by Heracleon, when commenting on John 4:14, of the verb *epichorēgein*, but while noting the use of *chorēgein* in B 26.22, fails to refer to the even more apposite *epichorē*[*gei*] of III 7.7f.[53] Tardieu's allusion in the apparatus to a fragment of the *Gospel of the Hebrews* which speaks of the whole fount of the Holy Spirit descending and resting on the Lord at his baptism and addressing him as 'my first-begotten Son who reignest for ever' is also apposite: another fragment speaks of the Holy Spirit as the Mother of Christ, so that this might add more support to seeing the triad of Father, Mother and Son as a Christian construction developing traditions found in Wisdom literature, Hebrews and Jewish Christian sources.[54]

Continuing the play on *noein*, the *Apocryphon* then has the Father's thought (*ennoia*) immediately realized and manifest as a distinct hypostasis.[55] The following list of titles of this figure, which vary between the recensions (as Pronoia, Barbelo, First Man, virginal spirit, Triple male, womb, Mother–Father (*mētropatōr*), etc.) forms a key element in any literary- and source-critical analysis of the *Apocryphon*.[56] As Tardieu recognizes, the original basis is the appearance of Barbelo and her praising the Father for her origin from him, and the hymnic passage with the titles derives from later redactions.[57] He rightly points to the unified character of the doxological formulae and their association with Sethian texts like *Trimorphic Protennoia*, the *Three Steles of Seth*, *Zostrianos*, *Allogenes* and the *Untitled Treatise* in the Bruce Codex.[58] But because he refuses to consider that Irenaeus' account could have influenced the *Apocryphon* directly, hypothesizes a pre-Christian Chaldaean-Platonizing source for both Irenaeus 1.29 and the Sethian texts, and considers the Pronoia hymn original, he cannot use Irenaeus as a control.

If one does, and works from the hypothesis that the Pronoia figure and hymnic material form part of a later redaction (a^2), then one can accept many of Tardieu's insights while making even more sense of the overall picture. Thus it would seem from Irenaeus' account supplemented and at times corrected by the Greek of Theodoret, that Barbelo is the virgin Spirit in whom there is an aeon which is never-ageing (*nunquam senescentem*: Theodoret, *anōlethron*).[59] If difficult to interpret because of the character of the sources, this is a simpler and probably more original picture than in the *Apocryphon* which, particularly in LR, confusingly applies the epithet of virginal Spirit to both Barbelo and the Father.[60] Irenaeus' account goes on to mention an unnameable Father who wished to reveal himself to Barbelo and how this Ennoia came forth and stood in his sight.[61]

However, the two accounts are by no means identical or entirely reconcilable. Whereas Irenaeus depicts Barbelo as a distinct hypostasis within whom there is an aeon whose relation to the Father is not entirely clear at this point, and the wish of the latter to reveal himself to Barbelo, that wish being hypostatized as Ennoia, the *Apocryphon* has the much more sophisticated concept of the self-conception and objectification of the single supreme Being as his image. Sevrin may well be right to argue that the *Apocryphon*'s monistic conception and imagery is likely to be more original than Irenaeus' confusing hovering between an original monad and a dyad, perhaps influenced by his desire to demonstrate the origins of Ptolemy's dyad.[62]

The self-unfolding and self-revelation of the supreme Being continues in a stereotyped ternary pattern of request (*aitein*), divine assent (*kataneuein*) and emergence of an aeon who praises its originators. Here the system underlying Irenaeus and the *Apocryphon* seems to be the original, developed in later Barbelognostic–Sethian treatises.[63] Thus Barbelo requests (*aitein*) that she be given Prior Knowledge (*prognōsis*/*shrp n̄sooun*).[64] Theodoret's version of Irenaeus also has Barbelo request (*aitein*) *prognōsis*, whereas in the Latin it is the Father's Ennoia who appears and makes the request.[65] After her request, the Father nods assent (*kataneuein*) and Prior Knowledge appears and takes up position with the earlier emanation, here the Ennoia which is the Pronoia (SR), or the Pronoia which originates from the Thought (*meeue*, i.e. *ennoia*)[66] of the invisible virginal Spirit (LR),[67] praising the Invisible Spirit and Barbelo since it came into being through her.[68]

SR evidently feels the need to equate Ennoia with Pronoia (and Barbelo) at this point, although just previously it had seemed to distinguish them, speaking of Barbelo as the Pronoia and First *ennoia* who emerged from the Father's Pronoia![69] Similarly LR, while distinguishing Pronoia and Ennoia here, had apparently previously identified them.[70] Again both recensions appear to distinguish Barbelo from Ennoia when they come to speak of the Father's pentad of aeons.[71] Further, B 28.13f. has a plural verb form, implying that both Ennoia and Prior Knowledge came into being because of Barbelo. For these reasons and from a comparison with Irenaeus' account in 1.29.1, Till, in his note on B 28.9, argues for *two* original Ennoia figures.[72] However, it seems best to leave any attempt to resolve the ambiguities until the end of this process of divine self-unfolding.

Continuing that process she again (i.e. the subject must be Barbelo) makes a request, this time for Incorruptibility (*aphtharsia/mntattako*); the Father consents and Incorruptibility appears and takes her stand with the others, praising the Father and Barbelo.[73] Once again Barbelo makes a request, this time for Eternal Life, with the same result.[74] At this point SR adds to the formula about their origin, namely that it was through the self-revelation of the Invisible Spirit,[75] and concludes this stage by stating that this is the Fifth (pentad?) of the aeons (B) or the five aeons (III) of the Father.[76] This pentad is identified as the First Man, the image of the invisible, i.e. Barbelo and Ennoia and Prior Knowledge and Incorruptibility and Eternal Life, and qualified further as androgynous, the Tenth of the aeons (B) or ten aeons of the Father.[77]

However, at this point LR adds a further emanation, Truth.[78] And significantly it exactly repeats the previous formula; *they* took up position and praised.[79] This last would appear to be the concluding one embracing all the aeons, and so one might have expected LR to have used a singular verb in the previous case of Eternal Life, as with Prior Knowledge and Incorruptibility, if LR were original here. Moreover the concluding motif in II 6.1f. unexpectedly has the singular: 'through whom *she* had come into being', despite the plural form in the previous two instances. The first plural might be a mistake,[80] but the singular form ('she came into being') is very odd after the plural ('they praised') and one cannot easily understand why, if it had originally been plural, it was ever changed to the singular.

LR then inserts the passage about the group of five aeons.[81] It has the term *pentas*, speaks of the First Man as the image of the Invisible Spirit, and adds 'that is the Pronoia' prior to the mention of Barbelo. Both of these are set in double apposition to the First Man and image and separated off from the other aeons, Thought, Prior Knowledge, Incorruptibility, Eternal Life and Truth, by the same or a similar conjunction to that which separates off each aeon.[82] Thus unless, as with Giversen, one equates Barbelo/Pronoia with Thought (or Ennoia), one has six, not five aeons! Indeed, the first figure in the pentad would appear to be the First Man with whom one must equate Barbelo/Pronoia/Thought.

Which recension is the more original, SR which omits or LR which includes the figure of Truth? We have indicated the confusion in the stereotyped pattern of the emergence of Truth in LR, which might point to its secondary character, but in fact there does seem to be similar confusion over that pattern in previous instances in both recensions. Ideally one would have expected each aeon to appear, take up its position, and praise the supreme Being and Barbelo to whom it owed its origin. The pattern actually begins with the Father's Ennoia appearing and taking up position before the Invisible Spirit.[83] Now this precisely echoes the Latin of Irenaeus' account: 'Ennoeam autem hanc progressam stetisse in conspectu eius.'[84] But whereas Irenaeus does eventually appear to distinguish Ennoia from Barbelo, as Till points out,[85] the *Apocryphon* ties itself in knots over whether Barbelo, Pronoia and Ennoia are one and the same or two distinct figures, as we saw. It would seem as if the combination of an originally distinct Barbelo, the Father's consort, with his Ennoia as the first projection of his wish to reveal himself to her, can plausibly be shown to be partly responsible for the present confused state of our *Apocryphon.*

The other confusing factor is plainly the figure and concept of Pronoia. That this figure is so frequently a gloss, a characteristic sign of later literary activity,[86] and that she occurs in what are evidently later additions which do not fit the context, e.g. the hymnic passage to Barbelo where SR has Barbelo emerge from her/it, while LR, evidently conscious of the awkwardness, omits mention of her,[87] and above all the concluding Pronoia hymn, which SR may have omitted because it was conscious of a certain lack of continuity, all suggest the secondary character of the Pronoia material, the subject, I have argued, of redaction (a^2).[88]

As regards the questions of whether there were originally two Ennoia figures and a final aeon, Truth, the account in Irenaeus, despite its brevity, may cast some light here. Thus although Irenaeus makes no mention of individual praise as each figure emerges, and appears to mess up the pattern by having Incorruptibility appear at the joint request of Ennoia and Prior Knowledge, he does mention that once the four female aeons (including Ennoia!) have been united with their male consorts they glorified (*magnificabant*) the Great Light and Barbelo.[89] And that SR with its Barbelo and the four female aeons including Ennoia is more original than LR, appears to be confirmed by the evidence of the *Gospel of the Egyptians.* It presents the first emanations from the Invisible Spirit, in all probability under the influence of the (a^2) redaction of the *Apocryphon* and its triple power designation of Barbelo, as the three powers or ogdoads of

Father, Mother or Barbelo and Son.[90] Now the ogdoad of the Father consists of the four female aeons of Irenaeus' account and SR of the *Apocryphon* (*ennoia, aphtharsia,* Eternal Life, and *prognōsis*) plus three of the male (or neuter) aeons later to appear in both sources (*logos, thelēma, nous*), but does not include Truth.[91] Here too Barbelo is distinct from Ennoia, who is part of the ogdoad and self-revelation of the Father, which might be further confirmation of the originality of Irenaeus' version.

If indeed, as we have argued, the figure of Truth is secondary, why was it added in LR? Again reference to Irenaeus' version may supply a clue. It recounts the later emanation of Truth (*alētheia*) as the female consort of Autogenes.[92] Now, as we shall discover, the *Apocryphon* has apparently fused the two distinct figures of Christ and Autogenes of Irenaeus' account.[93] Thus it has had to reinterpret the mention of Truth as the consort of Autogenes, and has simply represented it as an element (or figure) in the Autogenes/Christ which (or who) is made subject to him.[94] The redactor of LR, faced with the Sethian pentad of aeons, which, since he identified Barbelo/Pronoia with the Thought, only came to four, must have felt that one was omitted and searched for a suitable (female) candidate. Having come across the mention of Truth at the end of the list of aeons as present in Christ/Autogenes and among the beings subject to him, and reflecting the continuing Johannine influence on the *Apocryphon* (cf. John 14:6), he must have felt that here was the errant aeon and added it.

If the version in LR was original, as Giversen argues and Tardieu assumes,[95] and SR omitted it, first by accident then apparently deliberately a few lines later, why does this aeon, unlike the others, play no part in the rest of the work apart from its relation to precisely the figure with whom it is associated in Irenaeus' account? And why in the *Gospel of the Egyptians* is it absent from the list of aeons of the Father, but preserved precisely in relation with the Autogenes figure distinct from Christ, as in Irenaeus?[96] Once again Irenaeus' version would seem closer to the original, which, paradoxically, is better preserved in the later, dependent *Gospel of the Egyptians* despite its idiosyncrasies, than in one of its sources, our *Apocryphon*.

Finally, as regards the mysterious androgynous pentad or decad identified as the Father, Tardieu's explanation of it as an editorial gloss to assist the memory (of the bewildered reader?), seems persuasive.[97] It sums up the process so far of the emergence, at the request of Barbelo, heavenly Wisdom, pure virginal Spirit and first emanation of the Invisible Spirit, of appropriate feminine sapiential aspects of the supreme Being (Thought, Prior Knowledge, Incorruptibility, Eternal Life). What is rather striking about this process is the priority of the feminine and of Wisdom concepts treated in a positive way and the lack of any obvious Platonic influence at this point, apart from the general concepts of emanation and the hierarchy of being and perfection. Even the concept of the pentad itself, rather than being directly derivable from Platonic–Neopythagorean speculations, would seem to echo Sethian concerns, and be part of the Sethian reworking.[98]

(c) The Son

The self-unfolding of the supreme Being now finds its completion in the generation of the third member of the divine triad, the Son, and in the emanation of a tetrad of male aeons/attributes of the Father to balance and complement the females in a series of syzygies. The uniqueness of the Son, his likeness to but distinction from the Father, is expressed in the fact that he is generated, not emanated, even if by a spiritual process, a form of virgin birth (by the virginal Spirit!).[99] That does mean, however, as we shall see, that he is not coequal or perfect.[1] Here SR is closer in some details to Irenaeus' version than LR. Thus the latter has the Father (i.e. the Invisible Spirit?) look at Barbelo in the pure light and brightness which surrounds the Invisible Spirit (*sic*). She conceives by him and he begets a spark of light which is like the blessed light but not equal to it in magnitude. This is the only-begotten of the Mother–Father (*mētropatōr*), the only-begotten of the Father, the pure light.[2]

SR conversely seems less awkward and repetitive, and closer to Irenaeus. Thus it has Barbelo look intently at the pure light, turn to it and bear a spark of light like the blessed light but not equal in magnitude. It describes him as the only-begotten (*monogenēs*) who appeared to (B) or in (III) the Father (cf. John 1:18), the divine Autogenes (*autogenēs/-ētos*), the firstborn son of the All (cf. Col 1:15) from the spirit of the pure light (B), or of all who belong to the Father, the pure light (III).[3] Irenaeus has Barbelo look intently (*prospicientem*) at the Magnitude (*magnitudinem*) and, filled with pleasure at the conception of it (*conceptu delectatam in hanc*), bear a light like him (*generasse simile ei lumen*).[4] But if Irenaeus' version is more like SR in its general picture, it shows differences, such as light instead of spark of light, and no mention of the inequality of the light, but above all in the fact that whereas both recensions of the *Apocryphon* (followed by *Trimorphic Protennoia*) equate this figure with Autogenes/Monogenes, Irenaeus and the *Gospel of the Egyptians* do not.[5] Yet conversely the apparent gloss in Irenaeus that Barbelo thus initiated the illumination and generation of everything very much sums up what the *Apocryphon* is attempting to say about the Son/Autogenes as firstborn son of the All and light.[6]

The Invisible Spirit rejoices over the light which had come into existence from Barbelo and anoints him with his own goodness (abbreviations of *chrēstos*),[7] so that he becomes perfect (*teleios*), free of deficiency and Christ (or good, *chrēstos*?).[8] The Son receives the anointing, stands before the Father and praises or glorifies him. Tardieu points to the Johannine echoes and interprets the triple mention of anointing as given by the Father, the Invisible Spirit, by the mediation of the Mother, the virgin Spirit, as equivalent to the Trinitarian invocation in Christian baptismal practice.[9] And this is precisely the point. Despite the ambiguities of the wordplay *chrēstos/christos*, present but obscured by the Latin of Irenaeus (*benignitas*, i.e. *chrēstotēs*),[10] the anointed one is clearly Christ, as also in the *Gospel of the Egyptians*[11] and *Trimorphic Protennoia*.[12] Indeed the double play on *chrēstos/christos* may be deliberate: the original sense of each word is drawn upon to express both the ultimate goodness of the Father and the bestowed goodness and Christ character of the Son. The Son is perfected by the Father through the Mother.

Sevrin, who is the only commentator to investigate this episode in detail, largely because he is concerned with the liturgical implications, also insists on the originality of the wordplay, which LR has obscured by omitting the name Christ, and appeals to similar examples in contemporary Christian writers.[13] He also emphasizes the spiritual, metaphorical character of this episode and compares two Valentinian parallels, but unfortunately declares himself unwilling to follow Orbe in asking whether the transcendent unction of Christ might not underlie this whole development.[14] Surely this is precisely the case! Wilson, noting the absence of the name Christ in II at this point, thinks that SR may therefore be more original here.[15] But his question is rather whether the versions represent a process of Christianization or, indeed, a movement away from Christianity.[16] To her credit, King clearly sees that the anointing and perfection of the Son, Christ, provides the complete model of salvation for the later lower beings, but she has already accepted the Christianization hypothesis of Arai and Schenke.[17]

Certainly the term 'Christ' need not necessarily be due solely to Christian influence: its ultimate background is probably the Jewish concept of the Messiah, but that such an exalted heavenly being should require anointing reflects not the Jewish concept of kingly or priestly anointing, but *Christian* speculation about the heavenly Christ and his anointing as a transcendent event and reality not dependent on the earthly baptism of Jesus by John. Wilson alluded to the New Testament echoes of this passage without illustration, but we might cite Acts 2:36; 4:27; 10:38; Luke 4:18 (= Isa 61:1 LXX); Heb 1:8f. (= Ps 44(45):6f.).[18] Again, Hebrews is the key, alluding to Christian speculations about the pre-existent heavenly Son, his superiority to the angels and primal unction as Christ, based on passages in the Psalms and Wisdom literature. Sevrin's suggestion that the redactor of LR altered the more primitive text form (III modified by B) because of the demands of an actual ritual,[19] which he deduces was more an affusion or perfusion than a chrismation, and part of the five seals baptismal rite,[20] I find unconvincing; the evidence, Gnostic and 'orthodox' Christian, rather suggests that the five seals rite was precisely a postbaptismal chrismation, patterned on the anointing, perfection and elevation of Christ.[21]

Following the customary ternary pattern (*aitein/kataneuein/doxazein*) and to complete the self-manifestation of the Father, the Light/Christ asks (*aitein*) for a helper to be given him, namely Nous (*nous*). As female attributes/aeons were appropriate to the female, Barbelo, so male (or neuter) are for the male. At the assent of the Invisible Spirit the Nous appeared and took up position by Christ, praising him and Barbelo.[22] Irenaeus' account echoes elements of this: he has Christ again (*rursus*) ask for a helper (*adiutorium*) to be given him, namely Nous, and Nous came forth (*progressus*).[23] But the *Apocryphon*, instead of completing the doxological formula ('because he had come into being . . .'), has a gloss which appears to mark the end of this particular pattern of emanation and open the way to a new development. 'All this' says SR, ' happened in silence (*sigē*) and thought (*ennoia*)',[24] whereas LR only seems to mention silence and make thought the subject of the next sentence, rather than the Invisible Spirit of SR.[25]

Thus there is undoubted confusion in our texts here and neither recension seems to offer a trouble-free or persuasive interpretation of events. Whereas SR has the Invisible Spirit initiate a new series of emanations by deciding to complete a work by a word, with the consequent hypostatization of that as Will (*thelēma*), his appearance, position beside Nous and the Light, and praise of him (presumably the Spirit),[26] LR has Thought (i.e. Ennoia) decide through the word of the Invisible Spirit to complete a work, which then emerges and praises him (i.e. the Thought).[27] Yet neither is satisfactory. Why should the Invisible Spirit suddenly intervene, as in SR, to do what is properly the responsibility of Christ, namely to request the emergence of the Father's male attributes/aeons? And conversely, although Thought/Ennoia has already been responsible for the production of all preceding aeons, and the emergence of Will (and Word) from immanent thought is a plausible one, recalling Valentinian theories and the immanent/ expressed Word concept of contemporary Christian Apologists,[28] following the earlier pattern of emanations one would expect a male figure (i.e. Christ) to request male attributes/aeons.

And indeed Christ appears again a line or so later, where after all four texts come together again in agreeing that Word followed the Will,[29] they add 'for through the Word Christ, the divine Autogenes, created everything'.[30] This is an unmistakable allusion to John 1:3, and if we combine this with the evidence offered by Irenaeus' account, followed by Theodoret, which speaks of the Father in addition to these emitting Logos, but with no mention of Will, who yet appears a line or two later united with Eternal Life,[31] we are driven to conclude that the confusion was already present in Irenaeus' source, and that it was somehow associated with the influence of Johannine material. The symmetrical pattern of emergence and doxology we are led to expect (three male attributes/aeons (Nous, Will, Logos) along with Christ corresponding to the three female (Prior Knowledge, Incorruptibility, Eternal Life) along with Ennoia), reflected in Irenaeus' syzygies and the Father's ogdoad in the *Gospel of the Egyptians* (*ennoia/ logos, aphtharsia/*Christ, Eternal Life/*thelēma, nous/prognōsis*),[32] has been disrupted, evidently by speculations about the Logos of the Prologue of the Fourth Gospel.

As a tentative preliminary hypothesis to suggest how the confusion might have arisen, one might suppose that John's Gospel had already begun to influence the original *Apocryphon* (our source (*a*)), leading to the substitution of the Father for Christ as emitting the Word by an act of will.[33] This was the version (our (*a*[1])) which Irenaeus used, which might account for his omission of Will. The next redaction (our (*a*[2])), perhaps under Valentinian influence, added the gloss ('this all happened in a silence (*sigē*?) and a thought (*ennoia*)') to round off the emergence of Nous,[34] reinstated the Will as an aeon followed by the Word, and added the Johannine allusion as a mistaken attempt to 'correct' the doxology.[35] SR goes back to this source. Finally LR took Thought rather than the Invisible Spirit as the subject.

All four texts refer unambiguously to Christ here and all identify him with Autogenes. However, Giversen thinks that the latter term in its root meaning of 'self-alone-begotten' cannot properly apply to Christ here, but only to the action of the Invisible Spirit, and therefore both he and Janssens agree that in this case the Son is given the name of the Father, appealing to Charlotte Baynes' detailed analysis of the term in her edition of the *Untitled Treatise* in the Bruce Codex.[36] But, as Janssens admits, the title does not even fit the supreme Being properly since he did not produce the Son alone without a partner. Indeed, as she notes, *autogenēs* in other Gnostic systems, such as that of the Peratae, applies to the intermediate being of the descending triad, Unbegotten (*agennētos*), Self-begotten (*autogenēs*), and Begotten (*gennētos*).[37] Moreover, on the only occasion where the appellation 'the divine Autogenes' is applied to the Invisible Spirit (III 11.4) the text is evidently corrupt, for this figure is immediately identified as the *Son* of Barbelo. Everywhere else the divine Autogenes is equated with Christ.[38]

Pétrement, in her detailed discussion of the problem of the appropriateness of the term,[39] which begins by accepting that it is undoubtedly a name of Christ in the *Apocryphon*, refers to the researches of J. Whittaker into its possible pagan background.[40] Whittaker notes that pagan philosophers came to apply expressions meaning 'begotten of himself' not to the first principle but to a second principle or second god, or more generally to derived principles. So Porphyry refers to the Nous, the second principle of Neoplatonist metaphysics, as *autogennētos* and *autopatōr*, although he proceeds from the first principle. This is because for these philosophers the supreme principle cannot move and thus cannot beget. But, as Pétrement argues, although this idea may be found in Numenius (second half of the second century), there is no proof it appeared in philosophy prior to its occurrence among the Barbelognostics. And she even claims to detect it in the *Autophues* aeon of the Valentinian Ptolemy.[41] She also makes the pertinent comment that all the Valentinian male aeons are more or less figures of Christ, and appeals to the *Tripartite Tractate*, despite its obscurity, to illuminate what this idea of self-begetting might mean.

But this is surely to explain *obscurum per obscurius*, and there is little evidence to suggest that the *Tripartite Tractate* is early enough or close enough to the original Valentinus to be used to illuminate the use of the concept in Irenaeus and the *Apocryphon*. Which brings us to Irenaeus' account. Here the Autogenes is not identified with Christ but is a later emission from the union of the aeons Ennoia and Logos.[42] Similarly, in the *Gospel of the Egyptians*, the term *autogenēs* is not applied to Christ, the Son of the silence (*sigē*) who came forth from the Invisible Spirit, but to the Word, the son of Christ.[43] We have already suggested the significance of the term and concept for the Gnostics in that it represents a primary aspect and stage of their experience of salvation: after being enlightened about their state of exile and repenting, they are reborn, they literally beget themselves. In this the Autogenes aspect of Christ is their pattern. And in this sense Pétrement is right to appeal to Autogenes (and other titles) as a figure of Christ.

This may partly explain the identification of the two in the *Apocryphon* and other works dependent on it, but that such an identification is one of the main reasons for certain confusions in our present text is undeniable. The problems caused in our versions by the figure of Truth, the consort of the later emission Autogenes in Irenaeus, is one obvious piece of evidence for this hypothesis.[44] And that same identification would seem to be largely responsible for the confused nature of the following passage in the *Apocryphon* and might go some way towards explaining its differences from Irenaeus' version.

Thus while the latter relates how syzygies were then formed between the female and male aeons, Ennoia with Logos, Incorruptibility/Aphtharsia with Christ, Eternal Life with Will/Thelema and Nous with Prior Knowledge/Prognosis, and how these praised the Great Light and Barbelo,[45] the *Apocryphon* suddenly and without explanation lists four of the aeons, Eternal Life and Will, Nous and Prior Knowledge, as standing and praising the Invisible Spirit and Barbelo because they had come into being through her (i.e. Barbelo).[46] This last point is not strictly true of the male aeons, which tends to cast further doubt on the originality of this presentation. Giversen also senses some degree of corruption here, referring to Schmidt's conclusion that the text of B should be emended in line with Irenaeus and Theodoret, since the two pairs correspond to the last two of Irenaeus and the

Autogenes is completely isolated.[47] Countering Till's rejection of such an emendation, despite its attractiveness, on the grounds that only a few were mentioned and that there was no question of them being arranged in pairs(!), Giversen appeals to the previous mention of the androgynous pentad of aeons as a basic structure of the world of light.[48]

All this evidence seems further confirmation of my hypothesis that the *Apocryphon* does not represent the original version of the myth in this section, whereas Irenaeus does, in that, despite omissions and gaps, he does represent the original symmetry of first female then male aeons emerging and forming syzygies, each of which will be responsible for later emanations. The originality of this and the faithfulness of Irenaeus' account is attested by the remarkable parallel in the *Gospel of the Egyptians*, which lists the aeons precisely as do Irenaeus and Theodoret, like them reversing the expected chronological order (female–male) in the case of the last two, *nous* and *prognōsis*.[49] Why then did some redactor of the *Apocryphon* fail to preserve that original symmetry and its syzygies at this point? Again I think we can best make sense of the situation if we assume that the redactor of (a^2) identified the originally distinct figure of Autogenes, produced by the union of Ennoia and Logos according to Irenaeus' version,[50] with Christ. This is precisely what van den Broek argues has happened in the case of Autogenes and Adam.[51] Such an identification led to the suppression of the Ennoia/Logos figures and their role, both later and here, where they are the only figures (apart from Christ's consort, Incorruptibility) omitted from the abrupt list in the *Apocryphon*, which starts, significantly, with Christ, the Autogenes.

This conjecture finds further confirmation in the following passage in the *Apocryphon*. LR has the Holy Spirit perfect the divine Autogenes and Barbelo(?),[52] despite the fact that the former, as Christ, has already been perfected through his anointing![53] His subsequent taking up position by the Invisible Spirit, etc. also appears to be a doublet, since similar events have already been described,[54] unless, as I surmise, we have here the description of the original appearance of Autogenes as an aeon distinct from Christ, as in Irenaeus. Significantly the versions of SR are even more confused. III has Autogenes, identified with the Invisible Spirit, perfecting himself to stand beside the latter(!),[55] while B refers to the Spirit of Autogenes being praised by the aeons because he stood before the Invisible Spirit. Both versions are evidently nonsensical.

But the continuation in SR, which has the Autogenes greatly honoured by the Invisible Spirit because he had originated from his first *ennoia*(!), set as god over all things (III) or the All (B),[56] makes good sense and is strikingly similar to Irenaeus' version. It has Autogenes emitted from Ennoia and Logos to 'represent' (?*ad repraesentationem*) the Great Light, and greatly honoured (*valde honorificatum*), with all things subject to him (*et omnia huic subjecta*).[57] LR would appear to be less original here in that it has the Autogenes honoured with a loud voice (cf. Matt 3:17) and appearing through the Pronoia.[58] But it, like SR, seems to be under the particular influence of New Testament passages about the pre-existent and exalted Son at this point, for it has the Spirit appoint him as head of the All (cf. Eph 1:22f.),[59] while SR refers to the true God giving him all power (*exousia*; cf. Matt 28:18) and subordinating (*hypotassein*) the truth in him to him to enable him to comprehend (*noein*) everything.[60] LR has all power subjected (*hypotassein*) to the Autogenes as well as the truth in him and adds that he was called by a name more exalted than every name.[61] If the echo of Matt 28:18 is thus obscured, it is balanced by an allusion to Phil 2:9 which SR in turn fails to recognize, with its reference to the name as one to be spoken to those who are worthy.[62] Finally, as argued above, the original consort of Autogenes, Truth, has been both subordinated and promoted to an earlier aeon as a result of the identification of Autogenes with Christ.

Van den Broek is right to argue for the original distinction of the Autogenes from Christ, for the confusion in our texts of the *Apocryphon* as arising from the identification of the two, and for the exalted station of the Autogenes as hinted at by passages such as the above, but his further speculations about the Autogenes as heavenly Anthropos seem not entirely necessary to explain his status in the *Apocryphon* as a figure or aspect of the heavenly pre-existent Son, Christ of Phil 2:9f., Eph 1:21f. and Heb 2:6–8, etc. Tardieu's interpretation of this passage as demonstrating, on the basis of Phil 2:9–11 in particular, the true name of the Son as Christ, not Jesus; that this name is hidden, alien to the earthly Jewish and Christian Messiah; and that its institution does not date from the earthly baptism of Jesus, but from eternity, is more apropos.[63] In the distinct yet coalescing figures of Christ and Autogenes, as with Barbelo and Ennoia, we find that characteristic tendency of Gnostic theology to project several hypostases of one and the same entity, that fluidity and ambiguity which so annoyed both Irenaeus and Plotinus.

3　The completion of the divine unfolding: Illuminators, ministers, Adamas

The divine self-revelation first to and through the Mother, Barbelo, by four female aeons representing feminine attributes of the Spirit, then complemented by the appearance to and through the Son, Christ, of four male aeons representing masculine (or neuter) attributes, leading to their doxology and union in syzygies, now culminates through the fruits of each union. Thus from the male aeon the Light, identified as Christ, and the female Incorruptibility, the four great illuminators (*phōstēr*) appear.[64] This has a precise echo in Irenaeus,[65] but the *Apocryphon* adds that this took place through the Spirit from the Autogenes, a clumsy pleonasm which adds further support to the hypothesis of van den Broek and myself that it has artificially combined the two.[66] The four then take up position by the Autogenes, echoing the pattern of previous emanations and the Latin of Irenaeus (*ad circumstantiam Autogeni*).[67]

But whereas Irenaeus recounts the emanation from Will and Eternal Life of four beings, Charis, Thelesis, Synesis and Phronesis, to assist (*subministratio*) the four illuminators,[68] the *Apocryphon* abruptly mentions three aeons, Will, Ennoia and Life,[69] whose precise grammatical or syntactical link with what precedes or follows is not at all clear.[70] Tardieu's ingenious attempt to interpret them as part of an arithmological concordance of the faculties of the self-begotten Son (1+2+3+4=10) seems a counsel of despair, forced on him because of his refusal to use Irenaeus' account to help interpret the *Apocryphon*.[71] Van den Broek tries to unravel some of the confusion by suggesting that the mysterious *ennoia* dividing the pair Will/Eternal Life was a mistake for the *aiōnia* of the Greek source, but despite that he seems forced to suppose that *ennoia* stood in the original all the same.[72] So we are still left with the mysterious three aeons and the equally enigmatic continuation in the *Apocryphon* which has SR speak of the four (B) or his four (III), namely *charis, synesis, aisthēsis*, and *phronēsis*,[73] and LR refer to the four powers as prudence, *charis, aisthēsis*, and *phronēsis*.[74] As Giversen notes, prudence is an apt translation of *synesis*, and since II proceeds to list *charis* first, there is no real disagreement between the recensions.[75]

However, Irenaeus' account does appear to diverge here in that it has Thelesis second. But this divergence is partly lessened by the fact that in the ensuing attribution of aeons to the four illuminators in the *Apocryphon* the order is *charis, aisthēsis, synesis*.[76] Moreover the *Gospel of the Egyptians*, that syncretistic yet faithful preserver of older, particularly Barbelognostic traditions, lists the consorts of the four great illuminators (*phōstēr*) in the order *charis, aisthēsis, synesis, phronēsis*.[77] Further, as Harvey notes, the Clermont MS of Irenaeus reads *Enthesin* at this point and *Thesin* later, in association with the second illuminator, Raguel.[78] Thus Irenaeus' Greek original may have read *aisthēsis*, which was misunderstood or miscopied in the Latin.[79] Although the *Gospel of the Egyptians* differs from Irenaeus' account (and the *Apocryphon*) over the origin of the four illuminators (they are produced by the power of the great Light, the Manifestation (*prophaneia*) at the request of the Autogenes Logos and Adamas),[80] it bears out Irenaeus' presentation of the great illuminators and their female consorts. The *Apocryphon*, on the other hand, evidently lacks an element explaining the relation of the three abruptly-mentioned aeons to the four powers and the origin of the latter.

The secondary nature of the *Apocryphon* at this point is also borne out by further signs of confusion and of the likely combination of sources in what follows. Thus although, like Irenaeus' account and the parallel in the *Gospel of the Egyptians*, it associates *charis* with the first illuminator, Harmozel (B) or Armozel (III, II, IV), glossed as the angel of the first aeon (SR) or first angel (LR),[81] it proceeds to abandon this pattern of ascription in the cases of the other three powers. And it betrays great ambiguity over the nature of the powers/aeons and their relation to the illuminators, now treating them as locations, now as hypostases, with the illuminators now over, now under and now identified with them! Thus SR associates three aeons (hypostases?) with the first aeon (in which the illuminator is, i.e. a location), which it names as *charis*, truth and form (*morphē*),[82] while LR, having identified the illuminator with the aeon, associates them with it.[83] With the second illuminator, Oroiael, who is set over the second aeon there are (another: LR) three aeons, *pronoia* or *epinoia, aisthēsis* and *mnēmē*.[84] But why, one wonders, has the power *aisthēsis* been put second whereas *charis* came first?

With the third illuminator, Daueithe, who was set over the third aeon, we find three more aeons, *synesis, agapē* and *idea*,[85] while SR goes on to speak of the fourth illuminator, Eleleth, as set over the fourth aeon, with his three aeons, perfection (*-teleios*), *eirēnē*, and *sophia* (*sic!*).[86] LR diverges at this point and has the fourth aeon set over the fourth illuminator,[87] but this reverses the pattern up to now and is clearly secondary. Yet the logic of that pattern is not clear: why the random occurrence of the powers, *charis*, etc., and the deliberate substitution in all four of *sophia* for *phronēsis*? Attempts by Giversen and Tardieu to claim that the two are synonymous are unconvincing,[88] particularly in the light of the evidence in Irenaeus and the *Gospel of the Egyptians* of a fixed tradition of the four powers/consorts and their names. And further signs of the possible combination of traditions or sources is furnished by the repetitive character of the continuation in the *Apocryphon* dealing with the assignation of responsibility for the illuminators and aeons.

Thus both recensions first mention the four illuminators who stand beside the Autogenes, then the twelve aeons (are the illuminators no longer aeons, as before?) who take up position beside the Son, the Autogenes, through the resolve of the Invisible Spirit,[89] but then immediately go on to refer to the twelve aeons who belong to the Autogenes again.[90] This redundant statement might be further evidence of my hypothesis, supported by the inconsistencies in the treatment of the illuminators and aeons by the *Apocryphon*, that the original Barbelognostic scheme of the four angelic illuminators and their consorts, attested by Irenaeus and the *Gospel of the Egyptians*, has been combined with a system or systems involving four aeons as locations associated with twelve aeons as hypostases. Now the system of four aeons as locations, hierarchically ranked abodes of the elect and their heavenly ancestors/prototypes, is of course a basic Sethian doctrine, about to occur in the *Apocryphon*,[91] while what strikes one about the twelve aeons is not only the random character of the names, but the insistence on the number twelve with *sophia* as the last. Might this not suggest a degree of Valentinian influence, as well as the need to have a group of twelve aeonic entities as model for the twelve powers created by the Demiurge, Ialdabaoth?[92]

This then is further evidence in support of my historical sketch in chapter two, whereby the redaction (a^2) in all likelihood incorporated material about Ialdabaoth and the archons and their creation of the Zodiac, etc. on the model of a heavenly archetype, the twelve aeons, the last of whom, under the influence of Valentinian ideas, was Sophia, demoted from her original derivation from the first angelic illuminator, Harmozel (as we shall see), to be the last product of the fourth angelic illuminator, Eleleth. This picture then underwent a Sethian reworking in redaction (a^3) whereby the four illuminators were related to or transformed into hierarchically ranked aeons. And traces of this process can be detected particularly in *Trimorphic Protennoia* and the *Gospel of the Egyptians.*

Thus *Trimorphic Protennoia* has the Son, Christ, identified as self-begotten, reveal himself to the (four) aeons who originated through him and establish them over four aeons(!), each of which is given three names, the last being that of the four illuminators in the usual order.[93] In what follows, the fourth illuminator Eleleth appears in connection with the manifestation both of Sophia (also called the Epinoia of Light) and her offspring, Ialdabaoth, as saviour of the former and responsible for the latter's self-assertion and creation of humanity.[94] Here we have the transition of illuminators to aeons, the number twelve, and the transfer of Sophia, but conversely, the illuminators/aeons do not appear to be ranked, salvation is simply into the light,[95] and there is no mention of Seth and his seed, the immovable race.

On the other hand the *Gospel of the Egyptians* is undoubtedly a Sethian document. It promotes Adamas as father of heavenly Seth higher up the hierarchy, presents the illuminators (and Seth) as emerging in response to the request of Autogenes/Logos and Adamas for four aeons for Autogenes and a son for Adamas, and has the illuminators form an ogdoad with the four female consorts.[96] This last clearly reflects its own characteristic ogdoadic theology, so that it is led to replace the male/female pairing of individual illuminators and ministers as in Irenaeus and the *Apocryphon*, but its Sethian character and dependence on the Sethian reworking of the *Apocryphon* are made abundantly clear when it too presents the illuminators as the stratified aeonic abodes of Seth and his seed.[97] We find the same phenomenon further developed in *Zostrianos*, but significantly it always seems to preserve a distinction between the four aeons and the four illuminators over them.[98] Finally the *Untitled Treatise* of the Bruce Codex, despite its late date and luxuriant mythology, still preserves a distinction between the twelve aeons, the Autogenes aeon and the four illuminators.[99]

The evident confusion in the texts of the *Apocryphon* and the evidence from the related Nag Hammadi documents thus suggests that Irenaeus' scheme of four illuminators and their consorts, which the *Gospel of the Egyptians* has preserved and expanded in its own way, was nearer the original pattern. The redactors of the *Apocryphon* were led to distort and modify that scheme by introducing new material, converting the four ministers into twelve aeons to act not only as the heavenly archetype for the signs of the Zodiac, but to make room for Sophia as the last aeon, furthest from the Father, the point of transition, as Tardieu aptly puts it, from the transcendent Wisdom who is Eternity (Aeon) to the demiurgic Wisdom who is Time.[1]

4 The origin of heavenly Adamas and Seth

The *Apocryphon* concludes the previous stage with the summary formula: all things (B) or the All (II) were confirmed according to the will of the Holy Spirit through the Autogenes.[2] The first part of B's version finds an exact parallel in the Latin of Irenaeus: 'Confirmatis igitur sic omnibus' (1.29.3), while the second half bears out the earlier statement that the Autogenes was set over everything and reasserts the theme of divine providence. The stage is thus set for a new emanation to complete the self-revelation of the divine triad. The *Apocryphon* thereupon relates how from Prior Knowledge and the perfect Nous (i.e. a male/female syzygy) through the good pleasure of the Invisible Spirit and the Autogenes, [there originated] the perfect true Man, the first revelation.[3] Irenaeus' version, however, has him emitted by the Autogenes, with no mention of Nous and Prognosis, who alone of the four pairs are not made responsible for anything.[4] Here the *Apocryphon*'s version is undoubtedly the more original, supplying Nous and Prognosis with the role proper to them but associating the Autogenes with the action. But against van den Broek at this point, I consider that Adamas was part of the original Barbelo-gnostic scheme and that the interloper here is the Autogenes, in association with Ennoia and Logos. And whereas Irenaeus attests his more developed role as excluding Nous and Prognosis and assuming sole responsibility for Adamas,[5] the *Apocryphon* com-promises. But again there is no need to evoke the heavenly Anthropos to explain the Autogenes, as van den Broek does. The logic of the system, as Pétrement has shown, is that all these figures, Light, Autogenes, Adamas, are hypostatized aspects of Christ, the Son.[6]

The versions disagree over the precise name of the heavenly Man. While B 35.5 has him called 'Adam',[7] III 13.4 prefers 'Adamas',[8] and II 8.34f. has the at first sight strange form 'Pigeraadaman', which in fact does occur in other Sethian treatises.[9] Opinions differ as to the possible derivations of this term, but it seems a deliberate Sethian formation to distinguish the heavenly from the earthly Adam, for we find a similar phenomenon with the heavenly Seth.[10] Irenaeus' source appears to provide a Greek derivation: he was called 'Adamas' because neither he himself nor those from whom he originated were subjugated (*domatus*).[11] That he is dubbed the first revelation, apparently contradicting what has already been said of Barbelo,[12] need cause no concern; the application of the title to Barbelo is part of our redaction (a²); it identified Barbelo/Pronoia as the First Man, etc. who revealed herself to the archons of Ialdabaoth in the form of the first, perfect Man, so that they created earthly man in the image and with the name (Adam) of the heavenly Man.[13] As Janssens also notes, we have here the *first* manifestation of the heavenly Anthropos in the sense that he will be the first aeon to be revealed ouside the world of light.[14]

SR has him set over (or on) the first aeon with the Autogenes Christ, in the first aeon with (III), or of (B), Harmozel along with his powers,[15] while LR, perhaps conscious now of the evident contradiction, simply has Adam set over the first aeon with the Autogenes Christ alongside the first illuminator Armozel with his powers.[16] Irenaeus' account here diverges slightly in that the Latin appears to suggest that Adamas is separated along with the first light from Armoges ('remotus est cum primo lumine ab Armoge').[17] Although Schmidt's comment that Irenaeus is totally mistaken in having Adamas separated with the first light from Armoges/Harmozel since the first light *is* Armoges/Harmozel, is plausible at first sight, he has overlooked the careful distinction made in the Latin between light/*lumen*/*phōs*, i.e. the Father (the Great Light) and Christ (the (first?) Light), on the one hand, and illuminator/*luminarium*/(*phōstēr?*) on the other.[18] I would argue that the peculiar reading in Irenaeus reflects the original Gnostic mythologoumenon, based on christological speculations centring on Hebrews 1–2, of the pretemporal elevation of heavenly Adam/Man and Christ above the angels. The Sethian reworking of the myth set Adamas firmly in the first aeon, with Seth in the second and so on.[19]

The *Apocryphon* then relates how the Invisible Spirit gave Adamas an invincible intellectual (*noeros*) power,[20] which is echoed by Irenaeus,[21] but prior to this the latter again differs from the *Apocryphon* in that it relates the emanation by Autogenes along with Man of Perfect Knowledge as his consort, whereby Man gained knowledge of the being above everything.[22] Later this pair produce an offspring called *lignum* or *xylon*, who is himself also called

'Gnosis'.[23] Adamas and Perfect Knowledge can best be understood as archetypes of earthly Adam and Eve, and the Tree/Knowledge as the archetype of the tree of knowledge in Paradise, evidently a soteriological character like the Instructor of the *Hypostasis of the Archons*,[24] or the Epinoia of the *Apocryphon*, who is identified as the tree of knowledge.[25] But there is no trace of that at this point in the *Apocryphon*. Instead we suddenly hear of the heavenly Seth son of Adamas being set over the second aeon, with no indication of how he originated.[26] Here we have the tell-tale sign of the later Sethian reworking, the mention of Seth and his seed, and the illuminators/aeons hierarchically ranked and possibly periodized as world ages and abodes for Adamas, Seth, his seed, and others not repenting at once, respectively.[27]

However, just prior to that, there is one final possible parallel with Irenaeus. The *Apocryphon* has Adamas honour and praise the Invisible Spirit because everything originated on account of him and everything will return to him,[28] ending with the words: 'Now I praise you and the Autogenes and the aeons, the three, the Father, the Mother, the Son, the perfect power.'[29] According to Irenaeus' account all things (*omnia*) rest in the virginal Spirit, praising the Great Aeon. Hence(*hinc*) was manifested the Mother, Father, Son.[30] The last phrase would appear to refer to the supreme triad/trinity of Barbelo, the unnameable Father, and Christ, the Son, whose full manifestation is completed by this doxology; the Great Aeon probably designates the supreme Being.[31] In the case of the *Apocryphon*'s doxology, which is ascribed to Adamas alone, Till and Janssens prefer the reading in III 13.15 ('the aeon'), as supposedly referring to the Barbelo and thus to the Barbelognostic triad.[32] But the plural of B 35.18 and II 9.10 may be preferable not only as the more difficult reading but also because it adds further support to my hypothesis that the *Apocryphon* has combined the original Barbelognostic scheme of the triad of Father, Mother Barbelo and Son Christ, the four angelic illuminators and Adamas, with the figure of the Autogenes and his four aeons.

With this culminating doxology the self-revelation and manifestation of the supreme Being, the Great Aeon, the triad of Father, Mother and Son, is complete: the female and male aspects of the Father as requested by and appropriate to Barbelo and Christ respectively, have been united and borne fruit in the attributes of the Son, Christ (Autogenes and Adamas), and his angelic bodyguard, the four illuminators with their female consorts. Adamas and his consort Perfect Knowledge sum up this process in his possession by this union of the full revelation of Father, Mother and Son, a perfect intellectual and light power. But Father, Mother and Son remain distinct from the other aeons who are emanations, and thus it is appropriate to speak of a heavenly triad or even trinity. However, Böhlig would see this triad of Father, Mother and Son as an originally pagan formula, developed by the Gnostics to reflect their own metaphysic and then, in some cases, combined with the Christian trinity of Father, Son and Holy Spirit in the order Father, Spirit, Son.[33] But his procedure is flawed in that (*a*) he already admits the unique Gnostic character of the triad and merely appeals, without citing evidence, to the existence of such a triad in Near Eastern paganism; (*b*) he analyses the triad on the basis of what we have argued are later derivative texts like the *Three Steles of Seth*, and the *Gospel of the Egyptians*, and not on the basis of the more original treatments, such as Irenaeus 1.29 and 30 and the *Apocryphon*.

Thus Böhlig begins by speaking of Greek interpretation of the supposed pagan mythological formula of the triad in the Gnostic period as Father, the great Invisible Spirit, Mother as *ennoia* or *pronoia*, and Son as Logos. But, as we have already suggested, *ennoia* and *pronoia* are later interpretations, and Böhlig is wrong to designate the Son as Logos; the earliest systems do not make this identification.[34] Again, while suggesting a pagan, Stoic background for the Invisible Spirit, he ignores a more likely basis in Genesis and John, and his appeal to Jewish traditions to illuminate the figure of the Mother contradicts his overall explanation of the triad as pagan. Finally, as regards the Son, his attempt to interpret the clearer and more original picture of the *Apocryphon* in terms of the fragmentary and ambiguous evidence of the *Gospel of the Egyptians* leads him to further dubious assertions, e.g. that Christ takes over in the *Apocryphon* the responsibility for the origin of the four illuminators ascribed to the Logos in the *Gospel of the Egyptians*, whereas the evidence points precisely in the opposite direction![35]

Conversely, Böhlig correctly points to a trinitarian characteristic of the *Apocryphon* in that in the frame story Jesus presents himself to John as simultaneously Father, Mother and Son, and notes that the figure of Protennoia in *Trimorphic Protennoia* is designated as a trinity.[36] He asks why it is Barbelo who is the protagonist here and not the Son, which he sees as demonstrating the difference from the original Christian Trinity. The answer is that in fact *Trimorphic Protennoia* has borrowed the Saviour/Pronoia figure of the (a²) redaction of the *Apocryphon* with its three modalities of Father, Mother and Son.[37]

But Böhlig is right to point to the importance of the concept of triplicity in the *Apocryphon* and related treatises as linked to triad and trinity, if not as an intermediary in a causal chain:[38] this is a further development of the ternary scheme underlying the text. And he is also justified in noting the fluidity of early Christian trinitarian formulae. But he and his partners in the Yale discussion fail to take that fluidity sufficiently into account either in terms of the possible Christian character of the Barbelognostic triad, or in terms of the figures of the Holy Spirit and Wisdom in second-century Christian thinking. Thus Pearson is inaccurate to claim as another point of differentiation between 'orthodox' Christianity and Gnosticism that the Jewish figure of Wisdom lies behind Christ as Logos while in Gnostic circles Wisdom becomes the Mother: Wisdom lies just as much behind the Spirit in the former.[39] And all equally tend to overlook the doxological and liturgical character of the triad, bound up with saving *gnōsis* and baptismal initiation.

APPENDIX

The etymologies of Barbelo, the illuminators and Adamas

I consider that the etymologies of all these figures original to the Barbelognostic system cannot be dealt with or solved in isolation: the meaning of each, if there is any, must be sought in terms of the context and must cohere with all the rest.

(a) The name 'Barbelo'

Debate continues about the possible etymology of the name, and no consensus appears to have been reached. The main proposals are:

(1) from the Hebrew *barba' 'eloh*, 'in the four is God' (so H. Leisegang, *Die Gnosis* (Stuttgart: Kröner, 1955[4]), 186; cf. W. W. Harvey, p. 221, n. 2 of vol. 1 of his edition, suggesting the same derivation, but from the Syriac, and H. Lewy, 'God is in four [letters]', i.e. the tetragrammaton, in his art. 'Gnosis' in *Encyclopädia Judaica* VII 455f. cited by G. Stroumsa, *Seed* 61. Böhlig, 'Triade' 624, also refers to the Greek tetraktys and to the phrase 'the virgin with the four breasts' in *GE* III 56.8f.);

(2) from the Hebrew *barah ba'lo*, 'daughter of the Lord' (fille du Seigneur (so J. Matter ap. Harvey; cf. M. Scopello, 'Youel et

Barbelo dans la traité de l'Allogène', in Barc, *Colloque* 378f., who cites the *bar baal*, 'daughter of the Lord' of Isaac de Beausobre, *Histoire critique de Manichée et du Manichéisme* 2 (Amsterdam, 1739), 327). As a variant Pétrement, *Séparate* 92f., suggests the Aramaic *bar belo*, 'son of his husband/lord';

(3) from the Hebrew *chaber baal*, 'companion of the Lord' (so Quispel, 'Gnosticism and the New Testament', *VC* 19 (1965), 73);

(4) the derivation suggested by M. Tardieu, *Écrits* 259, presumably from Hebrew, of *bar bala*, 'the heart (spirit) has shone brightly (le coeur (l'esprit) a resplendi)';

(5) from a corruption of the Greek *parthenos*, 'virgin' via *Barthenos*, the wife of Noah according to the Gnostics of Epiph. *Pan.* 26.1.6 (so Bousset, *Hauptprobleme* 14, n. 3);

(6) from the Coptic *belbile*, 'seed' (so F. C. Burkitt, *Church and Gnosis* (Cambridge, 1932), 54, 58–61: cf. 59, 'a term ... neither Greek nor Semitic');

(7) from incantatory *voces magicae*, as in the *Barbarbelo* of PGM 12.157, or *Berbeloch* of PGM 5a.1 (so H. M. Jackson, 'The Origin in Ancient Incantatory *Voces Magicae* of Some of the Names in the Sethian Gnostic System', *VC* 43 (1989), 74f).

If we are to assume that the name must make sense in its original context, as Giversen argues in his discussion (165f.) but which may be debatable, as we shall see, then it is vital to try to determine that context. Our reconstruction of the original myth has Barbelo emanate from the Father and request three aeons, not four as in Irenaeus 1.29.1, and this would tie in with the underlying ternary scheme of the myth. Further, we have suggested an origin for the myth in Syria, and these hypotheses would appear to rule out or weaken both suggestions (1) and (6). In any case, appeal to esoteric Jewish traditions about the name of God might be excluded by the anti-Jewish animus of the Gnostics and their myth, and, as Giversen points out, the phrase 'in four is God' does not seem to fit the context in the *Apocryphon* (165). Suggestion (5) also seems implausible; the proposed corruption seems far-fetched and the figure of Noah's wife is not comparable with the supreme Mother.

Tardieu's suggestion (4), derived from what he admits are secondary glosses attached to Barbelo as glory titles, but without any linguistic support or detail (e.g. the language involved or the basis for understanding *bar* as heart/spirit), is also unconvincing. Quispel's suggestion (3) is neither very illuminating nor likely in the light of the comments of Pétrement, but her appeal to the various forms of Barbelo which Quispel claims to find in his magic manuscript as representing variations on *bar* and names of the Jewish God, perhaps tips the balance more in favour of Pétrement's own suggestion (2), already hinted at by Matter and de Beausobre and supported by Scopello. Jackson's similar appeal to Greek magical papyri, if more convincing in the case of Ialdabaoth (see below), is less happy with Barbelo; the incantatory *voces* do not refer to a heavenly female divinity, but to a subordinate male figure, and if it makes sense for anti-Jewish Gnostics to derive their name for the Jewish Creator God from magic, it surely would not in the case of their supreme female figure!

If we are to accept that the name 'Barbelo' does have some significance for the Gnostics, Pétrement's suggestion has some attraction. In the earliest system as attested by Irenaeus, the Mother is a virgin Spirit who gives birth to the Son by a purely spiritual process, i.e. she is androgynous. But her proposal is not entirely problem-free since it assumes knowledge of Aramaic among the Gnostics and is a rather odd and forced expression. Thus it may be best to assume that the name is an imaginative invention of the creative genius (or geniuses) responsible for the myth, sufficiently evocative of the kind of etymologies scholars have suggested to have seized the imaginations of generations of later Gnostics and survived various reinterpretations, Sethian, Valentinian, and Neoplatonic.

(b) The four illuminators

As with Barbelo, the names of the four can only be determined in the light of their role in the original myth underlying Irenaeus 1.29 and the *Apocryphon*. Thus Schenke and those such as Colpe, Poirier and Tardieu who accept his 'Sethian' corpus and the existence, if not of a system, yet of certain fixed mythologoumena such as the concept of Seth and his seed, base their case very largely on the interpretation of the four illuminators as representing horizontal divisions of the world year, and thus as abodes of, in turn, heavenly Adamas, Seth, his seed and the historical Sethians. But in the light of our demonstration of the secondary character of this Sethian material and of the primary character of the illuminators of the Barbelognostic myth as angelic revealer/redeemer figures, not spatio-temporal aeons, this interpretation is flawed and unconvincing. Similarly, Pétrement's attempt to derive the four from Valentinianism as aspects of the Saviour, Jesus, the star and fruit of the Pleroma, although very plausible and offering an explanation that tries to do justice to the phenomenon as a whole (*Separate* 388–406), appeals to the role of the four as not merely to surround the Autogenes Christ as angelic body-guards (cf. *1 Enoch* 40, also 9 and 71), but also as spatio-temporal aeons, i.e. to the *Sethian* interpretation of them. This later reworking cannot contribute to the original meaning of the four.

Further Pétrement admits her failure to give a satisfactory explanation of Eleleth, and tends to appeal to later Valentinian evidence, e.g. from Ptolemy, the *Gospel of Truth* and the *Tripartite Tractate* to support her case. If, as I have argued, the original myth is contemporary or even slightly earlier than Valentinus, brought to Alexandria at the time of, perhaps even by the likes of Basilides, then we would have to discount Valentinian influence on the names of the four. Further, the firm picture, the distinctive cosmogonic as well as revelatory and salvific roles of the four in Irenaeus and the *Apocryphon* and related texts, and the evident Jewish and Jewish–Christian apocalyptic background, suggest an already existing mythologoumenon hardly derivable from the generalized Valentinian account of the Saviour and his angelic bodyguard. I admit that I cannot suggest more plausible etymologies for the four names than Pétrement, although I consider there are good grounds for rejecting the Poirier/Tardieu explanation as lacking in solid evidence for an exclusively Iranian provenance, involving a needlessly complicated history of transmission, and in any case totally dependent on Schenke's 'Sethian' thesis. For my part, I would venture to suggest that, as with Barbelo, the four names are imaginative, evocative inventions, intended to designate the archetypes of the four archangels of Jewish apocalyptic (hence the Hebrew sounding names Theodoret remarks upon in *Haer.* 1.13 (364A), which again, as with Barbelo, appear neither pure Greek nor Semitic, but seem a combination of Greek and Semitic, with the characteristic Hebrew angelological suffix -*ēl*). The traditional names of the four archangels of *1 Enoch*, etc. are not used, perhaps as pertaining more to the sphere of the Protarchon, the Creator God of the Old Testament. Thus one of the two names of his demonic serpentine son in Irenaeus 1.30.9 is Michael.

(c) Adamas/Pigera(a)damas

There has also been debate about the meaning of the latter term, which again can only be resolved by considering the context. The most detailed discussion is in H. M. Jackson, 'Geradamas, the

Celestial Stranger', *NTS* 27 (1980/81), 385–94. He notes first Giversen's proposed Coptic etymology 'now the name is Adamas', *Apocryphon* 186f., rejecting it on grammatical and palaeographical grounds (see also the review of Giversen by A. K. Helmbold, *JNES* 25 (1966), 263f.). Jackson also rejects the Greek etymology of Tardieu in his translation of *Steles Seth*, *RSPT* 57 (1973), 545–75: 'ô vénérable (*geras*) Adamas', on grounds of absence of onomastic parallel and unsuitability of meaning. Schenke's proposal ('System' 170, taken up by his pupil K. Wekel, *TLZ* 100 (1975), 571–80, esp. 573, and his 1977 doctoral dissertation), that it was a Coptic distortion of *ho hieradamas*, 'the holy Adamas' of *OW* 108.23, is subject to the criticism of Böhlig ('Zum "Pluralismus" in den Schriften von Nag Hammadi: die Behandlung des Adamas in den Drei Stelen des Seth und im Ägypterevangelium', in M. Krause ed., *Essays on the Nag Hammadi Texts in Honour of Pahor Labib* (NHS 6) (Leiden: Brill, 1975), 25f.), in terms of Coptic rendering of Greek, and of Jackson in terms of the lack of real parallel in the *OW* passage. The inappropriateness in terms both of grammar and meaning of the Greek substantive *geras* or any of its equivalents would also appear to rule out the appeals to it or an equivalent by Böhlig (art. cit.). Shenke's more recent suggestion, 'Phenomenon' 594, n. 17, abandoning his earlier one, of *ho geraros Adamas*, 'the majestic Adamas', is better in that unlike forms of *geras* it is an adjective, but the abbreviation required is still problematical.

Jackson, rightly insisting on an etymology that both relates directly to the context (for him the Sethian system) and can find firm onomastic corroboration, suggests the Semitic term, *gēr*, 'stranger', a common prefix in Phoenician and Punic divine names and a term for proselytes in later Hebrew and Aramaic usage. His hypothetical reconstruction involves Samaritan Gnostic sectarians, acquainted with the Phoenician meaning of the term, coining the designation 'Geradamas' to distinguish the heavenly Adamas, like them a stranger, from the earthly. The sect and its teachings were later Christianized and the name survived as an occult designation whose true significance had long been forgotten. The Semitic derivation is plausible (see above for treatment of Barbelo and the four illuminators), but the fact that Irenaeus' account has the term Adamas with a Greek etymology and the doubts I have cast on the Sethian/Samaritan hypothesis might suggest that the term is part of the later Sethianization process, occurring only in *AJ* II 8.34; *Steles Seth* 118.26; *Zost.* 6.23; 13.6; 51.7; *Melch.* 6.6. So once again I would suggest that the original title was 'Adamas', deliberately coined by the author(s) of the Barbelognostic myth to suggest both a Greek and a Semitic background, as certainly was the case with the four illuminators, and possibly with Barbelo.

Notes

[1] *Écrits* 26. It may be significant that neither Krause nor Helmbold have published their theses on the *Apocryphon* and the relations between the versions, and neither Krause's promised synopsis (*Drei Versionen* 3f., cf. 37), nor Werner's nor that of the Coptic Gnostic Library series has yet appeared!

[2] 'The *Apocryphon of John*: A Case Study in Literary Criticism', *JETS* 13 (1970), 173–9 esp. 174.

[3] Appearance of revealer figure in brilliant light and varied form to recipient in a vision; revelation of secret mysteries about the past, present and future; instructions about preserving and communicating the revelation to those worthy to receive it, etc. On the Gnostic 'Dialogue', see K. Rudolph, 'Der Gnostische "Dialog" als literarisches Genus' in P. Nagel ed., *Probleme der koptischen Literatur* (Wissenschaftliche Beiträge der Martin-Luther-Universität Halle-Wittenberg 1) (Halle, 1968), 85–107.

[4] B 19.6–22.16; II 1.1–2.25. Tardieu, *Écrits* 33–5, 239–46.

[5] Cf. W. J. Blackstone, 'A Short Note on the "Apocryphon Johannis"', *VC* 19 (1965), 163, who notes the parallel to the phrase 'turn [you] from the traditions of [your] ancestors' in *Acts of Philip* 19 (14).

[6] *Apocryphon* 152.

[7] Cf. B 75.7–10/III 39.8–11; II 30.9–11. Note the same expression as in B 20.1.

[8] The choice of John as protagonist and the evident influence of Johannine material with its anti-Jewish bias, would suggest familiarity and spiritual kinship with the Johannine community.

[9] *Écrits* 34, 241.

[10] B 20.3–19; II 1.17–29. Note the battery of Johannine references detected by Tardieu, *Écrits* 84.

[11] B 20.19–21.3; II 1.30–2.9. Cf. e.g. *Acta Petri* ch. 20f.; *PS* Book 1, chs 4–6 (Schmidt–MacDermot 6.24–8.21).

[12] B 21.3–13; II 2.1–9. B has omitted the youth by mistake; the text continues with a mention of three forms (21.13; II 2.9, *morphē*). Tardieu is surely incorrect to classify this vision as a dream (*songe/somnium/oneiros*; *Écrits* 242f.).

[13] B 21.13–22.5; II 2.9–18. Note again the clear echoes of John and Revelation indicated by Tardieu.

[14] B 22.8–17; II 2.19–25. Cf. B 75.12–76.1/III 39.15–18; II 31.28–32/IV 49.9–13.

[15] Cf. B 35.3ff. and par and 49.5ff. and par (perfect Man Adamas); 71.12ff. and par (immovable race of the perfect Man of light). Cf. *Zost.* 6.23ff.; 30.4f. (mention of Adamas or Geradamas as perfect Man and of the immovable race); *Steles Seth* 118.11f.,26; 121.14ff.; *Melch.* 6.5f.(Man of light, immortal Aeon Pigeradamas).

[16] Cf. B 65.2f. and par; III 36.24f.; B 73.9f. and par; B 75.20–76.1 and par.

[17] Cf. *GE* III 51.8f. and par; 59.13–15; 61.19f. and par; *Steles Seth* 118.12f.; *Zost.* 51.15(?). *SJC* III 97.8f./B 88.8f. probably got the phrase, like so much, from *AJ.*

[18] Cf. *AJ* B 27.13–28.4 and par; II 30.11–31.25; *TP* 37.20–30; 42.4–27.

[19] See ch. 2, pp. 30ff.

[20] See ch. 1, p. 3.

[21] Against Tardieu, *Écrits* 31, who sees this first part as an exegesis of the Saviour's statement. See ch. 7, section 3.

[22] B 22.17–19; II 2.26f. One might add to Tardieu's Pythagorean parallels the fact that the Valentinians of Hippolytus describe the supreme Father as 'the monad' (*monas: Ref.* 6.29.2).

[23] Cf. e.g. *Tri. Trac.* 51.1–11; Hippolytus' description of the Valentinians in *Ref.* 6.29.2: for them the beginning (*archē*) of everything is a Monad (*monas*), unbegotten, imperishable, inconceivable, incomprehensible etc.

[24] B 22.19–23.3; II 2.28–32. See ch. 2, pp. 30ff.

[25] B 22.17–25.22; II 2.26–4.10. Cf. Tardieu's illuminating analysis, *Écrits* 248–53.

[26] See ch. 2, p. 52, nn. 58–9, p. 68; Tardieu, *Écrits* 250.

[27] See ch. 1, n. 37; ch. 2, pp. 42ff.

[28] Cf. ch. 1, p. 9f.

[29] Cf. 1.11.3 and 5 and ch. 1, p. 9.

[30] Cf. 1.11.5 in Epiphanius: *Proarchē,* Anennoētos, *Arrhētos, Aoratos,* Archē, Akatalēptos, *Anonomastos,* Agennētos, and *AJ* B 23.5–24.6: *Archē* over whom no-one rules, eternal, unperfectible, illimitable, indivisible (*adiakritos*), immeasurable, *invisible, inexpressible, unnameable.*

[31] Greer, 'Dog' 170.

[32] Cf. W. C. van Unnik, 'Die Gotteslehre bei Aristides und in gnostischen Schriften', *TZ* 17 (1961), 171.

[33] 51.1–55.40.

[34] *Ref.* 7.20.2–21.1.

[35] C III 71.13–73.3 and par.

[36] The relation between the two suggested above is the consensus view going back to M. Krause, 'Das literarische Verhältnis des Eugnostosbriefes zur Sophia Jesu Christi: zur Auseinandersetzung der Gnosis mit dem Christentum', *Mullus: Festschrift Theodor Klauser* (JbAC Ergänzungsband 1) (Münster: Aschendorff, 1964), 215–23. See Rudolph *TRu* 34, 208–10; C. Scholten, *Martyrium und Sophiamythos im Gnostizismus nach den Texten*

von Nag Hammadi (JbAC Ergänzungsband 14) (Münster: Aschendorff, 1987), 240–61, criticizing the attempt of Tardieu (*Écrits* 60, 65–7, 388, etc.) and myself ('The Epistle of Eugnostos and Valentinianism' in M. Krause ed., *Gnosis and Gnosticism* (NHS 17) (Leiden: Brill, 1981), 66–75) to derive the Valentinian Doctrinal Letter (Epiph. *Pan.* 31.5.1–8.3) from *Eug,* and suggesting that the latter was more likely itself influenced by Valentinianism. The attempt to interpret *Eug* as a Jewish–Gnostic text from Alexandria of the first century BCE or CE by R. van den Broek ('Jewish and Platonic Speculations in Early Alexandrian Theology: Eugnostos, Philo, Valentinus, and Origen' in B. A. Pearson, J. E. Goehring eds., *The Roots of Egyptian Christianity* (SAC 1) (Philadelphia: Fortress, 1986), 190–203; cf. D. M. Parrott ed., *Nag Hammadi Codices III, 3–4 and V, 1* (NHS 27) (Leiden: Brill, 1987)), seems too speculative: the internal evidence, comparison with e.g. Monoimus (and Irenaeus 1.30?), and the relationship with Valentinianism seems to point to a later date, in the late second or early third century CE. On the striking parallels between *AJ* and *SJC,* see Tardieu, *Écrits* 60–5. He omits the reference to the 'immovable race' in B 88.8f./III 97.9. However, van Unnik, 'Gotteslehre' 172f., is right to deny *SJC* depends on the apophatic theology of *AJ.* It comes, of course, from *Eug.*

[37] Cf. e.g. R. M. Grant, *The Early Christian Doctrine of God* (Charlottesville, 1966), 14–28; van Unnik, 'Gotteslehre'.

[38] 24.13–15/III 6.8–10. Cf. II 3.22 and Krause's apparatus ad loc./IV 5.6.

[39] 63.1–5. *Allogenes* has one or two minor differences.

[40] II 4.1–10/IV 5.25–6.9.

[41] Cf. B 24.6f./III 5.2f. and II 3.17/IV 4.28–5.1.

[42] B 25.14f./III 6.6f.

[43] Cf. *Écrits* 89 translating B 25.14f. 'lumière dispensatrice de *vie*'!

[44] B 26.1–6/III 6.13–19; II 4.10/IV 6.9f.

[45] 253.

[46] Giversen's interpretation, *Apocryphon* 164, against Till in his edition (93 note to 26.3) that the reference is to the Revealer not to John, and that he is not limited in his knowledge but (*a*) simply lacks words to describe what he can grasp, and (*b*) cannot describe in a manner John could understand, seems strained, although it may well explain why, as I think, LR omitted all but the first sentence: the redactor could not accept that the Revealer was in any way limited.

[47] Cf. B 26.6–14/III 6.19–7.2; II 4.10–19/IV 6.10–20. A connection of sorts is possible in SR but scarcely in LR.

[48] On the problems of identification caused, see Y. Janssens, 'L'Apocryphon de Jean', *Muséon* 83 (1970), 165. If one removes both passages the text runs very smoothly.

[49] Tardieu, *Écrits* 254, takes it in the former sense as the divine Wisdom.

[50] *Scriptures* 14f.

[51] B 26.15–27.4/III 7.2–12. Cf. II 4.19–26/IV 6.20–7.

[52] *Écrits* 262–3.

[53] *Muséon* 84, 43 on fragment 17 of Heracleon.

[54] Cf. Novatian, *De Trin.* 29.14, who echoes the *Gospel of the Hebrews* fragment about the whole fount of the Spirit (frag. 2 in W. Schneemelcher, *New Testament Apocrypha* vol. 1, rev. ed., ET ed., R. McL. Wilson (Cambridge: James Clarke, 1991), 177).

[55] B 27.4–8/III 7.12–15; II 4.26–29/IV 7.1–5.

[56] B 27.8–28.4/III 7.15–8.5; II 4.29–5.11/IV 7.5–27.

[57] *Écrits* 256–9. For possible etymologies of Barbelo, see Appendix (a).

[58] 256–61.

[59] 1.29.1/Theodoret, *Haer.* 1.13. Could there be an echo of this in *AJ*'s phrase (B 26.6–8 and par) about the imperishable (*atteko*) aeon resting in Silence, the Valentinian equivalent of Barbelo? Cf. Iren. 1.1.1 (an eternal aeon in rest with his partner Ennoia/Sige).

[60] Cf. e.g. II 4.35 (Father?); 5.11–13 (Barbelo); 6.19; 7.19 (= B 32.7f.), 23; 8.34; 14.4 (Father). In B 30.20–31.1 it applies to Barbelo, and in 37.5f. to Sophia's male consort.

[61] 1.29.1. Cf. the very similar wording in *AJ* B 27.5–7 and par. Theodoret has Barbelo for Ennoia.

[62] *Dossier* 15–17.

[63] Cf. *GE* III 50.17–55.11/IV 62.16–66.25 which is evidently a later development, setting the process later in the theogony and jumbling the entities and processes together.

[64] B 28.4–7/III 8.5–7; II 5.11–14/IV 7.27–8.1. SR uses *shrp ñsooun* here but varies between it and *prognōsis*. LR consistently reads the Greek loanword, a characteristic of later Coptic translation from the Greek according to Kasser, *Muséon* 77 (1964), 6f.

[65] Cf. Theodoret *Haer.* 1.13 and Iren. 1.29.1.

[66] Cf. II 5.4, 24; 6.6; 7.4 which read the former for the latter of B 27.18; 29.12; 31.11 and par.

[67] B 28.7–10/III 8.8–10; II 5.14–18/IV 8.2–7. Giversen, *Apocryphon* 170, is clearly wrong to identify the Thought and the Pronoia.

[68] B 28.7–13/III 8.7–13; II 5.14–20/IV 8.1–8.

[69] Cf. B 27.10f./III 7.16f. and B 27.18/III 17.22 with B 28.4.

[70] Cf II 5.4 and 4.32 in Krause's reconstruction.

[71] Cf. B 29.8–14/III 9.3–10; II 6.2–10.

[72] 297–9. Giversen, *Apocryphon* 170f., argues for an identification of Barbelo, Pronoia and Ennoia but, as we shall see, his appeal to the originality of the pentad of C II as including Truth is not persuasive.

[73] B 28.13–21/III 8.13–20; II 5.20–6. Giversen, *Apocryphon* 170f., although attacking Till's first argument for two Ennoias (298) namely that in B the pattern of praise is that the (second) Ennoia and Prior Knowledge praise the Father and Barbelo, then the three do the same,

on the grounds that in B 28.10 and 19 the MS has the singular form of the verb, fails to note that in the parallels to the latter (III 8.18f. and II 5.24–6) the verbs are in the plural.

[74] B 28.21–29.6/III 8.20–9.3; II 5.26–32/IV 8.20–4. LR refers to Barbelo to remove any doubts about the subject. Again Giversen has failed to note the plural verbs in all except III.

[75] B 29.7f./III 9.1–3.

[76] B 29.8f./III 9.3f. II 6.8 reads *pentas* which is the likely original. Cf. *AnonBru* ch. 15 (Schmidt–MacDermot 255.24).

[77] B 29.9–18/III 9.4–10. B's reading 'of the unoriginate Father' at 29.17f. seems nonsensical and may, as Janssens suggests, *Muséon* 84, 48, incorporate a marginal note.

[78] II 5.32–4/IV 8.24–7.

[79] II 5.35–6.2/IV 8.27–9.

[80] Although the plural is attested in both II 5.35 and IV 8.27.

[81] II 6.2–10/IV 9.8–11.

[82] Cf. B 29.12–16/III 9.6–8 where Barbelo and Ennoia are separated off from each other by the same copula (*mn*) as separates off each in the list.

[83] B 27.4–7/III 7.12–14; II 4.26–9/IV 8.1–4.

[84] 1.29.1.

[85] Cf. 1.29.1 and Till's edition (299). He may be too hasty in identifying the original Ennoia with Barbelo (298), and in that case would have no need to explain why the account of her origin was supposedly omitted by Irenaeus.

[86] Cf. e.g. B 27.10/III 7.16f.; II 4.31f.; B 28.10/III 8.10; II 5.16/IV 8.4f. (here LR, which particularly stresses the role of the Pronoia, has reversed the order); II 6.5; 23.24, 29; 24.14f. (here LR adds Pronoia). On the literary–critical principle involved, see Krause, 'Der Stand der Veröffentlichung der Nag Hammadi-Texte' in Bianchi, *Origini* 75.

[87] Cf. B 27.17–28.4/III 7.22–8.5 and II 5.5–11/IV 7.20–7.

[88] Conversely, SR is evidently secondary in its avoidance of the (a^2) theme of Barbelo/Pronoia as the androgynous Mother–Father (cf. B 27.19f. and par; 30.6 and par; 48.2 and par; 51.6 and par; 52.18 and par; 71.6 and par where SR prefers 'Father' or 'Mother' to LR's 'Mother–Father'; but cf. B 75.11/III 39.11f. and par where SR has the term and LR omits it!). See ch. 7, n. 23, p. 294.

[89] 1.29.1. Note that Theodoret, *Haer.* 1.13 (361C) preserves the singular *authis aitēsasēs* which, as we argued above, would seem to refer to Barbelo.

[90] Cf. B 27.17–28.4; II 5.4–11 and *GE* III 41.7–42.4/IV 50.23–51.22.

[91] III 42.5–11/IV 51.22–52.2. Cf. Iren. 1.29.1 and *AJ* B 31.5–18 and par. Note that the *GE* text echoes the syzygy pairing of Iren. 1.29.1: *ennoia/ logos, aphtharsia/* (Christ omitted as the subject of the third ogdoad), Eternal Life/*thelēma, nous/prognōsis*, and retains as the final member the androgynous Father (cf. *AJ* II 6.8–10).

[92] 1.29.2.

[93] Cf. B 30.4–9/III 9.15–19; B 32.8–14/III 11.6–11; II 7.15–24 and Iren. 1.29.1f.; Theod. *Haer.* 1.13 (362CD–364A).

[94] Cf. B 32.14–18/III 11.12f.; II 7.25–7/IV 11.18–22, an evident distortion of Iren. 1.29.2: 'et omnia huic subjecta. Coemissam autem ei Alethiam.' Cf. *GE* IV 60.2f. See n. 91 above.

[95] Giversen, *Apocryphon* 171; Tardieu, *Écrits* 262f. He ignores the evidence of *GE* and explains the supposed omission by homoeoteleuton – but was it likely that SR, having omitted it by mistake at B 29.6f. and par, should have not noticed and thus blithely omitted it when it appeared again only eight or so lines later at B 29.14 and par?

[96] Cf. III 65.11f./IV 77.9f. (also the fragmentary IV 60.2f.) and *AJ* B 32.14–17/III 11.12f.; II 7.25f./IV 11.18–21.

[97] *Écrits* 264.

[98] Cf. on a supposed Sethian 'Quinity' reflected in the five seals ritual, Schenke, 'Phenomenon' 603f. and Turner, 'Sethian Gnosticism' 77–9, with a valuable analysis of the structural significance of the number five for *GE*. The five androgynes may be based on the five illuminators and seals. In the original myth, of course, the figures are feminine, to be paired with their masculine counterparts.

[99] See my analysis in 'John' 52f.

[1] Cf. King, 'Sophia' 162. However, her claim that this is because he originated without the Father's permission is perhaps exaggerated: he is the outcome of Barbelo's ecstatic vision of the Father's self-revelation.

[2] II 6.10–18/IV 9.11–23.

[3] B 29.18–30.9/III 9.10–19. B 29.20 has mistakenly identified Barbelo with the pure light, and omitted the mention of the light being like the blessed light by homoeoteleuton.

[4] 1.29.1. This appears to be mistranslated by Krause and Wilson, *Gnosis 1* 104, to make the Father generate in her (Barbelo) a light like her. But surely *in hanc* cannot mean 'in her', and Theodoret's *apotekein* (*Haer.* 1.13: 361C) confirms that for Irenaeus Barbelo is the subject and that she bears the light.

[5] Cf. Iren. 1.29.1–2 and *GE* IV 59.13–60.11 with *AJ* B 30.4–17 and par, and *TP* 38.17–24.

[6] Cf. Iren. 1.29.1 and *AJ* B 30.7–9 and par. King, 'Sophia' 167f. also sees SR as more original in having Barbelo, not the Father, produce the Son: LR omits elements and does not supply a suitable paradigm of salvation.

[7] B 30.15 m̄ntc̄hs; III 9.24 m̄ntc̄hrs; II 6.23 m̄ntc̄hr̄s.

[8] B 30.17 nc̄hs; III 10.2 n̄chr̄s. On the debate over the wordplay here, see Till, 40; A. Böhlig, P. Labib eds, *Die koptisch-gnostische Schrift ohne Titel aus Codex II von Nag Hammadi im Koptischen Museum zu Alt-Kairo* (Deutsche Akademie der Wissenschaften zu Berlin. Institut für Orientforschung 58) (Berlin: Akademie, 1970), 46; Janssens, *Muséon* 84, 49–51.

[9] *Écrits* 266. Cf. A. Orbe, *Unción* 108–12, esp. 112, where he identifies four stages in the unction of the Son: (*a*) born as Nous or Intellect of the Father; (*b*) anointed with the virginal Spirit of the Father; (*c*) contemplates the Father as a consequence of the unction; (*d*) is deified by the life of the Father, at the root of the paternal intuition. The ultimate basis of this conception of unction in the Valentinians and Barbelognostics Orbe finds in John 1:3c-4a.

[10] 1.29.1: 'et videntem Patrem lumen hoc, unxisse illud sua benignitate, ut perfectum fieret. Hunc autem dicunt esse Christum.' Cf. Theod. *Haer.* 1.13.

[11] III 44.23–4.

[12] 37.30–3. The same verb is used here as in *GE* III 44.23 and *AJ*, and it also may have had Christ anointed with goodness. Line 33 preserves the first three letters of a substantive (*mnt-*) which the editor, J. D. Turner, restores as [goodness], *NHLE* 463.

[13] *Dossier* 41f. He refers to Justin, *1 Apol.* 6.1; 46.4; *2 Apol.* 2.6; Theoph. *Autol.* 1.10; Tert. *Apol.* 3.5; *Ad nat.* 1.3; Clem. Alex. *Protr.* 67.123; *Strom.* 2.14.18. But some of these are irrelevant or erroneous (e.g. Justin, *1 Apol.* 6.1, *2 Apol.* 2.6; Theoph. *Autol.* 1.10). More germane are texts reflecting the link of Christ/anointing/Christian, based on exegesis of Ps 45:7f., and Isa 61:1, e.g. Justin, *Dial.* 63, 86.3; *2 Apol.* 6.3; Theoph. *Autol.* 1.1,12; Lact. *Div. inst.* 4.13.9. Severin entirely overlooks Lampe's claim that it was Gnostics who initiated post-baptismal chrism (see ch. 1, section 3; ch. 2, section 2).

[14] *Dossier* 43f., referring to Orbe, *Unción*, 100.

[15] *Gnosis* 107.

[16] 107f.

[17] 'Sophia' 162f., 160. See following note.

[18] S. Arai, 'Zur Christologie des Apokryphons des Johannes', *NTS* 15 (1968/69), 305, would see this passage as a Gnostic interpretation of Jesus' *baptism* (Mark 1:9–10 and par), but the resemblances are not close and the latter does not explain the title 'Christ'. For an implied heavenly pre-temporal anointing, cf. Justin, *2 Apol.* 6.3; Lact. *Div. inst.* 4.13.9; for the Christological issues raised, cf. Gregory of Nyssa, *Antirrh.* 52f. (MPG 45.1249f.).

[19] *Dossier* 40, 45f.

[20] 46. Thus the form of B 30.19, *ntafouoth̠ naf ebol*, is to be retained, against Till, and the reading of III 10.4, as referring to the process of perfusion.

[21] See chs 1, section 3, and 2, p. 31f. Both the Marcosian rites in Iren. 1.21.3–5 have postbaptismal chrism. All this excludes attempts to treat this motif as a later Christian interpolation into an original non-Christian work, as e.g. Arai, 'Christologie' 305. King, 'Sophia' 162f., has rightly grasped the soteriological significance of the anointing, but given too negative an interpretation of Barbelo's act of generation as defective.

[22] B 31.5–9/III 10.9–14; II 6.33–7.3/IV 10.12–18. The 'him' must be Christ, not the Spirit. The redactor of III 10.13, who has both Nous and Christ praising, may have been confused by the earlier pattern of female aeons praising the Spirit and Barbelo.

[23] 1.29.1.

[24] B 31.10f./III 10.14f. Cf. *GE* III 42.2/IV 51.19f., where the Spirit produces the three ogdoads in silence (*sigē*) and providence (*pronoia*).

[25] II 7.3–6/IV 10.18–22. Cf. B 31.11f./III 10.15–18. The attempt of Giversen, *Apocryphon* 173, and Tardieu, *Écrits* 99, to take the thought of II 7.4 with the preceding silence founders on the facts (*a*) that in that case thought ought to have the indefinite article, and (*b*) the following sentence lacks an identifiable subject. Janssens, *Muséon* 84, 54f., is right to argue that the indefinite article suggests these are abstract nouns, not emanations, and that therefore they are unlikely to be periphrases for the Invisible Spirit and Barbelo.

[26] B 31.11–15/III 10.15–20. B 31.12f. has omitted mention of 'word'. It may be significant that Barbelo is omitted and the stereo-typed doxology formula broken, as it was in the case of Nous previously.

[27] II 7.4–8/IV 10.20–5.

[28] Cf. e.g. the relation of *ennoia* and *thelesis* in certain Valentinians, Iren. 1.12.1; Epiph. *Pan.* 31.5.4f., and the theories of e.g. Theoph. *Autol.* 2.10, 22.

[29] B 31.15f./III 10.20f.; II 7.9/IV 10.26f.

[30] B 31.16–18/III 10.21–3; II 7.10f./IV 10.27–9. B 31.18f. seems to regard the Autogenes as the subject of the following sentence.

[31] 1.29.1. Cf. Theod. *Haer.* 1.13 (364A).

[32] Cf. Iren. 1.29.1 and *GE* III 42.7–10/IV 51.25–52.1.

[33] For such a view of the generation of the Word by the Father, cf. e.g. Justin, *Dial.* 61; 100; 127–8.

[34] Cf. Iren. 1.1.1.

[35] If we assume the original pattern with the Logos emerging and praising Christ and the Barbelo 'since through him (i.e. Christ) the Logos came into being' (Greek: *hoti di'autou ho logos egeneto?*), the change to the present text of *AJ* under the influence of John 1:3 becomes only too understandable.

[36] Giversen, *Apocryphon* 174f.; Janssens, *Muséon* 84, 56; C. A. Baynes, *A Coptic Gnostic Treatise contained in the Codex Brucianus* (Bruce MS. 96, Bod. Lib. Oxford) (Cambridge, 1933), 33–5.

[37] 56f., with reference to Hipp. *Ref.* 5.12.3. Cf. also the Hermetic *Discourse on the Eighth and Ninth* (C VI,6) 57.13–18; *Eug* III 74.20–75.9; 82.7–15.

[38] Cf. B 30.6 and par; 31.18 and par; 32.5,9 and par; 34.10–18 and par; 35.3,17 and par; 51.9.

[39] *Separate* 412–16.

[40] 'The Historical Background of Proclus' Doctrine of the *Authupostata*', *Entretiens sur l'Antiquité classique* 21 (Vandouevres, 1975), 193–237; 'Self-Generating Principles in Second Century Gnostic Systems', Layton, *Rediscovery* 1.176–89.

[41] *Separate* 414, Iren. 1.1.2.

[42] 1.29.2. Cf. Theod. *Haer.* 1.13 (364A).

[43] IV 60.1–11. *TP* follows *AJ* in calling the Son, Christ, the Coptic equivalent of *autogenēs*, 'he who came into being by himself' (38.22f.).

[44] See p. 81f.

[45] 1.29.1/Theod. 1.13 (364A).

[46] B 31.19–32.2/III 10.23–11.2; II 7.11–15/IV 10.29–11.5. B 31.19 wrongly links Autogenes and Eternal Life. Janssens, *Muséon* 84, 57, points out that in the Coptic the aeons are treated as pairs by the use of conjunctions, particles and asyndeton.

[47] Giversen, *Apocryphon* 175f., referring to Schmidt, 'Irenäus' 325.

[48] 175f. referring to Till 299f. However, his reconstruction of the pentad with a supposed original *chrēstotēs*, read by Irenaeus as *christos*, paired with Incorruptibility, and with Autogenes and Truth, is not supported by the evidence, and is redundant on my hypothesis of the pentad/decad material as a later gloss.

[49] Cf. *GE* III 42.7–10/IV 51.25–52.1 and Iren. 1.29.1/Theod. 1.13 (364A). R. van den Broek, 'Autogenes and Adamas: The Mythological Structure of the Apocryphon of John' in Krause, *Gnosis and Gnosticism* (NHS 17) 17, suggests this points to a fixed, literary tradition. *GE* IV 51.26–52.1 has evidently and understandably taken *aphtharsia* to qualify Eternal Life.

[50] 1.29.2/Theod. 1.13 (364A).

[51] See, n. 49 above.

[52] II 7.15–17/IV 11.6–9.

[53] Cf. II 6.23–6 and par.

[54] Cf. II 6.15–22, 26f. and par.

[55] III 11.3–6.

[56] B 32.8–14/III 11.6–11. Cf. Rom 9:5.

[57] 1.29.2. Cf. Phil 2:9–11; 1 Cor 15:27–8; Eph 1:22; Heb 2:6–8. Van den Broek, 'Autogenes' 21, would see this as rendered by the *parastasis* of III 11.5, but such an identification is weakened by the fact that the Latin translator later seems to render the latter by *circumstantia* and *adstare* (see n. 63 below, p. 112). I see Autogenes as the heavenly archetype of John the Baptist and this as an attempt to render John 1:8b ('John' 53).

[58] II 7.20–2/IV 11.11–14. This may be a further example of its preference for Pronoia. Again note possible New Testament allusions (Eph 1:22; Col 2:10) in his being appointed head of the All: II 7.22–4/IV 11.15–18.

[59] II 7.22–4/IV 11.15–18. Cf. Col 2:10.

[60] B 32.14–18/III 11.12f. Cf. Wilson, *Gnosis* 106. Krause, *Drei Versionen* 63, suggests III 11.11 omitted the *exousia* phrase through homoeoteleuton.

[61] II 7.25–9/IV 11.18–24.

[62] B 32.18f./III 11.13f.

[63] *Écrits* 267f. This precisely ties in with our interpretation of the primal chrismation of the Son.

[64] B 32.19–33.2/III 11.14–19; II 7.30–3/IV 12.2–6. For the possible etymologies of the four, see Appendix (b).

[65] 1.29.2. Theod. 1.13 (364A) refers to other emanations 'tas ek tou Phōtos kai tēs Aphtharsias'.

[66] Schenke, 'Nag-Hamadi–Studien III', *ZRGG* 14 (1962), 359, in support of his claim that the aeons of *AJ* were originally unpaired, tries to argue that Christ and Incorruptibility are secondary, and that the original probably read: 'From the Light . . . through the divine Autogenes . . .', entirely overlooking the identification of the two here. The mention of the consent of Christ, the Spirit and the Father here may be an echo of the Valentinian account of the production of the Saviour and his angelic bodyguard, cf. Iren. 1.2.6.

[67] B 33.3f./III 11.19 (*parastasis*); II 7.34–8.1. II 7.34 reads: 'he saw that they . . .' The *parastasis* of III 11.19 evidently lies behind the *circumstantia* of Irenaeus. Cf., n. 57 above, p. 111.

[68] 1.29.2.

[69] B 33.4f./III 11.20f.; II 8.1f. IV omits this while III 11.20 has Eternal Life second.

[70] Giversen, *Apocryphon* 180, sees as a link the conjunctive *de* in II 8.1 and the indefinite *n* of B 33.4, but III 11.20 has no conjunctive at all. His suggestion that the three plus Christ and Incorruptibility represent five androgynous aeons and thus the decad, is unconvincing. Perhaps in desperation the redactor of IV has omitted all mention of the three.

[71] *Écrits* 268f. He is forced to interpret the Christ of the text as *chrēstotēs*, a figure distinct from Christ/Autogenes, contradicting his earlier pairing Christ/Incorruptibility (264), and to concoct a mixed male/female triad of which there is no evidence elsewhere.

[72] 'Autogenes' 18, n. 6. Thus he explains the awkward fact that III 11.21 has *ennoia* third as looking like a partial return to the original. Cf. Giversen, *Apocryphon* 181, who suggests that a copyist confused the Life at the end of the list of five aeons with the mention of Life who with Will reveals the four ministers.

[73] B 33.5–7/III 11.21–3.

[74] II 8.2–4/IV 11.21–3. IV starts abruptly with prudence.

[75] *Apocryphon* 181. Cf. II 8.4.

[76] Cf. B 33.7–34.1/III 11.23–12.11; II 8.4–16. Neither *phronēsis* nor a Coptic equivalent occur among the aeons of the fourth illuminator, which are perfection, peace and *sophia* (cf. B 34.6f. and par).

[77] *GE* III 52.9–13/IV 63.2–6.

[78] 223 of vol. 1 of his edition.

[79] Thelesis might have seemed more appropriate as alluding to an intellectual, spiritual process, more suitable at this stage. Harvey's suggestion, 223, that it might have been suggested by the Hebrew equivalent of Raguel, will of God, seems far-fetched. Giversen, *Apocryphon* 184, prefers 'friend of God'. The second illuminator in *AJ* and *GE* is Oroiael, which might be derived from the Hebrew '*ōr* and '*ēl*, i.e. illumination of God. See Appendix (b).

[80] Cf. *GE* III 50.17–51.19/IV 62.16–63.14. See Böhlig–Wisse, *Gospel* 33, 178f.

[81] B 33.7–10/III 11.23–12.1; II 8.4–6/IV 12.9–11. Cf. Iren. 1.29.2, *GE* III 52.8–10 and par. LR, by reading *phōstēr-aiōn* (II 8.5/IV 12.9f.), has evidently combined two entities which are distinct in SR at this point and which LR itself later distinguishes (cf. II 8.8f.), and thus has been led to refer to the first angel with no mention of the aeon. The phrase 'of the light' in B 33.9 is probably a redactional gloss.

[82] B 33.10–12/III 12.1–3.

[83] II 8.6–8/IV 12.11–14.

[84] B 33.12–17/III 12.3–8; II 8.8–12/IV 12.14–20. II 12.5 has 'in' rather than 'over' (cf. 12.9, 11); the 'other three *aeons*' associated with each *illuminator* in II 8.7, 11, 15, 19/IV 12.12(?), 18, 24; 13.2 again suggests the attempt to fuse together a scheme (or schemes) involving aeons understood as hypostases and/or locations with the four illuminator scheme.

[85] B 33.17–34.1/III 12.8–11; II 8.12–16/IV 12.20–6. The reading of III 12.8f.: 'in the third illuminator he(?) was set in the third aeon' which is nonsense and omits the illuminator's name, must be secondary.

[86] B 34.1–7/III 12.11–16. III 12.11f. repeats its peculiar form, omitting the illuminator's name.

[87] II 8.16–20/IV 12.26–13.3.

[88] Giversen, *Apocryphon* 182, makes the claim without any evidence. Tardieu, *Écrits* 271, appeals to Prov 8:1 and Dan 2:23 LXX, in both of which the two terms retain distinctive meanings.

[89] B 34.7–13/III 12.16–22; II 8.22–5. III 12.19–20 is a scribal doublet, and there is some confusion in the versions over the figure of the Invisible Spirit: B 34.12f. talks of the good pleasure of God, the Invisible Spirit; II 8.24f. has through the decision and God, the Invisible Spirit; and III 12.21f. through the resolve of God and the good pleasure of the Spirit.

[90] B 34.13–15/III 12.22–4; II 8.25f. B 34.15 has the form *autogenētos* (cf. 30.6) and III 12.20 *autogenetōr*.

[91] Cf. *AJ* B 35.20–36.15 and par; *GE* III 65.12–22 and par; *Zost.* 6.7–7.28; 29.1–20.

[92] Cf. the Valentinian twelve aeons with Sophia as last in Iren. 1.1.2; Epiph. *Pan.* 31.5.8 (the list also includes *synesis* and *agapē*!), and

Ialdabaoth's union with *aponoia* and creation of twelve *exousiai* according to the *typos* of the incorruptible aeons in *AJ* B 39.4–10/III 16.7–11. Since LR omits any mention of Ialdabaoth's imitation of the heavenly model at this point (II 10.26–8), simply referring to his general imitation later (II 12.33–13.1), it seems secondary.

[93] 38.16–39.13.

[94] 39.13–40.29. Cf. the role of Eleleth in *HA* and *GE*.

[95] Cf. e.g. 37.18–20; 41.4–20; 45.12–20; 48.26–35; 50.17–20.

[96] III 50.17–51.22 and par.

[97] Cf. III 65.12–22 and par. However, its listing of *mnēmē*, *agapē* and *eirēnē* along with eternal life as consorts of four further ministers of the illuminators, Gamaliel, Gabriel, Samblo, Abrasax, III 52.6–16 and par, might be an echo of the twelve female aeons of *AJ*.

[98] Cf. 6.7–7.22 (ascent by baptism through the four aeons); 29.1–20 (aspects of truth related to the four aeons in reverse order). *Melch* 6.2f. has Christ as commander-in-chief of the four illuminators, who are evidently angelic figures. See Pétrement, *Separate* 403f.

[99] Cf. ch. 20 (Schmidt–MacDermot 263.22–264.6).

[1] *Écrits* 271.

[2] B 34.15–18; II 8.26–8. III has omitted this through homoeoteleuton.

[3] B 34.19–35.5/III 12.24–13.1; II 8.28–33. The version in II 8.30f.: 'through the revelation of the will of the Invisible Spirit', is preferable to the 'through God and the good pleasure ...' of SR, B 34.20–35.2/III 12.25f., which repeats III 12.19f., 21f. The 'through the good pleasure of the Autogenes' of B 35.2f. and II 8.31f. is preferable to the 'before the Autogenes' of III 13.1. II 8.33 adds 'and the truth' to revelation rather than have it qualify the Man as in B 35.4, III 13.2 (which adds 'holy') and Iren. 1.29.3. See Giversen, *Apocryphon* 186. Janssens, *Muséon* 84, 60, n. 27, finds echoes of Eph 1:5 and Luke 2:14 here.

[4] 1.29.3. Theodoret preserves the Greek *probalesthai* (1.13: 364A). *AJ* does involve the Autogenes, if only in terms of his agreement.

[5] Cf. e.g. *Zost.* 30.4–9. In *GE* Autogenes Logos appears to be responsible for the origin of Adamas (cf. esp. IV 60.30–61.10 – note the phrase 'the eye of the l[ight]', in *SJC* III 105.14/B 100.14, omitted in *Eug*, and probably derived from the identification of the Autogenes with the Light, Christ, and a natural evolution from *Zost.* 30.5f.: Adamas as eye of the Self-begotten).

[6] Cf. *Separate* 391, 412, etc.

[7] Cf. *Eug* III 81.12 = *SJC* III 105.12/B 100.14; *OW* 108.21, etc.

[8] Cf. Iren. 1.29.3/Theod. 1.13 (364AB); *OW* 108.23; *GE* III 49.19; 50.20f./IV 62.19, etc.; *Zost.* 6.26; 30.4; 33.17; 51.14.

[9] Cf. *Steles Seth* 118.26; *Zost.* 6.23; *Melch.* 6.6.

[10] Cf. *Steles Seth* 118.26–8 (Geradamas and Emmacha Seth); *Zost.* 6.23–6 (Geradamas and Seth Emmacha Seth). H. M. Jackson, 'Geradamas, the Celestial Stranger', *NTS* 27 (1980/81), 385–94, seems

justified in rejecting attempts to derive the term from Greek (mainly variations of *gēr*, 'old') or Coptic, and his proposal of a Semitic origin from *gēr* 'stranger' appears plausible. On the proposed etymologies for Adamas and Pigeradamas/Geradamas, see Appendix (c).

[11] 1.29.3. Cf. the similar wordplay in *OW* 108.23–5: Adamas, of which the interpretation is 'the holy adamantine earth', and *AnonBru* 46.4 (Baynes; cf. Schmidt–MacDermot 252.9f.).

[12] Cf. B 27.8–10 and par; II 5.11, Giversen, *Apocryphon* 186.

[13] Cf. B 47.20–49.9 and par; II 14.18–15.13 and par, and Giversen, ibid. See ch. 7, section 3.

[14] *Muséon* 84, 61.

[15] B 35.6–10/III 13.4–9. III 13.5 has 'in' following its pattern of installation (cf. 12.5, 9, 12f.), as B and II follow theirs. III 13.5 also has 'his aeon'. B 35.8 again reads *autogenetōr*.

[16] II 8.35–9.3.

[17] 1.29.3. Theodoret is no help here.

[18] 'Irenäus' 329. Cf. Iren. 1.29.1–3/Theod. 1.13 (362C/364A). Only LR is aware of the distinction and always uses the Greek loan-word of the illuminators (cf. II 7.32f.; 8.5 (combined with *aiōn*), 9, 12f., 18, 20f.; 9.2 and par).

[19] Thus the reading of B 35.6–9, which has Adam first set *over* then *in*, might point to that reworking, which LR, as usual, has 'tidied up'.

[20] B 35.10–13/III 13.9–11; II 9.4f./IV 14.1f.

[21] 1.29.3: 'virtutem quoque ei invictam datam a virginali Spiritu.'

[22] 1.29.3/Theod. 1.13 (364B).

[23] Ibid.

[24] Cf. *HA* 89.31–90.12.

[25] Cf. B 57.8–12 and par.

[26] B 35.20–36.2/III 13.17–19; II 9.11–14.

[27] B 36.2–15/III 13.19–14.9; II 9.14–24. Note too the Valentinian term *plērōma* (III 14.4; II 9.20).

[28] B 35.13–16/III 13.11–13; II 9.5–8/IV 14.2–6. SR starts the direct speech immediately with Adam addressing the Spirit in the third person, then switching to the second. LR seems to tidy this up. III 13.13 has omitted 'and because of you everything will return' through homoeoteleton. Cf. *GE* III 49.8–12/IV 61.8–14. Giversen, *Apocryphon* 188, doubts an allusion to John 1:3 here, and prefers Rom 11:36. Janssens, *Muséon* 84, 61, also cites Rom 11:36 and adds 1 Cor 8:6.

[29] B 35.17–20/III 13.14–17; II 9.9–11.

[30] 1.29.3/Theod. 1.13 (364B).

[31] Cf. 1.29.1 where the aeon dwells in the virginal Spirit (i.e. Barbelo).

[32] Till, 111 of his edition, Janssens, *Muséon* 84, 61.

[33] 'Triade und Trinität in den Schriften von Nag Hammadi', in Layton, *Rediscovery* 2.617–34, and discussion, 640–2.

[34] Cf. Böhlig, 'Triade' 622; Iren. 1.29.1, *AJ* B 31.11–18 and par (the Logos as distinct from the Son and produced through him). So too with *GE* IV 60.1–8 (the Autogenes (Word) as son of Christ). On Logos as added to *AJ*, etc. see P. Perkins, 'Logos Christologies in the Nag Hammadi Codices', *VC* 35 (1981), 379f.

[35] 'Triade' 629.

[36] 629, 631.

[37] Cf. ch. 7, section 3. This pattern of transcendent God made known in three modalities is strikingly similar to the roughly contemporary efforts of the Modalist Monarchians attacked by Hippolytus and Tertullian!

[38] 622.

[39] Pearson, 'Triade' discussion, 642. Cf. on Wisdom = Holy Spirit, e.g. Athenag. *Leg.* 10.3 (cf. Wis 7:25f.); Theoph. *Autol.* 1.7; 2.15,18.

4

Gnostic Theogony and Cosmogony 2: The Lower World

1 The fall of Sophia

With the abrupt mention of the aeon Sophia by the *Apocryphon*,[1] a new section begins, involving cosmogony and anthropogony. This will trace to her error the origin of this present world of deficiency, ruled by an ignorant and arrogant Creator God or Platonic Demiurge and his seven archons, who created the visible universe and human beings in the image of the heavenly world, in order to gain control over that world and its aeons. The idea that a female heavenly being, often the – ironically named – Wisdom, was responsible for the tragic split in the heavenly world which gave rise to the present situation of the Gnostic as a divine spark or self trapped in matter and oblivion, is a very common Gnostic theme,[2] and forms the basic presupposition of the Valentinian system in particular.[3] But in the case of the Barbelognostics, Sophia's wanton if innocent act of giving birth to the Demiurge without a consort or the agreement of the supreme deity (i.e., a virgin birth again) is a characteristic negative reflection of Barbelo's conception of the Son. Once more we meet the fundamental themes of female initiative with or without male permission and co-operation, and of knowledge and obedience over against ignorance and recklessness.

That Sophia is called 'our sister' relates her to humanity and to the Gnostic elect in particular as source and archetype;[4] that she is designated an aeon is evidently meant to identify her as the last of the three aeons associated with the fourth illuminator Eleleth, and thus the twelfth in order of appearance and the furthest removed in the heavenly world from the Invisible Spirit. We have argued in the previous chapter that this represents part of redaction (a²) in which Sophia, perhaps partly under Valentinian influence, is demoted from her original status and active saving role. Evidence of this can be found in the omission of one of the consorts of the illuminators, *phronēsis*, to allow room for her, and from comparison with the parallel in the *Gospel of the Egyptians*, which added a further ogdoad of male ministers and female consorts, including three of the *Apocryphon*'s twelve, in addition to the three helpers of the illuminators (*charis, aisthēsis, synesis*). Thus the list has the appearance of an artificial construct, in which only the number (twelve) and the last aeon (Sophia) are important, the number, as we suggested, producing a heavenly archetype for the ensuing creation of the twelve signs of the Zodiac by the Demiurge, Sophia being identified as the female aeon responsible for the production of that Demiurge, and hence of the created order beneath the heavenly world.

This conception, I noted, naturally recalls the Valentinian duodecad of paired male and female aeons produced by Man and Church, of which the last couple is Desired (Theletos) and Sophia.[5] However, Scholten, while detecting considerable Valentinian influence on the *Apocryphon* both generally as regards the Sophia myth and at this point in particular, feels that the *Apocryphon*'s presentation of the twelve aeons as four times three ought not to be compared with the Valentinian arrangement of twice six.[6] But this is bound up with his acceptance of the Sethian character of the *Apocryphon* and the priority of its understanding of the structure of the heavenly world over against Irenaeus. Conversely he finds Valentinian influence precisely in the fact that although Sophia is presented in the *Apocryphon* as one of three female aeons with no trace of a male consort, as is usual in Sethian texts and as Irenaeus' version attests, such a figure suddenly appears and plays a major role in what follows.[7] Indeed Scholten traces the syzygy motif in general, which he finds strikingly absent in the *Apocryphon* where we meet it in Irenaeus, to Valentinian influence, while eschewing any attempt, such as that of Schenke, to claim that the myth underlying Irenaeus' account in 1.29 originally lacked a developed syzygy structure. He is content to suggest that Valentinian ideas may have been responsible for the concept of a consort in the *Apocryphon*, as they led Irenaeus to stress the syzygy structure of his Barbelognostic source, in his desire to explain the origins of Valentinianism.[8]

However, we attempted to explain in the previous chapter how the original syzygy structure of the myth underlying the *Apocryphon* was progressively distorted and obscured by the introduction of the Autogenes figure and Truth as part of the continuing Johannine interpretation, and by the identification of that figure with Christ, and we pointed to a trace of that structure in the *Gospel of the Egyptians*. Scholten's preference for texts of the *Apocryphon* lacking mention of that structure is not justified. But on the other hand he is surely right to identify Valentinian influence as being to some extent responsible for the *Apocryphon*'s concept of Sophia having a consort, and, as we shall see, for her failure to act with his consent as an explanation of her 'fall'. Such influence may also have contributed to the theme of the twelve female aeons, the last of which was Sophia.

As we have seen, SR calls Sophia 'our sister', whereas II 9.25 describes her as 'the Sophia of Epinoia'.[9] The former is echoed in the *Second Treatise of the Great Seth*,[10] while the Epinoia of the latter may be a reference to the first of the three aeons with the second illuminator, but is more likely to signify the revealer/redeemer of the latter part of the *Apocryphon*, dispatched to help Adam in his struggle with the powers of darkness and to correct Sophia's deficiency.[11] However, Giversen's suggestion that this phrase presupposes an unknown account which has disappeared may be even nearer the truth, in the light of the evidence of *Trimorphic Protennoia* about the origin of Sophia and her relation to Epinoia.[12]

Thus, after describing the appearance and establishment of the four aeons, the *Protennoia* relates how, in response to a word from the great illuminator Eleleth proclaiming his kingly role and asking who belongs to chaos and the underworld, his light appears endowed with Epinoia (a reference to Sophia?). This leads to the manifestation of the great demon Saklas, i.e. Samael, Ialtabaoth, who according to the text had taken power from the guileless one (i.e. Sophia). He had at first over-powered the Epinoia of light who had descended (i.e. Sophia again), from whom he had come forth from the first.[13] The text then speaks of the request of the Epinoia of light, apparently to Eleleth, for a better order, the consequent agreement of the higher order, and of how, when the great demon begins to produce aeons in the likeness of the real aeons, the Protennoia calls on him to desist, since she is about to descend for the sake of her portion imprisoned there since the guileless Sophia who had descended was conquered.[14] Despite a certain degree of ambiguity, the text appears to be describing the origin of Sophia, the Epinoia of light, from Eleleth, and her descent and production of Saklas/Ialdabaoth.

We shall consider the close parallelism of the whole passage
with the *Apocryphon* in due course, and the way the *Protennoia*
evidently presupposes and develops the myth underlying our
version of the latter, but at this point wish to draw attention to
certain features of the description of Sophia in these various
accounts, particularly in relation to Irenaeus' summary of the
Barbelognostics. The motif of the twelve aeons in the image of
the heavenly world, absent in Irenaeus, we have suggested
represents a tradition involving Ialdabaoth, his seven archons and
twelve powers (as types of heavenly archetypes) which the
Apocryphon has incorporated as redaction (a^2) into the original
scheme, which comprised four angelic illuminators and their
consorts. This involved the demotion of Sophia, perhaps also as a
result of Valentinian influence, to be the twelfth and last offspring
of the fourth illuminator, Eleleth, rather than, as apparently in
the allusive treatment of Irenaeus, of the first, Harmozel. The latter
is evidently the first angel standing beside Monogenes whom
Irenaeus records as emanating the Holy Spirit, also called 'Sophia'
and 'Prunicus'.[15] The term 'Monogenes' although not used
previously, would appear to apply to the Autogenes, as in the
Apocryphon,[16] which refers to the first illuminator, Harmozel, who
forms the bodyguard of Autogenes with the other three, as the
'first angel'.[17] Both Irenaeus and the *Apocryphon* thus appear to
represent a tradition which derives Sophia from one of the four
great illuminator angels, a tradition alluded to in more detail in
Trimorphic Protennoia and the *Gospel of the Egyptians*.

But both versions of the origin of Sophia appear to display a
certain degree of reserve or ambiguity, as if trying to play down
or conceal the tensions implicit in such a figure.[18] In Irenaeus'
all-too-brief account Sophia would appear to be the offspring of
Harmozel with or without the co-operation of Charis, his consort,
and herself to lack a consort. Significantly perhaps, the
Barbelognostics insist on calling Harmozel 'Saviour', which might
imply the soteriological significance of his emanation of Sophia.[19]
Now in the evidently related *Hypostasis of the Archons* we find even
less explanation of the origin of Sophia, here called Pistis, but
the appearance of the great angel Eleleth, who calls himself
Understanding (i.e. *phronēsis* rather than *sophia*),[20] as revealer/
redeemer and his account of how Sophia was eventually
responsible for the production of the Demiurge, is suggestive.[21]
It links Eleleth to the process of Sophia's fault and salvation. And
the pattern of Norea's call for help and the promised rescue

echoes that of Sophia in *Trimorphic Protennoia* and Norea in the *Thought of Norea*,[22] as the pattern of Sophia's ignorant but guileless action in producing the Demiurge and her subsequent repentance and elevation recalls (and perhaps even represents the archetype of) the souls who remain ignorant for a while but then repent and rest in Eleleth, according to the Sethian reworking of the *Apocryphon*.[23]

Here the *Hypostasis of the Archons* may cast some light on the development of the myth of Sophia, which by the allusive way it is presented, with almost no reference to her origin, suggests both its developed and problematic character. The *Hypostasis*, by its use of the figures of the great Invisible Spirit, the four illuminators, Sophia, Norea, and the kingless race or generation, is obviously dependent on and indeed a variant of the Barbelognostic myth, which develops earlier elements of Jewish provenance (the Saklas/ Samael and Ialdabaoth/Sabaoth material) which themselves have influenced later redactions of the *Apocryphon*, as we shall see. It reflects the transition from Sophia's origin from Harmozel, as in Irenaeus, to her origin from Eleleth, as in *Trimorphic Protennoia*. Thus one can surmise that in the *Hypostasis* Eleleth is identified with his consort, *phronēsis*, perhaps even called *sophia*, and that the offspring of this androgyne, Sophia, has been given the designation 'Pistis' to distinguish her.[24] Certainly this at least supplies an explanation for the title lacking up to now. Both the *Apocryphon* and the *Protennoia* stress her innocence, and *Zostrianos* emphasizes her action without prior reflection: she acts in blind faith, out of guilelessness.[25]

Furthermore, the evidence of the *Protennoia* that Epinoia and Sophia are apparently synonymous might suggest that the *Apocryphon*'s ensuing distinction between the two, with the former as revealer/redeemer and the latter as entirely in need of redemption, represents later theological reinterpretation of an earlier tradition, such as found in the 'Ophites' of Irenaeus and the Valentinians, that Sophia was responsible for the original fault or defect yet also acted as a redeemer.[26] Again, as *Epi*noia, Sophia appears as the afterthought, in contrast to *Pro*noia or Barbelo, the Father's first thought, appropriately linked with the fourth illuminator and later taken as the prototype for the fourth Sethian category, those souls who only finally gained knowledge and repented.

Since Sophia is an aeon, the *Apocryphon* continues, she conceived a thought out of herself and through the thought (*enthymēsis*) of the Spirit and Prior Knowledge, and willed to reveal her image.[27] As Scholten points out, this theme appears at first sight to combine the two main Valentinian versions of Sophia's fall: the more metaphysical one of trying to conceive the inconceivable Father (A, mainly in Irenaeus), and the more biological one of producing an offspring without her consort (B, mainly in Hippolytus), but differs subtly from both.[28] In accordance with the basic pattern of the myth, one would expect Sophia's disobedient (virginal) conception to be the negative reflection of Barbelo's obedient (virginal) conception. The two recensions seem to attest this while revealing some confusion and divergence. SR has this happen although the Spirit had neither agreed to this nor nodded assent (*kataneuein*), nor had her consort (*syzygos*), the male virginal spirit (*parthenikon pneuma*), joined in agreeing (*syneudokein*).[29] LR has this happen without the wish of the Spirit, since her consort had not agreed (*eudokein*), and without his thinking (*enthymēsis*), since the person (*prosōpon*) of her masculinity had not joined in agreement.[30]

Now the preceding pattern of aeonic emanation has certainly involved the union of male and female aeons and the agreement of the Invisible Spirit.[31] But the uncertainty in our texts over this consort (the male virginal spirit according to SR), who only appears here and can hardly be identified as Barbelo, as Janssens claims,[32] and who is the occasion of a very cumbrous paraphrase in LR, adds further support to the hypothesis that the theme of the consort is a later attempt to reconcile the paradoxes of Sophia and her guileless misconception along Valentinian lines.[33] LR, while accepting that Sophia has a consort, as we shall see tends to play down or reinterpret the consort/syzygy concept, whereas in Irenaeus the syzygies are primary, but Sophia lacks a consort. Corresponding to Sophia's predominantly *passive* role in our present *Apocryphon*, she needs a consort to help her correct her deficiency, whereas the logic underlying the Barbelognostic system, as attested by the 'Ophites' of Irenaeus and the Epinoia of the *Apocryphon*, dictates a more *active* role in revelation/redemption, as with the Valentinian Sophia. But the latter, in turn, like the 'Ophite' Sophia, needs a consort for ultimate salvation. Here again the various versions are attempting to reconcile the paradox of Gnostic experience projected in Sophia: the need for external revelation to ensure genuine salvation, on the one hand, but equally the fact that salvation is ultimately self-salvation, on the other.[34]

This might lead us to identify the male virginal spirit with the Epinoia, since we later hear that her consort descended to correct her deficiency,[35] that he will be sent out to her,[36] and that it is the Epinoia who will correct her fault.[37] The two aspects of Sophia, active and passive, are represented by Epinoia and Sophia respectively. But this Pronoia–Sophia–Epinoia scheme is a later attempt to resolve the paradoxes of Gnostic experience projected in and by the Sophia myth: in Irenaeus' version the motivation for the fall is simply that Sophia has no obvious partner as the others do, and seeks one without the agreement (*bona voluntas*, i.e. *eudokia*) of the Father.[38] There is some hint of this in the continuation in the *Apocryphon* that since she had not found her partner she consented, all this without the agreement (*eudokia*) of the Spirit and knowledge of her partner.[39]

The *Apocryphon* then has Sophia produce her conception through the wantonness (? *prounikon*) in her (B 37.10f.), or through her watchfulness (*phrourikon*: III 15.2f.), or through her invincible power (II 9.35–10.1). B's reading obviously echoes Sophia's title in Irenaeus: 'Prunicus', and can be seen to be more original than the evident emendations in III and II.[40] The 'invincible power' of the latter, as Giversen suggests, is best seen as further evidence of the tendency of LR to a more exalted, less crude and anthropomorphic portrayal of the world of light.[41] *Prounikos*, on the other hand, meaning 'lustful', 'lascivious' or 'wanton', or perhaps 'impetuous', 'prodigal',[42] supplies a very satisfactory motivation for Sophia's action here.

In Irenaeus' account 'Prunicus' is clearly a title for the Holy Spirit, derived from her wanton and impetuous action of seeking a consort by extending herself and looking down to the lower regions, and when that failed, of leaping forth and finally, driven by innocence (*simplicitas*, i.e *akakia*) and goodness (*benignitas*), generating a work in which was ignorance and audacity.[43] This again is a negative counterpart of Barbelo's procreative conception: here innocence and goodness lead to a downward, not an upward, gaze and a deficiency which is not corrected. In the 'Ophite' system of the following chapter (1.30), too, the power which overflows from the Holy Spirit, the First Woman, as a result of her union with First Man and his Son, is also fitly dubbed 'Prunicus' as well as Sophia from the wanton way (*petulanter*) she stirs up the waters of chaos into which she descends in innocence (*simpliciter*).[44]

M. P. Nilsson, followed independently by Pétrement, has argued
that the term *prounikos* has the primary sense of 'bearer' in popular
classical usage, and that the same sense applies to the Gnostic use
of it. The Church Fathers, he and Pétrement feel, are responsible
for giving the word an obscene connotation to discredit the
Gnostics, and both cite Epiphanius' own definition.[45] But, as
H. Chadwick has pointed out, it is probable that the Gnostics used
the term because of its double meaning,[46] and the fact that it
occurs in a Gnostic primary document, the *Apocryphon*, and has
proved awkward enough to require reinterpretation, suggests that
its sexual meaning has not been foisted on the Gnostics by the
heresiologists. Pétrement may be justified in querying R. A.
Bullard's translation of the term as 'whore' in the *Second Treatise
of the Great Seth*,[47] appealing to Celsus' reference to a certain *virgin*
(*parthenos*) *Prounikos* as a Valentinian title for Sophia,[48] but the
paradox of the wanton virgin is a well-attested Gnostic theme. It
is at the heart of the *Thunder*,[49] and is reflected in the Valentinian
doctrinal letter where the wantonness and procreative power of
the supreme female aeon Silence or Ennoia and her emanations
is a key theme.[50]

Epiphanius supplies further information about the figure
Prunicus. Discussing the Simonians he quotes a passage in which
Simon, the great power, describes his descent to his prostitute
consort, Ennoia, also called *Prounikos* and 'Holy Spirit': this figure,
comments Epiphanius, is called Barbelo or Barbero in other
heresies.[51] This comment would appear to refer to the Nicolaitans,
some of whom revere Barbelo (who, like the Ennoia/Helen/
Prunicus of the Simonians, is responsible for the seduction of the
archons), and some of whom honour Prunicus.[52] Barbelo and
Prunicus would appear to be akin, if not synonymous. Prunicus
also appears in Epiphanius' account of the Ophite heresy, based
on Irenaeus, in which the former gives an explanation of the term
as 'bad' (*achrēstos*).[53] This evidence not only confirms the
originality of the reading of B 37.11, but also the sexual connotation of the term and its possible influence on Valentinianism.
It may also, if we accept the reliability of Epiphanius' information
and judgement, add some weight to the hypothesis that Sophia
and Barbelo were originally identical.

Sophia's thought, the *Apocryphon* continues, could not remain
idle (*argon*), and her work (*ergon*) appeared incomplete and unlike
her form because she had created it without her consort.[54] This
motif of procreation/emanation by Sophia without a partner

underlies a number of Gnostic systems; what distinguishes them is whether she has a partner and what explanation for her action is offered. Thus Irenaeus' account of the Barbelognostics has Sophia seek a partner in vain and thereafter, impelled by guilelessness and generosity, procreate a work (*opus/ergon*) in which was ignorance and boldness (*authadeia/audacia*).[55] The *Hypostasis of the Archons* simply relates how Sophia, called 'Pistis', wanted to make a work by herself without her partner, and that work (*ergon*) became the images of heaven. The shadow which came into being beneath the curtain thus formed became matter and finally materialized as the arrogant beast-like Demiurge, Samael/Ialdabaoth.[56] Here Sophia's responsibility for the Demiurge is lessened by the curtain motif which may derive from the 'Ophite' system described by Irenaeus.[57]

Hippolytus' account of Valentinianism reflects a more sophisticated version of the motif: Sophia attempts to imitate the Father in procreating like him without a consort, but because of the difference in nature she, as begotten, emanated a shapeless (*amorphos*) and incomplete (*akataskeuastos*) substance (not the Demiurge but the lower Sophia, outside the Pleroma).[58] The Ptolemaeans have an even more demythologized and metaphysical account which explains Sophia's motivation as a desire to comprehend the greatness of the supreme Father, a passion she suffered apart from the embrace of her consort.[59] Nevertheless both of these teach a *double* Sophia. However, Valentinus himself, whom Stead justifiably argues probably only envisaged *one* erring Sophia figure,[60] shows traces of the mythologoumenon of Sophia imitating the Father in creating without a consort. Thus in a fragment of a homily Valentinus likens Sophia to a painter, producing as her creation (*plasma*) the Demiurge who is an image (*eikōn*) since he originates from one, not from a syzygy.[61] Although the precise terms are different, the whole theme recalls the *Apocryphon*'s version.[62]

That version, which in B presents Sophia as acting without her consort because of the wanton creative passion (*prounikon*) within her, can credibly be seen as an early stage in the process of development whereby the attribute ('wanton') became a title (as among the Barbelognostics and 'Ophites' of Irenaeus, the Simonians, Nicolaitans/Gnostics and Ophites of Epiphanius, and perhaps even among some Valentinians, as Origen and Epiphanius attest), and the exclusively sexual and mythological understanding of Sophia's action became increasingly sublimated

and demythologized (as in the long recension of the *Apocryphon*
and the various schools of Valentinianism). In any case, the
deliberate ambiguity of the term and the stress on Sophia's
guilelessness help exonerate her and cloak the negative character
of this 'fall'.

The *Apocryphon* then relates how Sophia saw that her offspring
was of a different type (*typos*), with the face of a snake and a lion
and eyes gleaming like a fire.[63] Sophia cast it away from those
regions lest any of the immortals see it, because she had produced
it in ignorance. She surrounded it with a cloud of light and placed
a throne in the middle of the cloud to ensure that no one saw it
except the Holy Spirit, who is called 'the Mother of all living',
and she called it 'Ialdabaoth'. This, says the *Apocryphon*, is the First
Archon.[64]

Now Irenaeus' account of the Barbelognostics simply names
the work of Sophia 'First Archon' (*Protarchon*), with no mention
of its appearance or proper name, although his reference to the
ignorance present in it recalls the *Apocryphon*'s statement that
Sophia had produced her abortion in ignorance.[65] However, the
first offspring of Sophia Prunicus, according to the 'Ophite' system
in the following section in Irenaeus, is called Ialdabaoth.[66] This
would suggest that the *Apocryphon* has here combined two distinct
traditions, the one dealing with the anonymous chief or first
archon, the other with Ialdabaoth/Saklas/Samael and his offspring, as we hypothesized in reconstructing the development of
the myth.[67] And if we again apply the principle that the meaning
of mythical names must be determined from their context, we
find, despite differences of opinion, that the characteristic
ambiguity of Barbelognostic divine names, suggesting both Greek
and Semitic elements, is lacking here.

In her treatment of possible meanings,[68] Pétrement first
considers and rejects Bousset's identification with the god
Saturn on the basis of Origen's assertion,[69] but without herself
offering an etymology. One recent popular suggestion she
notes, which goes back to J. Matter, is to derive it from the
Aramaic roots *ialad* 'child' and *baôth* 'chaos': Ialdabaoth is
the child of chaos.[70] She accepts Scholem's criticisms of this
proposal, as of Harvey's Aramaic *ia ēl dabahōth*, 'Lord God of
the fathers' and Giversen's suggested derivation, *ia ēl tabōth*,
'ruler of the God of the desires', based on the form Ialtabaoth.[71]
Scholem's own proposal, taking up suggestions by E. Preuschen
and A. Adam, is to take *iald* not as 'child' but as 'father', 'begetter',

and see Abaoth as the equivalent of Sabaoth: Ialdabaoth is *ialda 'abaōth*, 'Father of Sabaoth', the latter meaning 'hosts', summed up in the figure Sabaoth.[72] But both Pétrement and M. Black criticize this in that Ialdabaoth is the father of six sons, of whom Sabaoth is only one, if the most important in the *Hypostasis* and *On the Origin of the World*.[73] Black, whom Pétrement omits to mention, also suggests an Aramaic root: *ialda behūta*, 'son of shame', which is possible, but does not really fit the context, which involves Sophia's wanton and ignorant act, if committed in innocence and goodness.[74]

Pétrement herself prefers the suggestion made by R. M. Grant but criticized by Scholem: to derive it from the Hebrew *Ia El Sabaoth*.[75] She is right to stress that this figure is obviously intended to be the God of the Old Testament, and if we take the 'Ophite' system as among the earliest, and a probable source for the speculations about Sophia, the shadow/curtain, and Ialdabaoth and his offspring, which are developed in the *Hypostasis* and *On the Origin of the World*, then this last derivation would fit the context as well as any.[76] But that this mythologoumenon of Ialdabaoth and his offspring has been grafted on to the Barbelognostic cosmogony is suggested by Irenaeus' account, which identifies the Protarchon with the God of the Old Testament as the Creator of this visible world, the *maker* (not father) of powers, angels, firmaments, etc. the source of evil (cf. Isa 45:7 LXX), and by his arrogant exclusivist boast (cf. Exod 20:5; Isa 45:5f., 46:9) the jealous God of the Jews.[77] He is not explicitly the demonized figure Ialdabaoth of the *Hypostasis*; indeed it may be that, as Irenaeus himself hints, the Barbelognostics as well as the 'Ophites' included a left-hand ruler, the Devil, whose traits we find reproduced in Ialdabaoth.[78]

Finally, on the question of the origin of this myth of Sophia and its relationship to Valentinianism, MacRae has pointed to the striking parallels with Jewish Wisdom motifs and concepts in Gnostic texts and in the *Apocryphon* in particular, and attempted to derive the 'fall' of Sophia, clearly lacking in Jewish texts, from Gnostic interpretation of the figure of Eve.[79] Similarly Stead has appealed to the possible influence of Philo and his views of Sophia and Logos on the original myth of Valentinus of the one errant Sophia,[80] if ignoring the relationship of the Barbelognostic and 'Ophite' systems to that myth. Pétrement, criticizing both for not adequately explaining the fall element in terms of Jewish sources, suggests, as we have seen, that Gnosticism and the myth of Sophia can best be understood against a Christian background, and that the Valentinian version of the myth is probably prior to that in the *Apocryphon*.[81]

But in arguing that the fall of Sophia can only be explained by Gnosticism prior to Valentinus, i.e. by the anti-Jewish, anti-cosmic attitudes of Saturninus and Basilides, and pointing to the Valentinian 'turning point' in giving a more positive evaluation of Judaism and finding elements of truth in the Old Testament, she has once again been led by her pan-Valentinian thesis to reject the pioneering role of the Gnostics of Irenaeus 1.29 and 30. It is they who appear to have developed a myth or myths of Sophia, virgin and wanton, undoubtedly based on speculations about Jewish Wisdom and Eve, which splits her into heavenly perfect consort (Barbelo, the virgin Mother), and lower creative Wisdom, the dynamic figure of Proverbs, Wisdom of Solomon and *1 Enoch*, who is responsible for the production of this world by the Creator God of the Old Testament, and who descends but finds nowhere to rest. It is they too who pioneer the idea that the divine power of light is channelled through Sophia into the Demiurge, and in the case of the 'Ophites', the concept of a lower Sophia who falls from the heavenly world and whose passions solidify to form the material elements of this visible world. Thus while the Barbelognostics anticipate Valentinus' single errant Sophia, the 'Ophites' anticipate the double Sophia of Ptolemy and others. And both to some extent rehabilitate the Jewish Creator God, apparently teaching a demonic counterpart and, in the case of the 'Ophites', suggesting that Sophia inspired some of the Old Testament prophecies.

That the Barbelognostic version of the Sophia myth as suggested by Irenaeus is independent of and prior to (perhaps even a possible influence on) Valentinus rather than vice versa might be suggested by the evaluation of Sophia's role in it as (*a*) not produced last of twelve (or thirty) aeons of a Pleroma with its Limit figure; (*b*) lacking a consort, which the later redactions have added under Valentinian influence; (*c*) not associated with Christ, as in Valentinianism; (*d*) identified as the Holy Spirit, a separate figure paired with Christ in Valentinianism; (*e*) a single entity able to rescue herself; and (*f*) directly responsible for the Demiurge whom she battles against rather than working through secretly via Achamoth, as in Valentinianism.

2 The creation of the world of darkness

(a) The Twelve

With the production by Sophia (without the consent of the supreme deity) of an incomplete being, whose unlikeness to his mother is particularly stressed, a negative counterpart of Barbelo's bearing of an incomplete being (but with the consent of the Father, hence like him and perfected by him), we enter a new stage, that of the lower beings, the even more imperfect creations of a Demiurge and his subordinates. Thus the *Apocryphon* relates that Ialdabaoth took a great power from his mother, removed himself from her and turned away from the region (*topos*) in which he had been born, taking possession of another.[82] This is closely paralleled in Irenaeus' account which talks of the Protarchon as creator (*fabricator*) of this present condition, which certainly fits his role in the *Apocryphon*, seizing a great power from his mother and departing from her into the nether regions.[83] SR relates how he created for himself a flaming fiery aeon in which he now lives,[84] which is slightly closer to Irenaeus, who has him create a *firmamentum coeli* in which he is said to dwell (*habitare*),[85] than LR, which speaks of other aeon*s* and has him in the gleaming fiery flame.[86]

SR then has Ialdabaoth unite with his ignorance (III) or folly (B) and beget the powers (*exousia*) under him and (or as) twelve angels, each to his aeon, according to the pattern of the incorruptible aeons. He created for each of them (B), or they (the powers?) created for themselves (III), seven angels and the angels three powers so as to form 360 angelic beings, made according to the appearance of the first pattern (*typos*) before him, but ignorant of him who had made them.[87] LR, however, has Ialdabaoth stupefied in his folly and begetting for himself powers, which are then at once enumerated, the last being identified as over the depth of the underworld.[88] Only later do we have, in two separate passages, parallels to this enumeration of angels and powers (which, moreover, is different and adds up to 365),[89] and to the idea of creation after the heavenly pattern (which denies that Ialdabaoth actually saw the heavenly world).[90] Irenaeus' account here supplies a partial parallel which again appears to show closer affinities with SR. His text relates that since Ialdabaoth was ignorance he created (*fecisse*) powers (*potestates*, i.e. *exousiai*?) under him and angels and firmaments and all earthly things.[91]

Irenaeus' summary, despite its extreme condensation, may still be of some help in reconstructing the original sequence in the *Apocryphon*. Thus his order of powers then angels may confirm the originality of III 16.9 which has powers *and* the twelve angels. This distinction would also solve the arithmetical problem of arriving at 360 angelic beings.[92] Just who these beings are will become clear when we consider the list of twelve powers which then follows in both recensions. SR introduces them as appearing from the First Begetter (*archigenetōr*), the First Archon of darkness, and ignorant of him who begot them,[93] while LR plunges straight into the list, although it does have a similar allusion to Ialdabaoth later as an ignorant darkness, adding an excursus on light and darkness and the nature, names and boast of the First Archon, absent in the short recension.[94] The enumeration of the twelve powers differs slightly in the four versions, although what survives of IV appears to correspond to II.[95] The parallel in the *Gospel of the Egyptians* is unfortunately marred by lacunae (III) or very fragmentary (IV).[96] According to it, the great angel Saklas and the great demon Nebruel together begot twelve assisting angels, each with his aeon, and each to rule his world.[97] Its list is almost, but not quite, identical with that of the long recension of the *Apocryphon*.[98]

Just who these twelve powers or angels are is made clear by the continuation in SR. According to it, they all possess other names from desire (*epithymia*) and wrath (*orgē*), but also double names given them through the glory (B) or glories (III) of heaven; it is these latter which reveal their true nature.[99] Now Saklas, SR continues, called them by these (former?) names according to their appearance and powers. Through the glories (III) or the times (B) they grow distant and weak, but through these (former names?) they regain strength and wax (*auxanein*).[1] Till is clearly right to relate these twelve powers to the signs of the Zodiac, and Giversen to argue that the names given in the *Apocryphon* are the true names, given by the glory of heaven and revealing the true nature of these powers created by Saklas in imitation of the twelve heavenly aeons, whereas Saklas' names for them (the customary names of the Zodiac?) are the names of desire and wrath by which the signs gain strength.[2]

The picture presented by SR of this whole section involving the twelve powers created in the image of the twelve heavenly aeons with their double names whereby they wax and wane, and the 360 angelic beings deriving from them, makes good sense.

The twelve powers preside over the twelve constellations of the Zodiac, part of the circle of the fixed stars marking the first work of the Demiurge, which wax and wane through time, and the 360 angelic beings deriving from them represent the 360 degrees of the zodiacal circle (or the 360 days of the civil year).[3] This would explain the occurrence of the list of these beings at this point and the apparent lack of correlation of them with any later entities. They would correspond with the *potestates* and *angeli* of Irenaeus 1.29.4.

A. J. Welburn has attempted to link the twelve names as zodiacal signs with the Sun, Moon and five planets (or their rulers) which the *Apocryphon* then proceeds to mention, beginning with Leo (Iaoth/Athoth) associated with the Sun out to the sixth power (Sabaoth/Kain), i.e. Capricorn, and the seventh (Kainan/Abel), i.e. Aquarius, both associated with Saturn, then back in order to Belias, i.e. Cancer, who must be linked with the Moon.[4] This would supply a plausible explanation for the double occurrence of Iobel in fourth and ninth positions: Iobel would represent the Hebrew for 'Ram', both fourth and ninth signs (Scorpio and Aries) being governed by the same planet, namely Mars. Hermas would be Hermes/Mercury and the odd form Melcheiradonin, as equivalent to the double constellation *Basilis te kai Adonis* of Teucer Babylonius in Rhetorius, would, as Giversen has suggested,[5] represent Gemini.[6] Welburn also supplies a plausible solution to the question of which version of the fifth to seventh powers was original: the long recension identified Adonaios and Sabaoth and was thus forced to add another name after Kain/Cain, namely Abel.[7] And as he has also suggested, mention of 'the sun' in seventh place (as in B and III) rather than in sixth (as in II and *GE* III and IV), fits the division of twelve signs into seven day and five night signs.[8]

However, Tardieu, entirely ignoring Welburn and his case, is content to interpret the twelve in the more common order starting from Aries, attempting to find explanations of all the names which link them with the appropriate sign.[9] His efforts are once again ingenious and learned, but sometimes rather strained, and he perhaps does not offer the same degree of overall plausibility as Welburn does. A key to evaluating their rival claims may lie in their respective explanations of the gloss on Kain, 'whom men call "the sun"'. Tardieu would see this as originally a marginal gloss attached to the fifth name, Adonaios Sabaoth, i.e. Leo, which has progressively slipped from sixth in LR to seventh in SR, which mistakenly distinguished Sabaoth from Adonaios. Welburn, as noted above, conversely sees LR as having confused the original order by identifying Adonaios and Sabaoth. But while suggesting why the gloss might have been attached to the seventh sign as corresponding to the day/night division, he does not explain its appropriateness to the zodiacal sign, Aquarius, and its planetary ruler, Saturn, of his hypothesis. Again, as we shall see, it may be a case of two independent traditions, one involving twelve zodiacal powers, the other seven planetary rulers, which the redactors, in view of the overlap of names (Iaoth/Athoth, Adonaios, Sabaoth, Adonis) have attempted to combine.

Certainly the course of events in LR, which Tardieu has chosen to follow here without justifying his preference, is rather more complicated. It gives no indication of who or what the twelve are, apart from describing the last, Belias, as over the depth of the underworld.[10] It then has Ialdabaoth establishing seven kings over the seventh heaven in accordance with the heavenly firmament (*stereōma*) and five over the depth of Hell, giving them a share of his fire but not of the power of light he had taken from his mother, since he is an ignorant darkness.[11] Then follows the passage, unique to LR, on the mixture of light and darkness, the three names of the archon and his boast that he alone is God,[12] after which we have the enumeration of the angels. This passage speaks of the archons (the number is not given; twelve would not fit the arithmetic) creating seven powers for themselves, the powers creating six angels for each until they made 365 angels.[13] As Giversen admits, the sum is awkward and LR seems more concerned with the final total of 365 to which it remains faithful (as does B to 360) than with the precise arithmetic required.[14]

LR then gives the names and forms of appearance of the seven (archons?) who comprise the hebdomad of the week, repeats that Ialdabaoth gave them a share of his fire, alludes once more to his arrogant boast and enumerates the seven powers which he united with the (seven?) authorities.[15] Only then does LR parallel SR in asserting that all these beings (or perhaps only the last-named) have two names, the first according to the glory of heaven, which renders them powerless, the second the power names given by their First Begetter,[16] and that he organized everything after the pattern of the first aeons. But the tendentious hand of the redactor is again evident in that LR insists that Ialdabaoth did so, not because he had seen the incorruptible ones, but because of the power in him which he had stolen from his mother.[17]

Conversely SR offers a simpler and more coherent outline of events. After the enumeration of the twelve zodiacal powers with their names, it has Ialdabaoth command that seven kings rule over the (seven?) heavens and five over chaos and the underworld.[18] But that these are not the same as the twelve zodiacal powers, as Till and the redactor of LR appear to imagine,[19] is suggested not only by the new stage marked by 'and' and the new title 'kings', but by the fact that the seven glory names do not correspond to the first seven glory names of the twelve powers, with the possible exception of the first and fifth.[20] Who then are the seven and five? It has usually been assumed that they refer to the seven planets associated with the twelve zodiacal signs.[21] Certainly the seven are expressly identified as those over the seven heavens and as the hebdomad of the week, who control the cosmos.[22] But are they originally and fundamentally planetary rulers? Comparison with Irenaeus' account of the 'Ophite' system is instructive here; in it Ialdabaoth and his six sons similarly form a holy or perfect hebdomad, identified with the days of the week and in control of the seven heavens.[23] But they are only *secondarily* equated with the planets,[24] and this might cast some light on this section of the *Apocryphon*. For the primary role of these seven archons would seem to be the creation of psychic humanity.[25] Thus they alone are properly described as being given a share of Ialdabaoth's fire, but not of his power as is the case in SR.[26] That LR first attributes this to the twelve and then repeats it of the seven surely represents a later misinterpretation.

The two recensions then agree over the seven and their forms of appearance and over the seven powers united with them, but LR, with its passage about the double names, which (*a*) would suit the twelve zodiacal powers much better, (*b*) apparently implies that the seven are stars/planets and (*c*) most revealingly refers to the fact that they conform to celestial originals in the context of double names, and not, as in SR, in the context of the union of the seven rulers and powers (surely the more original),[27] does seem to represent a secondary reworking.

If then we assume that the version in SR (with its twelve zodiacal powers and 360 angels distinct from the seven heavenly rulers and five kings of the underworld assimilated to the planets) is original, how are we to account for the differences in LR? The two crucial factors I believe are the number 365 and the identification of the twelve powers with the seven and five. LR requires the first because of the mythologoumenon, not present in SR, of the creation of humanity by 365 angels.[28] It has been led to overlook the zodiacal significance of the 360 angelic beings, and interpret the 365 angels in terms of days of the year which are under the control of the seven (planetary) rulers. But since it had identified these rulers with the first seven of the twelve, it felt compelled to transpose the account of the creation of the 365 to after the mention of the seven and five.

This apparent identification by LR of the twelve with the seven and five is echoed in the *Gospel of the Egyptians*. Despite the fragmentary condition of the text, it seems to relate the production by Saklas and Nebruel of twelve assisting angels and twelve aeons for them, followed by his demand for seven (archons?) and for each of the twelve to rule his own (aeon? world?). The names of the twelve follow very closely those in LR, with the concluding gloss that they are over the underworld.[29] There are clear signs that this version is more likely to be secondary and dependent on the long recension of the *Apocryphon* than that it represents the original tradition echoed by the long and distorted by the short recensions.[30]

The twelve powers, we might note, appear to play no further part in the *Apocryphon*.[31] They are listed first among Ialdabaoth's creations both because they are the types of the twelve heavenly aeons, and because they represent the twelve constellations of the Zodiac which were considered part of the highest heavenly sphere, that of the fixed stars. Beneath them are ranked the seven planetary spheres. The ensuing mention of seven kings over the heavens plus five underworld rulers of whom we hear no more, whatever their provenance – whether representing the assignment of the Sun, Moon and five planets to the zodiacal signs (so Welburn and Tardieu) or not – was bound to be interpreted both in terms of the planets and as another dodecad. Thus it is perhaps not surprising that the two groups were confused, as in LR. Valentinian influence may again be in evidence in the idea in LR of the heavenly world being imitated by the Demiurge not because he saw it, but because of his mother's power working through him.

(b) The seven rulers

Having dealt with the twelve powers controlling the signs of the Zodiac, we should expect to pass to the creation and enumeration of the seven rulers controlling the planets, each set over a descending series of concentric spheres, to each of which was assigned a planet. But, as we have suggested, the seven heavenly kings appear to be only secondarily planetary rulers and primarily chronological entities, governing the days of the week (the 'holy hebdomad'), and ultimately responsible for the creation of humanity. This is the role they have in the 'Ophite' system of Irenaeus which appears to have been grafted on (redaction (a^2)) to the earlier Barbelognostic scheme, which simply spoke of the Protarchon creating powers and angels. SR retains traces of their distinct and original role, which LR has obscured by identifying them as planetary rulers assimilated to the first seven zodiacal signs. And significantly it is LR which continues that grafting process by developing a more demonized picture of Ialdabaoth than that of the 'Ophites', but akin to that in the *Hypostasis of the Archons, On the Origin of the World* and *Trimorphic Protennoia*.

Thus before it enumerates the seven LR presents a digression on Ialdabaoth as an ignorant darkness.[32] As Giversen admits, there is not even a similar idea to this in SR.[33] It is sparked off by the statement that Ialdabaoth gave a share of his fire but not of the power of light he had taken from his mother, because he is an ignorant darkness.[34] It relates how the light mingled with the darkness, causing it to shine, and how because of this mixture the light became darkened, neither light nor darkness but weak. This last term acts as a key to the second half of this digression, describing the nature of Ialdabaoth.[35] The archon who is weak, it continues, has three names, the first Ialtabaoth, the second Saklas, the third Samael.[36] And it dwells on the folly of his ignorant boast: 'I am God and there is no other god but me.' In saying this he had not confirmed the place from which he had come.[37]

The fact that both the opening passage (II 11.7–10 and par) and closing section (11.19–22 and par) are doublets or expansions of material found elsewhere as a unit in LR when in parallel with SR;[38] that the excursus on light and darkness has no parallel in SR; and the inclusion of Samael as a title that would suit LR's theological tendency to stress the ignorance and blindness of the Demiurge, all tend to undermine Giversen's arguments that LR represents a more original tradition here which SR abridged and rearranged.[39]

After its reference to the seven heavenly kings and five underworld rulers, SR supplies the glory-names of the seven, whereas LR abruptly lists their bodily names after its belated mention of the 365 angelic powers.[40] Both versions attest that these form the hebdomad of the week, SR adding the gloss, which might suggest their planetary nature, that it is they who control the cosmos.[41] But the names which follow and occur twice in the versions in B and II (with insignificant variations), as Tardieu has rightly demonstrated, do not correspond directly with the planets but represent the days of the week, as in the 'Ophite' system of Irenaeus 1.30.4f. and 10, with names of the Jewish God as found in magical sources.[42] However, if remarkably similar to the evidently related lists attested by Irenaeus, Origen and Epiphanius, a Greek magical papyrus and amulet, a Coptic magical papyrus, and a Nag Hammadi text,[43] its version remains distinctive.

Thus while the lists in Irenaeus, Origen, the Gnostic amulet and *On the Origin of the World* all begin with Ialdabaoth and then follow with versions of the Jewish names of God in the stereotyped order found in magical texts (Iao, Sabaoth, Adonaios, Eloaios), concluding with two more magic names (Oraios and Astaphaios),[44] the *Apocryphon*'s list omits Ialdabaoth (as the creator of the seven) and begins with the same name as in the twelve powers, Iaoth (B 41.18 and 43.13, cf. 40.5), or Aoth (III 17.22, but Haoth in 16.20), or Athoth (II 11.26 and 12.16, cf. 10.29).[45] SR assigns him the face of a lion, LR of a sheep.[46] Then comes Eloaios with the face of an ass,[47] followed by Astaphaios with the face of a hyena.[48] While all seem to agree on the name of the fourth, Iao or Iazo,[49] they differ on his face. B 42.2f. and II 11.30f. assign him the face of a snake with seven heads, III 18.2 a lion-shaped snake face.[50] The fifth figure is sometimes Adonaios, sometimes Sabaoth,[51] with a snake face, the sixth is Adoni(n) with an ape face.[52] Finally the seventh is variously named Sabbataios (B 42.6 and 44.4), Sabbadaios (III 18.6), Sabbede (II 11.33) or Sabbateon (II 12.25). That unlike all the rest he does not have an animal face but is described as a flaming fire, Tardieu has plausibly explained by the fact that in Origen and *On the Origin of the World* the seventh archon (Ialdabaoth) alone has an astrological association, namely with Saturn.[53]

Although, therefore, four of these names can be found in the *Apocryphon*'s list of twelve powers (Iaoth/Athoth, Adonaios, Sabaoth, Adonin), the real parallel is with the names of the seven heavenly archons, or hebdomad of the week, of the 'Ophites' of Irenaeus and Origen, of *On the Origin of the World*, and of the Gnostic amulet. This motif of the seven or hebdomad seems a fairly consistent one in that the first three texts mentioned suggest, as does the *Apocryphon*, a link with the planets, the middle two and the *Apocryphon* refer to the First Archon as 'lion-like', Origen and the *Apocryphon* ascribe animal faces or forms to them, and the last two associate Ialdabaoth with the name 'Ariel' ('lion of God' in Hebrew). Further, the version in *On the Origin of the World* not only appears to be aware of the different order of the seven in the *Apocryphon* but associates them with a list of abstract characteristics (providence, lordship, divinity, kingship, envy, riches, wisdom (*sophia*)) which, as we shall see, closely correspond to the seven powers in the *Apocryphon* which are later united with the seven heavenly rulers.[54]

The difference between the two lists of names would appear to be explicable in terms of two independent but overlapping traditions, one of which included Ialdabaoth as the first of the seven, the other of which had him as the creator of the seven. *On the Origin of the World* tends to confirm this by the way it begins with the latter but then abandons it and presents the former. But Tardieu's persuasive interpretation of the hebdomad as not astrological but chronological rather undermines the attempt of Welburn to reconcile both traditions as originally and essentially astrological.[55] However, Welburn may be justified in appealing to Origen's account of the Ophite diagram as a key to interpreting the evidence. Thus it seems to link the two traditions, that of the *Apocryphon* with its seven theriomorphic archons created by Ialdabaoth, the seventh apparently equated with Saturn, and that in Irenaeus, *On the Origin of the World* and the Gnostic amulet, which has Ialdabaoth, the lion-like archon equated with Saturn, as first and progenitor of six.

Certainly both Origen's account of Celsus' list of the seven and that of the *Apocryphon* agree in ascribing animal faces or forms, but Origen's list and names (lion/Michael, bull/Suriel, snake/Raphael, eagle/Gabriel, bear/Thauthabaoth, dog/Erathaoth, ass/Thaphabaoth or Onoel – Celsus; Onoel or Thartharaoth – Origen) differ from those in the *Apocryphon* (although the two share lion (SR only) as first, snake, dog or hyena, and ass). And Origen in the following chapter appears to confirm the astrological character of the seven in that he lists the Ophian formulae which allow the Gnostic to pass unscathed through the seven heavens with their archons in descending order, starting with the lion-headed Ialdabaoth, with whom Saturn (*ho Phainōn*) is in sympathy.[56] Conversely the *Apocryphon* has Sabbataios, with a gleaming fiery appearance (i.e. Saturn) as the *seventh*,[57] and thus the First Archon with the lion-like appearance must be equated with the Moon, on Welburn's hypothesis. Yet merely to reverse Origen's order does not help much in establishing a correlation with the *Apocryphon*, since the former obviously corresponds with those of Irenaeus, etc. which include Ialdabaoth as the lion-like archon. Further, far from representing a more original order, as Welburn argues, Origen's list with its odd features (the omission of Adonaios and the insertion of Astaphaios before Eloaios) actually suggests a deliberate rearrangement to fit into a planetary scheme: Adonaios as the Sun was overlooked, and Astaphaios as Venus was moved from seventh to its appropriate planetary position of fifth.

On the other hand, if Origen's list, like those related to it, was originally chronological, that of the *Apocryphon* may well, as Welburn argues, have been more astrological from the start, assimilating features from the Ialdabaoth tradition in redaction (a^2). Thus Welburn's explanation of the planetary features of the seven is quite illuminating and plausible, even if his attempt to use Origen's evidence as the hermeneutical key to resolve all the problems is not wholly successful.[58]

The *Apocryphon*, stimulated by the reference to the various forms of appearance of the seven, then relates how Ialdabaoth has a host of forms so as to appear in every form he wishes.[59] He gave the seven a share of his fire but not of the pure light, the power he had seized from his mother.[60] He was lord over them precisely because of what he had got from his mother, variously rendered in terms of glory, power and light.[61] For this reason, the text continues, he called himself 'god', thereby disobeying the being or reality (*hypostasis*) from which he had originated (SR) or the place from which he had come (LR).[62] Following the mythic pattern, the selfishness and arrogance of the Demiurge is an exact negative counterpart to the attitude of Adamas, giving birth to knowledge, being given an invincible power and consequently obediently praising the supreme deity.[63]

(c) The seven powers

The *Apocryphon* then proceeds to relate how Ialdabaoth combined with the authorities (i.e. the seven heavenly rulers) seven powers which originate from his speaking,[64] and how he named them, beginning from above.[65] To each of the seven rulers named in the form described above is united a power which (with one exception) is feminine in Greek and Coptic. But while the list of these in II 12.15–25 is identical with its second enumeration in II 15.14–23, that in B 43.11–44.4 differs slightly from its counterpart at B 49.11–50.4, which itself is virtually identical with the parallel in III 22.19–23.6.[66] Furthermore both recensions differ from each other. Thus B 43.12f. has providence (*pronoia*) with the first, Iaoth, but it comes fourth in B 49.16/III 23.1f., while it is second (with Eloaio) in II 12.17f. and 15.15f./IV 24.4f. But this is the only difference in order in the three versions in SR, and the remaining order is divinity second with Eloaios in B 43.14f., first in B 49.11; goodness (*mn̄tchs̄*) third with Astaphaios in B 43.15–17 and second in B 49.13 (although the parallel in III 22.21 appears to read lordship (*mn̄tj[oeis]*)) and Till has corrected his translation of B in line with III at this point);[67] fire (*kōht*) fourth with Iao in B 43.17–19 and third in B 49.14f./III 22.22f. (which appears to read [*kau*]*ma*); kingship (*mn̄trro*) fifth with Sabaoth in B 43.19f. and fifth in B 49.14f./III 23.2f.; [insight?] sixth with Adoni in B 44.1f. and sixth in B 50.2 (*syn[esis]*)/III 23.4; wisdom (*sophia*) seventh with Sabbataios in B 44.3f., and seventh in B 50.4/III 23.5.

LR presents a much less ambiguous picture. It has goodness (*mn̄tchrs̄*) first with Athoth (II 15.14 confirms this by giving the fuller form *mn̄tchrēstos*), providence second as indicated, then divinity third with Astaphaios in II 12.18f. and third in II 15.17/IV 24.7. Lordship (*mn̄tjoeis*) is fourth with Iao in II 12.19f. and fourth in II 15.18; kingship (*mn̄tero*) is fifth with Sabaoth in II 12.21f. and fifth in II 15.19./IV 24.10; envy (? *kōh*) is sixth with Adonein in II 12.22f. and sixth in II 15.21, while prudence (*mn̄trmn̄hēt*, i.e. *synesis?*)[68] is seventh with Sabbateon in II 12.24f. and seventh in II 15.22f./IV 24.13.

However, the second enumeration is complicated by the fact that it allots to each power the creation of one of the seven psychic substances of the human body. In this case both recensions appear to preserve the same order: bone, sinew, flesh, marrow, blood, skin, hair, over against the more traditional order found in a Zoroastrian text cited by R. C. Zaehner:[69] marrow (associated with the Moon), bones (associated with Mercury), flesh (associated with Venus), sinews (associated with the Sun), veins (associated with Mars), skin (associated with Jupiter), and hair (associated with Saturn). Tardieu, in a comprehensive discussion, has demonstrated the primary role of the *Timaeus* of Plato, as interpreted in Greek philosophical, astrological and medical traditions, in the development of this motif, and the way its presentation in the *Apocryphon* has influenced Manichaean and through them Mazdaean, as well as Syriac Christian (Audi) and through them Ismaili, sources.[70] Now Macrobius' list, based according to Tardieu on (*a*) the *Timaeus* and (*b*) the *De Hebdomadis* of Pseudo-Hippocrates, has the order marrow, bone, sinew, vein, arteries (i.e. respiratory canals), flesh, skin, that is, from the innermost to the outermost (*ab imo*),[71] and awareness of this order may be preserved in B's version which has providence, responsible for the marrow, first in its first list.

This at once recalls the very similar list of female names given to the seven androgynous powers in *On the Origin of the World*, also from Codex II: providence (Sambathas), lordship, divinity, kingship, envy (*kōh*), riches (? [*mntr*] *mao*) and wisdom (*sophia*), and the fact that the first of the seven powers, Ialdabaoth, created the head and *marrow* of the first man.[72] And finally the passage quoted by Theodore bar Konai from a certain Apocalypse in the name of John (which Puech thinks identical with our *Apocryphon*) ascribed to a schismatic Edessan deacon, Audi, and used by his followers, the heretical sect of the Audians, has Audi say of the powers responsible for his body: 'My wisdom made the hair, understanding the skin, Elohim the bones, and my sovereignty the blood, Adonai made the nerves, and zeal made the flesh, and thought made the marrow'.[73] These powers, Theodore maintains, Audi got from 'the Chaldaeans', i.e. astrologers.[74]

However, this evidently varied tradition seems to be even more confused here. First of all, both recensions assert that Ialdabaoth began from above, although, if we accept Welburn's attribution of the names and the Zoroastrian and other parallels, he began with the ruler of the lowest sphere, the Moon. Second, as indicated, one would have expected him to start with the marrow, as in the Greek philosophical and magical sources, and work outwards, rather than having the marrow fourth and separated from the bones. Third, there is the masculine term 'zeal' or 'fire' (*kōh*/ *kōht*) which occurs in a neuter form in III ([*kau*] *ma*) despite the fact that all the rest are feminine.[75] LR may be more correct and consistent in its clear distinction between 'goodness' and 'lordship',[76] but the version in B may be more original in that it appears to be aware that providence which creates the marrow did once come first. Furthermore, 'goodness' does not occur either in Theodore bar Konai's list nor apparently in the similar one in *On the Origin of the World*, whereas *sophia* or equivalent does, and both of these lists, like that of the short recension of the *Apocryphon*, attest a sequence which has providence or equivalent and *sophia* or equivalent at either end. The attribution of bodily parts and powers preserved by Theodore's quotation also reproduces that in SR, although this may be because, as Tardieu claims, the Audians got their version from the tradition found in that recension.[77]

Moreover, one could explain why the creation of the marrow comes fourth in the list better from SR than from LR. Thus providence occurs first in the first enumeration just as she is the female name of the first androgynous archon (Ialdabaoth) in the list in *On the Origin of the World*, who, as we saw, was responsible for creating the marrow.[78] The redactor of SR, however, aware that Iaoth in fact represented the Moon, may have felt the need to transfer providence as creator of the marrow to fourth place, the sphere associated with the Sun, most powerful and important of the planets. And against Giversen it could be argued that LR has omitted wisdom (*sophia*) as the last power, perhaps under the mistaken impression that its final name, *mñtrmñhēt*, stood for *sophia* rather than *synesis*. Thus it was compelled to add another power and inserted 'goodness' as the first.[79]

Of this whole section of the creation and naming of the twelve zodiacal powers, the seven planetary rulers united with their seven powers (and the five kings of the underworld, if distinct) Irenaeus appears at first sight to give little or no indication. However, he does refer to the Protarchon creating first the powers (*potestas*, i.e. *exousia*?) which are under him, which has a clear parallel in SR (B 39.6f./III 16.8f.) but not in LR, then angels, which could refer to the twelve angels mentioned with the powers by SR, or to the following total of 360, or even perhaps to the seven planetary rulers.[80] Once again SR would appear more closely related to Irenaeus' account than LR, which has separated the list of angels from the twelve powers. The firmaments (*firmamenta*) then mentioned by Irenaeus may correspond to the firmaments (*stereōma*) assigned to the seven powers in the *Apocryphon*.[81] Finally, Irenaeus refers to the creation by the Protarchon of all earthly things, which of course has not yet taken place in the *Apocryphon*'s version.

Again in a passage which appears to have no parallel in the *Apocryphon*, Irenaeus relates how the Protarchon united with Presumption (*Authadeia*) and begot Wickedness (*Kakia*), Envy (*Zelus*), Jealousy (*Phthonus*), Revenge (*Erinnys* or better *Eris*, Strife)[82] and Passion (*Epithymia*).[83] Schmidt argued that these can only be understood as the five rulers of chaos and the underworld whose names probably dropped out of the *Apocryphon*.[84] This is an attractive suggestion; certainly the origin of evil and of the underworld and its rulers would fit better at this point in the *Apocryphon* than earlier. The tendency to identify the seven planetary rulers and five underworld kings with the twelve zodiacal powers to which we drew attention may have led the redactors of the *Apocryphon* to move the five to their present position.[85] Certainly, as already indicated, they appear rather abruptly and play no further part, although the *Apocryphon*'s reference to them suggests some further knowledge. This tendency shown by Irenaeus' account of the Barbelognostics to make the Protarchon/ Ialdabaoth equated with the God of the Jews ultimately responsible for evil (cf. Isa 45:7 LXX), despite the possible presence in their system of a devil figure as outlined above,[86] has clearly been developed by the *Apocryphon* and the works related to it, i.e. the *Hypostasis of the Archons, On the Origin of the World,* the *Gospel of the Egyptians* and the *Apocalypse of Adam.* But the Protarchon is not entirely evil since he remains the channel of the divine light-power, as in the systems of the 'Ophites' and the Ptolemaean school of Valentinianism, which rehabilitate him and attribute the evil in creation to some other figure.[87]

3 Ialdabaoth's arrogant boast and Sophia's repentance

Irenaeus' account of the Barbelognostic system concludes with the reaction of Sophia to her son's generation of the five evil powers, her withdrawal above, and his arrogant boast that he is a jealous god and that there are no others apart from him. Full of grief she withdrew to the higher regions and became for those counting from below the Ogdoad (*octonatio*). After her withdrawal he thought that he was alone (or alone existed: 'se solum opinatum esse') and for this reason said: 'I am a jealous (*zelator*) god (cf. Exod 20:5) and beside me there is no one' (cf. Isa 45:5; 46:9).[88]

The *Apocryphon,* however, presents a different order and conception of these events. At this point it places Ialdabaoth's arrrogant boast that he alone is god, but what sparks this off is his gazing at the creation surrounding him and the host of angels created by him, which leads him to boast; 'I am a jealous god, beside me there is none' (B), or 'I, I am a jealous god, and there is no other god apart from me' (II/IV).[89] To make this identifica-tion of Ialdabaoth with the God of the Old Testament (and thus of course of the Jews) doubly clear it adds the ironic comment, pointing up the folly of such exclusivist claims, that in so doing he had immediately indicated to the angels under him that another god existed, for otherwise his jealousy would have no object![90] This identification also serves to mark the beginning of the *Apocryphon*'s reinterpretation or 'correction' of the opening chapters of Genesis, which provide the backbone of its anthropology and soteriology.

Sophia's reaction thus comes *after* Ialdabaoth's boast and is interpreted differently from Irenaeus' version. It is first seen in terms of the going to and fro of the spirit of God of Gen 1:2b LXX (*epipheresthai*),[91] suitably reinterpreted, the reasons being her realization of her deficiency in acting without her consort coupled with her awareness of the wickedness, apostasy and imperfection of her son.[92] Thus she is said to have repented, and her lament was heard by her brothers whose plea for help was granted by the Invisible Spirit.[93] The recensions seem to disagree over whether her consort was sent down to her, but agree that she was led up to the Ninth (or Ennead?) rather than being the Ogdoad as in Irenaeus, until she perfected her deficiency.[94]

Now Carl Schmidt appealed to the fact that Sophia's repentance follows Ialdabaoth's boast in the *Apocryphon* as evidence that the work excerpted by Irenaeus extended beyond the point where he concluded.[95] Schenke, however, pointed to the differences in motivation, etc. sketched above between the two accounts and the appropriateness of Irenaeus' order of events as weakening Schmidt's argument, also appealing to the literary seam he claimed to detect at B 44.19, precisely where Irenaeus' excerpt ended, in support of his view that Irenaeus had excerpted a complete work.[96] But Schottroff proceeded to criticize Schenke's claim of a literary seam on the grounds that the contradictions detected by him between the first and second parts of the *Apocryphon* do not necessarily prove a suture at this point, since there are similar contradictions within each part.[97] However, the important point he established was the appropriateness of Sophia's repentance prior to her son's boast in Irenaeus' account. Schottroff herself in her valuable analysis of this section of the *Apocryphon* suggests the secondary character of much of it, and this can assist us in determining which order is likely to be the more original.[98]

Signs of this secondary character include the repetition of the Demiurge's hubristic boast and Sophia's repentance,[99] the insertion in the first example of a question by John on the meaning of 'to go to and fro', which Schottroff would see as a piece of polemical exegesis ('correcting' what 'Moses' had said) added later and giving rise to the repetition.[1] Then there is the disagreement between the recensions over her going to and fro: SR first traces it to her awareness of her deficiency, namely that her consort had not concurred (*symphōnein*) with her when she was degraded from her perfection,[2] while LR, in a further piece of spiritualizing interpretation, speaks of the brightness of her light being diminished and her becoming dark because her consort had not agreed with her.[3] But both then go on to derive her movement from the wickedness and apostasy of her son which would take place (SR), or had taken place (LR).[4] LR has evidently 'corrected' SR at this point, seeing the difficulty, but could the future tense of SR betray an awareness that originally Sophia's withdrawal *preceded* Ialdabaoth's boast, as in Irenaeus' account of the Barbelognostics and *On the Origin of the World*?

Unlike the active, unrepentant figure of Irenaeus' version, Sophia here is presented as essentially passive and unable to reascend. Her going to and fro, interpreted as an allusion to Gen 1:2b LXX by the Saviour's reply to John that it was not as 'Moses' said 'over the waters', is thus understood by the *Apocryphon* as her restless movement in the darkness of ignorance, and her feeling ashamed and not daring to return.[5] Schenke's attempt to derive this whole mythologoumenon from an allegorical interpretation of Gen 1:2 by appeal to the various Gnostic exegeses of it (Valentinian, Barbelognostic, 'Ophite'),[6] has been rightly criticized by Schottroff who prefers to see here the mythologoumenon of the wandering Sophia. She draws attention to its associations with the Ennoia/Helen figure, the soul in the Naassene Preaching, etc. and finds what I consider a more likely origin in the idea of Wisdom's sojourn on earth (cf. *1 Enoch* 42.1–3).[7]

Further evidence that this passage with its anti-Jewish 'correction' of Genesis may not be original but was developed to harmonize the earlier Barbelognostic Sophia, who acts without a partner, with the more passive, repentant, Valentinian-influenced figure of the *Apocryphon*, who needs her partner, and tie this into the reinterpretation of Genesis which now follows, may be found in the obvious doublets in the second passage about her repentance. Thus after a further mention of Ialdabaoth's taking power from his mother coupled with reference to his ignorance of any power apart from her, and his self-exaltation at the sight of the angelic hosts created by him,[8] we hear once more of her repentance and weeping on realizing that the abortion (B) or cover (III) of darkness was not perfect because her consort had not concurred with her.[9]

But the final and perhaps most conclusive evidence of the secondary, Valentinian-influenced nature of this passage comes in its treatment of Sophia and her consort. Thus SR, echoing the normal ternary pattern of events (*aitein–kataneuein–doxazein* or equivalent), has Sophia's brothers (although there has been no explicit mention of such) plead for her and the holy Invisible Spirit assent (*kataneuein*) and pour a spirit over her from the Pleroma. Her consort (*syzygos*) by a providential resolve descends to correct her (III 'their') deficiency, but because of her ignorance she is not elevated to her aeon at once but remains in the Ninth until she corrects her deficiency.[10] However, LR again seems secondary here in that not only does it fail to recognize the ternary pattern, but it betrays considerable confusion and ambiguity, particularly over the descent of Sophia's consort. Thus II and IV, which normally show a high degree of unanimity, differ in that while both agree that the entire Pleroma of the Invisible Spirit blesses (rather than pleads for) her,[11] they divide and are confused over the ensuing action of the Spirit: II 14.5f. has the Holy Spirit shed over her (something?) from their whole Pleroma, while IV 22.5f., according to Krause's reconstruction, reads: 'And [he] nodded assent in the sp[irit]', attaching the reference to the shedding from the Pleroma to the following sentence about the consort.[12]

They then seem to deny that the consort came to Sophia while insisting that he (or something) *did* come down from the Pleroma,[13] but proceed to agree with SR that Sophia was not brought up to her own heaven but remained in the Ninth until she corrected her deficiency.[14] And it is not only these inconsistencies in LR, which may be partly due to its tendency to play down the anthropomorphic features, as Giversen suggests,[15] but the evident tension in both over the role of the consort and over who is ultimately responsible for correcting Sophia's deficiency, which, in the light of the unmistakable Valentinian colouring of this and related passages, further support my hypothesis that the *Apocryphon*'s version is not original here. The whole pattern of Sophia's repentance, the request of her brothers or the Pleroma to the supreme being, and the descent of a consort to perfect her deficiency is undoubtedly Valentinian, not Barbelognostic,[16] and this might also add weight to my suggestion that, as with Irenaeus' account of the latter, *On the Origin of the World* and *Trimorphic Protennoia*, Sophia's grief and withdrawal originally came before Ialdabaoth's boast.[17] Her initiative is once more denied by reinterpretation.

Finally, that Sophia is in the Ninth rather than in the Ogdoad, as in the Barbelognostic and Valentinian systems, is evidently a secondary interpretation.[18] Thus Schottroff, in an excursus on this idea, suggests that this is the heavenly region below the Pleroma but above Ialdabaoth and the seven archons, which other systems characterize as the Ogdoad.[19] But since according to the *Apocryphon* Ialdabaoth departed and created an aeon/heaven first for himself and then for each of the seven archons, the heaven above him would be the ninth.[20] LR has attempted to clarify the situation in that it speaks of the seven as *over* the seventh heaven,[21] and has Sophia in the heaven of, i.e. above, her son.[22]

Conclusion

On the question of the original form of the *Apocryphon* and the priority of the versions, we have attempted to demonstrate that in this section of the myth neither Giversen's thesis of the priority of the version in Codex II nor Tardieu's preference for its order adequately explain the clear differences between the recensions over the order of events and the number and nature of the powers created by Ialdabaoth. The evidence suggests, by and large, that it is the short recension which has remained closer to a more original order of events and interpretations of the powers and angels. The long recension, with its doublets and expansions, the passages unique to it, and its spiritualizing tendency, has obscured and altered the original order, particularly as regards the twelve zodiacal powers and the seven planetary rulers and five kings of the underworld. By equating them, while insisting on its own tradition of 365 angels responsible for the creation of earthly Adam, it has been led to change the order of events, alter the number of angels, add doublets and obscure the nature of the various heavenly beings involved. Conversely the short recension presents a logical and fairly comprehensible order which both makes clear the nature of and distinction between the twelve and seven and retains more echoes of Irenaeus' account at points where some similarity is demonstrable.

Thus while the overlappings and inconsistencies in the lists of powers suggest that the *Apocryphon* has taken over existing 'Chaldaean' traditions about the Zodiac and planets without complete understanding, and while it leaves much unexplained, some elements do recall Irenaeus' brief summary, e.g. the five underworld rulers in the former as perhaps akin to the Protarchon's five evil offspring in the latter. And the repetitions, confusions and clear signs of Valentinian influence in the passage on Sophia's repentance and her consort, leading into the Genesis reinterpretation, suggest that the *Apocryphon* may have altered a more original order which (as in Irenaeus 1.29.4, *On the Origin of the World, Trimorphic Protennoia* and Valentinianism) put Sophia's withdrawal and/or repentance before her son's boast.

Notes

[1] B 36.16f./III 14.9f.; II 9.25.

[2] Cf. e.g. the figure of Ennoia in Simonianism, Iren. 1.23.2f., which Haenchen, 'Gab es ein vorchristliche Gnosis?' *ZTK* 49 (1952), 316–49, argues is part of the original, pre-Christian Gnosis of Simon. See Rudolph, *TRu* 37 (1972), 323–43 on Simonianism and Pétrement, *Séparate* Part II, ch. 1 for a denial that Simon was a Gnostic. Cf. also Pistis Sophia in *HA* 94.5–96.15; *OW* 98.11–106.27; Sophia in *SJC* B 118.1–121.13; *Treat. Seth* 50.25–51.20, etc. See on the myth of Sophia in Gnosticism, C. Scholten, *Martyrium und Sophiamythos im Gnostizismus nach den Texten von Nag Hammadi* (JbAC Ergänzungsband 14) (Münster: Aschendorff, 1987), esp. part 2.

[3] Cf. the Ptolemaean view in Iren. 1.2.2–5.6; *Exc. ex Theod.* 44.1–53.5; 67–8; *Val. Exp.* 33.28–38; 34.23–37. See also W. Foerster, *Von Valentin zu Herakleon* (BZNW 7) (Giessen, 1928); F.-M.-M. Sagnard, *La gnose valentinienne et le témoignage de Saint Irénée* (Paris, 1947); G. Quispel, 'The Original Doctrine of Valentine', *VC* 1 (1947), 43–73; G. C. Stead, 'The Valentinian Myth of Sophia' *JTS* n.s. 20 (1969), 75–104; G. W. MacRae, 'The Jewish Background of the Gnostic Sophia Myth', *NovT* 12 (1970), 86–101; J. E. Goehring, 'A Classical Influence on the Gnostic Sophia Myth', *VC* 35 (1981), 16–23; D. Good, 'Sophia in Valentinianism', *Second Century* 4 (1984), 193–201; Pétrement, *Séparate* 85–92, 378–86.

[4] Cf. B 54.1–4/III 25.20–3; *Treat. Seth* 50.25–51.7; *TP* 47.29–34. Tardieu, *Écrits* 274, rightly stresses the sapiential character of this passage, but could have noted the obvious allusions to the Sophia of Wis 7:22–7 here, a spirit who permeates all intelligent spirits, entering holy souls, as well as Prov 7:4, cited as the basis of the expression 'sister' by A. Orbe 'Sophia

Soror' in *Mélanges d'Histoire des Religions offerts à H.-Ch. Puech* (Paris: Presses Universitaires de France, 1974), 355–63, esp. 360f., and MacRae, 'Jewish Background' 92f., who alludes to Sophia as sister of Christ in Iren. 1.30.11–12.

[5] Cf. Iren. 1.1.2; 1.2.2; Hipp. *Ref.* 6.30.5f.; Epiph. *Pan.* 31.5.8. In *Eug* the last female name of the six androgynous (i.e. twelve) beings produced by the Saviour and Pistis Sophia which form the archetypes of time and space, and which give rise to 'the defect of femaleness', is Pistis Sophia (III 81.21–85.9).

[6] *Martyrium* 209–13, esp. 212 n. 26. Certainly the Valentinian system has six male and six female aeons in syzygies, *AJ* four sets of female aeons in threes. Cf. also *Eug* III 82.7–83.2 (six androgynous aeons produced by the Saviour and Pistis Sophia with six male and six female names, who then appear as twelve powers, the archetype of time (year, months, days, etc.)).

[7] 212f. Cf. B 37.3–16 and par; 45.2–5 and par; 46.9–47.14 and par with Iren. 1.29.4.

[8] 209–13.

[9] See n. 4 above. Schmidt, 'Irenäus' 329, suggests that this may indicate that we are now in the lower world, since there is no indication in *AJ* of an upper and lower Sophia, as with the Ptolemaeans and 'Ophites' of Irenaeus.

[10] See n. 4 above. Sophia is also described there as a *prounikos* acting out of guilelessness (*mñtatkakia*) in l.28f. See further below.

[11] On the first possibility, cf. II 8.11/IV 12.19. B 33.16 reads *pronoia*. Cf. Giversen, *Apocryphon* 192. On the second, cf. B 53.4–54.4 and par. Giversen appears to identify the two Epinoias.

[12] Ibid.

[13] 39.13–32. On the likely identification of *epinoia* and Sophia, see Turner's comments ad loc. in Hedrick, *Nag Hammadi Codices XI, XII, XIII* 442. Cf. *GE* III 56.22–57.18/IV 68.5–10; 69.1–3, which has Eleleth request a ruler for chaos and the underworld, resulting in the appearance of a cloud called 'material (*hylikē*) Sophia', which issues in two monads, Sakla the great angel and Nebruel the great demon. This is evidently related to, and probably dependent on, the picture in *TP*, but also akin to Manichaean themes.

[14] 39.32–40.19.

[15] Cf. 1.29.4/Theod. 1.13 (364B).

[16] Cf. B 30.4–7 and par. Harvey's claim (225), that the phrase 'qui adstat Monogeni' is an interpolation, is not therefore justified. Indeed, as I have argued elsewhere ('John' 52f.), the title Monogenes is more original than that of Autogenes.

[17] Cf. B 33.9f./III 11.24–12.1 (the angel in the first aeon) and II 8.5/IV 12.10f. (the first angel in the first aeon). Cf. also *HA* 93.8f.,18f.; 94.3, where Eleleth identifies himself as 'the great angel'.

[18] Plotinus' Gnostics, *Enn.* 2.9.10, are ambivalent over Sophia and whether she actually declined or not. Cf. the reserve among the earlier Valentinians as noted by Good, 'Sophia' 193–201. *GE* III 59.9–60.2 evidently replaces Sophia with the more abstract figure of Metanoia, Repentance. See on this Perkins, *Gnosticism* 170ff.

[19] Cf. 1.29.2. He, with Autogenes and the other three illuminators does have a saving role later in *AJ* in being responsible for Ialdabaoth's inbreathing of his power of light into Adam (B 51.8–52.15 and par). We have already suggested the major significance of the four in the five seals rite, symbolizing the reception of spiritual illumination.

[20] 93.8f. *mñtsabe* = *phronēsis*: Crum, *Coptic Dictionary* 319ab; 93.19; 94.3f. *mñtrmñḥet* = *phronēsis*: Crum 715a. The former can render *sophia*, as in Crum 319b (1 Cor 3:19), but the usage is less common. One would have expected the Greek original to have retained the traditional term associated with Eleleth to avoid possible confusion, but on the other hand there may be an allusion here to the origin of the lower Sophia, deliberately designated 'Pistis', from Eleleth/*phronēsis*/*sophia*.

[21] 93.2–94.33.

[22] Cf. *TP* 39.32–40.4; *Norea* 27.21–29.5. Note the reference to the four holy helpers, i.e. the illuminators.

[23] Cf. B 44.19–45.5; 46.9–47.14 and par with 36.7–15 and par. Pétrement, *Séparate* 396, also cites *Zost.* 29.11f., where Eleleth is 'an impulse and a preparation for the truth', and compares Eleleth with the Ogdoad, the dwelling place of the psychics and of Sophia, according to the Valentinians (cf. Iren. 1.5.3, etc.).

[24] Cf. the similar title 'hylic Sophia' of *GE* III 56.26–57.1. According to Irenaeus, Basilides had Sophia originating from Phronesis (1.24.3).

[25] Cf. *AJ* B 51.4f./III 23.22 (not in LR); II 23.21f. (not in SR); *TP* 39.29; 40.15; 47.33f.; *Treat. Seth* 50.27–30; Iren. 1.29.4; *Zost.* 10.10f.

[26] Cf. Iren 1.30.3,6–13; Ptolemaeans of 1.4.1–5.6, etc. Note that for both Sophia has a consort/brother, Christ.

[27] B 36.16–37.1/III 14.9–14; II 9.25–29/IV 15.1–4. There may be a play on *enthymēsis* here. Sophia can conceive an *enthymēsis* since she is a heavenly aeon but, like all the preceding aeons, as an emanation of the Spirit can only do it in and with the consent of the Spirit's own prior knowledge.

[28] *Martyrium* 209f. Thus her thought does not encompass the Father (as in A) but produces an image, which is not represented as generation (as in B). Scholten compares *OW* 98.16–18, Sophia's work as a veil or curtain, which he considers 'Sethian', despite Schenke's exclusion of it from his corpus, 'Phenomenon' 597. He could have cited the more relevant *HA* 94.4–10. But the theme of the curtain also occurs in the non-Sethian *SJC* III 114.13–25, and perhaps in the 'Ophite' system of Iren. 1.30.3. Cf. also the shadow in Valentinus' system (Iren. 1.11.1) and the shadow/image of Theodotus (*Exc. ex Theod.* 31.4; 33.3f.).

[29] B 37.1–6/III 14.19–23. The copyist of III 14.14–19 has wrongly inserted a passage which rightly occurs at 15.4–9, perhaps misled by the same prepositional phrase * n̄ḥēts* at 14.14 and 15.3f.

[30] II 9.29–33/IV 15.4f. The latter has *syne[udokein]* at 15.5 to the *eudokein* of II 9.30.

[31] Cf. e.g. B 32.19–33.3 and par; 34.19–35.5 and par.

[32] *Muséon* 84, 63. Cf. Scholten, *Mysterium* 211, n. 21, who also refers to Schottroff, *Glaubende* 44, n. 4, as relating the title to the supreme Father. This seems even less likely.

[33] On Sophia as having a consort but acting without him, cf. Iren. 1.2.2; Hipp. *Ref.* 6.30.6–7; *Val. Exp.* 34.25–38. Cf. also *SJC* III 114.13–18.

[34] King, 'Sophia' 171, however, would interpret the evidence in terms of a tendency in LR both to give a larger soteriological role to the male and to devalue the feminine.

[35] Cf. B 47.3–7/III 21.8–11. Significantly, the parallel in II 14.7–9/IV 22.8–11 is confused over his descent, perhaps conscious of the original scheme of Sophia's self-salvation, or stressing more the independent role of the Epinoia/Pronoia figure.

[36] B 60.12–14/III 30.10–12 ('they sent'). Again, significantly, the parallel in II 23.14–22 is very confused, but essentially insists that it was Sophia who descended to correct her deficiency, not her consort.

[37] Cf. B 53.18–54.4 and par.

[38] 1.29.4.

[39] B 37.6–10/III 14.23–15.2; II 9.33–5. As Tardieu notes, *Écrits* 274, the latter's *mokmek* (i.e. *katanoein*) is a mistake for *kataneuein*.

[40] Cf. III 23.21 (= B 51.3) which has the Mother (i.e. Sophia) wanting to recover the power she had given the archon in wantonness (*prounikon*).

[41] *Apocryphon* 195. Cf. Schottroff, *Glaubende* 46, who argues that the versions in III and II clearly demonstrate the problems posed by sexuality and the way it is sublimated in *AJ* to exonerate Sophia. Such a process has gone much further in the latter than in Iren. 1.29, and the lack of explicit syzygies in *AJ* may be due to modesty as regards sexual matters as well as to the interpolations of Autogenes, etc. as argued above.

[42] Cf. for the first, Liddell and Scott, *A Greek–English Lexicon* (9th ed., Oxford, 1940), 2, 1537. For a more nuanced treatment, stressing the meanings 'impetuous' and a porter or peddler in new Comedy, see A. Pasquier, 'Prouneikos. A Colorful Expression to Designate Wisdom in Gnostic Texts', in King, *Images* 47–66, and for a response, giving more emphasis to the sexual meaning, see M. W. Meyer, ibid., 67–70.

[43] 1.29.4.

[44] 1.30.3.

[45] Nilsson, 'Sophia-Prunikos', in *Eranos* (APS) 45 (1947), 169–72; Pétrement, *Separate* 98–100. She suggests the meaning 'to carry in front', i.e. to promote, bring to light, thus in the Gnostic texts, to beget, and

criticizes the tendency of modern scholars to accept Epiphanius' interpretation uncritically. Pasquier, 'Prouneikos' 62, having suggested similar, non-sexual meanings, does admit the sexual implications of Epiphanius' evidence.

[46] In his edition of Origen, *Contra Celsum* (Oxford, 1953), 350, n.1.

[47] 50.28.

[48] Orig. *C. Cels.* 6.34f.; Pétrement, *Separate* 98f.; Meyer, art. cit. 70.

[49] Cf. 13.18–20: 'I am the whore and the holy one. I am the wife and the virgin', where the subject seems to be Wisdom, as both higher (Barbelo) and lower (Sophia); *OW* 114.7–11 (Eve as mother, virgin, pregnant one).

[50] Cf. Epiph. *Pan.* 31.5.7–9. Scholten, *Martyrium* 210f. nn. 17 and 18, while rightly pointing out that Prunicus is a name to the heresiologists but a characteristic in the texts, seems to accept the sexual connotations, rejecting other suggested etymologies. But he thinks the doctrinal letter may have been influenced by non-Valentinian material, denying Origen's claim that Prounikos was a Valentinian title for Sophia. The Valentinians may have borrowed the term, like so much, from the Gnostics.

[51] *Pan.* 21.2.3–5.

[52] 25.2.2,4; 3.2. Cf. 21.2.5–6. Epiphanius seems to have understood the Barbelognostics not as the distinct sect of Irenaeus, but as followers of Nicolaus.

[53] 37.3.2, etc. and esp. 6.2 for the definition. Cf. 25.4.1f. for a fuller treatment.

[54] B 37.12–16/III 15.4–8; II 10.2–5. Note the play on *argon/ergon* to which Tardieu compares Orig. *Hexapla* on Gen 1:2. The versions in III 15.6f.: 'it had no *morphē* in her *morphē*', and II 10.4: 'it was different from her form', seem preferable to B 37.14.: 'it was hateful in its appearance', and, significantly, echo the Valentinian conception, as Janssens notes, *Muséon* 84, 63, whereby the female supplies the essence, the male the form (*morphē*). Cf. e.g. Hipp. *Ref.* 6.30.6–8; *Exc. ex Theod.* 68. A parallel in *TP* 39.21–6 has the great demon Saklas having neither *morphē* nor perfection, but the *morphē* of those begotten in darkness.

[55] 1.29.4. On Sophia's guilelessness, see n. 25 above; on the arrogance and boldness (*tolma*) of this figure, cf. Plot. *Enn.* 2.9.11.

[56] 94.5–17. For a more elaborate treatment, probably dependent on *HA* or a common source, cf. *OW* 98.1–100.10. *SJC* III 114.14–25/B 118.10–119.16, also shares that mythologoumenon, but with echoes of the 'Ophite' myth of Iren. 1.30.3 (Man/Son of Man/Christ scheme; drop/ dew of light; Ialdabaoth). Plotinus' Gnostics, *Enn.* 2.9.10, have Soul (i.e. Sophia) illuminate the darkness, thus forming an image in matter, from which a material image of the image produces the Demiurge.

[57] Cf. 1.30.3. See previous note for the possible influence of this on *SJC*. On the shadow motif in Valentinus, etc. see n. 28 above.

[58] *Ref.* 6.30.6–8. *ektrōma,* 'abortion' is the Valentinian term. Cf. *HA* 94.15 and *AJ* B 46.10.

[59] Iren. 1.2.2.

[60] 'Myth' 84ff.

[61] Cf. Clem. Alex. *Strom.* 4.13.89.6–90.3. *Val. Exp.* 34.21–38; 36.24–38 also appears to present a single Sophia who renounces her consort, leaves the Pleroma and suffers in attempting to imitate the Father in giving form to things. Cf. the similar role of the Logos in *Tri. Trac.* 76.2–77.36.

[62] Scholten's rejection, *Martyrium* 213, of the parallel on the basis of the disparity between the description of the abortion in B 37.13f. as hateful, in contrast to the positive depiction of Sophia's motive in the Valentinus fragment as to glorify the invisible, is undermined by the secondary character of B, influenced by the later depiction of Ialdabaoth. Further, Valentinus' version of the origin of the Demiurge in the Greek of Iren. 1.11.1 has him produced (*proenegkasthai,* the root of *prounikos?*) by Sophia!

[63] B 37.16–38.1/III 15.8–12; II 10.6–11. All three differ slightly in detail, but the general sense is clear. On Sophia's offspring as lion-like, cf. *HA* 94.17; *OW* 100.7; Bullard, *Hypostasis* 105; *PS* Book 1, ch. 31 (Schmidt–MacDermot 46.14–16); Book 2, ch. 66 (141.21f.). On his fiery eyes, cf. the fiery god of the Naassenes (Hipp. *Ref.* 5.7.30). The attempt by LR to distinguish between the *typos* which is serpentine and the face which is lion-like may be due to the awkwardness of SR which simply combines the two.

[64] B 38.1–15/III 15.13–23; II 10.11–20/IV 16.1–6. Cf. *GE* III 56.26–57.16. SR refers to Ialdabaoth as born (*jpo:* B 38.5/III 15.15), LR, again avoiding any sexual connotations, as created (*tamio:* II 10.13). Cf. the Demiurge of Valentinus in Iren. 1.11.1 as produced (*emisse/proenegkasthai*). All three disagree over the title given to the Holy Spirit but clearly allude to Gen 3:20 LXX. Thus B 38.12f. has '*Zoe* the Mother of everyone (*nouon nim*)', III 15.21 'the Mother of all living', and II 10.18 'the Mother of the living'. Here the designation 'Holy Spirit' probably applies to the Mother, Barbelo (cf. II 5.7f.), since 'Holy' as applied to the supreme being elsewhere (cf. II 6.29; 7.16; 8.27f. = B 34.17; also B 46.19 and par), is merely a qualifier of his normal title, 'Invisible Spirit', and since it is the Mother, Barbelo, described as 'Holy Spirit' who will play a saving role later (cf. B 71.5–10 and par, glossing her as the Epinoia!). Cf. Iren. 1.29.1 on Barbelo as the origin of the illumination and generation of everything.

[65] Iren. 1.29.4. Cf. B 38.5f. and par.

[66] 1.30.5. On the name cf. Orig. *C. Cels.* 6.31f.; Epiph. *Pan.* 25.2.2f.; 3.4f.; 26.10.2f.; 37.3.6, etc.; *HA* 95.8, 11f.; 96.3f.; *OW* 100.14, 19, 24; 102.11f.; 103.1f.; *Treat. Seth.* 53.13f.; 68.29; *TP* 39.27f.; *SJC* B 119.16; *PS* Book 1, ch. 31 (Schmidt–MacDermot 46.16); Book 3, ch. 102 (258.13;

259.3); Gnostic gem in C. Bonner, *Studies in Magical Amulets* (University of Michigan Studies, Humanistic Series vol. 49) (Ann Arbor, 1950), 135.

[67] See ch. 2, p. 44.

[68] *Separate* 42–5.

[69] *Hauptprobleme* 351–5, referring to Orig. *C. Cels.* 6.31.

[70] Ibid. 43. Cf. for details Giversen, *Apocryphon* 199f. There might be some support for this in *HA* 94.10–19 and *OW* 98.23–100.10; 103.24, in that Ialdabaoth appears to emerge from chaos (see Böhlig–Labib ed. 42f.). The etymology offered by *OW* 100.12f.: 'O youth pass over here', is clearly specious; it might support the derivation of the first element from the Aramaic *ialad*, but does imply ignorance of a likely Semitic origin.

[71] 'Jaldabaoth Reconsidered' in *Mélanges Puech* 405–21; Giversen, *Apocryphon* 199–201. Ialdabaoth seems the earliest attested form.

[72] 'Jaldabaoth' 421.

[73] *Separate* 44; M. Black, 'An Aramaic Etymology for Jaldabaoth?' in A. H. B. Logan, A. J. M. Wedderburn eds, *The New Testament and Gnosis: Essays in Honour of Robert McL. Wilson* (Edinburgh: T & T Clark, 1983), 69–72, esp. 71. In *AJ* Sabaoth is the fifth archon (cf. II 11.31; B 43.20/ II 12.22), and in Iren. 1.30.5 Sabaoth is the son of Iao, not of Ialdabaoth directly.

[74] Ibid.

[75] *Separate* 45, with reference to Grant, *VC* 11 (1957), 148–9, who combines the proposals of Harvey and Burkitt, *Church* 38, viz. *Iao Sabaoth*, to produce the form *Ia-El-Zebaoth* (= *Yahweh Elohe Zebaoth*).

[76] In a most interesting article, 'Samaël-Saklas-Yaldabaôth. Recherche sur l'origine d'un mythe gnostique', in *Colloque* 123–50, Barc argues for the Ialdabaoth myth as a synthesis of materials from two existing myths, one involving Saklas, the other Samael, which the redactor of *AJ* has completely reinterpreted in terms of the fall and repentance of the Mother. But my reading of the evidence suggests that no such developed myths existed, but merely figures and themes which were incorporated into the more original Barbelognostic and 'Ophite' myths and developed separately. Thus the rivalry Ialdabaoth/Sabaoth is already hinted at in the Demiurge/left-hand ruler of the Barbelognostics and Valentinus; it is required by the ambivalent character of the Barbelognostic Demiurge – both a channel of the divine and the creator of this evil world.

[77] 1.29.4.

[78] Cf. Iren. 1.11.1. J. E. Goehring may be correct in finding influence from the classical myths of Typhaon and Hephaestus on the Gnostic figure of Ialdabaoth as presented in *HA*, etc. but this is not so obvious in the case of Irenaeus 1.30 and *AJ*.

[79] 'Jewish Background' *passim*.

[80] 'Myth' *passim*.

⁸¹ Cf. *Separate* 85–92 and 406–10. On 89 she admits the link, which she proceeds to argue is best seen in terms of *AJ* representing a very similar but later version.

⁸² B 38.15–39.1/III 15.23–16.4; II 10.20–24. Cf. *TP* 39.26–32; Plot. *Enn.* 2.9.10.

⁸³ 1.29.4. As Tardieu points out, *Écrits* 276, the Coptic of B 38.15 and III 15.23 rests on a metathesis in the Greek; II 10.20 preserves the original (*proselabe?*), echoed by the *abstulisse* of Irenaeus 1.29.4.

⁸⁴ B 39.1–4/III 16.4–6. Cf. *HA* 94.35–95.1; Hipp. *Ref.* 6.7.30.

⁸⁵ Ibid. The 'firmament of heaven' of Irenaeus could well be described as a flaming fiery aeon, since it is probably meant to represent the heavenly fiery realm beyond the circle of the fixed stars, the empyrean. Cf. Till's edition, 119. Giversen, *Apocryphon* 202, thinks that the firmament idea may be referred to by II 10.25: 'which he now is', but this appears to refer to the flame.

⁸⁶ II 10.24–6.

⁸⁷ B 39.4–40.4/III 16.7–19. III 16.13 has omitted the 360 through homoeoteleuton. The prominence of the theme of ignorance supports Tardieu's claim, *Écrits* 276f., that the 'ignorance' (i.e. *agnoia*) of III 16.7 (and Irenaeus 1.29.4, *ignorantia/agnoia*) is original and has been read as *aponoia* by II 10.26 (and B 39.5). As the Creator is ignorant of his mother Sophia, present when he creates (cf. Prov 8:27), so his offspring are ignorant of him.

⁸⁸ II 10.26–11.4.

⁸⁹ Cf. II 11.22–5.

⁹⁰ Cf. II 12.35–13.5/IV 20.10–18.

⁹¹ 1.29.4. The Coptic for beget in the *Apocryphon* can also be translated as 'create' (*poiein*: cf. Crum, *Dictionary* 779a s.v. *jpo*).

⁹² Thus by adding twelve powers to the twelve angels we get 360 rather than the 348 of Till (43). Cf. Giversen, *Apocryphon* 216ff.

⁹³ B 39.18–40.4/III 16.15–19. On *archigenetōr* as a title for Ialdabaoth, cf. II 12.29/IV 20.5; *SJC* B 119.14f.; 125.16/III 118.20; *OW* 102.11; 103.4f.; 104.12; 106.13, 19; *TP* 40.23 (it adds 'of ignorance'), etc. Janssens' note, *Muséon* 84, 403, that the term occurs in the same place in all four versions, is inaccurate. That the term is apparently associated in *SJC* and *OW* with Ialdabaoth's generation of seven sons and his arrogant boast that he is god might suggest the priority of LR, which links it with the double names of Ialdabaoth's seven sons, the planetary rulers, not with the twelve powers governing the fixed stars (i.e. the zodiac).

⁹⁴ Cf. II 11.10–22/IV 17.16–18.6.

⁹⁵ B 40.4–19/III 16.19–17.5; II 10.28–11.4/IV 17.1–5. For a detailed comparison (omitting IV), see Giversen, *Apocryphon* 205–8.

⁹⁶ Cf. III 58.7–22/IV 70.1–5.

[97] III 57.16–58.5/IV 69.1–5. This is evidently modelled on the twelve aeons of *AJ*, produced from Christ and Incorruptibility and standing round (B 34.9f.: *paristanai*; cf. *GE* III 57.20f.: *paras[tatai]*) the Autogenes.

[98] *Pace* Böhlig–Wisse, *Gospel* 184. The chief differences between the versions are: (1) over the form of the first name, Iaoth in B 40.5; 41.18; 43.13, Haoth in III 16.20 (Aoth at 17.22 with a parallel to B 43.13 missing), and Athoth in II 10.29; 11.26; 12.16 (= IV 19.17. Cf. *GE* III 58.8). Both II 10.29f. and *GE* III 58.8–10 add that he is called another name by men, but both are then lacunous; (2) over the form of the third name, B 40.8 and III 16.23 reading Galila and II 10.32 having Kalilaoimbri (*GE* III 58.12 has a lacuna which only Galila would fit. Cf. Böhlig–Wisse, *Gospel* 124); more significantly (3) different names for the fifth, sixth and seventh: B 40.9–13/III 16.23–17.1 have Adonaios, Sabaoth, Kainan, usually called 'Kain', i.e. the sun (B 40.11–13 has 'Kainan and Kae, called Kain . . .', III 16.25–17.1 has 'Kainan Kasin, usually called "the sun"'), while II 10.33–6/IV 17.1f. have Adonaios who is called 'Sabaoth', Kain, whom men call 'the sun', and Abel (in GE III 58.15,18/IV 70.1,4 the names 'Kain' and 'Abel' are in lacunae but their restoration by Böhlig–Wisse, ibid., would fit very well); (4) both II 11.2 and *GE* III 58.20 have a longer form than the Adonin of B 40.17/III 17.4, namely Melcheiradonin and Arch[eiradonin] (so Böhlig–Wisse, ibid.) respectively.

[99] B 40.19–41.6/III 17.5–12. This seems to be the sense of a confused passage.

[1] B 41.6–12/III 17.12–17. The version in III 17.15 'through the glories' is perhaps preferable to B 41.9 'through the times' since the sense is that these beings wane through the influence of and the names given by the heavenly ones, and wax through the influence of and names given by Saklas.

[2] Till 43; Giversen, *Apocryphon* 203–5. But he argues that Saklas' names are not necessarily the usual zodiacal names, but could be other prevalent ones.

[3] Cf. Giversen, *Apocryphon* 217. In *Eug* III 83.10–84.8 and par, we have a similar scheme whereby the twelve powers produced by the Saviour and his consort Pistis Sophia produce 360 powers so that the twelve are archetypes of the twelve months of the year and the 360 powers of the 360 (*sic*!) days of the year.

[4] 'The Identity of the Archons in the "Apocryphon Johannis"', *VC* 32 (1978), 241–54, esp. 248ff.

[5] *Apocryphon* 211. Giversen's derivation from *mlk* is preferable to Helmbold's suggestion, *JNES* 66 (1965), 269f., of the Phoenician *milkart*, the god of the underworld. For an alternative derivation of Melcheir from the Melcheira of the *Ascension of Isaiah* (2.12; 3.6 in Greek, etc.), and an identification with Aquarius, see Tardieu, *Écrits* 283.

[6] 'Identity' 249ff.

[7] Ibid. The very close similarity of the parallel passage in *GE* suggests it was influenced here by the long recension of *AJ*.

[8] Ibid., 251ff. Cf. Giversen, *Apocryphon* 212, for a suggested division in terms of the seven zodiacal signs on or above the celestial equator where it divides the ecliptic (Aries to Libra) and the five below (Scorpio to Pisces).

[9] *Écrits* 277–84. Cf. Giversen, *Apocryphon* 211f., on the two ways of enumerating the signs.

[10] II 11.3f. Cf. *GE* III 58.21f., which has all twelve set over the underworld [and chaos], again suggesting dependence on the long recension of *AJ*.

[11] II 11.4–10/IV 17.16f.

[12] II 11.10–22/IV 17.18–18.6.

[13] II 11.22–5.

[14] *Apocryphon* 216–18. Thus II 19.3 has 365, and B 50.18ff. 360, angels create man. Tardieu, *Écrits* 286, assuming twelve powers, is driven to deriving the confusion in II from a mistaken stigma (6) instead of a gamma (3), and adding the five epagomens to make up 365. But this does not affect the evidently secondary character of LR here.

[15] II 11.26–12.26/IV 18.18–20.1. Cf. B 41.16–44.9/III 17.20–18.25.

[16] II 12.26–33/IV 20.2–10. Cf. B 41.1–12/III 17.7–17.

[17] II 12.33–13.5/IV 20.10–18. Cf. B 44.7–9. See also *TP* 40.4–8. There is no trace in B of the last statement; it recalls the Valentinian conception of the Demiurge creating after the image of the Pleroma in ignorance since it was his mother who worked through him (cf. Iren. 1.5.1f.; Hipp. *Ref.* 6.33).

[18] B 41.12–15/III 17.17–20. The form in III 17.19f. 'chaos and the underworld' is preferable to B 41.15: 'chaos of the underworld' in the light of the similar formula in *GE* III 56.25; 58.22 and *TP* 40.24.

[19] See Till's note to B 41.13. Thus II 11.4–10, which comes immediately after the enumeration of the twelve, has the seven set *over* the seventh heaven (i.e. they are distinct from the planetary rulers each ruling one of the lower heavens up to the seventh), and the seven and five given a share of Ialdabaoth's fire, a process repeated with the seven planetary rulers later (II 12.4ff. and par), while the gloss in II 11.3 which has Belias as over the abyss of the underworld, evidently takes him as one of the five.

[20] Thus B 41.18 has Iaoth as in 40.5 and 43.13, Adonaios fifth as in 40.9. But III, although it has Adonaios fifth in 16.24 and 18.3, reads Haoth in 16.20 and Aoth in 17.22. II, although it has Athoth in 10.29 and 11.26, has Adonaiou fifth in 10.33, but Sabaoth in 11.31.

[21] Cf. e.g. Welburn's argument in 'Identity' and Tardieu, *Écrits* 285.

[22] Cf. B 41.16f./III 17.20f. and B 42.7–10/III 18.7–9; II 11.34f./IV 18.24f.

[23] 1.30.4–5; 10.

[24] Cf. 1.30.9: 'Sanctam autem hebdomadam septem stellas, quas dicunt planetas, esse volunt . . .' Cf. Pétrement, *Separate* 64–72.

[25] Cf. B 48.6–50.6 and par.

[26] B 42.13–43.2/III 18.12–19. Cf. B 50.15–52.8 and par on the impotence of the archons to raise Adam, until Ialdabaoth inbreathes the power from his mother.

[27] B 44.5–9. Cf. II 12.25f., 33–13.1 and par.

[28] Cf. II 15.29–19.10 and par. The 'Book of Zoroaster' referred to at the end may be the source.

[29] III 57.16–58.22 and par. See Böhlig–Wisse, *Gospel* 120–4, for proposed reconstructions. Doresse, '"Le livre sacré du grand Esprit invisible" ou "L'Evangile des Egyptiens"', *JA* 254 (1966), 384f., suggests a possible reference in ll. 1–5 to the division of the twelve into seven and five, the latter being commanded to rule over chaos. But there does not seem enough space for such a reconstruction and the text seems to indicate that all twelve are to rule over the underworld [and chaos].

[30] E.g. Nebruel, associated with Saklas in the Manichaean cosmogony (cf. Theodore bar Konai, *Lib. Schol.* 11 (CSCO 69 ed. A. Scher (Louvain, 1960), 317.9ff., etc.), and by Priscillian in his first tractate (CSEL 18 ed. G. Schepss (Prague/Vienna/Leipzig, 1889), 17.29; 21.6, see Böhlig–Wisse, *Gospel* 183); the striking similarity in the list, and the final gloss mistakenly applying to all twelve what *AJ* limited to the last, Belias.

[31] Giversen's appeal, *Apocryphon* 205, to the later passage where Ialdabaoth plots with his powers and brings forth Fate (B 72.2–4/III 37.6f.; II 28.11–15/IV 43.24–9) is unconvincing since the powers mentioned there are most probably the seven planetary rulers who are responsible for Fate according to the *Poimandres* (CH 1.9).

[32] II 11.10–15/IV 17.17–23.

[33] *Apocryphon* 212.

[34] II 11.7–10.

[35] II 11.15–22/IV 17.24–18.6.

[36] II 11.15–18/IV 17.24–18.2. Cf. *TP* 39.26–8; *HA* 87.3f.; 94.25f.; 95.7f. On these names, see Barc, 'Samaël' *passim.* The reading of II 11.16: *ialtaba[oth]* is confirmed by IV 17.26. Saklas is found in SR, cf. B 41.6f.; 42.10f. and par (III 18.10 reads Sakla), but not Samael. Saklas is used without explanation by *AJ* as an alternative name for Ialdabaoth, the name actually given him by his mother Sophia (cf. B 38.13f. and par). Barc's claim of a distinct myth of Saklas based on the *GE* version may be debatable, but his link of Saklas with astrology and the twelve zodiacal signs/aeons is illuminating, would explain the occurrence of Saklas in SR, cast light on his role in *AA* as god of the thirteen aeons/kingdoms (i.e. twelve plus his own, cf. *AA* 74.3f.; 77.27–82.19, etc.; *GE* III 63.18 and par), and tie in with our hypothesis of the twelve as originally distinct from the seven and five. The 'Soclan' who is ruler (*archōn*) of the twelve-houred night in the Peratic system (cf. Hipp. *Ref.* 5.14.6) may also be

equated with him. Although in *HA* 95.7f. Zoe's retort to the first archon's boast that he was God: 'You are wrong Sakla', is related to his creation of seven rather than twelve powers, that the interpretation of Saklas is Ialtabaoth (*not* Ialdabaoth as in Bullard's edition p. 36), as the text continues, might hint at the combination as found in *AJ* of the motif of Ialdabaoth and his seven sons with Saklas and his twelve powers. Cf. *TP* 39.26–40.8 where the name of the great Demon ruling over the lowest region of the underworld and chaos is given first as Sakla, that is Samael, Ialtabaoth, who creates (twelve?) aeons in the image of the heavenly ones. The customary derivation from Aramaic, *sakla* 'fool', would fit the contexts in all the above Nag Hammadi works. See further, Bullard, *Hypostasis* 107f.; Doresse, *Secret Books* 51, n. 125; 162, n. 30. Samael, coupled with Saklas and Ialdabaoth in *TP* as well as here in the long recension, is interpreted as 'the blind god' in *HA* 94.25f., and *OW* 103.18, or 'the god of the blind' in *HA* 87.3f., which would suit a derivation from סומאל. The Ophites of Theodore bar Konai set a blind satanic angel Samiel in the form of a pig in the first of ten heavens (*Schol.* 11), while in the *Acts of Andrew and Matthias* 24 (Lipsius–Bonnet *AAA* II/1 101), the devil is called Amael (or Samael) because he is blind. Samael along with Michael(!) is one of the two names for the devilish serpentine son of the Demiurge in Irenaeus' 'Ophites' (1.30.9: Theodoret, however, reads *Samanna*). In the Jewish pseudepigrapha Sam(m)ael occurs as a name for Satan (e.g. *Asc. Is.* 3.13; 5.15; 7.9; 11.41, etc.), while in rabbinic literature he is the angel of death (e.g. in *Deb. Rab.* 11.10; *Tg. Ps. J.* Gen 3:6). See Bullard, *Hypostasis* 51–4. Barc's appeal to a myth of Samael appears less well founded than in the case of Saklas, but Bullard's suggestion that Samael and Saklas are popular names taken from contemporary Jewish and magical circles to describe aspects of the archon whose secret name is Ialdabaoth, which appears far more often on magical amulets and in magical texts, is plausible. 'Saklas' would represent his folly (cf. *OW* 107.34f.), and 'Samael' his blindness. Since LR adds that he did not actually see the heavenly world (II 13.1–5 and par) it is not surprising that it added the name here.

[37] II 11.18–22/IV 18.2–6. This is evidently an expansion of II 12.8–10 and par, quoting Isa 46:9.

[38] Cf. II 11.7–10 and 12.4ff. with B 42.13–18 and par, and II 11.19–22 and 12.8–10 with B 42.18–43.6 and par.

[39] *Apocryphon* 215. Tardieu, *Écrits* 41f., also sees here the work of a later redactor (his (n²)). The treatment of the origin, nature and three names of the Demiurge in *TP* 39.13–32 would appear to be dependent on the form reflected in LR here.

[40] B 41.16–42.7/III 17.20–18.7; II 11.26–34/IV 18.18–24.

[41] B 42.9f./III 18.8f. This may be a marginal note incorporated into the text of SR (so Giversen, *Apocryphon* 223), or it may have been omitted by redactors of LR because they thought that the seven were the seven

powers immediately preceding (cf. II 11.23 and par) created by the archons, who thus could not be said to control the cosmos.

[42] *Écrits* 287f.

[43] Cf. Iren. 1.30.5; Orig. *C. Cels.* 6.31f.; Epiph. *Pan.* 26.10.1–3; *PGM* XIII 161–206 (A); Coptic magical papyrus XLVIII.38ff. (Kropp I x.16; II 201); *OW* 101.29–34. See Tardieu, *Écrits* 287–9.

[44] Origen's list needs emending since it omits Adonaios and has Astaphaios before Ailoaios (*sic* = Eloaios). The Gnostic amulet starts with Ia on the reverse, which obviously represents the Ialdabaoth of the obverse. Opposite the latter the amulet also has the name 'A(a)riel', as in *OW* 100.25f.: 'the perfect call him "Ariel" because he was lion-like'. On the amulet, see C. Bonner, 'An Amulet of the Ophite Gnostics' in *Commemorative Studies in Honor of Theodore Leslie Shear* (Hesperia, Supplement 8) (Athens, 1949), 43–6; *Studies* 135–8. Origen asserts, *C. Cels.* 6.31, that the Ophites took the names Iao to Eloaios from the names of God in Hebrew scripture and Ialdabaoth, Astaphaios and Horaios from magic. See Jackson, 'Origin' 71ff.

[45] However, the redactor of *OW* may have known *AJ*'s distinctive form as well as the other, more familiar one, in that in 101.10–22 he has the archon Ialdabaoth produce first Iao, then Eloaios, then Astaphaios. That he stops there may be because of the repetition of the fourth name, Iao again. This might suggest that the form in B's version of *AJ*, Iaoth, was the original one, converted by the redactor of the long recension into the Athoth of the twelve powers, confused by the author of *OW* with the more familiar Iao.

[46] B 41.18/III 17.22; II 11.27. On the first archon having a lion-like face or form, cf. Orig. *C. Cels.* 6.30 (the first of the seven in Celsus' diagram has a lion-like form and is called Michael, according to Origen, but Ialdabaoth in ch. 31); *OW* 100.25–7; *HA* 94.17; Manichaean *Kephalaia* 33.9. Earlier in *AJ* Ialdabaoth was described as in the form of a (snake and a) lion (B 37.20f. and par). The term translated 'face' (*ḥo* = *prosōpon*) probably applies to the head and not the whole figure, *pace* Giversen, *Apocryphon* 219. On the animal-faced archons, cf. Orig. *C. Cels.* 6.30 and 33; *PS* Book 3, ch. 126 (Schmidt–MacDermot 317.22–319.10); Theodore bar Konai's Ophites (*Schol.* 11: Pognon, *Coupes* 145f., 213f.); *HA* 87.27–9; the Gnostics of Epiph. *Pan.* 26.10.6 (Sabaoth, the archon of the seventh heaven, has the form of an ass or pig).

[47] Cf. B 41.19/III 17.23 and B 43.15 (Eloaios); II 11.27f. (Eloaiou); 12.18 (Eloaio).

[48] Cf. B 41.20f./III 17.24 (Astophaios) and B 43.17; II 11.29; 12.19 (Astraphaio).

[49] Cf. B 42.2; 43.19; II 11.30; 12.20 (Iao); III 18.1 (Iazo; see Tardieu, *Écrits* 287, for an explanation of the form).

[50] On the seven-headed snake, cf. *PS* Book 2, ch. 66 (Schmidt–MacDermot 137.18f.); 3, ch. 126 (318.25–7). The version in III 18.2 is

virtually a mirror-image of its description of Ialdabaoth in 15.11, which might suggest it misunderstood the reference to the seven-headed snake, or thought that Iazo represented Ialdabaoth. But, cf. *PS* Book 2, ch. 66 (141.22) where Sophia tramples on both the seven-headed snake and the lion-snake-faced power.

[51] Cf. B 42.3/III 18.3 (Adonaios); B 43.20; II 11.31; IV 19.23 (Sabaoth); II 12.22 (Sanbaoth). The confusion is easily understandable and has already taken place in II 10.33f. Cf. *GE* III 58.13–15.

[52] Cf. B 42.5 (Adoni); III 18.4f. and II 11.32 (Adonin); II 12.23 (Adonein).

[53] *Écrits* 289.

[54] Cf. 101.9–102.2 and *AJ* B 43.11–44.4 and par. While the latter preserves its characteristic conception of the heavenly aeons as male–female syzygies, the former presents these entities as androgynous.

[55] 'Identity' 241–7.

[56] Cf. *C. Cels.* 6.31.

[57] On Sabbataios as a transcription of the Hebrew for Saturn, Shabbathai, and thus a play on the Hebrew for 'Lord of hosts', 'seven', and 'Saturn', and Tacitus' association of Saturn with the God of the Jews, see Welburn, 'Identity' 245.

[58] Thus he is justified in interpreting Eloaios as Mercury and Astaphaios as Venus in both lists, and his interpretation of the seven-headed snake united with Ia(z)o in terms of the Sun is illuminating. But the two lists remain ultimately distinct. For parallels to *AJ*'s planetary interpretation of the seven, cf. *Poim.* CH 1.9 (the Nous Demiurge fashions seven governors embracing the perceptible world in circles) and the Valentinians of Ptolemy in Iren. 1.5.2 (the Demiurge prepares seven intelligible heavens/angels above which he dwells as Hebdomad).

[59] B 42.10–13/III 18.9–12; II 11.35–12.4/IV 18.26–19.2. B 42.10f./III 18.9f. add 'Saklas', which the long recension may have omitted since it had already explained it as one of the common names of Ialdabaoth. It has him indwelling the various forms (II 12.1/IV 18.28), and adds a final gloss: 'while he is in the midst of the Seraphim' (II 12.3f./IV 19.2). This is probably less original, the Seraphim being the seven powers in a possible allusion to Isa 6:2. Cf. also Ezek 1:5–14 LXX and Rev 4:6–8.

[60] B 42.13–18/III 18.12–16; II 12.4f./IV 19.3f. B 42.15 adds to the gift of fire a share of Ialdabaoth's own power, and LR omits the reference to his withholding the light-power he got from his mother, since it has already mentioned it (II 11.8–10). On this motif, cf. Epiph. *Pan.* 37.3.6. Plotinus seems to allude to this in *Enn.* 2.9.5, 8 (no share of immortal soul given to the entire heaven and stars).

[61] B 42.18–43.2: 'because of the glory in him of the power of light of the Mother'; III 18.16–19: 'because of the glory of the light of the power which is in him of the Mother'; II 12.5–8/IV 19.4–6: 'because of the power of the glory which is light for him from his mother'. The variations

probably derive from differing interpretations of the several genitives of the original Greek.

[62] B 43.2–6/III 18.19–22; II 12.8–10. LR prefers him naming himself (II 12.8) to the implication of SR that his followers were involved (cf. B 43.3 which reads: 'he let himself be called' and III 18.20 which adds 'over them'). LR also, perhaps misunderstanding the Greek loan-words *peithein* and *hypostasis*, as is suggested by the doublet at II 11.21f., reads 'place' in both passages. Tardieu, *Écrits* 289, rightly considers this motif to be based on an exegesis of Exod 3:14; by such a hubristic claim the God of the Jews has betrayed the ground of his being. Cf. the parallel in *GE* III 58.26f., with the loan word, but apparently used positively (see Böhlig–Wisse, *Gospel* 126 and 184), unlike in *AJ*, perhaps because the former has taken over the demonized figure of Saklas and his demonic counterpart Nebruel, whereas the latter still preserves a more positive evaluation of Ialdabaoth. Cf. also *HA* 86.28–32; 94.19–23; *OW* 103.8–15 (Ialdabaoth's boast and sin against the All); *Treat. Seth* 53.27–33 and 64.17–33 (the archon's empty boast and disagreement with the supreme Father). The allusion to him calling himself 'God' is of course proleptic; the actual boast does not occur till B 44.14f. and par.

[63] Cf. Iren. 1.29.3; *AJ* B 35.11–20 and par. The Valentinians also have the Demiurge's boast but characteristically trace it to his weakness and ignorance rather than his disobedience (Iren. 1.5.4; Hipp. *Ref.* 6.33).

[64] B 43.6–8/III 18.22–4; II 12.10–13/IV 19.10–13. LR adds that it was through his thought as well as his speaking that they (II 'he') came into existence (II 12.12f./IV 19.12f.), again reflecting its tendency to greater internal harmony and consistency: as the supreme Being brought his offspring into being by mental conception (*ennoia*), so too with Ialdabaoth. Cf. Saklas' creative word calling forth twelve aeons and seven beings in *GE* III 57.21–58.2. Janssens, *Muséon* 84, 404, alludes to Genesis 1, Tardieu, *Écrits* 290, to magical as well as biblical parallels of this divine creative word and its consequences.

[65] B 43.9–11/III 18.24f.; II 12.13–15/IV 19.13–15. II 12.14/IV 19.14 has 'every power', and B 43.9f.: 'he named them and established (*kathistanai*) powers (*exousia*)'. III 18.25 breaks off at 'established', the following two pages being lost. SR's version may rest on a mis-interpretation of the Greek (*katestē/hekastēn exousian?*).

[66] The parallel to II 12.15–25 in IV 19.15–26 is very fragmentary, but appears to be identical, as is the better-preserved parallel to II 15.14–23 in IV 24.3–14.

[67] On p. 139 of his edition. See his note ad loc. on the preceding page.

[68] Cf. Giversen, *Apocryphon* 181. On the translations of *mntrmñḥēt*, see the remarks of Wilson in his articles in *NTS* 9 (1963/64), 297ff.; *Les textes de Nag Hammadi* (NHS 7) (Leiden: Brill, 1975), 36f.

[69] *Zatspram* 30.5–11 in Zaehner, *Zurvan: A Zoroastrian Dilemma* (Oxford, 1955), 162, n. 1. Cf. Puech, 'Fragments retrouvés de

l'Apocalypse d'Allogène' in *Mélanges Franz Cumont 2* (Brussels, 1936), 938, n. 2, referring to the Chronicle of Michael the Syrian on Bardaisan, which has each planet as creator of the marrow, bones, sinews, blood, flesh, skin, hair respectively, and to the Manichaean *Kephalaia* ch. 42 (ed. Böhlig I.1 107.9–32) which has the order marrow, bones, sinews, flesh, veins, blood, skin.

[70] *Écrits* 300–8.

[71] *Commentarium de Somnio Scipionis* I.6.79 (Willis 33.17–20: 'medulla, os, nervus, vena, arteria, caro, cutis'). Cf. with *ab imo* the phrase 'from above' in B 43.11 and par.

[72] Cf. 101.23–102.2 and 114.34f.

[73] Theodore, *Schol.* 11; Puech, 'Fragments' 936ff., 942, n. 2, 952, n. 4; see also Hennecke–Schneemelcher–Wilson, *NTA* 1 318ff.

[74] Ibid. Puech, 'Fragments' 938, n.1, notes that 'powers' corresponds to the Greek *exousiai* and designates the seven planetary archons. In n. 2 he accepts the emendation of *sa'ra*, 'skin', for the *besra*, 'flesh', of the MSS, and in n. 3 the emendation of *binta*, 'understanding' (i.e. *synesis*), as in B instead of the incomprehensible *bi'ta*, 'egg', of the text. However, we should note that no such piece of direct speech is found in our *AJ*, although Audi may simply have been quoting a traditional passage. What is significant is that if we take wisdom as equivalent to *sophia*, understanding as *synesis*, Elohim as divinity, Adonai as lordship, zeal as fire and thought as providence (*pronoia*), we have the exact equivalent of the list in SR – accepting that the *mñtchs̄* of B 43.16 and 49.13 is a mistake for *mñtjoeis*.

[75] However *kōh* occurs among the otherwise exclusively feminine Greek and Coptic names in *OW* 101.26–102.2 which designate the seven powers of the seven heavens. The terms *kōh, kōht* and even *kauma* may represent independent attempts to render a Greek substantive like *zēlotēs* or alternatively *kausis*, as Giversen, *Apocryphon* 227, suggests.

[76] Cf. the arguments of Giversen, *Apocryphon* 227f., and Welburn, 'Identity' 247f. Comparison with Theodore bar Konai's list shows that B 43.16 has mistakenly read 'lordship' (*mñtjs*) as 'goodness' (*mñtchs̄*). Tardieu, *Écrits* 292, suggests that the unparalleled 'riches' ([*tmntrm*] *mao*) of *OW* 101.33f. rests on a mistake of the abbreviated loanword *c̄hr̄t* (= *chremata*, riches) for *chrs* (= *chrēstotēs*, goodness).

[77] Cf. *Écrits* 44, 301f.

[78] See n. 73, above.

[79] Giversen, *Apocryphon* 227f., evidently understands *sophia* to be rendered by *mñtrmñhēt* here in II, although earlier (181) he had argued for *synesis* as the relevant term. If one removes 'goodness' then LR and SR agree over the first three powers (providence, divinity, lordship), reverse the next two (zeal, kingship), and agree over the next (*synesis*/*mñtrmñhēt*).

[80] Cf. Iren. 1.29.4 and *AJ* B 39.6–18/III 16.8–15.

[81] Cf. B 44.5f. and par.

[82] Cf. Rousseau–Doutreleau SC 263 303 *notes justicatives* on 264 363, n. 2.

[83] 1.29.4. Cf. the similar list of evils produced by the snake-like son of Ialdabaoth in 1.30.5: 'oblivio, malitia, zelus, invidia, mors.'

[84] 'Irenäus' 333. Foerster, *Gott* 136, also accepts that Irenaeus has supplied the names of the five underworld kings and suggests that the archetype for this may be the pentad of aeons beneath the supreme God (B 29.14–16), an unlikely hypothesis in the light of our claim that the pentad concept is secondary.

[85] The same tendency in *GE* III 57.20–58.22 and par may explain why we hear little or nothing about the seven and five in it, although a reference to them may be concealed in 58.1f., as Doresse has suggested. The compression of the whole passage concerning Sakla's creation and subsequent boast probably derives in part from this tendency, further confirming its dependence on *AJ*.

[86] See p. 127f. Although Irenaeus attributes a left-hand ruler to Valentinus' system, the latter and Theodotus share with the Barbelognostics not only belief in a single Sophia but also a more negative evaluation of the Demiurge and his angels. Cf. e.g. Valentinus frag. 1 (Clem. Alex. *Strom.* 2.8.36); *Exc. ex Theod.* 33.3–4.

[87] E.g. Ialdabaoth's snake-like son according to the 'Ophites' (Iren. 1.30.5f.), or the left-hand power, world ruler or Devil according to the Valentinians (cf. Iren. 1.5.4; Epiph. *Pan.* 33.7.3–7, etc.). In line with this, 'Saklas' appears as a nickname for Ialdabaoth suggesting his foolish and demonic character in *AJ* and related works, but not in the earlier Barbelognostic system summarized by Irenaeus, while 'Samael', another such name, is ascribed to Ialdabaoth's snake-like son rather than himself in Irenaeus' 'Ophite' system (1.30.9). Thus Valentinus is not so different from these Gnostics as Edwards claims, 'Gnostics' 43f.

[88] 1.29.4: 'Ego sum Deus zelator et praeter me nemo est.' On Sophia's withdrawal prior to the boast, cf. *OW* 100.26–33 and possibly *TP* 39.32–40.8; on her forming the Ogdoad, cf. the 'Ophites' of Iren. 1.30.3f. and the Valentinians of 1.5.2–4. The former have the Mother occupy the eighth place, the latter dub her 'Ogdoad' and have her dwell in the supercelestial region (i.e. the Middle). If she is the Ogdoad for the Barbelognostics, this implies there are seven heavens and rulers below her, as in the 'Ophite' and Valentinian systems described by Irenaeus.

[89] B 44.9–15; II 13.5–9/IV 20.18–24. The same combination of Exod 20:5 and Isa 46:9 or 45:5 occurs in *GE* III 58.24–26. Cf. also *Treat. Seth* 64.19–23 ('I am God ... and there is no other apart from me. I am a jealous god ...': cf. Isa 45:5; 44:6; Exod 20:5). For a conspectus of all the Nag Hammadi texts with a similar quotation from Isaiah, see Kasser 'Citations' in Krause, *Essays* 60. The form in LR has probably been harmonized with the earlier boast of Ialdabaoth echoing Isa 46:9 in II

11.20f. and par, part of its later redaction. The version in *GE* III 58.24–26, while taking up the redoubled 'I' of LR, is closer to B's version as regards the latter half. On this theme of the hubris of the Demiurge, cf. Schottroff, *Glaubende* 50, n. 1.

⁹⁰ B 44.15–19; II 13.9–13/IV 20.24–9. Cf. my article 'The Jealousy of God: Exod 20:5 in Gnostic and Rabbinic Theology', in *Studia Biblica*, 1978, 1: Papers on Old Testament and Related Themes (*JSOT* Supplement Series 11: Sheffield, 1979), 197–203.

⁹¹ B 44.19–45.19 and par. B alone preserves the Greek which makes the allusion to Genesis more explicit.

⁹² B 44.19–45.5; 45.11–19; 46.9–13 and par. Cf. the echo of this in Plot. *Enn.* 2.9.4, 8.

⁹³ B 46.13–20 and par.

⁹⁴ Cf. B 46.20–47.14/III 21.6–16; II 14.5–13/IV 22.6–15.

⁹⁵ 'Irenäus' 333.

⁹⁶ 'Nag-Hamadi–Studien I' 59f.

⁹⁷ *Glaubende* 50.

⁹⁸ 49f.

⁹⁹ Cf. B 44.9–45.19 and par and B 45.19–46.15 and par. The latter with its mention of Ialdabaoth the *authadēs* taking power from his mother is also a doublet of B 38.15ff. and par.

¹ Ibid. Cf. B 45.5–19 and par.

² Cf. B 45.2–5.

³ II 13.14–17/IV 20.30–21.3. Cf. also the earlier insertion in LR about the character of Ialdabaoth, II 11.11–15.

⁴ Cf. B 45.11–13; II 13.21–3/IV 21.8–10. Against Giversen, *Apocryphon* 233, the references to *kakia* and *apostasia* in B surely apply to her son's action and boast rather than to Sophia's sense of being diminished in light-power. Cf. her designation as *akakos*/innocent in related texts (*TP* 39.29; 40.15; *Treat. Seth* 50.25–30).

⁵ B 45.13–19; II 13.23–6/IV 21.10–15.

⁶ *Gott 'Mensch'* 79–87, with reference to *Exc. ex Theod.* 47; Iren. 1.18.1; *OW* 100.29–101.2; 104.11–13; Iren. 1.30.1.

⁷ *Glaubende* 51, 53–5. Cf. also *Exeg. Soul* (C II,*6*) 127.19–129.5.

⁸ B 45.19–46.9; II 13.26–32/IV 21.16–22. Cf. B 38.15–39.10 and par which has him imitate the heavenly archons!

⁹ B 46.6–15; II 13.30–14.1/IV 21.20–22.1. In making Sophia realize she had not concurred with her consort at the moment she recognized the imperfection, LR is probably secondary: she was aware of acting without him from the outset. On the Valentinian term 'abortion' (*ḥouhe*, i.e. *ektrōma* in B 46.10), cf. Hipp. *Ref.* 6.31.2.

¹⁰ B 46.15–47.14/III 21.2–15. Note both the concentration of Valentinian technical terms, e.g. *plērōma* (III 21.7f. 'their Pleroma'), *syzygos*, and 'deficiency' (*shta* = *hysterēma*), and the Valentinian theology of Sophia, whose deficiency is precisely her action without her consort,

which will only be cured by her eschatological rescue of her seed and union with her consort.

[11] The appropriate response here is a request (*aitein*), not a blessing, and Tardieu, *Écrits* 296, is not justified in equating the *eine ou smou* of II and IV with *parakalein*. The pattern in *TP* 39.35–40.4, of Sophia's request for a superior location (*taxis*) and its blessing, probably reflects dependence on *AJ*.

[12] II 14.1–6/IV 22.1–7. The Coptic verb *eiōrm* in IV 22.6 does not mean 'be amazed' (so Krause 219), but is evidently the Sahidic of *jōrm*, which represents the Greek *neuein, kataneuein*, etc. (cf. Crum, *Dictionary* 785b), and thus IV is closer to SR here.

[13] II 14.7–9/IV 22.8–11. However, the two appear to distinguish between 'come' and 'come down', as Krause does, but not Tardieu or Wisse in their respective translations. Note the very Valentinian colouring which might explain the oddness: her consort did not unite with her at the beginning but was sent later from the whole Pleroma (cf. the Valentinian Jesus of Iren. 1.4.5, etc.).

[14] II 14.9–13/IV 22.11–15.

[15] *Apocryphon* 235, 238.

[16] Cf. e.g. Iren. 1.4.5; *Exc. ex Theod.* 43.5; *Tri. Trac.* 80.11–81.35; 86.4–87.31, etc.

[17] See p. 163, n. 89.

[18] Giversen's rejection, *Apocryphon* 236f., of Till's translation of the Ninth as a collective (135) is unjustified. Coptic does form a collective precisely in this way, as with its rendering of the *hebdomas* of III 18.7 and par by the *tmehsashfe* of B 42.8. However, IV 22.14 does add *pe*, 'heaven'.

[19] *Glaubende* 55f. To her references one should add Iren. 1.29.4; Epiph. *Pan.* 25.2.2; 40.2.3; *Poim.* CH 1.26; *HA* 95.33f.; *OW* 104.30f.; 105.22f.; 106.7f.; 112.12, 20.

[20] Cf. B 38.17–39.4 and par (II 10.24 mistakenly reads 'aeons' since the following reference (l. 25) is in the singular); II 11.4–6; B 44.5–9. This reinterpretation is further evidence of *AJ*'s combination of two originally independent systems, that of the Barbelognostic Protarchon (with his own heaven and his mother above him in the Ogdoad) and that of the 'Ophite' hebdomad of Ialdabaoth and his six offspring, one to a heaven, by equating the Protarchon with Ialdabaoth.

[21] Cf. II 11.4f. with B 41.16f. and par and B 44.5f., which speak of seven heavens with a ruler to (*kata*) each.

[22] Cf. II 14.11/IV 22.13.

5

Gnostic Anthropology and Anthropogony

Introduction

The famous and much-quoted definition of the essence of *gnōsis* in the Valentinian *Excerpta ex Theodoto* 78.2 reads:

> Now it is not merely the washing (*loutron*) which liberates, but also the knowledge (*gnōsis*): Who were we? What have we become? Where were we? Into what place have we been cast? Whither are we hastening? From what have we been delivered? What is birth? What is rebirth?

This encapsulates the heart of the Gnostic problem: the nature, origin and destiny of the elect, estranged from their heavenly home and origin, imprisoned in this visible universe under the domination of ignorant and hostile powers, in need of a heavenly revealer/redeemer to rouse them from its oblivion, reveal their true origin and destiny, and ensure their ultimate escape from the world in the context of a rite of initiation. But the elect form part of humanity; human existence is the context and condition of their salvation, and so anthropology forms the heart and pivot of Gnostic theology. But it cannot be properly understood apart from both cosmology and soteriology. Thus in our treatment of Gnostic anthropology in the 'classic' Gnostic myth and investigation of how and why it developed, we will necessarily have to overlap with the previous cosmological chapter as well as dealing with material which properly belongs to the following soteriological and christological chapter.

If there is one point of agreement in the fantastic plethora of Gnostic systems, it would appear to be that human beings are composite, a mixture of heterogeneous elements, light and darkness, good and evil, spirit and matter, corporeal and incorporeal. Salvation is a matter of unscrambling this mixture, of distinguishing the various kinds.[1] Such a mixture can result from an original monism or from an original dualism, and the power or powers responsible for the creation of earthly man[2] can be seen both as hostile, as in the *Hypostasis of the Archons*, and as unwitting agents in the divine plan of salvation, as with the 'Ophites', the *Apocryphon of John* and the Valentinians of Ptolemy's school. Thus, too, we can find dichotomous and trichotomous anthropologies, sometimes a combination of both and even a fourfold scheme.[3]

At the heart of this bewildering variety, however, lies the same basic conception: humanity is a mixture of divine and anti-divine elements, and the various, often inconsistent, anthropologies represent attempts to do justice to this insight and dilemma: to allow for the fact that humanity is the creation of – and under the sway of – cosmic forces hostile to the unknown Father, the ultimate origin of man's divine spark, yet to try to delimit as far as possible the extent of that sway and preserve the divine uncontaminated. The text which gives classic and prototypical expression to this situation is of course the opening chapters of Genesis, read with Platonic, but more importantly, Gnostic spectacles. For it is not simply that humanity consists in the Platonic sense of a divine soul trapped in an earthly body; Gnosticism is much more pessimistic about human nature. No, the Gnostic claim is that not only is the human form, made 'in the image of God', not the divine element but an inferior copy made by lower powers ignorant of or hostile to God, if nevertheless in imitation of a heavenly archetype; neither is the 'divine' soul, since it too originates from these same powers. The real divine element for the Gnostics is the spirit, seed, 'inner man' or whatever, which is not a natural endowment but an alien element from the supra-heavenly sphere, present only in the elect or to which they alone respond.

Gnostic anthropology, then, does have a certain underlying unity despite the varieties alluded to above, in that it presupposes a central 'self' or 'I' present in addition to the natural twofold or threefold structure, and present as gift or grace. Here Irenaeus' sketch of the system of Saturninus, however brief, contradictory and tendentious, can help us structure our analysis of the paradoxes of Gnostic anthropology and assist us to understand it better.

Thus on the surface Saturninus appears to teach a dichotomous anthropology: man's body is created by angels in imitation of a heavenly archetype (cf. Gen 1:26), and animated by the spark of life from heaven descending to occupy its copy and remaining until death.[4] But, as Pétrement points out, there is a contradiction here: on the one hand man needs the spark to stand upright (implying that all possess it), on the other it later transpires that not all possess it, only those who believe in Christ.[5] Further, man without the spark is not inanimate: he wriggles like a worm. Pétrement's consequent interpretation of man's elevation as figurative[6] is not entirely convincing since the spark is explicitly said to equip him with limbs (*articulare*).[7] And the later assertion that there are two types or races of humanity, one good, the other bad,[8] seems hard to reconcile with the divine spark theory; one cannot simply argue that all the good possess it. And finally there are inconsistencies between the two theories as regards the opponents: in the case of the spark theory it is the hostile God of the Jews and his angels, in the latter the evil angels and Satan, who is already independent of and hostile to the Old Testament God and his fellow creator-angels.

Assuming the general accuracy of Irenaeus or his source, we are driven to conclude that Saturninus has not resolved the dilemma and paradox of Gnostic anthropology: all need the divine spark to be fully human, only the elect possess it through faith, yet it is apparently a lifelong possession. What our account presents is at least three key but not entirely consistent anthropological themes which recur in Gnostic texts and cast light on that dilemma. The first is that of the divine spark descending to animate Adam, the Golem of Jewish legend, created by angels in the image of a heavenly being reflected in the waters of chaos. It occurs in various guises, often involving the theme of the seduction of the archons, with either a female or a male figure,[9] or, as in the *Poimandres*, involving the Narcissus motif whereby Primal Man descends to enter his irrational reflected form.[10] The second is the idea found in the Christian Adam books and the Sethians of Epiphanius, that originally angels, perhaps divided into good and bad, created two human types or races, one evil, the other good (i.e. Cainites and Sethians).[11] The third theme is that of three original principles or three substances and races, and is found in such varying forms as Valentinianism and the three-principle systems described by Hippolytus, particularly that of the Naassenes.[12]

The other major theme in Gnostic anthropology, which Irenaeus' summary of Saturninus only hints at, is that the heavenly image seen by the angels is none other than that of the supreme being (or an emanation of his) called 'Man'. Indeed Schenke has claimed that the concept and myth of the God 'Man' is fundamental to Gnostic mythology, arguing that it developed directly out of exegesis of Gen 1:26f.[13] Here he is building, if critically, on the theories of scholars since the turn of the century who have claimed to detect the figure of Primal Man behind the various Gnostic systems. These theories have tended to select one or two of the central themes outlined above. Thus there is (1) the idea of the descent or fall of Primal Man, either (*a*) directly, as in the *Poimandres*, or (*b*) in the form of his reflection being seen and copied, leading to the descent of a divine spark, as in Saturninus and the *Hypostasis of the Archons*. Others, however, have taken (2) the motif of man made in the image of the divine Man reflected in the waters of chaos, as the central Gnostic anthropological tenet. Others have insisted that the fundamental Gnostic theme is (3) the idea of the consubstantiality of the *salvandus* and the *Salvator* or Redeemer. That is, that either the supreme God himself, or, since this is an impossible thought for Gnostics, his primary emanation and image, the heavenly Primal Man, is actually present in earthly man, i.e. a variation on motif 1(a), or, avoiding that dangerous conception, his image or reflection is somehow present in earthly man and thus Primal Man does not fall, i.e. motif 2, or a divine spark or seed from heavenly Man is present in earthly man, i.e. motifs 1(b) and 3.

The first thesis was represented by Bousset and Reitzenstein.[14] Bousset claimed there had been an archaic cosmogonic myth which derived the world from the body of the sacrificed Primal Man. This formed the basis of the Gnostic myth of the divine Man who fell into matter and this was then adapted to express the origin of earthly man.[15] But, as Schenke points out, the only Gnostic texts in which the Primal Man occurs as a cosmogonic principle are Manichaean.[16] Reitzenstein argued that the Gnostic conceptions of a divine Man developed on the basis of pre-Christian Iranian ideas according to which the soul or inner man, seen as a divine being, was sent down from the world of light into matter, freed from it and recalled to heaven.[17] Primal Man is here essentially a 'redeemed Redeemer'. Now both Bousset and Reitzenstein had claimed support for their theory of a pre-Christian cosmogonic (only secondarily anthropogonic) Anthropos myth from the Naassene Preaching,[18] which Reitzenstein claimed had been interpolated.[19] This claim has been contested by Schottroff and others,[20] who also cast doubt on the whole assumption of a Primal Man–Redeemer, or a 'redeemed Redeemer (*salvator salvandus*)' myth underlying Gnosticism and Christianity.[21]

The hypothesis of an Iranian Primal Man as proposed by Reitzenstein and others of the *religionsgeschichtliche Schule* had already been attacked by Quispel.[22] He argued that the original Primal Man myth had been a myth of Sophia, the virgin of light, casting her shadow image (*eidōlon*) on to the primal waters, from which the hostile archons created the world and the human body.[23] The original female Sophia, the *anima mundi* of late Platonism, later became the male Anthropos figure.[24] Thus Quispel simply reverses the Bousset–Reitzenstein thesis and takes as the key to Gnostic cosmology and anthropology the second theme, humanity made in the image of God, as found in the *Apocryphon*.[25]

J. Jervell also sees the relationship between heavenly image and earthly copy as the key to understanding the Gnostic systems,[26] but rejects both the Bousset–Reitzenstein and Quispel theses. Against the former he claims that pre-Christian Gnosis such as that underlying the *Poimandres* most probably did not know of a redeemer figure called Anthropos; only under Christian influence did he become such.[27] Against Quispel he argues that it is not Sophia but the Anthropos figure who is primary in Gnosis: he is the Father himself as he projects himself as *eikōn*, and all the Gnostic systems are variations on this self-projection theme, itself based on Gen 1:26, outlining the heavenly birth of Primal Man. Earthly man is a copy of the heavenly: being in the image means that the divine spirit lives in man.[28] But against Jervell, (1) because the *eikōn* motif is not universal in Gnostic texts, he is forced to include the concept of the divine spark or seed in that motif; (2) the motif is frequently used in a negative and polemic fashion, particularly in cosmogonic contexts, to explain how this hostile world arose and how the divine became enmeshed in matter; being in the image of a divine being does *not* imply or guarantee life and salvation, but rather imperfection.[29]

It is noticeable how central the theme of Primal Man/Anthropos is in all this. If the Bousset–Reitzenstein thesis is generally rejected, both a Jewish and a Christian origin have recently been canvassed. Thus van den Broek has argued on the basis of his analysis of *Eugnostos* for the existence of a Platonized Jewish–Gnostic myth of both Anthropos and Sophia underlying not only *Eugnostos* and the *Apocryphon* but also Valentinianism.[30] On the other hand we find Pétrement claiming, in defence of her thesis of the Christian origins of Gnosticism, that the title 'Man' used of God derives from Gnostic misunderstanding of Christ's title 'Son of man'. She points to the almost invariable association of 'Son of man' with 'Man' in the myths of the creation of earthly man and in passages where the name 'Man' is given to God, and the fact that speculations about God being called 'Man' do not occur in the earliest systems described by the heresiologists.[31] And she claims to find *Eugnostos* not as pre- or non-Christian, but only to be understood in connection with Valentinianism.[32] We shall therefore have to consider the origin and centrality of the figure of Primal Man/Anthropos in our analysis.

But in any case, whatever the truth about the origin of the speculation about 'Man', it would seem that the most common, if not universal anthropological and soteriological theme, which recurs in all the Gnostic texts presently available, is our third: the idea of the consubstantiality of Redeemer and redeemed, of a divine spark, spirit, intelligence or seed (even sometimes 'inner man') present in humanity, or rather the elect. This motif expresses the basic anthropological dualism of Gnostic theology to which Jonas, Schottroff and Rudolph have drawn attention;[33] of the Gnostic 'self' or 'I' (however that may be expressed) over against the soul (or psychic element) and body (or however the hostile element in humanity is understood).[34]

As will become clear from an analysis of Gnostic anthropology, the theme of the divine spark or Gnostic 'self' can and does embrace the motifs of heavenly Primal Man somehow present in earthly man, of heavenly Anthropos and humanity made in his image, and of the three races, types and substances. How far the spiritual element or substance is a natural endowment which ensures salvation 'by nature', which Bultmann would see as the essence of Gnostic soteriology;[35] or a means of expressing the certainty of divine grace, a consequence of revelation, as Quispel has argued;[36] or simply a way of expressing the fact that the Gnostic is saved by grace but that salvation is not an assured possession, as Schottroff insists,[37] will have to await the next chapter. But in the meantime one cannot fail to be struck by how closely the three respective interpretations express the paradox of Gnostic anthropology and soteriology mirrored in the three inconsistent theories in Irenaeus' account of Saturninus (a divine spark in all; a lifelong *possession* of believers; only a *gift* to believers).

Now since Irenaeus' summary of the Gnostic myth in 1.29 concludes with the boast of the Demiurge marking the end of the cosmogony but with no explicit anthropology or soteriology, we cannot proceed from now on exactly as before. However, because the 'Ophite' version of the Gnostic myth in the following chapter in Irenaeus is evidently related to that of the *Apocryphon*, and was bracketed by Irenaeus with the Barbelognostic system as a source of Valentinianism, we can use it with the *Apocryphon* to supply our basic framework.[38] What is more, since our main thesis is that in chapter 29 Irenaeus only excerpted the first part of what was a complete myth, we will also be looking for possible surviving traces of that myth by comparing the present form of the *Apocryphon* with related texts, particularly the *Hypostasis of the Archons*. Indeed, it is our thesis that the *Apocryphon* has combined elements from both the Barbelognostic and 'Ophite' systems, probably when it was also being influenced by Valentinian ideas (i.e. redaction (a^2)) and before it underwent its Sethianization process (i.e. redaction (a^3)).

1 The initial anthropogonical impulse: Ialdabaoth's arrogant boast and the response from heaven

N. A. Dahl claims to detect a pattern of vain claim by a Demiurge or similar figure and heavenly response in the setting of the Genesis creation story in a special group of texts (*HA, OW, AJ, GE*, Iren. 1.29 and 30).[39] Its complete but non-existent form included ten items ((1) setting, (2) introduction, (3) vain claim, (4) comment, (5) rebuke, (6) disclosure, (7) challenge, (8) appearance of image (cf. Gen 1:2b and 3), (9) proposal to create man (Gen 1:26), (10) formation of man (Gen 1:27 and 2:7)). He notes that only *On the Origin of the World* has all the elements, but interspersed with others, while in the *Hypostasis* and the long recension of the *Apocryphon* some of them recur several times.[40] And he rightly points to the fact that the last three items are directly related to the creation story in Genesis 1–2, and that the focus of interest is the creation of humanity, not of the world.[41]

The pattern Dahl has identified is undoubtedly there, but his own comments about its incompleteness, repetitions and central focus on the creation of humankind might suggest that in the most complete form (*OW*) we have a combination of two originally distinct versions of the heavenly image-reflection motif, the one cosmogonic (Gen 1:2b and 3; i.e. items 3–8) the other (and more original form?) anthropogonic (Gen 1:26f. and 2:7; i.e. items 3–5, 8–10). More detailed analysis of the pattern and its elements is therefore required.

The motif of the hubris and vain claim of the Demiurge clothed in the language of the God of the Old Testament (Isa 45:5f.; 46:9) recurs frequently in very varied forms in the heresiologists' accounts and in the Gnostic texts from Nag Hammadi, as Dahl has demonstrated.[42] Thus while virtually all the texts attest the allusion to Isaiah: 'there is no other [god] beside me', only four begin with Ialdabaoth calling himself a jealous god in allusion to Exod 20:5 (*AJ, GE, Treat. Seth* and Iren. 1.29).[43] Yet despite the differences, a number of texts agree in having Ialdabaoth's claim immediately followed by a voice from heaven in rebuke, generally associated with Sophia, indicating his error and in several cases affirming the existence of a superior heavenly being or beings, Man and the Son of Man (e.g. Iren. 1.30, *HA, OW, GE*).

But although the *Apocryphon* does contain the motif of the heavenly voice affirming the existence of Man and Son of Man,[44] this is separated from the claim of Ialdabaoth by the passage concerning the repentance and partial restoration of the Mother. Furthermore she is not the author of the rebuke as in Irenaeus 1.30 and *On the Origin of the World*: it comes to her and Ialdabaoth also hears it (despite being in a lower realm!) and thinks that it came from his mother.[45] In the light of the evidence already adduced to suggest the secondary nature of the passage between Ialdabaoth's claim and the heavenly rebuke, our hypothesis that the *Apocryphon* has changed the order of events at this point and destroyed the original unity of claim and reply, partly to adapt better to the Genesis reinterpretation, would appear to receive further confirmation. That the voice should come *to* Sophia is, as Schottroff has convincingly demonstrated, explicable in terms of the *Apocryphon*'s consistent reinterpretation of her to remove all trace of the idea that she was a redeemer.[46] That Ialdabaoth thinks that the voice came from his mother not only suggests his ignorance but also that the voice was female, and that in the original it did indeed come from her.[47]

The formula 'Man exists and the Son of Man' occurs in two of the three texts which unite the two titles, the *Apocryphon* and the *Gospel of the Egyptians*, spoken anonymously and in almost identical wording in the five documents involved.[48] The 'Ophite' version is rather more circuitous: it has Sophia cry out: 'Do not lie,

Ialdabaoth, for above you there is the Father of All, the First Man (*primus Anthropus/prōtos Anthrōpos*) and Man the Son of Man (*Anthropus filius Anthropi/huios anthrōpou*).'[49] Conversely the parallel passage in *On the Origin of the World* has Pistis as the speaker refer to Man only: 'You are in error, Samael . . . an immortal light Man exists before you!'[50]

The question inevitably arises as to which is primary. F. H. Borsch, while allowing some arguments for the priority of the *On the Origin of the World* version (its brevity, the existence of comparative material about Man in e.g. *Poimandres*, the addition of the Son of Man through Christian influence), prefers the opposite supposition, in view of the preponderance of versions with the Son of Man, and the earlier date of Irenaeus' account.[51] He suggests Irenaeus' peculiar version may be the result either of his attempt to combine two variants of the heavenly retort or his use of a version which had interpolated a reference to the Son of Man, or alternatively of his conscious or unconscious attempt to interpret the statement he found by identifying the Son of man, Jesus, with the Man.[52] His final suggestion is that Irenaeus may have preserved a more Semitic understanding whereby the Son of Man is taken as a counterpart or appositional way of speaking about the Man and not a distinct entity.[53]

Despite their value, however, these suggestions do not supply an explanation of the two basic versions of the retort, with or without the Son of Man, in terms of the texts themselves. We have to ask (*a*) what is the significance of the rebuke in its context; (*b*) who the figure or figures are and what part they play in the rest of the system; and (*c*) what the background is to the figures of Man and Son of Man in Gnostic theology as revealed by these and other texts which deal with them.

As regards (*a*) we should note that in all but the 'Ophite' version the blasphemy of the Demiurge and the heavenly rebuke are immediately followed by the appearance of a heavenly being, whose image is almost invariably reflected in the waters below, and that this initiates the creation of earthly man in accordance with the heavenly image.[54] However, the 'Ophite' version prefers the idea of a mental image of man supplied to the archons by Sophia when they respond to Ialdabaoth's exhortation 'Let us make man in our image!'[55] Valentinus too, perhaps influenced by this, seems to have envisaged the angelic creators not having seen a heavenly image but fashioning Adam in the name of heavenly pre-existent Anthropos.[56]

As regards (*b*), the figure of heavenly Man is both prominent and easily recognizable in the last two systems mentioned: in Irenaeus 1.30 Man is the supreme Father, while in Valentinus and the Valentinians Man is either one of the original Ogdoad or even, according to some, the highest deity, deduced from the fact that Christ is called 'Son of Man'.[57] Thus the versions in Irenaeus 1.30 and Valentinus which do not employ the motif of the heavenly image could be interpreted as secondary attempts to avoid the implication that the supreme being could possibly be seen by the angelic creators.

In *On the Origin of the World* too, the figure of the heavenly immortal man of light is equally visible, and is hinted at in the *Hypostasis*.[58] Again Son of Man in Irenaeus 1.30 is plainly Ennoia, Second Man, offspring of First Man, although Christ, the son of First and Second Man, can also be called 'Son of Man'![59] But who exactly is Man and, more to the point, Son of Man in the *Apocryphon*? Janssens argues that Man here is clearly the First Man, the manifestation of Pronoia and consort of Sophia,[60] the image of Barbelo, the virginal spirit, the threefold male, androgynous,[61] and that his son is the Autogenes or Monogenes who is also the Saviour.[62] Giversen also identifies Man with Barbelo or Pronoia on the basis of the occurrences of the term *Mētropatōr* in II,[63] and his son with Christ who, as he notes, is called the son of Metropator.[64] But none of these candidates, Barbelo, Sophia's consort and Christ, are immediately recognizable as Man and Son of Man or as appropriate as the first two figures of Irenaeus' 'Ophites'.

Moreover, what are we to make of the figure of Adamas, described by the *Apocryphon* as 'the perfect, true Man, the first manifestation'?[65] How is he related to the First Man we have been discussing? Full clarification of this situation will have to await our treatment of the motif of Adam made in the divine image, but it is worth recalling once more the apparent secondary character of the references to the First Man in the *Apocryphon*: Barbelo becomes First Man, or the bisexual pentad of female aeons is First Man.[66] And while the *Gospel of the Egyptians* seems uncomplicated in its derivation of Adamas from the First Man,[67] it does not imply that Adamas is his son, the Son of Man of the heavenly rebuke, nor does it appear to identify Barbelo and Christ with Man and the Son of Man as the *Apocryphon* evidently does.

What we would seem to have here is, as we argued in our suggested reconstruction of the development of the myth in redaction (a²), the combination of two originally separate themes and motifs: that of Man and Son of Man associated with the 'Ophite' system of Irenaeus 1.30, in which Sophia rebuts the arrogant Demiurge Ialdabaoth's boast by referring to the supreme figures of the system, but no heavenly image appears; and that of the original Barbelognostic myth where in response to the Protarchon's claim Sophia rebukes him and appears in the guise of the heavenly Man Adamas. We shall develop this when we come to examine the image motif.

But in the meantime some support for this hypothesis may come from (c), our examination of the background of Man and Son of Man (and Adamas) in the Gnostic texts and systems where they occur. Pétrement has devoted a chapter of her book to the theme of the God 'Man', and given a persuasive critique of Schenke's thesis that the Gnostics deduced from (a) the consubstantiality of humanity and the divine related to (b) Gen 1:26f., its creation 'in the image of God', that the supreme God was called 'Man'.[68] She rejects Schenke's consubstantiality thesis as not confirmed by the evidence and points out that 'Son of Man' is best explained in terms of the Christian title of Christ in the Gospels: if he is called Son of man it is because God the Father ought to be called Man.[69] And she points out that there is no proof that the name Man was given to God before the Saviour was called Son of Man; that the earliest Gnostics according to the heresiologists do not speculate on Man; and that those who do almost invariably link together Man and Son of Man.[70] She cites the 'Ophites' of Irenaeus, certain Valentinians (Iren. 1.12.4), the Naassenes and Monoimus of Hippolytus, the *Apocryphon, Sophia of Jesus Christ* and *Eugnostos,* the *Gospel of the Egyptians* and the *Gospel of Philip.*[71]

But if all these have the association of Man and Son of Man, reference to Adamas is only found in the Naassenes, the *Apocryphon,* the *Sophia* and *Eugnostos* and the *Gospel of the Egyptians,* and, what is more, in the last three in the stereotyped form 'Adam the eye of the light'.[72] Moreover Adam is found in the same kind of context and in association with light in such related works as *On the Origin of the World,*[73] the *Three Steles of Seth,*[74] and *Melchisedek.*[75] All this, as well as other shared elements such as signs of Valentinian influence,[76] and the Sethian character of several of the texts which promote Adamas up the hierarchy as son of Barbelo or descendant of First Man and father of Seth,[77] suggest the existence and development of a cluster of mythologoumena involving Man, Son of Man and Adamas.

Now if we take as a possible key to the present state of the texts and their complicated mythologoumena the combination of two originally distinct motifs, one of Man and Son of Man, the other of heavenly Adamas, we can make sense of and fruitfully link together a whole series of texts and systems in which these figures occur. Thus systems which appear to have Man and Son of Man only as the supreme heavenly figures include the 'Ophites' of Irenaeus and Monoimus of Hippolytus. The former we have argued is fundamentally Christian, attempting to develop a form of Trinity in which Christ is the offspring of Man and bisexual Son of Man's union with the Holy Spirit, who ascends to join it and form the heavenly Church. Monoimus' system is very hard to interpret, but its presentation of Man as the unoriginate eternal monad comprising all opposites and his son as originate and susceptible to suffering, yet generated without time, will or forethought and responsible for creation, being the image of his father and wrongly thought to have been born of a woman,[78] does suggest similarity to Christian ideas, particularly those of Hebrews.[79] It also contains numerous parallels to the Naassene system, which we will be dealing with shortly.[80]

Speculations on Man and Son of Man also occur among the Valentinians, perhaps partly under the influence of the 'Ophite' myth, as Irenaeus suggests. Thus, as we have noted, he refers to certain Valentinians as teaching that the Forefather of all things was called 'Man' and that this was why the Saviour designated himself 'Son of Man'.[81] And the figures of Man and Son of Man who is the Lord also occur in the *Gospel of Philip*. Thus in a passage dealing with the way each species produces its own kind we hear how the elect, the children of the bridal chamber, are called 'the chosen people of [the Father of the All?] and the true Man and the Son of Man and the seed of the Son of Man'.[82] The last designation would appear to refer to the Gnostics. This seems to be echoed elsewhere where there is mention of the Son of Man and the son of the Son of Man. The Lord is the Son of Man (who has power both to create and beget) and the son of the Son of Man is created through him.[83] The Lord is evidently Christ, the Son of Man with creative power from God, and the son of the Son of Man is the Gnostic believer created by him.[84] Finally there is reference to the coming of the Son of Man in the context of dyeing, which may be a reference to baptism.[85]

What is striking in all these cases is both the way the figure and activity of the Son of Man recall Christ in his creative and saving roles, and the way no allusion is made to heavenly Adamas in relation to Man, who is either the supreme or next to supreme being. Valentinus does refer to *earthly* Adam in relation to heavenly Man, but significantly he has him made in the name of pre-existing Man, i.e. Anthropos *not* Adamas, which implies that for him at least the two motifs have not yet been combined and that he is only aware of the theme of Man (and Son of Man?).[86] Interestingly, too, he combines the motif of the seed with the idea of the presence of Man in Adam.

Adamas, on the other hand, does appear in the Barbelognostic system summarized by Irenaeus, as the perfect, true man, long after the generation of Christ, the Only Begotten Son, and with a female consort and offspring.[87] And to him there evidently corresponds the heavenly light-Adam(as) of *On the Origin of the World*, who is first referred to obliquely by Pistis in her rebuke of Ialdabaoth's vain claim,[88] then appears in a light in further response to another demiurgic retort as the angelic light-Adam/Adamas.[89] Now unlike the Barbelognostic figure he is not given a partner and may even be androgynous, as are the creatures such as Eros for whom he is responsible,[90] but he is the archetype for the creation of Adam, which suggests his role in the continuation of the Barbelognostic myth, and Pistis hints that it is he who will appear in human bodies to confront and confound Ialdabaoth and his archons.[91] In both these texts and systems there does not seem to be a place for the couple Man and Son of Man of Sophia's rebuke. Conversely, both seem to represent developments of the motif in Irenaeus' sketch of Saturninus' system.[92]

Now if we recall the secondary character of the figure of Man in the *Apocryphon*, identified with Barbelo, and Son of Man with Christ, in contrast to the obvious primary character of Adamas, the perfect true man and first manifestation, as receptacle of light-power and archetype of earthly Adam, this would suggest an early if not the earliest attempt to combine the two motifs, the 'Man and Son of Man' of Sophia's rebuke along with Ialdabaoth and his six sons from the 'Ophite' system of Irenaeus 1.30, and the Adamas motif of the Barbelognostics of 1.29, to form our redaction (a^2) with its Valentinian colouring. *Norea*, despite its allusive character, may preserve evidence of this fluid stage: it makes no mention of Man and Son of Man or of Ialdabaoth, uses Valentinian themes like 'Pleroma' and 'deficiency', and has Adamas as Father of the All and present in all the Adams.[93] Certainly the Naassene Preaching, whatever the precise genesis of that complex document, clearly combines the two themes and also echoes Valentinian ideas, presenting bisexual Adamas as Man and Son of Man, composed of three elements (intellectual/psychic/hylic), archetype of earthly Adam and source of the 'inner man' (also Adamas) who descends into human bodies.[94] Hippolytus' presentation of Man and Son of Man as a single supreme figure may represent a very excusable misunderstanding on his part.[95]

And it is perhaps in this line of development we can best place that most enigmatic and much contested document, *Eugnostos*. It presents a hierarchy of Forefather or Father of the All, immortal First Man, Son of Man and Saviour, the last three bisexual each with a female counterpart called Sophia. Now not only does the pattern recall that of the 'Ophites' of Irenaeus and the formula quoted above from the *Gospel of Philip*,[96] and First Man's designation 'Adam [the eye] of the light'[97] suggest the combination of the two themes perhaps initiated by the *Apocryphon*, but the striking parallels in the work to the Valentinian doctrinal letter preserved by Epiphanius are best interpreted, as Scholten has argued, as evidence that the author has constructed his system on a predominantly Valentinian background.[98]

Further, in the peculiar designation, 'Adam, the eye of the light', may lie the key to the connection we have hypothesized between these texts. For it also occurs in a passage in the *Gospel of the Egyptians* which appears to be aware, if clumsily, of a distinction between Adamas as 'the eye of the light' and the First Man, the Light, a figure who only occurs here and appears to be the supreme being.[99] Not only therefore does this text supply further support for our hypothesis that the *Apocryphon* has combined two originally distinct motifs, but it offers a clue to the designation 'eye of the light'. This enigmatic expression surely only makes sense if the Adamas who reveals himself to the creator archons of our hypothesized original Barbelognostic myth is understood as the vehicle for the revelation of the supreme Light–Man of the 'Ophite' system. The absence of a supreme light figure in *Eugnostos* as referent of the designation and its application to First Man, on the one hand, and the virtual absence of First Man in the *Gospel of the Egyptians* suggest that both are attempting to fit the existing combined motif and peculiar designation of Adamas into their own systems.[1]

Such a hypothesized combination also helps to answer the questions about which form of the heavenly rebuke is more original and about the origin of the figures of Man and Son of Man. If we assume that the heavenly rebuke was originally anthropogonic and associated with the Man and Son of Man scheme, then the cosmogonic versions, such as in the *Hypostasis*[2] are in all likelihood later variants, and the version involving immortal light-Man/Adam, which *On the Origin of the World* expands into several episodes, is evidently dependent on the combined motif as found in the *Apocryphon*.[3] Further, since *Eugnostos* (and the *Sophia* which is dependent on it) equally implies the existence of the combined motif, reflects 'Ophite' and Valentinian speculations about Man and displays other parallels with Valentinianism, it seems that the earliest speculations about Man and Son of Man are to be associated with the 'Ophites' and Valentinians.

We have already argued for the Christian character of the 'Ophite' system and its attempt to present a kind of Trinity, with Christ begotten of the Father, Son and Holy Spirit as a fourth (also Son of Man?) and elevated with the Holy Spirit to form the heavenly Church. He is clearly the central figure in revelation and salvation, along with First Man, and he ultimately descends to be united with his sister Sophia, who is the vehicle of interim salvation of the divine and of the revelation of First Man and Christ via the prophets in a continuing struggle with Ialdabaoth, at whose right hand Christ sits until he rescues all the souls akin to him. The figure of the Second Man, the Son of Man, an emanation of the Father, seems largely redundant. Now what this picture recalls is not the later Christianization of Schenke's God – 'Man' myth developed on the basis of allegorization of Gen 1:26f., or van den Broek's hypothetical Platonized Jewish Anthropos–Sophia myth as underlying *Eugnostos*, but Christian speculations based on the very Wisdom and Psalms texts the early communities used to construct their theology and Christology, on the foundation of the four Gospels and Paul. The clearest example is of course Hebrews, to which we have drawn frequent attention.

Thus if we consider the role of the Son of God in Hebrews 1–2, and in particular the interpretation of Ps 8:5–7 in Heb 2:5–10, we find the Father (variously attested by the Old Testament prophets) giving his final self-revelation through his son and heir (1:1–2, cf. Ps 2:7f.; 2 Sam 7:14), by whom he created the ages (aeons!). This son, moreover, is the express image (*charaktēr*) of his being (1:3, cf. Wis 7:25f.); superior to and worshipped by angels as begotten by him (1:4–6, cf. Ps 97:7); depicted as eternally enthroned, righteous and therefore anointed by God (1:8f., cf. Ps 45:6–7); the original and eternal creator (1:10–12, cf. Ps 102:25–27); elevated to God's right hand with his enemies under his feet (1:13, cf. Ps 110:1).

Even more striking, however, is the identification of this son as man and son of man, subordinated for a while to the angels, but glorified, having everything under his feet (2:5–8, cf. Ps 8:5–7 LXX). Further, the continuation could be read as implying a distinction between the heavenly Son and Jesus who is later rewarded for his sufferings, as in the 'Ophite' system.[4] And it is surely significant that the latter does not include among the prophets chosen as mouthpieces of Ialdabaoth and his archons David (author of the Psalms) and Solomon (author of Proverbs and Wisdom):[5] what the prophets truly proclaim about God (i.e. First Man) and Christ they unwittingly derive from Sophia.[6]

Again, the fleeting Valentinian references to Man and Son of Man also fit into this Christian framework: if they do not have the motif of the heavenly rebuke, they do present the vain claim of the Demiurge,[7] seem to interpret the figure of Man as the supreme deity in the light of Christ's title 'Son of Man', evidently no longer understood in its New Testament sense,[8] and represent Christ as Son of Man with creative powers.[9] And it is this picture of Man as supreme or next to supreme being associated with the Son of Man who has creative and redemptive roles as a couple or sometimes a single figure, frequently combined with Adamas in an anthropogonic context, or distinct from him in an eschatological context, which permeates the texts which refer to Man and Son of Man.[10]

Finally, the eschatological motif of the heavenly true Man and his elect trampling on the Demiurge and his powers at the final consummation, which occurs in several texts, once again recalls Hebrews 1 and its redoubled mention of the Son's enemies being put under his feet (1:13 quoting Ps 110:1 and 1:8 quoting Ps 8:7),[11] and the paradigmatic character of Ps 8:5–7 in its Hebrews 1–2 context for the whole theme of Man/Son of Man as creator/ redeemer, might suggest that here we have a – or the – basis for the Gnostic mythologoumenon of the Demiurge's vain claim to his angels and the heavenly rebuke 'Man exists and the Son of Man'.

Thus I would argue that both the heavenly true man Adamas of the original Barbelognostic myth and Man and Son of Man of the 'Ophite' version originate in Christian Gnostic systems; appeal to pagan Anthropos figures or myths or to Philo's celestial Man and double creation account and Jewish Adam legends do not really account for them, whatever contribution such sources may have made to their subsequent development and colouring.[12] Adamas represents the characteristic Gnostic back projection of the Adam figure as heavenly archetype for the earthly version, the protological counterpart of Christ, the Pauline second or eschatological Adam, the true perfect man, while Man and Son of Man derive from Gnostic speculations based on the figure of Christ and his title in the Gospels and on the sources used by early Christians (the Psalms in particular) to construct their distinctive theology and Christology.

2 The appearance of the heavenly image and its consequences

Once again the best way to structure our discussion of this part of the myth is by reference to Irenaeus' sketch of the views of Saturninus. In it we can discern three main motifs: (1) the appearance of the luminous heavenly image; (2) the reaction of the angels; and (3) their creation of man in the divine image but as a wriggling Golem.

As regards the first motif, the luminous heavenly image, whereas its identity is unclear in Irenaeus' sketch of Saturninus – one might deduce from the fact that the heavenly being later takes pity on the inanimate man because of his having been made in its likeness that it is male, but the passage equally recalls the theme of the seduction of the archons by a female figure as in e.g. the allied *Hypostasis*[13] – in the case of the short recension of the *Apocryphon* the figure who appears is the Father, the First Man in the form of a man. He reveals his likeness to the seven powers who bend down and see the form (*typos*) of the image (*eikōn*) in the water and say to one another: 'Let us make a man in the image (*eikōn*) of God and in his likeness' (cf. Gen 1:26).[14] The long recension considerably expands this. It has the holy Mother–Father (*mētropatōr*), the perfect Pronoia, the image (*eikōn*) of the invisible, the Father of the All through whom everything came into being (cf. John 1:3), the First Man, instruct them that it was in a man-like (*andreas*) form (*typos*) that he (First Man?) revealed his likeness.[15]

This evidently represents an attempt by the redactor of LR to make it clear that it is Barbelo, the first emanation and self-reflection of the totally transcendent Father who is the subject, and not the Father, as SR appears to suggest: it is she who appears in a masculine form. And the continuation in LR, which records the usual accompaniments to a theophany: trembling of the archon's aeon, shaking of the foundations of the abyss, illumination of the underside of the waters above matter through the appearance of the image (*eikōn*) which enables the archon and his henchmen to see it in the water,[16] is a further attempt by the redactor to increase the distance between the Demiurge and the heavenly world and emphasize the sublime and spiritual character of the latter.[17] As we shall see, LR may be more original than SR in making Barbelo the subject, but the evident awkwardness of both versions would further confirm our hypothesis that the original Barbelognostic myth lacked the supreme Man figure and had Adamas, the first true Man (or Sophia disguised as him), and not the Father or Barbelo, appear to the Protarchon and his powers at this point.

Indeed that Adamas, the light-Man, *was* the original subject of the theophany is implied by LR through its repeated association of the man-like image with light,[18] a point which SR only suggests later when it has the archons exclaim: 'Let us call him [their creation] Adam, that his name and power may become a light for us.'[19] Now this only makes sense on the basis of a combination of two distinct motifs; (1) the Greek wordplay on *phōs* (= man/light) and (2) the identification of heavenly Man as Adam(as). The first of these is found in the 'Ophites' of Irenaeus 1.30,[20] the second in his Barbelognostics![21]

But what of the similar motifs in the *Hypostasis* and *On the Origin of the World*, which not only have a female figure appear in response to Ialdabaoth's vain claim,[22] but also present the light being called forth by Ialdabaoth's taunt entirely independently of the revelation of a heavenly figure in whose image earthly Adam is fashioned,[23] or distinguish the image from the light?[24] The appearance of a female figure certainly recalls Irenaeus' sketch of Saturninus and the motif of the seduction of the archons, while the motif of light reflected in the dark waters of chaos suggests a Gnostic interpretation of Gen 1:2 LXX. Whereas the former appears primarily anthropogonic (certainly in Saturninus' version), the latter is plainly cosmogonic. But which came first?

In his analysis of the motif in *Poimandres* of the reflection of the image of heavenly Man/Anthropos in the waters of chaos and the desire produced in Nature to unite with it,[25] Jonas claims to detect three different ideas adroitly combined which are germane to this issue. They are (1) that of Darkness becoming enamoured of Light and getting possession of it; (2) that of Light becoming enamoured of Darkness and voluntarily sinking into it; and (3) that of a radiation, reflection or image of the Light projected into the Darkness below and there held fast. Version (1) he finds in Manichaeism, (2) in a quotation from Macrobius,[26] and (3) in the Sethians and Peratae of Hippolytus, the Gnostics of Plotinus and the 'barbarian' system recorded by Basilides according to Hegemonius.[27] But only the third is really relevant here, allowing the presence of light in some form in the midst of darkness without having to admit a genuine fall. It can be projected as a ray,[28] or if issuing from a divine figure like Sophia or Man can appear as an image of the divine in the dark medium.[29] Jonas' analysis thus suggests why the motif can be used both cosmogonically and anthropogonically.

But his examples are late and the priority of the anthropogonic version of the motif in the texts relevant to us is suggested not only by the consistent version of the Demiurgic vain claim: 'There is no other [god] apart from me!' which demands the appearance of a pre-existent divine being to refute him, but also by the early and primitive character of Saturninus' system and the way the other versions of the motif of the heavenly voice, image and response seem to be dependent variants of the anthropogonic one.[30]

As regards our second element, the reaction of the archons to the appearance of the heavenly image, SR has the archons say to one another: 'Let us make a man in the image (*eikōn*) of God and in the' (B) or 'his (III) likeness',[31] whereas LR has Ialdabaoth say to the powers beside him: 'Come let us make a man in the image (*eikōn*) of God and in our likeness, that his image (*eikōn*) be for us a light'.[32] Clearly this is an allusion to Gen 1:26 which gives a satisfactory answer in Gnostic terms to the awkward plural of the text – the archons are responsible – and supplies the appropriate scriptural grounding to their view that earthly man is made in the (external) likeness of a divine being, heavenly Man. However, the interpretation of both has to adjust the original (i.e. the LXX version), for SR ignores the 'our', preferring the 'in the image of God' of v. 27, and thus interprets the archontic action, for which it supplies no immediate motive,[33] as simply copying the divine image, while LR ascribes the address to Ialdabaoth,[34] supplies a motive (getting control of the source of light), and distinguishes between image and likeness (*eine* = *homoiōsis*).[35] Earthly man is made (externally) in the likeness of God, but also (internally) in the image of the archons. However the archontic response in both versions presupposes the figure of Adamas in association with light as the archetype, and suggests the motive of the creation of Adam as to gain control of the power of light.

That externally the archontic creation looks like its heavenly original while in essence it belongs to its creators is understood in the *Hypostasis* and *On the Origin of the World* in terms of the Narcissus motif: the archons hope that the heavenly archetype will fall in love with the earthly copy and thereby be captured[36] or neutralized.[37] This not only depicts Ialdabaoth and his archons as essentially negative, demonic figures, but it implies, as the texts later confirm, that the divine element or Man is not yet present in the earthly copy. In an obvious attempt to counterbalance this demonized view of the Creator, both texts proceed to stress the divine initiative and overall plan in all this, and separate the later descent or inbreathing of the divine from any Demiurgic contribution as suggested by Gen 2:7.[38] In contrast the *Apocryphon* gives a much more positive interpretation of the image–reflection motif and the role of the Demiurge, in that the former is interpreted not in terms of capture or neutralization but of illumination, and the Demiurge is the vehicle of the divine light-power which he withholds from his offspring.[39] They alone are responsible for creating earthly (or psychic) man, who, although made in the image of heavenly Man, remains an immobile Golem until Ialdabaoth is prevailed on to inbreathe something of his light-power.[40]

Here we have a two-stage process of the formation and animation of Adam, evidently echoing Gen 1:26 in combination with 2:7, but based on the Barbelognostic myth and not constructed directly from speculations on Gen 1:26f. as Schenke has argued. However, the two texts do function as paradigms for Gnostic anthropology and anthropogony, and we shall have to explore further what role they play and how they are interpreted. Clearly what distinguishes the *Apocryphon*'s treatment of the two texts from that of the *Hypostasis* and *On the Origin of the World* is the different evaluation of Ialdabaoth, but which is more original? Again, comparison with Irenaeus' account of Saturninus may help decide this.

Now in this account, the most basic presentation of the image–reflection motif, neither the theme of light-Adamas reflected in the waters below nor the motive of gaining control of light by creating earthly Adam in the image and with the name of his heavenly archetype is explicit, nor is there any obvious allusion to Gen 2:7. It has Adam created by seven angels 'after the image (*eikōn*) and after the likeness (*homoiōsis*)' (of the heavenly light-image, i.e. no distinction between archontic image and divine likeness) as a result of their inability to detain the heavenly image. The result, whether willed or not by the angels, is the descent of a spark of life from the heavenly power to elevate the wriggling Golem and give it limbs, because of its similarity.[41]

This account is paralleled more or less closely by Pseudo-Tertullian, Filaster, Epiphanius and Theodoret,[42] but Filaster and Epiphanius, unlike the others, supply desire as a motive, perhaps conscious of the seduction of the archons motif, Epiphanius not unexpectedly bringing out the sexual element.[43] But the sketch remains incomplete: there is no attempt to explain why the light appeared, no explicit identification of the image (is it perhaps bisexual Anthropos?) linking it with cosmogony as in the *Apocryphon* and *Hypostasis*, no trace of Ialdabaoth and no adequate explanation of the angelic motivation apart from the later hint in Filaster and Epiphanius. Finally there is a version of the Golem motif with no obvious allusion to Gen 2:7: the heavenly power sends down a spark of life out of pity.[44]

Now while the *Hypostasis* represents one of the closest parallels to Saturninus' scheme, it presupposes, as we have seen, the developed Barbelognostic myth of the *Apocryphon* while pursuing its own concern, the origin and nature of the archons, which often leads to an exegesis of Genesis 1–2 closer to the original text. More explicitly than Saturninus' system it presents the motif of the seduction of the archons: a female heavenly figure looks down to the lower watery regions causing her image (*eine*) to appear in them. The powers of darkness fall in love with it but cannot reach it because of their weakness.[45] The text immediately stresses the divine initiative: it is part of the plan of the supreme Father to unite the All with the light.[46] The (seven?) archons hold a council and say 'Come let us make a man of dust (*chous*) from the earth'.[47] That this represents a combination of Gen 1:26 and 2:7 is confirmed by the continuation: man is formed (*plassein*) from dust according to the body (*sōma*) of the archons and [according to the likeness?] of God which appeared [to them] in the waters. Their motive is then made explicit: to trap the heavenly image in their moulded form (*plasma*), the co-image, which is thus to act as a visual lure.[48]

The secondary character of this is evident in such features as the glosses (female heavenly figure glossed as masculine pneumatic; archons glossed as bisexual to reconcile female archetype and male copy), the uneasy combination of Gen 1:26 and 2:7 which implies awareness of the Barbelognostic motif of Adam's creation in the likeness of heavenly Adamas, and the insistence on the priority of the divine initiative. The peculiar interest of the *Hypostasis* is evident in the way Gen 2:7 is further reinterpreted: the Demiurge breathes into the man's face so that he becomes psychic, but a Golem whom the powers cannot raise because of their weakness, even as, despite their persistence, they cannot trap the image which had appeared to them because of their ignorance of its power.[49] And it is only after the Spirit sees the psychic man on the earth, comes forth from the adamantine (*adamantinos*) earth, descends and settles in him that man becomes a living soul (*psychē*, cf. Gen 2:7) and is named Adam since he was found moving on the ground.[50]

This version of Adam's creation and animation in three stages (moulded as choic by the archons in their (bisexual) image and in the likeness of the divine being who appeared to them, inbreathed as psychic by Ialdabaoth/Saklas, animated as pneumatic by the Spirit from above) represents an obvious conflation of elements from Gen 1:26f. and 2:7 in addition to the image–reflection motif, which suggests further influence from Genesis 1 (reflection in the waters of chaos). Gen 2:7 is employed not only to suggest humanity's original incomplete choic stage but also a second psychic stage through the inbreathing of the Demiurge.[51] But this stage is really irrelevant; the psychic element he contributes makes no appreciable difference. The real animating element is the spirit sent down from heaven as a gift. What is new and awkward in comparison with Saturninus is precisely the introduction of Gen 2:7 into the motif with its reference to the choic element and the inbreathing Creator. Although the effect is to create a three-fold cosmological and anthropological scheme which suggests Valentinian influence,[52] the more obvious source of the use of Gen 2:7 in connection with 1:26 is the *Apocryphon*, particularly its (a²) redaction combining 'Ophite' and Valentinian ideas. The same goes for *On the Origin of the World*.[53] Even though both texts seem at times closer to Saturninus' scheme than the *Apocryphon* does, overall they suggest an ultimate awareness of and dependence on the latter.[54]

3 The multiple creations of Adam

Although the series of divine moves and archontic countermoves in the creation and animation of Adam, as presented by the *Apocryphon* and related texts, properly belongs to soteriology,[55] the variety of creations has a strong claim to be treated in the context of anthropology. We shall look briefly therefore at the way the creation of Adam is presented, first in terms of his formation by seven powers,[56] then of his arrangement by 360 (or 365) angels but as a Golem unable to move,[57] and finally of his being trapped in a material body composed of the four elements, earth, water, fire and air.[58]

On the first point, man's creation by the seven powers, unlike the author of the *Hypostasis* and certain Valentinians who in accordance with Gen 2:7 have the archons create him from dust as choic,[59] the *Apocryphon* presents this first creation as psychic. According to SR each power (the archons appear to be the subject)[60] creates a soul from his own power after the divine image in imitation of the first perfect man.[61] LR speaks instead of the powers creating by means of each other's powers in accordance with the signs given them, each power supplying a characteristic according to the form (*typos*) of the image (*eikōn*) he had seen in its (or from his) psychic (form? nature?).[62] And LR adds that each created a hypostasis after the likeness of the first perfect man.[63] This latter version looks like yet another attempt by the redactor of LR to separate the Demiurge and his henchmen and their creative activity from the supreme divine world: they do not see even the original image, the first man, merely the form (*typos*) reflected in the waters which, as Tardieu suggests, they interpret in terms of the only form they know, their own.[64]

Then follows the archontic naming of Adam, which, as we noted above, implies that the original image they saw was indeed heavenly light-Adamas. Here the LR version ('Let us call him Adam so that his name may be a power of light for us')[65] is evidently preferable to SR which associates power with the name.[66]

The powers begin the process, but while all four texts are in almost total agreement about the psychic substances created, respectively bone, sinew, flesh, marrow, blood, skin and hair,[67] the two recensions differ in their list of the powers, LR reproducing its earlier order (goodness, providence, divinity, lordship, kingship, zeal, understanding (*m̄ntrm̄n̄hēt*)),[68] SR presenting its earlier order with the first-mentioned power in fourth position (divinity, lordship, zeal, providence, kingship, understanding, wisdom (*sophia*)).[69] As we have already argued,[70] the list of psychic substances ought to begin with the marrow, as SR seems to be aware by its change of order in the case of providence. Certainly the version preserved in Theodore bar Konai and attributed to the fourth-century Audians appears closer to SR.[71] Similarly *On the Origin of the World* has the seven archons form man in their image but in the likeness of light-Adam. Each was responsible for a part of his moulded body (*plasma*, cf. Gen 2:7), their chief (i.e. Ialdabaoth) creating the head and marrow.[72] Man thus formed is described as becoming psychic (*psychikos*),[73] although the text stoutly denies that he yet has a soul.[74] He is a lifeless Golem, first animated by Sophia Zoe's inbreathing.[75]

Here, as with the similar picture in the *Hypostasis*, man's creation is painted in dark colours; he is a Golem, made of earth by seven powers which are hostile and demonic, despite their positive names. We may have traces here of what Jonas has described as the planetary equipping of the soul.[76] The seven appear to be planetary powers, as they have become in redaction (a^3) of the *Apocryphon*, and as are the seven governors of the *Poimandres* who, although presented in a positive light in the cosmogony, later appear much more hostile. Hence heavenly Man is given something from and so shares the nature of each of the seven governors, offspring of the second highest divine being, identified with the planetary spheres and responsible for fate (*heimarmenē*),[77] but his earthly counterpart, enslaved to fate, in his ascent must strip off the negative characteristics belonging to each of the spheres.[78] And in the *Apocryphon*, as we shall see, the production of fate by the First Archon and his powers is described as a wicked and perverse plan.[79] But because the Barbelognostic and 'Ophite' myths underlying the *Apocryphon* represent Ialdabaoth as the vehicle of the divine light-power which he inbreathes into Adam, they have a much more positive view of him at this point, and utilize Gen 2:7 to express that (spiritual) inbreathing and suggest that Adam was first created psychic.

But that the *Apocryphon*'s depiction of the first archontic creation as a psychic one is not original, and rather part of the 'Sethian' redaction (a^3), is suggested by the fact that in both *On the Origin of the World* and the Audian excerpt preserved by Theodore bar Konai, there is no hint of such a psychic creation. Nor is there in the extensive lists of Manichaean, Mazdaean and other passages that Tardieu adduces as influenced by our *Apocryphon*.[80] He may be correct to detect the influence of a 'Book of Zoroaster' on the passage about the seven soul substances, but he is not justified in deriving the whole passage, and with it the underlying Barbelognostic myth, from his 'Chaldaean' source. Conversely, the centrality of Seth with his seed as spiritual in Valentinian systems, and their interpretation of the Demiurge as psychic and responsible for the psychic element, may well have considerably influenced those responsible for the 'Sethian' reinterpretation of the Barbelognostic myth.[81]

The *Apocryphon* then proceeds to involve the angels associated with the powers in this psychic creation. The version in II is the clearest at this point: it has the multitude of angels receive from the powers the seven psychic substances to create the composition of the limbs and the interconnection of all the parts.[82] SR compresses their activity into a single sentence while LR goes into elaborate detail.[83] Here Tardieu is probably right to see the source of this description of the parts of the psychic body as the 'Book of Zoroaster' mentioned by LR: SR has omitted the detailed description of the activity of 360 angels, while LR, which speaks of 365, has made selective use of it.[84] The preference of LR for 365 is, as I have already suggested,[85] thus due to its anthropological source: SR remains faithful to its astrological 360.[86]

But despite their efforts Adam remains inert (LR adds 'and immobile') for a long time, SR explaining that this was because of the inability of the seven powers and 360 angels to raise him up.[87] Here finally we have the *Apocryphon*'s version of the Golem motif, the third anthropological element in Irenaeus' sketch of Saturninus. But in contrast to it and the 'Ophite' version of Irenaeus, Adam here, despite being psychic, remains immobile, as in the *Hypostasis, On the Origin of the World* and Naassene Preaching.[88] Only later, as we shall see in the following chapter, does he move when inbreathed by Ialdabaoth with his light-power (i.e. Gen 2:7).[89]

Finally the *Apocryphon* relates how the archons and their powers, disturbed by the superiority of the animated Adam, formed another creature of the four elements and put it on Adam as a tomb or fetter.[90] This is one of a series of moves and countermoves by the Demiurge and his powers in reaction to the animation (i.e. redemption) of Adam by a series of redeemer figures and redemptive acts which we will examine in detail in the following chapter. Suffice it to say that Sophia had asked for help for immobile Adam. The Autogenes Christ had descended with the four illuminators, disguised as angels of the First Archon, and persuaded him to breathe some of his spirit (the light-power) into Adam. As a result he moved and became superior to his creators. They in turn brought him down to the regions beneath matter, to which the supreme Father responded by sending as a helper (cf. Gen 2:18?) the Epinoia of light who once more elevates him above his creators.[91]

Then follows the motif of psychic man being trapped in a material body composed of the four elements. The archons and their powers mingle fire, earth and water with the four fiery winds, bring Adam into the shadow of death and form another creation as a cave or tomb, the fetter of oblivion, from the four elements characteristically reinterpreted as matter, darkness, desire and the opposing (B, II) or counterfeit (III) spirit.[92] The psychic man is thus trapped in the material body. This explanation of earthly man's origin may represent further reinterpretation of Gen 2:7,[93] although it also suggests Greek ideas.[94] But certainly the other texts in which we find it, namely the *Poimandres*,[95] Zosimus (who sees it as Chaldaean lore),[96] and certain Christian apocrypha,[97] suggest a combination of Jewish and Greek influences.[98]

This picture of an original incomplete psychic creation involving a multitude of creators, followed by a material creation as a trap for the creature animated from above, is one way of explaining how man came to be a union of soul and body in which was also present a divine spark or spirit which represented his true essential self. Another explanation more in line with the Fall account in Genesis 3 is offered by the 'Ophites' of Irenaeus. When originally created, Adam and Eve had as it were spiritual bodies, but once cast out of paradise these became more sluggish, as did their souls, since their creator had only inbreathed a worldly breath. Sophia Prunicus took pity on them and restored a whiff of the sweetness of the dew of light whereby they recognized their nudity, material bodies and mortality.[99]

We find a similar motif in the *Apocalypse of Adam*, where Adam and Eve, although created of earth, possess through Eve a glory from the aeon from which they had derived and knowledge of the eternal God, and thus are superior to the Demiurge who had created them. When the Demiurge in wrath divides them they lose that glory and knowledge and become slaves of the Demiurge, under the power of death. But Adam is awakened from his oblivion by three revealer figures who foretell the future of the Gnostics, the seed of Adam's son, Seth.[1]

The last two texts are clearly influenced by Jewish traditions about Adam, but all three, despite their different ways of presenting man's fall into the world of matter, insist that the divine is something in addition to his natural endowments of body and soul, the handiwork of the Demiurge. It comes to him from above, be it described as the Epinoia of light, a dew of light or glory and knowledge. And precisely the same is true of Valentinian anthropology. The spirit or seed is sown from above and is not a natural endowment.[2] Very few in fact possess it.[3]

4 The creation of Eve

It would not be proper to conclude a treatment of Gnostic anthropology without some reference to the creation of the first woman. But despite the crucial importance of the feminine principle for the *Apocryphon*, the 'Ophites', the Valentinians and others, the earthly Eve does not play a significant role in Gnostic anthropology. She occurs in the Gnostic Paradise accounts which are best interpreted as soteriological rather than anthropological statements. They represent our human plight and redemption in terms of the events of Genesis, the trees of Paradise, the naming of the animals, Adam's sleep and the creation of Eve, the serpent, Adam and Eve's transgression and expulsion, the birth of Cain, Abel and Seth and so on. Earthly Eve is frequently transmuted into the heavenly spiritual woman, the Instructor, who comes to sleeping Adam, awakens him and raises him up.[4]

However both the *Apocryphon* and the 'Ophites' of Irenaeus relate the creation of earthly Eve as a device of Ialdabaoth to empty Adam of his light-power.[5] The former has him cast oblivion (not sleep as in Gen 2:21) over Adam in an attempt to bring out the Epinoia of light concealed in him. This fails and so he tries again. But here the versions differ. The short recension simply has him decide to take the power from Adam, make another creature in female form and raise her up before him, not, as Moses said, 'he took a rib . . .' (a further correction of Gen 2:21f.).[6] The long recension, however, in an attempt to clarify and improve this, has Ialdabaoth take part of his power, fashion a female in the likeness of the Epinoia and transfer into her the part (not his rib as in Gen 2:21f.) he had taken from the man's power.[7] In rather similar fashion the 'Ophites' of Irenaeus have Ialdabaoth, full of jealousy, devise a scheme to empty the man by means of a woman. He brings forth from his (i.e. Adam's) thought (*enthymēsis*) a woman whom Prunicus invisibly empties of power.[8]

The *Hypostasis* also appears to envisage Eve's creation as an archontic plan to empty Adam of his spirit. Following Genesis more closely, it has them cast a deep sleep, similarly interpreted as ignorance, over Adam. They then open up his side like a living woman and build it up with flesh in her place (Gen 2:21). Thereupon Adam becomes completely psychic.[9] Bullard is probably correct to interpret this in terms of the original bisexuality of Adam: his female side is removed and formed into a living woman, the spiritual woman, thus depriving him of spirit, and the gap is filled up with flesh.[10] But the spiritual woman at once awakens and animates Adam,[11] and later appears in the guise of the serpent Instructor,[12] which suggests that her role is more soteriological than anthropological. The abrupt mention of the fleshly woman indicates that the text has not worked out a satisfactory way of combining the Gnostic interpretation of Eve as the spiritual woman with the account in Genesis to which, nevertheless, it tries to remain faithful.

On the Origin of the World solves this problem by abandoning the idea that Eve was in any sense formed from Adam, while developing the idea of Eve as the spiritual woman who produces psychic Adam and as the Instructor awakens him. The archontic reaction to this is to try to ravish her so that once defiled she will be unable to return to her light. They will then bring an oblivion over Adam and mislead him into believing that she originated from his rib, thus making her subservient to him.[13] Needless to say, Eve is well aware of their plans and leaves her (psychic?) likeness behind for them to defile. What in fact they do defile is their own body![14]

In these Gnostic texts Eve is interpreted in two ways: (1) she is a redeemer figure, the spiritual woman awakening Adam from his stupor (*Apocryphon, Hypostasis, On the Origin*); and (2) her separation from Adam marks the beginning of the processes of generation, decay and death (Valentinians,[15] *Apocalypse of Adam, Poimandres*). Indeed, some texts attempt to relate both ideas. In the *Apocryphon* and Irenaeus' 'Ophites' on the one hand, Eve is a vehicle of light-power but also the originator of reproduction, whereas on the other, *On the Origin of the World* distinguishes the spiritual Eve who remains unaffected by the archons' sexual overtures, from the psychic or fleshly Eve, her likeness, who is the actual object of them.

Conclusion

Having concluded our analysis of the fundamental mytho-logoumena of Gnostic anthropology and anthropogony, let us summarize our findings. As a result of our preliminary analysis we noted three basic anthropological theories: (1) that heavenly Primal Man or his image fell or descended into matter; (2) that earthly man was made in the image of God, or heavenly Man, an emanation from God; and (3) that a part of earthly man is consubstantial with the Godhead. The last appeared to us to be the most comprehensive and the one best suited to express the basic anthropological dualism of divine spirit versus body and soul which characterizes Gnostic theology.

We then considered the initial anthropogonic impulse, the vain claim of the Demiurge and the response from heaven, examining the significance and background of the figures of Man and Son of Man. We concluded that the originally independent motifs of 'Ophite' Man and Son of Man and Barbelognostic Adamas had been combined by our *Apocryphon*, a hypothesis which enabled a whole spectrum of texts dealing with these figures to be understood and interrelated. And we argued for the Christian background to such figures based on speculations such as are found in Hebrews 1–2. We further suggested the priority of the anthropogonic version of the motif of Demiurgic boast and heavenly response to the cosmogonic version, and the essentially Christian character of the earliest forms of it, those of the 'Ophites' and Valentinians.

Then, as regards the appearance of a heavenly image and its consequences, we noted three motifs; (1) the appearance, (2) the angelic response; and (3) the creation of Adam as a Golem. Here we pointed to the centrality of Gen 1:26 in combination with 2:7 as pioneered by the *Apocryphon*, and the difference of interpretation arising from the varied evaluation of the Demiurge, more positive in systems where he is the vehicle of the divine, more negative where he is not.

We went on to analyse the multiple creations of Adam attested in the *Apocryphon*, suggesting that its picture of an initial psychic creation of Adam as Golem might represent part of the later 'Sethian' redaction, borrowing from a 'Book of Zoroaster'. We noted the likely influence of both Jewish and Greek sources on the following account of a material body created from the four elements as a trap for Adam animated from heaven. And finally we considered the motif of the creation of Eve as a device to empty Adam of his power, noting the two interpretations of her as (1) a heavenly redeemer figure (possibly based on the Barbelognostic consort of Adamas and/or Sophia), and (2) representing the beginning of separation and death, the object of archontic lust.

This picture of multiple creations of Adam, the ambiguity of the Eve figure in the context of divine move and archontic countermove, is evidently meant to illustrate and explain the Gnostic sense of being a divine spirit trapped in a body with a soul, governed by demonically inspired passions and fate and buried in matter, to whom revelation/salvation comes not as a permanent possession or natural endowment but as a gracious gift or series of gifts. This again confirms the centrality of the theme of the consubstantiality of redeemed and redeemer, of the divine spirit, spark, 'self' or 'inner man' in the Gnostic elect.

Notes

[1] This definition is able to encompass even such an uncharacteristic system as that of the Basilidians of Hippolytus (*Ref.* 7.21.1–4; 27.11f.); cf. W. Foerster, 'Das System des Basilides' *NTS* 9 (1962/3), 233–55; *Gnosis 1* 62–4.

[2] In what follows 'man/he' is used to include male and female purely for convenience and as a common translation of the Greek *anthrōpos* which, of course, means 'human being'.

[3] Dichotomous: e.g. Saturninus in Iren. 1.24.1 (body plus spark of life – but see below); the system described by Zosimus, *Omega* 12 (Scott–Ferguson, *Hermetica* 4.107 (man of four elements plus inner spiritual man)); *Poimandres*, CH 1.15 (mortal body and immortal inner man); and in Manichaeism according to the *Kephalaia* 65; Theodore bar Konai, *Schol.* 11 (A. Adam, *Texte zum Manichäismus* 22f.); Ibn al Nadim, *Fihrist* (ed. Flügel, (Leipzig: Brockhaus, 1862), 101), etc. (mortal body and immortal soul); trichotomous: e.g. the *Baruch* of Justin (Hipp. *Ref.* 5.26.7f.: body, soul and spirit); the 'Ophites' (Iren. 1.30.13f.: body, soul and spirit or trace of light, but see below); and *AJ* (B 48.14, 55.13 and par.: material body, psychic body and light-power, but see below).; in combination in e.g. the Naassenes of Hippolytus where we hear both of the soul or inner man imprisoned in the earthly body (*Ref.* 5.7.30, 36), and of the three elements or types of soul in man (5.6.6f.; 8.2–4); fourfold in, e.g. the Ptolemaic school of Valentinians according to Iren. 1.5.5f. and *Exc. ex Theod.* 50.1–52.3; 53–55.1 (hylic soul, psychic soul, spiritual soul and flesh). But here only the hylic and fleshly are natural; the psychic and spiritual are gifts. This Valentinian division may reflect the

Platonic scheme of body plus threefold soul (irrational/spirited/rational divine). Cf. *Tim.* 69B–71A; 73B–D. See on this G. Quispel, 'La conception de l'homme dans la gnose valentinienne', *Gnostic Studies 1* (Istanbul, 1974), 48ff. But more important surely is the influence of Christian anthropology and the desire to adapt to it, evident in the intermediate category of the psychics or Great Church Christians, saved by works, and the spiritual as a fourth element transmitted through the Demiurge and found only in a few elect by grace, not nature.

[4] Iren. 1.24.1.

[5] *Separate* 105. Cf. Iren. 1.24.1–2.

[6] 105.

[7] But, cf. Rousseau–Doutreleau SC 264, 323 and 263 *notes justificatives* ad loc., translating this 'le mit debout'.

[8] 1.24.2.

[9] Cf. e.g. *HA* 86.28–88.16 (Incorruptibility, a female figure); *OW* 103.2–32 (Pistis Sophia); 107.25–108.25; 112.25–113.10 (Light-Adam). On this, see Y. Janssens, 'Le thème de la fornication des anges' in Bianchi, *Origini* 488–94.

[10] CH 1.12–17.

[11] Cf. 'On the Evangel of Seth' in E. Preuschen, 'Die apokryphen gnostischen Adamschriften' in *Festgruß Bernhard Stade* (Giessen: Ricker, 1900), 199; *Die Schatzhöhle*, ed. C. Bezold (Leipzig: Hinrichs, 1883), 10ff.; 'The Books of the Rolls' ff. 102a–106a in *Apocrypha Arabica* (*Studia Sinaitica VIII*), ed. M. D. Gibson, 18–22; *The Book of Adam and Eve*, trans. S. C. Malan (London, 1882), 118–21. See also L. Ginzberg, *The Legends of the Jews* (Philadelphia, 1909–38), 1, 121ff.; 5, 149f., 172; Epiph. *Pan.* 39.2.1–7.

[12] Valentinians, cf. Iren. 1.6.1; 7.5; *Exc. ex Theod.* 54.1–3; *Tri. Trac.* 118.14–23; three principles systems, see Foerster, *Gnosis 1* chs 14–19; Rudolph, *Gnosis* 91f.

[13] *Gott 'Mensch'.*

[14] Bousset, *Hauptprobleme*, ch. 4, 'Der Urmensch' (160–220); R. Reitzenstein, *Poimandres* (Leipzig: Teubner, 1904), esp. 101–8, 249; *Das iranische Erlösungsmysterium* (Bonn, 1921), 116.

[15] *Hauptprobleme* 215.

[16] *Gott 'Mensch'* 19.

[17] *Erlösungsmysterium* 116. See Schenke, *Gott 'Mensch'* 20.

[18] Bousset, *Hauptprobleme* 167–70; Reitzenstein, *Poimandres* 81ff.

[19] Ibid. His reconstruction of the supposed original is on 83–97. On the Old Testament quotations inhering in this original, see Wilson, *Problem* 133, n. 27.

[20] *Glaubende* 18.

[21] *Glaubende* 59f., citing the criticisms of C. Colpe, *Die Religionsgeschichtliche Schule: Darstellung und Kritik ihres Bildes vom gnostischen Erlöser* (FRLANT 78) (Göttingen: Vandenhoeck & Ruprecht, 1961). Cf. also

Schenke, *Gott 'Mensch'* 16–33; 'Die neutestamentliche Christologie und der gnostische Erlöser" in K.-W. Tröger ed., *Gnosis und Neues Testament: Studien aus Religionswissenschaft und Theologie* (Berlin: Evangelische Verlagsanstalt, 1973), 210; Perkins, *Gnosticism* 30, 94, etc.

[22] 'Der gnostische Anthropos und die jüdische Tradition', *Eranos Jahrbuch* 22 (Zürich, 1954), 195–234 (= *Gnostic Studies 1* 173–95).

[23] 'Anthropos' 201f. (= *Studies 1* 178).

[24] 'Anthropos' 214 (= *Studies* 188).

[25] 'Anthropos' 197 (= *Studies* 174): 'Schon hier begegnet uns das eigentliche Thema der gnostischen Anthropologie, das Verhältnis vom göttlichen Urbild und menschlichen Abbild, welches als eine Einheit und Wesensgleichheit der Gegensätze aufgefasst wird. Dieses Thema kehrt nur . . . in tausendfachen Variationen in der Geschichte der Gnosis wieder.'

[26] *Imago Dei: Gen. 1:26f. im Spätjudentum, in der Gnosis und in den paulinischen Briefen* (FRLANT 76) (Göttingen: Vandenhoeck & Ruprecht, 1960), 122–70, esp. 122f. Similarly K. Rudolph, 'Ein Grundtyp gnostischer Urmensch Spekulation', *ZRGG* 9 (1957), 1–20. The interpretation of Gen 1:26 in *AJ* (the image of Primal Man appears to archons who create man in the image, but he is incomplete and is animated from heaven) represents the fundamental type of Gnostic anthropology.

[27] *Imago* 136f., n. 63.

[28] 169f.

[29] The same arguments also apply to Schenke, *Gott 'Mensch'* 38ff., who also sees the *eikōn* motif with reference to Gen 1:26 as fundamental, although he does interpret it in terms of the consubstantiality idea he finds in the texts, particularly *AJ*: man's essential unity consists as much in divine form (image) as in divine content (light-power).

[30] 'Jewish and Platonic Speculations in Early Alexandrian Theology: Eugnostus, Philo, Valentinus and Origen', in B. A. Pearson, J. E. Goehring eds, *The Roots of Egyptian Christianity* (SAC 1) (Philadelphia: Fortress, 1986), 190–203.

[31] *Separate* 103–7.

[32] *Separate* 450–61. Cf. Scholten, *Mysterium* 240–52, for a similar conclusion.

[33] Jonas, *Gnosis* 1[3], 143–6; Schottroff, *Glaubende* 36ff.; Rudolph, *Gnosis* 88f.

[34] Thus, as Schottroff points out, *Glaubende* 14ff., whereas the soul or psychic element is ambivalent in Valentinianism, able to share in an intermediate level of salvation, in the Naassene Preaching it is a hostile element. Cf. Rudolph, *Gnosis* 91, on the reversal of soul and spirit in Mandaeism.

[35] See e.g. his *Theology of the New Testament 1* (London: SCM, 1952), 168, 178, 182. On this whole problem, see Schottroff, 'Animae' 67ff.

[36] Cf. 'Conception' 249–86, esp. 274ff. (= *Studies 1* 50).

[37] 'Animae' esp. 65–8, 84–97. See E. Pagels, 'The Valentinian Claim to Esoteric Exegesis of Romans as Basis for Anthropological Theory', *VC* 26 (1972), 241–58, for a critique of the debate between Bultmann and Schottroff.

[38] The centrality of the 'Ophite' myth along with that of *AJ* for Gnostic anthropology is evident from their prominence in ancient and modern treatments. Irenaeus' account in 1.30 is by far the longest in his heresiological catalogue; Schottroff takes as the central theme of Gnostic theology the statement in 1.30.8: 'uti neque maledictionem participaret, neque opprobrium is qui esset a principalitate spiritus' (*Glaubende* 78, 82, 98); Quispel finds the original form of his projected Jewish–Gnostic myth readily recognizable in *AJ* and Iren. 1.30. Cf. also Rudolph, 'Grundtyp' *passim*; Schenke, *Gott 'Mensch'*; Turner, 'Sethian Gnosticism' 59f., etc.

[39] 'The Arrogant Archon and the Lewd Sophia: Jewish Traditions in Gnostic Revolt' in Layton, *Rediscovery* 2.689–712.

[40] 'Arrogant' 693f.

[41] 'Arrogant' 695–7.

[42] 'Arrogant' 693–9. They include Iren. 1.5.4; 29.4; 30.6; Hipp. *Ref.* 5.26.15; Epiph. *Pan.* 25.2.3; *AJ* B 44.14f. and par; *HA* 86.30f.; 94.21f.; 95.5; *OW* 103.11–13; 107.30f.; *GE* III 58.24–6; *Treat. Seth* 53.30f.; 64.19–26. See also Schottroff, *Glaubende* 50, n.1.

[43] Cf. *Testim. Truth* (C IX,*3*) 48.4–8, which also puts Exod 20:5 into the mouth of the Demiurge, but does not mention his claim to be God. On this theme, see Logan, 'The Jealousy of God: Exod. 20:5 in Gnostic and Rabbinic Theology', *Studia Biblica 1978* 1. Papers on Old Testament and Related Themes (*JSOT* Supplement Series, 11) (Sheffield Academic Press, 1979), 197–203.

[44] B 47.14–16/III 21.16–18; II 14.13–15/IV 22.17–20. All four texts appear to be identical in reading *fshoop ñji prōme auo pshēre mprōme*. The mention in LR that the voice came from the exalted aeon heaven implies both awareness that Sophia may originally have been the source and the need to exclude that – the voice comes to her from above – and the spiritualizing tendency of LR to emphasize the distance between Ialdabaoth and the heavenly world. The motif of the heavenly voice, the *bath qōl* of Jewish and particularly rabbinic sources (see G. F. Moore, *Judaism* 1 (Cambridge, Mass., 1950), 421f.), can be used by Gnostics both cosmogonically to explain how the primal mixture of light and darkness occurred, as e.g. in *HA* 94.23f., or christologically, as e.g. in *Treat. Seth* 51.20–54.16. But its most natural and probably original context is anthropogonical, since the consistent form of the claim 'there is no other [god] apart from me' requires the appearance of a pre-existing divine being to refute him.

[45] B 47.16–20/III 21.18–21; II 14.15–18/IV 22.21–5. SR has the voice come to Sophia, hence the omission of any reference to Ialdabaoth's

error. Janssens' explanation, *Muséon* 84, 409, that the voice is to encourage her is further evidence of the artificiality of *AJ*'s present scheme, since her consort, First Man, has just descended to her and she has been elevated. Against Tardieu's supposition, *Écrits* 120, that the voice came to the lower hebdomad, is not only the remoteness of the supposed referent and the fact that Ialdabaoth follows as the subject, but the omission by LR of any mention of the object addressed, evidently because of the awkwardness of the phrase. That Ialdabaoth did not recognize where the voice came from (II 14.18/IV 22.24f.), an element lacking in the lacunous and confused SR, may be a further attempt to emphasize the ignorance of Ialdabaoth and his distance from the heavenly world.

[46] *Glaubende* 22, 79. This, of course, is the thrust of redaction (a^2).

[47] *GE* III 59.1f. simply speaks of a voice coming from above (cf. *AJ* II 14.13f./IV 22.17–19), with no further identification apart from the fact that the image which appears simultaneously and descends is said to be like the voice. To make sense of the passage one has to infer the course of events found, e.g. in *AJ*: the heavenly voice and (male?) image corresponding to it which the archons see and imitate. On the fundamental theme of voice–image–response in *AJ* (and *TP*), see ch. 7, section 3.

[48] *AJ* B 47.14–16/III 21.17f.; II 14.14f./IV 22.19f. ('fshoop ñji prōme auo pshēre mprōme'); *GE* III 59.2 ('fshoop ñji prōme m̄n̄ pshēre n̄prōme'). This stereotyped formula suggests the Greek original: 'estin [ho] anthrōpos kai [ho] huios anthrōpou'.

[49] 1.30.6. Harvey supplies *kai Anthrōpos* to correspond to the Latin.

[50] 103.19f.

[51] *The Christian and Gnostic Son of Man* (SBT second series 14) (London: SCM, 1970), 107.

[52] Ibid.

[53] Ibid. n. 185. Unfortunately he does not suggest what the variants might have been or how the original statement might have read.

[54] Cf. *AJ* B 47.20–48.14/III 21.21–22.6; II 14.18–15.3/IV 22.25–23.18; *OW* 103.28–32 (Sophia appears; cf. 107.17–108.31, light and Light-Adam appear); 112.25–113.12 (Light-Adam is seen by the archons who decide to create earthly man in the divine image); *GE* III 59.4–10 (see n. 47 above). Cf. *HA* 87.11–33 which follows the Great Archon's blasphemy and the heavenly rebuke with the appearance of a female being, Incorruptibility, whose image is seen in the waters and copied by the archons.

[55] 1.30.6: 'sex autem virtutes audientes haec, matre dante illis excogitationem hominis . . . formaverunt hominem.'

[56] Frag. 1 in Clem. Alex. *Strom.* 2.8.36.

[57] Cf. Iren. 1.30 *passim*; Valentinus, frag. 1 (see previous note); Iren. 1.1.1; 1.12.4.

[58] Cf. *OW* 103.19–28; *HA* 96.33–97.9.

[59] Cf. 1.30.13.

[60] *Muséon* 84, 409. Cf. also 62f. On First Man, cf. B 27.19f./III 7.23f.; II 5.7/IV 7.17; B 29.10/III 9.4f.; II 6.3f./IV 9.3; II 15.10/IV 23.27f.

[61] 44f. referring to B 27.17–28.4/III 7.22–8.5; II 5.4–10/IV 7.20–7.

[62] Cf B 30 and *Muséon* 84, 49–54.

[63] *Apocryphon* 239f. Cf. II 5.6ff., 14.19ff. and n. 61 above. Tardieu, *Écrits* 298, makes the same identification, failing to recall his ascription of the title in II 5.6 to a later scholiast, and claiming that SR omitted the list of titles here.

[64] Cf. II 6.16/IV 9.19f. This passage is unique to LR.

[65] Cf. B 35.3–5/III 13.1–3; II 8.32f.

[66] Cf. B 27.19f. and par; B 29.10 and par. and Monoimus (Hipp. *Ref.* 8.12.6–13.4).

[67] Cf. III 49.8–12. The parallel in the often more accurate version in IV (61.8–14), although lacunous, appears to suggest that Adamas is himself the first man, but the description that follows applies best to the supreme Father. Cf. Böhlig-Wisse, *Gospel* 177.

[68] *Separate* Part 1, ch. 4, esp. 103–7.

[69] *Separate* 105f.

[70] 105f.

[71] 107: 'Ophites', Iren. 1.30.1, 13; Valentinians, Iren. 1.12.4; Naassenes, Hipp. *Ref.* 5.6.4; 10.9.1; Monoimus, Hipp. *Ref.* 8.12.2, 4; 13.3; 10.17.1; *AJ* B 47.15–16 and par; *SJC* B 98.11–12/III 104.1f.; *Eug* III 85.10–12.

[72] Cf. *SJC* B 100.14/III 105.12f., adding 'because he came from light'; *Eug* V 9.24 (in lacuna, but seems probable)/III 81.12 ('Adam of the light'); *GE* IV 61.8–10/III 49.8f. ('Adamas, the shining light' clearly a paraphrase of a misunderstood expression).

[73] Cf. 103.19–28; 108.20–24; 112.10, 25; 117.28f.

[74] 118.26–119.11.

[75] 6.5f.

[76] E.g. the theme of the three elements or types, spiritual, psychic and earthly in association with Adam found both in *OW* 117.28–118.3 (three Adams: spiritual, psychic, choic); 122.6–9 (three races) and the Naassenes (Hipp. *Ref.* 5.6.6f. (three elements in Adamas: intellectual, psychic, choic)), and the motif of 'kinglessness' in *OW* 124.33–125.11; 127.10–17 and the Naassenes (*Ref.* 5.8.30, which Bergmeier, 'Königlosigkeit' 322–8, has argued is only explicable from Valentinianism). *Gos. Phil.* is usually classed as Valentinian, and we have already noted the Valentinian influence on *AJ*. J. Frickel, 'Naassener oder Valentinianer?', in Krause, *Gnosis and Gnosticism* (NHS 17) 95–119, considers the Naassenes and Valentinians as dependent on an older Christian Gnostic tradition, while Pétrement, *Separate* 357, would argue for the dependence of the former on the latter. Edwards, 'Gnostics', etc. would, however, distinguish the Gnostic Naassene Preaching from

Valentinianism. On the likelihood of *Eug* being dependent on Valentinianism rather than vice versa, see ch. 3, n. 36, p. 104.

[77] Cf. e.g. *Steles Seth* 118.24–121.25 (Pigeradamas as the Self-Begotten aeon, above which is the First-Appearing aeon Barbelo); *Zost.* 6.21–29; 13.1–6 (hierarchy of supreme Hidden One, First-Appearing One (Barbelo), Self-Begotten Geradamas, his son Seth Emmacha Seth); *Melch.* 6.5f. *GE* III 49.1–16/IV 60.30–61.18 has Adamas derived via a female entity, Mirothoe, from First Man, and the latter descend to annul the deficiency, a favourite Valentinian theme.

[78] Hipp. *Ref.* 8.12.1–13.4.

[79] The editor of Hippolytus, Wendland, detects possible allusions to John 1:1–3, Matt 5:18; Luke 16:17; Col 1:19; 2:9, and Matt 11:27 in this passage.

[80] On the parallels, identity of the systems and possibility that Monoimus was the author of Hippolytus' Naassene source, see R. P. Casey, 'Naassenes and Ophites', *JTS* 27 (1926), 374f.

[81] 1.12.4. Cf. also the Valentinian doctrinal letter in Epiph. *Pan.* 31.5.5 (Father of Truth as 'Man' as antitype of the supreme being), and Valentinus frag. 1 in Clem. Alex. *Strom.* 2.8.36.4 (Adam with the name of a god, the pre-existent Man).

[82] II 75.25–76.4. On the reconstruction 'Father of the All', cf. 71.4 also concerned with the bridal chamber and Jesus, the anointed. *Eug* has the pattern 'Father of the All' (III 73.1f.), 'Man' (III 76.23f.), 'Son of Man' (III 81.13), and even 'son of Son of Man' (V 13.12f.).

[83] 81.14–21.

[84] So Borsch, *Son of Man* 81f.

[85] 63.29f. The text has a reference to a second 'son of' marked for cancellation, which Borsch, *Son of Man* 78, argues for, appealing to 81.15 and *Eug.* But both Wilson, *The Gospel of Philip* (London: Mowbray, 1962), 115, and Ménard, *L'Évangile selon Philippe* (Paris: Letouzey & Ane, 1967), 70, 170, reject it as dittography.

[86] Frag. 1.

[87] 1.29.3.

[88] *OW* 103.8–24.

[89] 107.25–108.25.

[90] Cf. 109.1f.

[91] Cf. 103.19–28; 113.5–10. However, the subject here is more probably Christ, the eschatological light-Man. See below.

[92] Cf. 1.24.1: a light image (*phōteinē eikōn*) appears from the heavenly power and vanishes; the angelic creators respond 'Let us make man in the image . . .' (Gen 1:26), and the heavenly power because of the likeness sends a spark into the wriggling Golem. Later Christ comes as a man only in appearance to destroy the God of the Jews.

[93] 28.21–29.1. Cf. *OW* 103.19–28. The continuation (29.1–5), with its reference to the Adams possessing the thought of Norea who speaks

concerning the two names which create a single name, strikingly recalls the Naassene hymn to bisexual Adamas: 'From thee, Father, and through thee, Mother, the two immortal names, parents of the aeons, . . . Man of the mighty name' (Hipp. *Ref.* 5.6.5).

[94] Cf. Hipp. *Ref.* 5.6.4–7; 7.6; 7.36. On Valentinian influence on the text, see Bergmeier, 'Königlosigkeit' 322f., 327.

[95] Cf. *Ref.* 10.9.1f.

[96] II 75.35–76.4. See p. 178.

[97] Cf. *Eug* III 81.10–12/V 9.21–25 and *SJC* B 100.12–16/III 105.11–14.

[98] *Martyrium* 249–52. Cf. Epiph. *Pan.* 31.5.5 where the first emanation, Father of Truth, is called 'Man' as an antitype of the supreme being. This last surely reflects the inference of the Valentinians of Iren. 1.12.4 that the supreme being is called 'Man' because of the Saviour's title 'Son of Man'.

[99] Cf. IV 61.8–18/III 49.8–16 and Böhlig–Wisse, *Gospel* 177. They note the play on *phōs*, 'light', and *phōs*, 'man', which underlies this passage. Certainly the Invisible Spirit or Father is designated 'light' in III 40.15–41.4/IV 50.6–15. Note also the Valentinian echo: the unknowable Father descending to annul the *deficiency* (III 49.13–16/IV 61.14–18).

[1] For later similar and probably dependent formulations involving Adamas, cf. *Zost.* 13.6 (Pigeradamas the eye of the child); 30.4–13 (Adamas as [perfect] man, as the eye of the Self-Begotten); *Steles Seth* 118.26–119.18 (Geradamas as light, Mirotheos, Self-Begotten); *Melch.* 6.5f. (Pigeradamas as man of light); *AnonBru* ch. 20 (Schmidt–MacDermot 354.3). The obscure reference in *TP* 38.1–7 to the 'eye of the light' may be to the Barbelognostic Adamas who 'gives aeon (?) to the Father of all the aeons'. Cf. Iren. 1.29.3 where Adamas joins in praising the great Aeon.

[2] Cf. *HA* 86.27–87.11; 94.8–95.13.

[3] Cf. *OW* 103.2–32 (Pistis' rebuke and revelation of her image); 107.17–109.1 (the fearful and arrogant response of the Archigenetor and the appearance of a light with a human form in it, that of the angel light-Adam, with whom Pronoia falls in love); 112.10–113.10 (light-Adam before his withdrawal above is seen by the archons who decide to create a man in his image to enslave him).

[4] Cf. Heb 2:8f. and Iren. 1.30.13.

[5] Cf. Iren. 1.30.10–11.

[6] Cf. 1.30.11. The allusions to Man probably derive from Ezek 1:5, 26; Dan 10:16–21; to Christ from Amos 4:13; Hab 3:13; Dan 9:25; 7:13, and to the incorruptible light from Isa 60:19f.; 9:1f.; 42:6; 49:6 (cf. Luke 2:32; Acts 26:23). Cf. on these prophecies Justin, *Dial.* 113, 126, etc.

[7] Iren. 1.5.4 (spoken through the prophets: Isa 45:5); Hipp. *Ref.* 6.33 (Isa 45:5). Cf. *Exc. ex Theod.* 49.1 (with reference to his ignorance only); 53.4; Iren. 2.9.2. See Dahl, 'Arrogant' 692f.

[8] Cf. Iren. 1.12.4; Epiph. *Pan.* 31.5.5; Marcosians in Iren. 1.15.3 (Christ, the Saviour, who descends on Jesus, confesses himself Son of Man and is Man as possessing the whole Pleroma in himself).

[9] Cf. Heracleon frag. 35 (distinguishing the Son of Man above the Place (i.e. the Demiurge) who sows from the Saviour, Jesus, also Son of Man, who reaps); *Gos. Phil.* 75.25–76.4; 81.14–21.

[10] Cf. Monoimus in Hipp. *Ref.* 8.12.1–13.4 on the creative role of the Son; the Naassene Preaching in Hipp. *Ref.* 5.6.5–11.1 on Man/Son of Man (Christ/Logos)/Adamas in both anthropogonic and redemptive roles; *OW* 103.19–28; 107.25–108.25; 112.25–113.10; 117.28–30; 123.15–125.23 on both light-Adam as an anthropogonic principle and the immortal eschatological Man (i.e. Christ); *GE* III 49.8–16/IV 61.8–18 on Adamas as derived from Man who is the supreme being and cause of both creation and redemption; *Eug* V 5.30–6.4/III 76.19–24; V 6.19–7.2/III 77.13–78.2; V 8.27–9.13; V 10.5–10/III 81.21–82.3 on the emanations Man, Son of Man, Saviour as creative powers.

[11] Cf. *OW* 103.19–28; *HA* 96.33–97.9; *SJC* B 125.19–126.16/III 118.22–119.8. The last, however, may be more dependent on Luke 10:17–20, as may Zosimus, *Omega* 14 (Scott–Ferguson, *Hermetica* 4.108). On *katapatein* and *kerameus*, cf. Isa 41:25; Ps 2:9.

[12] See on this Schenke, *Gott 'Mensch'*, Borsch, *Son of Man*, etc. Pétrement makes a persuasive case, *Separate* 118–26, for seeing the pagan gnoses of *Poimandres* and of Zosimus, *Omega*, with their Anthropos/Adam figure as combining Platonism, Philo's celestial Man and Genesis and as not representing early forms of Gnosticism, but as unable to avoid Christian Gnostic influence even when disguising it. And she too points to the syncretistic character of such gnosis.

[13] Cf. *HA* 86.27–87.23. The following passage (87.30–35) has man made in the image of God, but the reference is still to the female figure of Incorruptibility, in accordance with the seduction motif. Is the gloss that the bodies of the archons who create man in their image are androgynous (87.27f.), an attempt to overcome the apparent anomaly of female archetype and male copy? On the theme, see Janssens, 'Thème' 488–94; Stroumsa, *Seed*, esp. Part 1. He would derive it as well as a cluster of related mythologoumena from the descent of the 'sons of God' in Gen 6:1–4.

[14] B 47.20–48.10/III 21.21–22.6. The reading in B 47.20: '[he ins]tructed them' might appear more original than the 'he revealed to them' of III 21.21 in that it is echoed in LR (cf. II 14.19/IV 22.25), seems the more difficult reading, and makes more sense than III which has the Father reveal himself twice (cf. III 21.21–24). But the text is problematic in that (1) the pronominal suffix 'them', as Tardieu admits, *Écrits* 298, cannot apply to the previous plural subject, but only to the seven archons not mentioned till later; (2) while B 48.1 has an object, 'about him (? masc.)' which LR omits, both read clumsily, which may

have led the redactor of III to change the verb; the following verb (*eiōrm/ kataneuein*) perhaps suits revelation better than instruction.

[15] II 14.18–24/IV 22.25–23.2. Compare the Naassene description of Adamas, Hipp. *Ref.* 5.6.5f. (bisexual, called 'father ... mother', progenitor of aeons, in three parts).

[16] II 14.24–34/IV 23.3–23.14. Cf. *OW* 108.2–13 (a light from the ogdoad in response to Ialdabaoth's own insolent response, in which is seen the light-Man).

[17] Against Tardieu, *Écrits* 298, who sees LR as original. Cf. Giversen, *Apocryphon* 240f.; *AJ* B 20.19–21.2; II 1.31–3. On the motif of archontic terror and the shaking of foundations at a theophany or heavenly voice, cf. *Treat. Seth* 51.24–31; *TP* 40.8–22; *PS* Book 1, chs 2–3 (Schmidt–MacDermot 4.20–6.24). Cf. also Isa 24:18; *1 Enoch* 1:5; 60:1; *As. Mos.* 10:3f. and W. C. van Unnik, 'Die "geöffneten Himmel" in der Offen-barungsvision des Apokryphons des Johannes', *Apophoreta: Festschrift Ernst Haenchen* (BZNW 30) (Berlin: Töpelmann, 1964), 269–80.

[18] Cf. II 14.26–30/IV 23.5–9; 15.1–5/IV 23.14–20.

[19] B 49.6–9/III 22.15–18. Cf. II 15.11–13/IV 23.29–24.2. As Janssens points out, *Muséon* 84, 410, this recalls and confirms that the perfect Man is an aeon of light, and she cites *OW* 108.21; 112.10, 25; 117.28. That the first man is called 'Adam' by the angels is the gist of a gloss in Zos. *Omega* 11 (Scott–Ferguson, *Hermetica* 4.106.24).

[20] Cf. 1.30.1 (*Lumen/Homo*). Cf. Clem. Alex. *Strom.* 1.6.28; Zos. *Omega* 11 (Scott–Ferguson 4.107.7–11).

[21] 1.29.3.

[22] Cf. *HA* 86.27–87.23; *OW* 100.10–29; 103.2–32.

[23] Cf. *HA* 94.19–33.

[24] Cf. *OW* 107.36–108.13.

[25] *Religion* 161–5.

[26] *In somn. Scip.* 2.11. Jonas, *Religion* 158.

[27] Sethians in Hipp. *Ref.* 5.19 (cf. *Par. Shem* 1.25–4.21); Peratae in Hipp. *Ref.* 5.12ff.; Gnostics in Plot. *Enn.* 2.9.10; Basilides' 'barbarians' in Hegemon. *Acta Archelai* 67.2–11.

[28] Cf. *HA* 94.28–33.

[29] Jonas, *Religion* 162. Cf. *OW* 103.28–32; 108.3–13.

[30] For versions of the claim, see above p. 174, n. 42. The variants include cosmogonic, as in *HA* 94.23ff. and christological, as in *Treat. Seth* 51.20–54.15.

[31] B 48.10–14/III 22.3–6.

[32] II 15.1–5/IV 23.14–20.

[33] This comes several lines later in B 49.6–9 par.

[34] The rabbis explained the plural in terms of God addressing or consulting the council of angels (cf. *Gen. Rab.* 8.4f.). Philo interpreted Gen 1:26 in terms of God taking others as his fellow workers (*Opif.* 75; *Fug.* 68–72; *Conf. ling.* 171–5). Does the lack of explicit reference in

both versions to Ialdabaoth's taking part in the first act of man's creation suggest that LR is trying to combine the motif of man's creation by (seven) angels with a picture more acceptable to Christians of the Great Church – God creates through intermediaries? The 'Ophite' version (Iren. 1.30.6), which has Ialdabaoth utter Gen 1:26 and his six offspring do the actual creating, may point to an earlier stage of this process in which Ialdabaoth is distinguished from the original seven creators, as in Saturninus. Cf. Plato (*Tim.* 69C) as another source of the motif of both Demiurge and archons being involved in man's creation. On Gen 1:26, see R. McL. Wilson, 'The Early History of the Exegesis of Gen. 1:26', *Studia Patristica 1*, ed. K. Aland and F. L. Cross (TU 63) (Berlin: Akademie, 1957), 420–37.

[35] Cf. Crum, *Dictionary* 80b s.v. *eine.*

[36] *HA* 87.33–88.1.

[37] *OW* 112.25–113.2.

[38] In *HA* 88.11–15 the Spirit descends from the adamantine earth and settles in man, so that he becomes a living soul (cf. Gen 2:7); in *OW* 115.9–15 after 40 days Sophia Zoe sends her breath into the soulless Adam so that he begins to move but cannot stand upright.

[39] Cf. B 48.10–49.9 and par (man made in the heavenly likeness and named Adam to be a power of light for the archons); B 42.10–43.6 and par (Ialdabaoth gives his underlings something of his own power but nothing of his mother's light-power).

[40] Cf. B 48.14–52.1 and par. In the related 'Ophite' myth both Ialdabaoth and his six offspring possess the dew of light but, to avoid the danger of them seeing an image of the supreme deity, they are given a mental image of man in response to Ialdabaoth's vain claim and the heavenly rebuke. The motive for his citation of Gen 1:26 is to rally and deceive his offspring, the heavenly motive to empty them all of the dew of light. As created by the six Adam is a wriggling Golem until inbreathed by Ialdabaoth with the 'breath of life' (Gen 2:7), including the light-power.

[41] Iren. 1.24.1; Hipp. *Ref.* 7.28.2.

[42] Ps. Tert. *Adv. omn. haer.* 1; Fil. *Div. haer. lib.* 31; Epiph. *Pan.* 23.1.1–10; Theod. *Haer.* 1.3.

[43] Fil. *Div. haer. lib.* 31 ('concupiscentia . . . cupidi luminis'); Epiph. *Pan.* 23.1.5f. ('erethismos . . . pothos . . . erasmiotēs').

[44] Despite Jervell's arguments, *Imago* 152, there is no indication that the spark of life is to be equated with the inner man, Anthropos, thought of as the supreme God himself. Such an identification – always guarded – is only explicit in Valentinian texts (e.g. Val. frag. 1; Iren. 1.5.6), the Naassene Preaching (where Adamas does appear to descend), and *Poimandres.* The Valentinian version has Sophia inbreathe the seed (Gen 2:7) as the Demiurge creates, and we have suggested the signs of Valentinian influence on the Naassene Preaching.

[45] *HA* 87.11–20. Note the Valentinian-sounding gloss which also implies the male character of the image: 'for the psychics (*psychikos*) will not be able to reach the pneumatic (*pneumatikos*) because they are from below, but he is from above.'

[46] 87.20–23.

[47] 87.23–6.

[48] 87.27–88.1.

[49] 88.3–10.

[50] 88.6–17. As Bullard notes, *Hypostasis* 68, a Jewish etymology is apparent here: Adam (*'dam*) is named from Adamah (*'damah*), virgin earth. Cf. *OW* 108.24f. But in 115.1–3 Adam is named after Light-Adam.

[51] Although this two-stage version – the archons/angels create man in God's image but he is an inanimate Golem until the Creator breathes the breath of life into him – may reflect the views of supposed 'heterodox' Jewish groups of the first and second centuries CE based on a distinction between Gen 1:26 and 2:7 (cf. *Gen. Rab.* 14.8; 8.1; Justin, *Dial.* 62; *Tri. Trac.* 112.35–113.1; Philo, *Opif.* 75; *Fug.* 68–70; *Conf.* 171–5), Jewish sources could not readily have presented the creator angels as in ignorance of and ultimately hostile to the Creator God. *HA* is dependent on the Christian Barbelognostic myth and is merely utilizing Jewish traditions to illustrate its main theme, the evil character of the archons.

[52] Cf. the frequent references to the three Valentinian classes of hylic, psychic, pneumatic (and even to the pneumatic character of evil) in *HA* 86.25 (cf. Eph 6:12 and Iren. 1.5.4; *Exc. ex Theod.* 48.2); 87.15–20; 88.3–17; 89.10f., 31–90.18. For other claimed Valentinian influences, see Pétrement, *Separate* 440.

[53] Thus in it, as in *HA*, we find the image–reflection motif involving two archetypes (female Sophia, male light-Adam), the arrogant Demiurge Ialdabaoth, his seven archontic offspring and obedient son, Sabaoth, further versions of the Narcissus and seduction of the archons motifs, conflation of Gen 1:26 and 2:7, insistence on divine overall control, Adam as Golem animated in stages, and a threefold cosmological and anthropological pattern of pneumatic, psychic, hylic, etc.

[54] Thus Tardieu, *Écrits* 299, would see the phrase in *OW* 108.32, *ḥitn mmoou* ('through the waters'), as recalling *AJ* II 14.23–30 (esp. 27). The very allusive and fragmentary version of the entire constellation (vain claim of Saklas, heavenly rebuke, image–reflection motif, archontic response creating man) in *GE* III 59.1–9, is also evidently more dependent on the picture presented by *AJ* and *OW* than on the similarly brief and elliptical version of Saturninus.

[55] So Schottroff, *Glaubende* 9–12, 36–8.

[56] B 48.14–50.11/III 22.6–23.11.

[57] B 50.6–51.1/III 23.7–19; II 19.2–15. LR gives a very detailed account of the activity of 365 angels over against the very brief summary in SR which involves only 360.

[58] B 54.11–55.13/III 26.6–25; II 20.33–21.13/IV 32.7–27.

[59] 87.24–33. Cf. *OW* 112.33–113.1 and the Valentinians of Iren. 1.5.5; *Exc. ex Theod.* 50.1–3.

[60] In B 48.6ff./III 22.1ff. the entire archonship of the powers (*exousia*) is the subject, whereas II 14.30f./IV 23.9f. only mention all the powers (*exousia*), adding the Protarchon.

[61] B 48.17–49.6/III 22.9–14.

[62] II 15.5–11/IV 23.20–28. 'From his' makes more sense. Krause interprets the *tephpsychikē* of II 15.9 (IV 23.26 has *tepsychikē*) to mean the soul.

[63] II 15.9–11/IV 23.26–8. The reference to *hypostasis* may be an echo of the concluding summary in B 50.9f. and par.

[64] *Écrits* 300.

[65] II 15.11–13/IV 23.29–24.2.

[66] B 49.6–9/III 22.14–18. Giversen, *Apocryphon* 243, also argues for the priority of LR, but his ground, namely that SR is anticipating, is not convincing. Possession of the name was thought in the ancient world to give one control over the power of the one named.

[67] B 49.9–50.6/III 22.18–23.7; II 15.13–23/IV 24.2–14.

[68] Cf. II 12.15–25/IV 19.15–26.

[69] Cf. B 43.11–44.4. For an extremely similar list, cf. *OW* 101.26–34.

[70] See ch. 4, section 2c.

[71] *Schol.* 11.

[72] *OW* 114.29–35.

[73] 114.36–115.1, an obvious allusion to Gen 2:7.

[74] This is repeated no less than four times (115.5, like an abortion without *pneuma*, 10f., 13f., 34), evidently to avoid misinterpretations of the earlier allusion to Gen 2:7.

[75] 115.3–15.

[76] Cf. his *Gnosis 1* 181–5; *Religion* 156–69.

[77] Cf. CH 1.9, 12–14.

[78] Cf. CH 1.24–26. The negative side of their planetary nature is evident in the term *zōnai*. Cf. Servius, *in Aen.* 6.714 and Origen's description of the descent of the Gnostic through the seven planetary spheres in *C. Cels.* 6.31.

[79] B 72.2–12 and par. Cf. the Mandaeans who represent the creators of man as the Demiurge Ptahil and the seven planets (*R. Ginza*, Lidzbarski 108.4ff.).

[80] *Écrits* 301–4.

[81] Cf. Iren. 1.5.1–6; 7.5; *Exc. ex Theod.* 47–50; 54. See ch. 1, section 3.

[82] II 15.23–29/IV 24.15–21. On *psychikē hypostasis*, cf. Ptolemaeans in Iren. 1.5.4.

[83] Cf. B 50.6–14/III 23.7–14 and II 15.23–19.2/IV 24.15–29.5.

[84] *Écrits* 300f. Cf. II 19.6–10, against Giversen, *Apocryphon* 281, and Kasser, *RThPh* 14, 144, who assume it was added by the redactor of LR. For details of this passage, see Tardieu and Giversen.

[85] See ch. 4, p. 133.

[86] But according to Epiph. *Pan.* 24.7.6, Basilides derived man's 365 bodily parts from the 365 heavens, each corresponding to an individual power. Cf. also *PS* Book 3, ch. 132 (Schmidt–MacDermot 340.15) on the 365 servitors inserting soul compounds into the body of the matter of the world, and the phrase in the Naassene Preaching on Adam's creation by many powers severally described at great length (Hipp. *Ref.* 5.7.6).

[87] B 50.15–51.1/III 23.14–19; II 19.13–15/IV 29.22–4. LR probably omitted the reference to the angels because of its preference for 365.

[88] Cf. Iren. 1.24.1 (Saturninus: unable to be raised up but crawling like a worm); 1.30.6 ('Ophites': the six form him of immense length and breadth, but he only wriggles); *HA* 88.3–17 (psychic man incapable of being raised through archontic weakness until the Spirit settles in him and he becomes a living soul; but the text then suggests Adam could move: the Spirit names him Adam 'because he was found moving upon the earth' (88.16f.)); *OW* 115.3–15 (Adam left in a vessel for 40 days as a breathless, soulless abortion till Sophia breathes into him and he begins to move); Hipp. *Ref.* 5.7.6 (the Chaldaean Adam produced by the earth lying without breath (*apnous*), without motion (*akinētos*), without a tremor (*asaleutos*), like a statue, an image (*eikōn*) of the heavenly Man Adamas). The spiritual Man (*Phōs*) of Zos. *Omega* 12, who is inbreathed by Fate (*heimarmenē*), is described as guileless (*akakos*: cf. the Barbelognostic and 'Ophite' Sophia Prunicus of Iren. 1.29.4 and 30.3) and inactive (*anenergētos*).

[89] Cf. B 51.1–52.1 and par.

[90] B 55.2–13 and par.

[91] Cf. B 50.15–54.11 and par.

[92] B 54.11–55.15/III 26.6–27.1; II 20.33–21.14.

[93] So Janssens, *Muséon* 84, 414; Tardieu, *Écrits* 320, suggesting as the source a midrashic exegesis such as in the *Targum Ps. Jonathan.*

[94] Cf. Plato, *Tim.* 42E–43A; Philo, *Opif.* 146. However, Tardieu, *Écrits* 320, sees this passage in *AJ* as an echo of the midrashic exegesis of Gen 2:7 (*Tg. Ps. Jon.*).

[95] CH 1.16f.

[96] *Omega* 11; the parallels with *AJ* are striking.

[97] Cf. *Book of the Rolls*, ed. M. Gibson 5f.; *Schätzhohle*, ed. Bezold 3.

[98] Cf. also the picture in the Naassene Preaching: Adam as a Golem produced by earth, an image of heavenly Adamas, made by many powers (5.7.6); enslaved by a soul (5.7.7), the elect souls or inner men brought down into the moulded figure of clay to serve the Demiurge (5.7.30f.; 37); the moulded creature being made of hostile elements (5.8.19).

[99] 1.30.9. This account, which recalls the animation motif in Saturninus, etc., cannot be satisfactorily harmonized with 30.6, according to which the six powers created Adam and Ialdabaoth inbreathed his dew of light ensuring Adam's salvation.

[1] 64.6–67.14.

[2] Cf. Iren. 1.5.6; Val. frag. 1; *Val. Exp.* 37.32–8.

[3] *Exc. ex Theod.* 55.1–56.2.

[4] Thus *HA* 89.11–17, 31ff.; 90.12; *OW* 113.21–114.15; 115.30–116.8; and *AJ* B 53.4–10 and par deal in their own characteristic ways with the figure of the spiritual woman Zoe/Eve who awakens and instructs Adam. Despite evident Jewish influence, the Gnostic archetype of this figure could be seen as on the one hand the consort of heavenly Adamas, Perfect Knowledge (an echo of the Hebrew/Aramaic wordplay *hawwah/ hawja*?) in the Barbelognostic system and, on the other, Sophia in her second decisive intervention (see ch. 7, section 3 and Iren 1.30.7).

[5] *AJ* B 58.10–60.16/III 28.25–30.14; II 22.18–23.26/IV 35.9–36.21; Iren. 1.30.7.

[6] B 59.12–19/III 29.18–24.

[7] II 22.32–23.4/IV 35.14–24. By this reworking the redactor of LR can (*a*) avoid implying that Adam was deprived of all his power, and (*b*) suggest how the Epinoia might be lured out by and into her counterpart, as in the similar motif involving Adam in Saturninus and *HA*.

[8] 1.30.7. The Latin has 'from his own thought (*sua Enthymesi*)', which appears to refer to Ialdabaoth. But that is surely a mistake on the part of the translator since (1) to make sense the plan must have woman brought out of man and (2) man has just been described as having *Nous* and *Enthymesis* which are the elements which are saved (30.6).

[9] *HA* 89.3–11.

[10] *Hypostasis* 75–80.

[11] 89.11–17.

[12] 89.31–90.12.

[13] *OW* 115.30–116.25. On the archontic attempt to ravish Eve, cf. *HA* 89.17–31; Audi's 'Book of the Requests' and 'Book of the Aliens' in Theodore bar Konai, *Schol.* 11.

[14] 116.33–117.15. The mythologoumenon of the ravishing of Eve appears in various forms, e.g. Iren. 1.30.7 (powers ravish Eve and produce the angels); *AJ* B 62.3–63.2 and par (Ialdabaoth ravishes Eve and produces the archons Iave and Elohim (Cain and Abel)); Archontics of Epiph. *Pan.* 40.5.3 (the devil begets Cain and Abel by Eve). Cf. *Tg. Ps. J.* Gen 4:1; 5:3; *Pirqe R. El.* 21, etc. See on this Ginzberg, *Legends* 5, 133, n. 3; Bullard, *Hypostasis* 84; Stroumsa, *Seed, passim.*

[15] Under this heading I include *Exc. ex Theod.* 21.1–3 and *Gos. Phil.* 70.9–22.

6

Gnostic Soteriology 1:
The Reinterpretation of Genesis 1–4

Introduction

If we wish to know what second-century Gnostics understood by salvation (as opposed to twentieth-century interpretations and hypotheses) we can do no better than once again turn to the classic Valentinian definition preserved by Clement in his *Excerpta ex Theodoto* 78.1–2. Up until baptism, says Clement, the Valentinians assert that Fate (*heimarmenē*) is true; after it the astrologers are no longer right. However, it is not baptism alone which sets us free, they say, but also the knowledge (*gnōsis*) of our origin, nature and destiny, a knowledge which tells Gnostics who they really are and frees them from their present state of ignorance and imprisonment in an alien body and a hostile world governed by Fate. Salvation is *gnōsis* in this special sense and its cosmic and metaphysical implications are summed up most concisely in the Marcosian formula reproduced by Irenaeus:

> The perfect redemption is said to be the knowledge of the ineffable Greatness. From ignorance both deficiency and passion arise; through 'knowledge' will the entire substance derived from ignorance be destroyed. Therefore this 'knowledge' is redemption of the inner man.[1]

This finds a precise echo in the *Gospel of Truth*.[2] And the soteriological significance of knowledge, specifically of self-knowledge, is not limited to Christian Gnostic sources. In the *Poimandres* God proclaims: 'Let man who has Nous recognize himself as immortal',[3] and Poimandres himself continues, 'If then you learn that you consist of life and light and that you come from these, you will go back to life.'[4] Salvation, then, is special knowledge of one's true self, of one's kinship with the unknown transcendent God and of the true nature of the visible world. But the mention of baptism is also significant, as we shall see: without the divine initiative symbolized by such a rite of initiation full revelation and salvation would not be possible.

For we do not come to such knowledge by rational investigation and philosophical enquiry;[5] it is religious knowledge; it has ethical connotations; and above all it is a matter of revelation.[6] Thus although it might appear from the *Poimandres* that everyone can save themselves by the mere possession of Nous – the conclusion drawn by the recipient – this is explicitly denied: the saving revelation is only near to those who by their conduct deserve it, and who are thereby enabled to perceive the truth.[7] Saving *gnōsis* is thus revelation from above or outside. It can be summed up by the frequent Gnostic motif of the 'call' which Foerster at least would see as the kernel of Gnosis,[8] which comes to the Gnostic self trapped in matter, 'drunkenness', 'oblivion', etc. and awakens it so that it is enabled to recognize its true nature and escape from imprisonment in the body and matter.[9] Thus, contrary to the arguments of e.g. Quispel and Colpe,[10] salvation would not appear to be simply or primarily a matter of self-redemption.

If then we are unable to save ourselves and need revelation and salvation from outside, does that mean that *gnōsis* is something entirely new, a matter of sheer divine grace, as e.g. Quispel has argued, appealing to a statement of Tertullian about Valentinianism?[11] This would certainly go against the traditional interpretation of Valentinian (and *a fortiori* of Gnostic) soteriology, found both in ancient heresiologists like Irenaeus and Clement of Alexandria and in modern commentators like Bultmann, which seized on the Gnostic claim that they were being saved by nature (*physei sōzomenos*) as the key to understanding their view of salvation as essentially determinist.[12] It would also contradict what we have been arguing is a fundamental idea in Gnostic theology, the consubstantiality of God and the divine element in humanity – if the saving knowledge be interpreted as recognition of one's essential heavenly nature. However, the deterministic interpretation of salvation as a matter of nature and substance has been criticized particularly by Schottroff, who has argued that the *salvandus* is not assured of salvation as a substance, it is rather a matter of grace and free will: the indicative of salvation is balanced by an imperative.[13] The idea of salvation by nature or substance she ascribes to inaccurate heresiological polemic.

However, the idea does occur in the *Tripartite Tractate*,[14] and E. Pagels has argued, on the basis of an analysis of Valentinian exegesis of Romans, that both the traditional view and that of

Schottroff are misleading since they are cast in terms of the antithesis free will–determinism, rather than of an experience of election through grace which she finds as the basis of the Valentinian three nature concept.[15]

We have already touched on this debate in the previous chapter, noting how all three positions (salvation 'by nature'; by divine grace as a lifelong possession of believers, and as a gift to believers, capable of being lost) were present in unresolved tension in Irenaeus' sketch of Saturninus' views, expressing the paradox of the Gnostic understanding of salvation.[16] And it is worth noting that the heresiologists do preserve alongside the Valentinian concept of substance or nature the ideas that education is necessary even for the pneumatics,[17] and that they are sown as seed, both of which suggest that same paradox: although they are assured by the grace of revelation that they are by nature elect and divine, yet they have to work out their own salvation (in terms of formation and perfection), a process not complete until the consummation (*apokatastasis*).[18] Thus *On the Origin of the World* concludes: 'each one by his deed (*praxis*) and his knowledge will reveal his nature.'[19] We shall have to examine what our texts say on this question of nature and grace.

If salvation is to be understood in terms of the awakening call, the saving revelation, allowing us to do what we cannot of ourselves, i.e. recognize our essential divine nature, this surely implies a revealer/redeemer. Although it has been argued that Gnosticism has no need of a redeemer, being essentially a religion of self-recognition and a redeemer being first introduced under the impact of Christianity,[20] Schenke and others have shown convincingly that this presupposes too limited a view of the nature and role of a Gnostic redeemer. Schenke contends that there is practically no Gnostic work or system without a redeemer in some form as an integral element, from the concrete historical figure of Simon Magus at one extreme to the abstract concept of the 'call' at the other.[21] Rudolph has reinforced this argument by pointing out that the ancient concept of 'redeemer' corresponds more to the term 'liberator' or 'rescuer', and that this precisely describes the Gnostic redeemer whose infinite variety he has charted.[22] And Filoramo has appealed to the existential situation of the Gnostic, longing yet unable to escape this closed universe unless a superior power intervenes: 'The descent of the Nous Illuminator is the necessary counterpart of the ascent of the soul.' The Gnostic concept of soteriology is the result of these two vectors and poles in continuous tension.[23]

This at once raises the very vexed question of a pre-Christian redeemer myth, conceived of in terms of a 'redeemed redeemer' or *salvator salvatus* or *salvandus*.[24] We cannot enter this much-debated subject at length here, but we can ask what light our texts throw on it, particularly since those such as Rudolph who still consider it as part of the logic of Gnosticism find support for this concept in the variety of saviour figures and saving entities found in the 'Sethian' group of texts, which he would see as essentially non-Christian – indeed pre-Christian.[25] In this vein Arai has attempted to show that all sections of the *Apocryphon* in which Christ appears must be considered interpolations, and Schottroff and others would see the Pronoia hymn at the end of LR as, if not original, yet containing a concept of a Gnostic redeemer independent of Christianity.[26] Schenke too would see in the subject of the Pronoia hymn and in the figure of Sophia in Irenaeus 1.30.3–11a the outline of the non-Christian redeemer as the heavenly Mother saving her children.[27] In the light of these claims we shall have to submit our thesis of an essentially Christian origin for the myth underlying the 'Sethian' and related texts, and thus for their various saviour figures, to further scrutiny.

Finally there is the question of when exactly salvation takes place. If we take the concept of the 'call' as central, this might lead us to conceive of the Gnostic understanding of salvation as essentially timeless, or in other words existential, as indeed Schottroff argues, appealing to the inconsistencies in the Gnostic *Heilsgeschichte*. But appeal to inconsistencies overlooks the paradoxical character of the Gnostic understanding of salvation such as we found exemplified in Irenaeus' account of Saturninus, and recourse to the existentialist analysis as *the* hermeneutical key to unlock the mysteries of Gnosis, however valuable it has been, is not justified. The existence of Gnostic texts with a kind of *Heilsgeschichte* beginning with Adam and incorporating a threefold system of ages, advents of the Saviour, etc. linked to events like the Flood, does suggest that history is of some importance for the Gnostic as the locus of revelation. Thus Schenke has argued that, for the Gnostics, redemption and a redeemer existed from the beginning of human history and that the redeemer has therefore a twofold task: original revelation and continuous revelation throughout history. He appeals to Manichaean and Mandaean evidence to demonstrate that this concept is independent of Christianity, post- as well as pre-Christian.[29]

This Gnostic redeemer concept, whether in its basic structure or its various concrete forms, has, according to Schenke, at times influenced the development of early Christology in that Jesus is seen either as the bearer of continuous revelation or as the primal redeemer.[30] Rudolph suggests a two-sided process whereby on the one hand Gnostic ideas were Christianized while on the other Christian concepts were gnosticized; Gnostic redeemer concepts were historicized and the Christian figure of Christ mythologized.[31] But such views presuppose the pre-Christian character of Gnosticism, as attested particularly in the *Apocryphon of John* and related 'Sethian' texts such as the *Apocalypse of Adam*, the *Gospel of the Egyptians* and *Trimorphic Protennoia* with their three ages and triple descent schemes of male or female revealer/redeemers, combining primal and continuous revelation.

However, we have argued that the Barbelognostic core scheme underlying these 'Sethian' texts was originally Christian and only later Sethianized and periodized in an attempt to counter 'orthodox' Christian taunts of novelty. Indeed one can find a striking precedent for our hypothesis of a Gnostic combination of primal and continuous revelation in response to a taunt of novelty in the Logos doctrine of Justin Martyr. He was able to answer pagan insinuations about the novelty (and therefore falsehood) of Christianity by claiming that the divine Son or Logos, known in all his fullness to Christians through the Incarnation, was yet partially known in his primal revelation in and through his activity in creation, and in his continuous revelation to choice souls (Abraham, Socrates, etc.) in history.[32] Schemes involving primal and continuous revelation, particularly the threefold systems of ages, of advents of the Saviour/Seth/Protennoia figure so characteristic of the 'Sethian' texts, only make sense in the light of a decisive revelation such as that of and in Christ, with whom Seth is identified.[33] Indeed the primal and continuous revelations can only be understood as preliminary stages, explaining how an elect seed or race was preserved until the present era of decisive and final revelation as salvation, involving the end of this present age and the ultimate restoration of all things to their original status.

In enquiring about the soteriological views of the Gnostics as found in the *Apocryphon* and related texts, and attempting to suggest how those views may have developed, we shall therefore have to ask (1) what understanding of salvation is present (is knowledge in the sense of revelation an adequate definition?); (2) what is the subject or object of salvation (i.e. the whole person, the soul or the spirit?); (3) how does salvation come (i.e. is it a matter of nature and/or grace or what?); (4) what picture of a saviour emerges; and finally (5) when exactly salvation takes place. In this first of two chapters on the soteriology of the *Apocryphon* we shall consider what light may be thrown on these questions by Gnostic treatment of what they consider their fundamental source on this matter: Genesis 1–4.

The Gnostic interpretation of the Genesis primal history

As we have already indicated, the Gnostic Paradise accounts are best interpreted as soteriological: they explain the origin and hence the nature of our present plight, but point to the presence of divine redeeming activity in terms of a kind of Gnostic *Heilsgeschichte*. The different motifs in the early chapters of Genesis are selected by the various documents to delineate the human situation and isolate the activity of various redeemer figures. Differences in selection, order, interpretation, etc. are therefore to be ascribed to different theological aims and tendencies (where they are evidently not the result of errors in transmission). But the presence of certain common elements, tendencies and influences may help further to confirm our proposed reconstruction of the literary and formal relationships between the texts and illuminate our questions about the Christian character of the original myth, the relationship with Valentinianism and our hypothesis about the 'Sethian' reworking.

1 The original soteriological impulse

Both the *Apocryphon* and the 'Ophites' of Irenaeus initiate the process of rescuing the divine power present in the Demiurge with the creation of earthly man. He is not simply an archontic device to retain or trap the divine light;[34] rather, he is the chosen instrument of the divine plan to recover the imprisoned divine element[35] and condemn the archons for their ignorance and audacity.[36] But whereas in the 'Ophite' system it is Sophia herself who initiates the creation of humanity by supplying the archons with the mental concept of Man to empty them of heavenly power,[37] in the *Apocryphon* the figure who reveals itself to the archons in the form of heavenly Man is not Sophia, who is increasingly relieved of any positive soteriological function, but, according to LR, the Mother–Father (*mētropatōr*) of the All, great in mercy, to whom Sophia prays when she wishes to recover the power she gave her offspring.[38]

However, in SR it is the Father of the All, the merciful, the light god, who had earlier appeared as the First Man, to whom Sophia prays,[39] and in the previous chapter I suggested that LR's version was more original; the version in SR probably finds the figure of Barbelo, the Mother–Father, problematic and almost always emends to either Father or Mother.[40] That priority is suggested both by SR's later ascription of the Father's designation 'rich in mercy' to the Mother (although the passage is evidently confused),[41] and by the striking parallel role of the lower Sophia in the 'Ophite' system: prior to the coming of Christ she calls in grief to her mother, First Woman, for help, and she asks First Man to send out Christ.[42]

Now the combination in the 'Ophite' system of Sophia's continuing revelatory/redemptive activity which is yet incomplete, with the decisive eschatological revelatory/redemptive descent of Christ, seems to find an echo – if a confused one – in the *Apocryphon* with its plethora of redeeming figures and final Pronoia hymn. Thus not only do we hear of the Mother–Father or Pronoia in a redeeming capacity, but also of the Holy Spirit, Zoe 'the Mother of the living', the Epinoia of light, Christ and even Sophia, in that she has to correct her own deficiency.[43] But the textual evidence just cited suggests that that plethora may conceal an earlier, simpler picture in that the Holy Spirit, the Epinoia of light and Zoe appear to be ultimately one and the same figure, originally to be equated with Sophia, as Janssens has claimed.[44] Indeed the phenomenon not only corresponds to the familiar Gnostic tendency to reduplicate heavenly figures (particularly Christ), but more importantly reflects, in the antithesis between the plethora of redeeming entities and the passive Sophia who requires redemption, her ambivalent character as *salvator salvandus*, the paradigm of the Gnostic's experience: he or she is saved from above but must work out that salvation in a continuing struggle with evil and ignorance until the final, eschatological denouement. The characters and events of the opening chapters of Genesis (the Spirit, Adam, Eve, the serpent) provide the necessary material for the Gnostic expression (via re-interpretation) of that experience.

The characteristic ambivalence over Sophia is well expressed, as we saw, in the confusion over the existence and descent of her consort; the earlier myth has no need of this, but the figure is added both through Valentinian influence and to ease the paradox by representing the erring Sophia as entirely passive. And the figure/figures of the Epinoia/Zoe/Holy Spirit are similarly presented in terms of Sophia's helper, better half or consort.[45] Not surprisingly we find various interpretations of this basic ambivalence in texts we would see as dependent on the *Apocryphon*. Thus *Trimorphic Protennoia* stresses the more passive aspect of both figures in that it identifies the Epinoia of light with the guileless Sophia who descends, produces Ialdabaoth and then begs to be elevated.[46] On the other hand the *Hypostasis of the Archons* represents Sophia unequivocally as a redeemer figure, yet alongside a similar range of redemptive entities developed from speculations based on passages in Genesis (particularly 2:7b, 2:18; 3:20), such as those in the *Apocryphon*, namely her daughter Zoe, the spirit which descends to animate Adam, and the spiritual Woman/Eve/Instructor.[47] The absence of the Epinoia of light or equivalent in the *Hypostasis* I would see as further evidence of the secondary character of the Pronoia–Epinoia scheme.[48]

Thus it may be that the 'Ophite' picture of Sophia as responsible for initial and continuing revelation/redemption, yet ultimately requiring the decisive redemptive Christ event, finds an echo in earlier versions of the *Apocryphon*, which later, under the influence of a Pronoia–Epinoia scheme developed round Barbelo, demoted Sophia to a more passive figure and replaced her with a more active one (Epinoia/Zoe/Holy Spirit).[49]

2 Ialdabaoth inbreathes divine power into Adam

In SR the Mother, wishing to recover the power she had given the First Archon in compulsive desire (*prounikos*), comes in innocence and makes her request to the Father.[50] The innocent wantonness whereby she originally acted without asking the Father is hereby corrected (or recapitulated) by the innocent obedience of her request. LR makes no mention of her motivation and since it appears to have suppressed any reference to the compulsive desire of Sophia it would appear to be less original here.[51] But it probably preserves a more original view in having the Mother–

Father dispatch five illuminators (II 19.18f./IV 29.27–30.1) over against B 51.5–10 which has the Father, the light-God, send out the Autogenes and the four lights, or III 23.22–24.3 which has the Father and the five lights send out an unnamed subject with his four lights.[52] Thus the original version would have the Mother praying to the Father and him sending the five illuminators, i.e. Christ/Autogenes and his four accompanying angels.[53] However, it is not at all clear whether the continuation in LR, that the five descend to the region (*topos*) of the angels of the Demiurge,[54] is preferable, as Tardieu argues, to that of SR which has them sent in the guise (*typos*) of those angels, a characteristic Gnostic motif.

Thus, in accordance with a holy plan, the Autogenes/Christ and his four illuminators advise the First Archon to breathe into the immobile body something of his breath (*pneuma*), i.e. the power of his mother, thereby emptying him of it, causing Adam to move and become superior to the Demiurge and his archons.[56] We have here an obvious allusion to Gen 2:7 LXX,[57] but with characteristic Gnostic overtones: the Creator inbreathes spirit (*pneuma*), not the breath (*pnoē*) of the LXX, and there is a conscious play on the themes of the compulsive desire/activity of Sophia and her creation versus the inactivity of the Demiurge and his.[58]

The presence in LR of certain features lacking in SR may be partly explicable in terms of the theological tendencies of its redactor. Thus it dwells characteristically on the ignorance of Ialdabaoth in this manoeuvre: 'he did not know since he is in ignorance.'[59] But its further reference to the Mother's power proceeding from Ialdabaoth into the psychic body created by the archons in the heavenly image[60] may preserve a more original reading which might explain the oddities of SR. Thus whereas both versions have Ialdabaoth breathe into Adam something of his spirit, glossed as the power of the Mother, III 24.11f. adds 'from the First Archon into the body', while B 51.20 only mentions the last phrase. Now that phrase is evidently redundant in SR but makes perfect sense in LR, which suggests that SR has omitted through homoeoteleuton the passage in LR relating how the power of the Mother went from Ialdabaoth into the body of Adam. LR has typically stressed the ignorance of Ialdabaoth, the psychic character of Adam's body and the fact that it was in the likeness of the first existent (i.e. First Man/Mother–Father), whose initiative in the salvation process is all the more comprehensible.

Man in the divine image is the appropriate receptacle for the divine power.[61]

The 'Ophite' system described by Irenaeus presents a similar general picture. To empty Ialdabaoth of the trace of light lest he rise up against heaven because of the power he has from Sophia Prunicus(!), his mother, she has him breathe the spirit (*spiritus/ pneuma*) of life into the wriggling man. Thus Ialdabaoth is secretly emptied of power and man thereby receives *nous* and *enthymesis*, the elements which are saved.[62] Only the Valentinians of the school of Ptolemy explicitly share this view of the Demiurge as unwitting transmitter of the divine, but for them the 'spirit of life' inbreathed by him is simply the psychic substance or man consubstantial with him; the heavenly element is the seed in man sown simultaneously with his inbreathing by or rather through the Demiurge.[63]

All three systems in fact distinguish between what the Demiurge contributes of his own nature and what is actually responsible for salvation. In the *Apocryphon* the Demiurge is responsible for the power of the Mother later identified as the soul, the principle of biological and rational life, which cannot save itself; it needs to be united with the spirit of life which is not a natural endowment but must descend.[64] The 'Ophite' system similarly appears to distinguish between the trace of light or power or rational intelligence (*nous* and *enthymesis*) which the Mother inserts via Ialdabaoth and can remove again at will,[65] and the 'worldly inbreathing' (*insufflatio mundialis*) which is what Adam and Eve received from Ialdabaoth as his own proper contribution, namely the souls which are consubstantial with him.[66] And in the system of the Valentinians of Ptolemy, when the Demiurge inseminates the psychic man consubstantial with himself into the hylic man, Sophia simultaneously sows the spiritual seed, which alone achieves the highest level of salvation.[67] Finally Valentinus himself betrays awareness of this conception when he refers to man, the immobile creation of angels, expressing sentiments superior to his created status because of the one who had invisibly deposited in him seed of the heavenly substance.[68]

This similarity of approach is surely further evidence of the links between the *Apocryphon*, the 'Ophites' of Irenaeus and the Valentinians, which would add more weight to the thesis of Irenaeus that the last-named developed from the Gnostics of 1.29 and 30. Indeed, certain features of the Valentinian system (or systems) found in the *Excerpta* and the fragments of Heracleon may themselves cast light on the *Apocryphon*'s account at this point and counter Pétrement's thesis that the latter developed from the former. If we accept the reading of SR that the Autogenes and the illuminators descended in the guise of the angels of Ialdabaoth and ask about the significance of it, a pointer may emerge from the Valentinian speculations about the mediating role of the Demiurge's angels in the creation of psychic man and the insertion of the pneumatic seed into him. Two groups appear to be involved here: (1) the male angels, consorts of Christ, who are responsible for Sophia's production of the spiritual seed and who minister to or 'reap' it when ripe,[69] and (2) the psychic angels of the Demiurge who mediate the inbreathing of the psychic element and the spiritual seed.[70]

If we then compare the *Apocryphon*'s picture of Christ the Autogenes and his four male angelic illuminators, the final destination of the redeemed, encouraging the Demiurge to inbreathe the divine power acquired from Sophia into psychic man, in the guise of his angels, with that of the Valentinians of the Saviour and his angels being responsible for Sophia's production of the spiritual seed then inserted into psychic man via the Demiurge and his creator angels, we might consider it more likely that the former, simpler picture inspired the latter, more complex one with its various ambiguous angelic groups and idiosyncratic theme of the Gnostic and his angel, than vice versa.

This episode, developing the Gnostic reinterpretation of Genesis 2, sets the scene for the struggle over humanity and its salvation between the heavenly world and Ialdabaoth and his powers. In the power of the Mother we possess the principle of life, biological and rational, which is the precondition of salvation. But this is only a precondition; a divine initiative is still required and the story is by no means over. Salvation has a history and a goal: the light-power resulting from Sophia's deficiency must be united with the eschatological Spirit given through the Saviour.[71] Thus alongside the Mother–Father we also have the Autogenes/Christ as a saviour on Sophia's behalf,[72] and the four illuminators so closely associated with him also clearly have soteriological functions.[73] We have suggested that the baptismal initiation (and particularly the fivefold chrismation) of the Gnostic was in the name of the Autogenes and the four, and this would correspond neatly to this opening soteriological action: as the five are responsible for the initial inbreathing of spirit, so they are invoked in the descent of saving spirit in the five seals rite of chrismation.[74]

3 The struggle over humanity between the powers of light and darkness

(a) The first archontic reaction and the heavenly response

Having received the power of the Mother, Adam moves. SR has an awkward lacuna at this point,[75] while LR relates how Adam's body became powerful and shone.[76] II 24.13f. appears to echo the first idea, but neither it nor B refer to the man shining. But since the archons' aim had been that Adam made in the image and with the name of heavenly Man might become a light-power for them,[77] and since this theme recurs in the continuation in SR[78] and is central to the *Apocryphon* and related texts,[79] it must be considered a necessary presupposition, whether wholly or partly omitted by SR or added by LR in the light of the continuation.

The seven archons are inevitably jealous of Adam in that, although he was their creation endowed with their psychic power, his intelligence (*phronēsis?*) was superior to theirs and the First Archon's.[80] Because of Adam's superior intelligence, light-power and freedom from evil,[81] they cast him down to the nethermost region of the whole of matter.[82] There then follows the episode alluded to above in which the beneficent Mother–Father (or Father) takes pity on the power of the Mother brought out from the First Archon to control the body of Adam. S/he sends out the good, merciful spirit, the Epinoia of light, as a helper (*boēthos*, cf. Gen 2:18 LXX) for Adam, whom he called 'Zoe' (cf. Gen 3:21 LXX).[83] Here we have the first appearance of the principal redeemer figure of the main body of the *Apocryphon*, in the closest association with the Mother–Father or Pronoia on the one hand, and explicitly identified with Eve, the helper and consort of the Adam of Genesis on the other. It is also clear from what follows that not only is she responsible for the primal revelation to Adam but she also represents the principle of continuous revelation. As we have already suggested, she is the positive counterpart of the passive Sophia, who recapitulates, puts right, all that had gone wrong in the case of the latter. She is thus Tardieu's 'anti-Sophia', part of the Pronoia–Epinoia scheme of redaction (a²), replacing a single active redeeming Sophia, as in the 'Ophite' system, or a double redeemer, Pistis Sophia and her daughter Zoe, as in the *Hypostasis*.

She is said to work at the whole creation (*ktisis*), which in fact from the context appears to signify Adam, since our texts continue that she takes trouble with him, restoring him to his perfection (*plērōma*). SR refers to his being enlightened about the descent of the deficiency (*hysterēma*) and his ascent, while LR talks of his descent to the seed (*sperma*) and being instructed about the way of ascent as identical to the way of descent.[84] Epinoia's revelatory activity is evidently to be understood as redemptive: the spirit labours on the creature to prepare it for its perfection and final ascent. This would suggest a universal eschatological perspective: humanity will not be completely saved until the end, and the presence of the Epinoia/spirit imparts only a readiness for that final redemption. The *Apocryphon* gives the idea of her presence a special interpretation: the Epinoia is concealed in Adam not just to escape the notice of the archons but above all to correct the Mother's deficiency.[85] Much of this picture and terminology (the passive Sophia, the work of her consort, the terms and concepts of restoration, *plērōma–hysterēma*) is strikingly parallel to Valentinianism and further confirms the hypothesis of its influence.

(b) The second archontic reaction: the material body and the trees of Paradise

Because of the shadow (or particle) of light in him, Adam shone and his intelligence elevated him above his creators.[86] They stared up and saw how superior he was,[87] and the whole band of archons, angels and powers decided on a counter-plan, mingling the elements of fire, earth, water and the four fiery winds in a great (con)fusion.[88] Man is brought into the shadow of death through a further creation from the four material elements which the *Apocryphon* characteristically interprets as matter (*hylē*), darkness, desire (*epithymia*) and counterfeit (*antimimon*: III), opposed (*antikeimenon*: B) or variegated (*etshbbiaeit*: II) spirit (*pneuma*).[89]

In typical Gnostic fashion this material body of ours is depicted as composed of evil hypostasized passions and hostile elements, described as 'the fetter', 'the tomb' (*spēlaion*) of the created form of the body imposed on us by the robbers (the archons) and summed up as 'the fetter of oblivion'.[90] Thus man becomes mortal and he is described as the first to descend and the first separation.[91] But as usual, lest we should feel too pessimistic about the human situation, our imprisonment in a body enslaved to the passions, ignorant and deficient, we are reminded of the continuous revelatory/redemptive activity of the heavenly light figure.

However, the versions differ in that while LR refers to the Epinoia of light who will be in Adam awakening his intelligence,[92] SR talks of the Ennoia of the pre-existent (III) or first (B) light as present in him.[93] Since such a figure could be identified as Barbelo,[94] adding more weight to the hypothesis that the various redeemer figures are fundamentally identical, LR may represent a further attempt to remove such a risky conception and, by its use of the future tenses, tidy up apparent inconsistencies (e.g. that the Epinoia does not awaken Adam's intelligence until later).[95]

Then follows the episode of the two trees of Paradise, reinterpreted in terms of the hostility, deceitfulness and evil character of our mortal existence, represented by the counterfeit spirit (tree of life) and the presence of the redeeming power of the Epinoia or holy spirit (tree of the knowledge of good and evil).[96] While SR remains more faithful to the Genesis account in having the First Archon set Adam in the garden which to deceive him he said would be a delight (*tryphē*, cf. Gen 2:15, 3:23f. LXX) for him,[97] LR has the archons put him in Paradise and command him to eat at leisure.[98] The difference seems to lie in alternative interpretations by both of the wordplay *tryphē/trophē* which underlies the whole passage, as Tardieu has noted.[99]

Thus the *Apocryphon* continues its interpretation of Genesis by explaining the Paradise episode as a further archontic trick: the delight, nourishment and beauty of the garden is bitter and lawless; it is a deceit. The trees are hostility and impiety, their fruit an incurable poison, their promise death.[1] For the archons' tree, the texts continue, is the tree of life in the middle of Paradise (cf. Gen 3:4), whose secret the Saviour promises to reveal. But both recensions then differ, SR glossing that secret as their counterfeit (*antimimos*) spirit intended to turn Adam away from recognizing his perfection, which LR, aware that this figure only appears much later, has been led to amend to refer to their mutual plan, namely the image of their spirit.[2]

The Saviour's description of the tree of life is quite similar to the previous one: its root is bitter, its branches shadows of death, its leaves hate and deceit, its sap a wicked ointment, its fruit death, its seed desire, and it grows in darkness. Those who taste it dwell in the underworld.[3] Conversely, the forbidden tree of the knowledge of good and evil is the Epinoia of light, about which, SR continues, command was given not to taste, i.e. not to listen to it (cf. Gen 2:17), to prevent man looking up to and recognizing his nakedness of perfection (cf. Gen 3:7).[4] LR, however, omits the references to Genesis and to Adam's lack of perfection and simply has the archons prevent him looking up, further demonstrating its tendency to avoid or tidy up seeming awkward-nesses and inconsistencies.[5]

The Saviour then suddenly interjects: 'But it was I who raised them (*sic!*) up and made them eat.' John is prompted to ask what is his second question arising out of the Genesis reinterpretation: Was it not the snake who was responsible? To this the Saviour smilingly replies that the snake taught the sowing (*spora*) of desire, defilement and destruction, i.e. sexual reproduction which would be useful to him.[6] Although the passage is clearly an insertion,[7] it may be regarded as anticipatory, stimulated by the mention of man recognizing his nakedness of perfection.[8] If it was not the snake who instructed Adam and Eve to eat of the tree of knowledge, i.e. listen to the Epinoia, who was it? The Saviour insists it was he. However, it later transpires that – at least according to SR – it was the Epinoia who instructed Adam to eat the knowledge, not as the tree but through the tree in the form of an eagle.[9] LR is even more complicated, having Adam taste the knowledge through the Pronoia, the Saviour (the eagle) and the Epinoia (the tree) respectively![10] As we shall see, LR may represent an attempt to make sense of the Saviour's interjection, that it was he who got Adam to eat, as also to integrate the redeemer figure, the Pronoia of the closing hymn, more thoroughly into the narrative.

What we have here are several not entirely consistent interpretations of the Genesis account of the trees in Paradise, the snake who instructs Adam and Eve, and the consequences of their eating. The garden is a deceit, the significance and effect of the two trees is reversed and the snake demoted. The underlying theological paradox which the passage is employed to illustrate is the presence of the possibility of salvation and the continuous revelation (represented by the power of the Mother and the Epinoia respectively) in the Gnostic's present situation, the fetter of oblivion, the tomb of the material body. But even the presence of the Epinoia itself is not enough, as we shall see; humanity needs the divine Holy Spirit itself to descend and grant decisive redemption, presumably in the context of the five seals rite.[11]

These episodes of the creation of a material body as a second stage (not explicit in Genesis)[12] and the two trees of Paradise (in Genesis but reinterpreted by the *Apocryphon*)[13] are developed to explain certain aspects of the Gnostic's existence: his or her material body and the influences it is prey to – desire and the passions, mortality, sexual generation, ignorance of humanity's spiritual nature and origin. Humanity is a battleground of two opposing spirits: the good spirit or Epinoia, and an evil spirit, imitating the good, which prevents humanity from gaining knowledge of its situation.[14]

(c) The third archontic reaction: the creation of Eve

Our human situation has not, however, been fully delineated: sexual division has not yet taken place. This is preceded if not initiated by Adam's recognition of his disobedience to the First Archon because of his superior wisdom,[15] attributed by LR to the light of the Epinoia present in him.[16] The First Archon thereupon decides to extract the power of the Mother given to Adam by him.[17] In fact such a decision is repeated on two more occasions in remarkably similar wording: it occurs after the episodes of Adam's oblivion and the Epinoia's concealment in him when Ialdabaoth is said to resolve to extract her, and again in SR before it describes how Ialdabaoth forms a female figure and raises it up before Adam.[18] Significantly, LR obscures the last parallel in its entirely different version, which has him take a part of Adam's power, create a female form like the Epinoia and insert the power into it.[19] But both recensions agree in rejecting the reference in Gen 2:21 to Eve's creation from Adam's rib.[20]

The difference between the recensions at first suggests the existence of two distinct Gnostic interpretations of Gen 2:21. The first, echoing the theme of the seduction of the creator archons in Saturninus and the *Hypostasis*, has Ialdabaoth try to empty Adam of his power (i.e. the Epinoia?) by creating Eve as a kind of lure, with no attempt to utilize the rib idea.[21] The second, which does make use of it, recalls the 'Ophite' version in which Ialdabaoth tries to empty Adam of his power by producing a woman from the thought (*enthymesis*) which Adam had derived from his inbreathing,[22] combining with it echoes of the related theme found in the *Hypostasis* and *On the Origin of the World*, the archontic attempt to ravish and subjugate the spiritual woman.[23] In this version Ialdabaoth creates Eve from the power he takes from Adam in imitation of the Epinoia (who was supposed to have concealed herself in Adam unobserved!), presumably in order to lure her out and seize her. In this case, the target is not the power, but the Epinoia, whereas in SR, as with the 'Ophites', the creation of Eve is apparently to be the means of removing the power. Here once again the version in LR seems to be attempting to resolve the inconsistencies or gaps of SR.

But the real key to the present state of the texts is surely to see them as resulting from the combination of two distinct traditions, one involving the power of the Mother only, the other including the activity of the Epinoia. This has led the redactors of SR and LR to their different interpretations of Gen 2:21. Such a combination would explain the awkward triple repetition of Ialdabaoth's decision to retrieve the power noted above, which LR has felt it necessary to modify to fit the Epinoia scheme. Further evidence of it is demonstrated by the way the episodes involving the Epinoia (being sent as helper, awakening Adam's thought and being present in Paradise as the tree of knowledge) evidently break the (original) continuity of the tradition about the Mother's power. This continuity has been preserved by the 'Ophites' of Irenaeus who relate how Ialdabaoth inbreathed the power of the Mother into Adam, how he was thus exalted above his creators, and how Ialdabaoth, full of jealousy, plotted to recover the power by producing a woman from him.[24] And comparison of the terminology involved tends to confirm the existence of the two traditions and the secondary character of the Epinoia tradition: passages concerning the Epinoia use terms reminiscent of the technical terminology of Valentinianism, while those involving the power speak in terms more reminiscent of 'Ophite' ideas, of man's thought being stronger, more powerful or more exalted than that of his creators.[25]

If then the original formulation only involved the power and the Epinoia tradition was later conflated with it, did the sleep/oblivion motif of Gen 2:21 (not present in the 'Ophite' version) belong to that original? Certainly both recensions agree in reinterpreting it: in pursuance of his plan to recover the power Ialdabaoth casts an oblivion over Adam.[26] This prompts John's third question, 'Lord, what is oblivion?' and the Saviour's 'correction' of 'Moses': he did not make him sleep but veiled and weighed down his senses in accordance with Isa 6:10.[27] However, far from this being the means for Ialdabaoth to remove the power, as we might have expected, we suddenly hear of the Epinoia of light concealing herself in Adam (despite the hint in LR that she was already there!),[28] and the resolve of the First Archon to extract her from Adam's side.[29] Although the oblivion theme may be original, this passage with its reinterpretation of the rib of Gen

2:21 is evidently a further intrusion into the power tradition by the Epinoia material, which continues with the Johannine gloss that despite the First Archon's resolve, the Epinoia is unattainable; although the darkness pursued her it could not reach her (cf. John 1:5).[30]

Comparison with the treatment of Gen 2:21 in the *Hypostasis*[31] and *On the Origin of the World*[32] is instructive here. In the former, which as usual follows the LXX of Genesis in a much more literal fashion, it is the archons who decide to bring oblivion (*bshe*) over the spirit-indwelt Adam so that he falls asleep. This oblivion is interpreted, as in the *Apocryphon*, as ignorance. They thereupon open his side as a living woman and build it up with flesh in place of her (cf. Gen 2:21f.). Adam thus becomes entirely psychic, but the spiritual woman thus formed awakens him so that when he sees her he exclaims: 'You will be called "the Mother of the living"' (cf. Gen 3:21).[33] Then follows the motif of the archontic rape, not of the spiritual woman but of her shadow.[34]

On the Origin of the World presents a rather different picture of events. According to it Zoe/Eve, the daughter of Pistis Sophia, is sent to waken the inert, soulless Adam. He is enabled to stand and when he sees her he exclaims (as in the *Hypostasis*) 'You will be called "the Mother of the living" because you gave me life' (cf. Gen 3:21). When the authorities hear of this they decide to seduce her to prevent her ascent. They plan to deceive Adam into thinking that she is from his rib, and thus subservient, by bringing an oblivion (*bshe*) over him and instructing him in his sleep (cf. Gen 2:21f.).[35] Then follows, as in the *Hypostasis*, the archontic attempt to seduce Eve, which fails. What they do defile is her likeness left secretly beside Adam.[36] As we have already observed, the same two motifs (Eve's appearance and her seduction by the archons) also appear side by side in the 'Ophite' system.[37]

What makes the *Hypostasis* and *On the Origin* different from the *Apocryphon* is the latter's more positive evaluation of the First Archon as an unwitting vehicle of the divine and consequent emphasis on the power motif. Thus the *Hypostasis* and *On the Origin* put their stress on the spiritual woman as the source of revelation and salvation (and thus properly entitled 'Zoe, the Mother of the living'), entirely distinct from Adam (and earthly Eve) and the object of the archontic attacks. The *Apocryphon*, on the other hand, at least originally (as with the 'Ophites'), focuses rather on the light-power, with Eve created as a means of emptying Adam of it, and the Epinoia added only later as the main target. This analysis is confirmed by their differing use of the oblivion motif, either literally, to assist Eve's creation, as in the *Hypostasis*, or as part of an archontic pretence, as in *On the Origin*. Both are more meaningful than that of our present *Apocryphon* with its abrupt reference to the Epinoia, suggesting that originally the *Apocryphon* was closer to the version found in the *Hypostasis*: God cast an oblivion over Adam, removed, not his rib but the light-power, and formed it into Eve, who is thus recognized by Adam as consubstantial.[38] This picture seems to be borne out by the continuation in SR: when Adam sees her he immediately becomes sober and applies Gen 2:23f. to her (i.e. she is the revealer/ redeemer rather than the Epinoia which SR has hastily inserted in an attempt to harmonize, and she is rightly entitled 'the Mother of all living', rather than the Epinoia, or even, as in LR, the abruptly-introduced Sophia).[39]

Our present version of the *Apocryphon* has obscured this by its introduction of the Epinoia. As we saw, she has been given the attributes of the spiritual woman of the *Hypostasis*, *On the Origin* and the 'Ophites', whom the archons attempt to seduce. Ialdabaoth's attempt to extract the light-power becomes his unsuccessful attempt to lure out the Epinoia, and it is she, rather than the light-power present as the spiritual Eve, who removes the veil from Adam's senses, and is called by Adam, 'Zoe, Mother of the living'.[40] And this interpolation also makes sense of the confused interpretation of Gen 2:23f. in the *Apocryphon*.[41] With the loss of the original reference to Adam's abandonment of his creators and union with his spiritual counterpart through the substitution of the Epinoia, the text required a new interpretation. The reference to the man was taken to apply to Sophia's consort (i.e. the Epinoia), that to the woman to Sophia, and man's leaving his parents to the future descent of the Epinoia to unite with Sophia and correct her faults. As we have seen, SR seems to retain a trace of the more original interpretation while LR has taken the feminine figure named by Adam as Sophia and not as the Epinoia.[42]

This complex episode enables the author(s) of the *Apocryphon* to explain how the division of Adam into male and female came about. Here we have a further element in our present situation, the existence of woman, which implies the further fettering of the divine through sexual reproduction and also explains (by appeal to the prevailing Jewish legends about the seduction of Eve) the existence of angelic intermediaries with control over the visible world. Characteristically, alongside the tradition of the First Archon attempting to remove the light-power from Adam and creating woman as a means, bait and receptacle for it, we have the presence of the Epinoia, just as in the 'Ophite' system we have both the trace of light and the redemptive activity of Sophia. Even if Ialdabaoth is successful as regards the presence of the light-power (which as we shall see is later interpreted as the soul or precondition for salvation) in Eve, there is still the revelatory and redemptive activity of the Epinoia.[43]

The tensions and contradictions visible in both recensions are to some extent the result of different traditions, but they also serve to express, as do the similar phenomena in the *Hypostasis* and *On the Origin of the World*, the classic Gnostic paradox: how to proclaim their certainty of being the elect, possessing the divine power within themselves, yet do justice to the elements in their own existence which threatened that assurance: the weight of matter and the senses, the fact of sexual differentiation, the lure of the passions and the burden of mortality and fate.

(d) The eating of knowledge and the expulsion from Paradise

Despite frequent anticipations Adam and Eve have not yet eaten of the tree of knowledge, already interpreted (if hesitantly by LR) as the Epinoia. Further, they are still in Paradise and not in this present world of ignorance, darkness and death, governed by the demands of nature and the inexorable drive of sexual reproduction, subject to the imperfect antitheses of justice and injustice and the conventions of morality. To account for such a situation the *Apocryphon* makes further use of the tree of knowledge motif, but in this case as it occurs in Genesis 3 rather than Genesis 2.

The heavenly initiative in getting Adam and Eve to eat is again stressed. We were told above that the snake had merely taught sexual reproduction: it was the Saviour himself who encouraged them to eat.[44] Now we hear that it occurred through heavenly authority and revelation.[45] But whereas SR has the Epinoia instruct Adam through the tree in the form of an eagle to eat the knowledge,[46] LR, after reference to their tasting pefect knowledge, suddenly has the Saviour interject: 'It was I who appeared in the form of an eagle on the tree of knowledge, i.e. the Epinoia from the Pronoia ... to teach them and awaken them from deep sleep.'[47] This passage is not simply part of the attempt of the redactor of LR to introduce more traditional elements of exegesis of Gen 3:6–7, as Tardieu claims,[48] but rather aims to confirm the Saviour's ultimate identity as the Pronoia.[49] By such an identification and description of the Saviour's redeeming activity as teaching and awakening from sleep, this passage is brought into harmony both with the Saviour's earlier interjection and the triple descent scheme of the closing Pronoia hymn.[50]

LR is thus led to 'correct' SR's representation of Epinoia in the form of an eagle on the tree (instead of herself *being* the tree as in the earlier passage based on Genesis 2) instructing Adam to eat the knowledge and thereby recognize his (or their) perfection.[51] And it again follows Genesis (3:8) in speaking of their fall and recognition of their nakedness, over against SR's description of their fault as ignorance.[52] But, conscious that the Epinoia was originally the subject, LR immediately reintroduces her as revealing herself to them and awakening their thought.[53]

This sparks the inevitable archontic reaction. According to its exegesis of Gen 3:6f., the *Apocryphon* has described how Adam and Eve came to 'eat' the knowledge and thus become aware of their perfection and fallen state of ignorance. Following Gen 3:8 (Adam's concealment from God) it relates how Ialdabaoth becomes aware that they have departed from him.[54] The same two motifs occur together in the 'Ophite' system: Adam and Eve after eating the tree of knowledge recognize the supreme power and depart from their creators.[55] The *Apocryphon* continues the Genesis reinterpretation with Ialdabaoth's curse. That LR has him curse Adam's earth rather than him and Eve, as in SR,[56] is probably due to its more literal interpretation of Gen 3:17.[57] And Tardieu has very plausibly traced LR's divergence from SR (in having Ialdabaoth discover the woman preparing herself for Adam, adding that he was lord over her although he did not know the mystery which had occurred through the holy counsel,[58] rather than, as in SR, that he added (*prospoieisthai*) of the woman that her husband would be lord over her (cf. Gen 3:16) etc.)[59] to its misreading of *prospoieisthai*.[60] Thus it failed to spot the reference and amended the text in the light of Ialdabaoth's subsequent rape of Eve.

The 'mystery of the holy counsel', of which Ialdabaoth is ignorant in ordaining the superiority of male to female, is probably the resolution of the Mother–Father whereby the Mother's power was inserted into Adam by Ialdabaoth.[61] But we might also recall the use of the terms 'mystery' and 'counsel' in the previous passage about the trees in Paradise. Over against the secret of the archons' plan revealed by the Saviour, i.e. the counterfeit spirit which leads to wickedness, desire and death,[62] there is the secret of the heavenly plan, the light-power hidden in Adam and Eve and the presence of the Epinoia, who continually awakens man from his oblivion to recognize his equal and consubstantial consort, Eve.[63]

In an ironic reversal of Genesis, the *Apocryphon* has Adam and Eve frightened to reprove their creator and thus reveal his ignorance to his angels.[64] Finally he casts them out of the garden (cf. Gen 3:23) and cloaks them in thick darkness.[65] Thus we have the depiction through the reinterpretation of selected motifs from Genesis 3 (eating the tree of knowledge, 'nakedness', the curse, man as lord of woman, the expulsion from Paradise) of further characteristics of our present situation. We do not live in Paradise; we are aware of our lack of perfect knowledge and of the tragic splitting of our original unity, of that mystery of the power found in us which seeks reunion, perfection. We live in a world under a curse, the creation of an ignorant demiurge, a dominant characteristic of which is the male's lordship over the female, despite their true but hidden equality and unity.[66] But the Gnostic is conscious, through the presence of the divine power within and the work of the divine Spirit, of the mystery of the heavenly plan of restoration and removal of the deficiency, the ignorance that drowns that divine element in oblivion.

(e)   *The seduction of Eve and the origin of human generation*

Besides the reality of sexual distinction there is a further determinant of human existence, the biological urge to reproduce. Sex and generation are presented as a further device of the creator and his satellites to keep us enslaved and blind to our true origin and destiny. To explain this the authors of the *Apocryphon* have recourse to the motif already mentioned, the archontic seduction of Eve. This appears in various guises in Gnostic texts. In the 'Ophite' system, for example, Ialdabaoth's offspring, sexually attracted by the woman created by their progenitor, call her Eve, and beget sons, i.e. the angels, by her. Her adultery (and claim to be Mother of all living?) leads to another heavenly rebuke from Sophia.[67] This is followed by a second use of the motif, in association with and partial explanation of, Adam and Eve's expulsion from Paradise. Ialdabaoth himself tries to rape Eve and beget sons by her, but is unable because of Sophia's secret opposition and evacuation of the trace of light.[68] This reveals the characteristic hallmark of 'Ophite' theology: the trace of light cannot be jeopardized and in both cases is removed beforehand.

Elements of both interpretations occur in the *Hypostasis* and *On the Origin of the World*. In both the archons, horrified to discover that the spiritual woman has awakened their Adam, attempt to seduce her, but in fact merely defile her earthly image.[69] The 'Ophite' distinction between defiled earthly Eve and the intact heavenly trace of light appears here as the distinction between the defiled image and the unscathed heavenly Eve. The *Hypostasis*, perhaps closer to the likely original form of the motif, has the archons motivated by infatuation,[70] whereas in *On the Origin* their intention is to defile her to prevent her return to heaven, thereby ensuring the subordination of her and her offspring to themselves and Adam.[71] In it the earthly Eve is raped and produces Abel first from the chief archon, then the rest from the seven powers and their angels.[72]

The background of this motif may indeed be Gen 6:1f., as Bullard, Janssens and Stroumsa suggest,[73] but we should carefully distinguish, as Jonas argues,[74] between the related but not identical mythologoumena of the fornication of the angels (of Genesis 6) and the seduction of the archons. The idea found in rabbinic and Gnostic sources that the Devil (in the guise of the snake) begot Cain (and Abel) by Eve[75] has clearly played some part along with speculation, Jewish and otherwise, on Genesis 6, in the development of both. But whatever the precise source or sources, the rape motif is used by the *Apocryphon* to explain the demiurgic origin of sexual reproduction and the nature of the archons who rule humanity and the cosmos, and who embody the kind of imperfect morality (righteous/unrighteous) which pertains in this world.

Ialdabaoth is once more the protagonist, as in the creation of Eve and the expulsion from Paradise. According to SR he saw the virgin standing beside Adam and became filled with ignorance since he wanted to raise up offspring (*sperma*) from her.[76] LR, in that it feels constrained to add as motivation that the First Archon had seen the Epinoia appear in Eve as life, seems secondary, a further sign of its tendency to stress the Pronoia–Epinoia pattern.[77] Thus it at once involves the Pronoia sending assistants to remove Zoe (i.e. the Epinoia) from Eve, presumably lest she be defiled.[78] This also precisely echoes the tendency noted above in the 'Ophite' system, the *Hypostasis* and *On the Origin*: to ensure that the divine redeeming element remains undefiled by at times removing it from its earthly vessel. Indeed the parallel to LR is more marked in the 'Ophite' system: Sophia secretly empties Eve of the trace of light lest the *spirit* from the *height* (*principalitas = authentia*) should share either in cursing or in (sexual) abuse (*opprobrium*) at the hands of Ialdabaoth.[79]

All four versions then agree in depicting Ialdabaoth raping Eve and begetting two sons.[80] But the two recensions reverse their names. Whereas LR first gives them as Eloim (i.e. Elohim) and Jave (i.e. Yahweh), assigning a bear face to Eloim and a cat face to Jave,[81] SR omits the primary identification and reverses the ascriptions.[82] Both recensions agree that one is righteous and the other unrighteous, but continue with their reverse identifications; Jave as righteous and Eloim as unrighteous in LR, vice versa in SR.[83] SR then has the righteous set over fire and spirit, the unrighteous over water and earth, while LR has Jave over fire and wind, Eloim over water and earth.[84] Finally, while SR has them called Cain and Abel by all the generations of men till today, LR makes Ialdabaoth responsible for naming them in view of his wickedness, apparently attaching the reference to the present day to the following sentence.[85] A few lines later we are told Ialdabaoth set them over the elements (*archai*) to rule the tomb (*spēlaion/ mhaou*), namely the material body.[86]

Despite the reversals in identification, the basic structure and thrust are clear. The powers which rule the elements, and thus material human bodies, are derived from Ialdabaoth's rape of Eve. The more elevated elements (fire and wind) are governed by the righteous archon identified as Cain by humanity, the less elevated (water and earth) by the unrighteous identified as Abel. They are not (as in Genesis, the 'Ophite' system, the *Hypostasis*, etc.) the sons of Adam: further, their characteristics are the reverse of the Genesis account.[87] And it is the Genesis connection which may explain the swapping round of the names Jave and Eloim. It is surely significant that these names alone are reversed, not their appearance, character, the elements they control, etc. What seems to have caused the trouble is the similar attempt by redactors of both recensions to accommodate the identification with Cain and Abel. Cain, the first son in Genesis 4, is yet unrighteous, Abel, the second, righteous. SR, with its original order Jave–Eloim (cf. Gen 2:4b), has identified Eloim with the righteous archon Abel, set over the superior elements, and Jave with the wicked Cain, associated with water and earth: LR, with its order Eloim–Jave, has done the same, identifying Jave with Abel and Eloim with Cain. It is difficult to judge which of these traditions is more original, but pointers to the priority of SR might be its more biblical order of the archons' names and the clumsier treatment of the naming of Cain and Abel by LR.[88]

It is in this context, sandwiched between the origin and activity of these archons who were the first product of sexual intercourse, that the *Apocryphon* relates how ordinary earthly intercourse began, the point being, of course, that it was Ialdabaoth and his powers who initiated, control and ensure the continuation of sex and human reproduction. Although the Saviour's previous attribution of this to the snake we suggested may be secondary and modelled on Ialdabaoth's action here,[89] the snake could be seen as an agent of or even the First Archon himself. Thus it was indeed through Ialdabaoth that sexual intercourse began and continues, in that he sowed a desire for reproduction in Adam.[90]

The gist of the following confused passage, in which B and III differ from one another as well as from LR, seems to be that by means of this desire and the operation of the counterfeit spirit human images were produced.[91] The key to the confusion may lie in the *ousia* of SR, which LR seems to avoid and has evidently understood here in a sexual sense and emended into the more comprehensible (and just mentioned) *synousia*.[92] What SR for all its disarray may be trying to express is that the desire for offspring sown in Adam and Eve and the counterfeit spirit represent two of the four evil substances from which Adam was re-formed by the archons; hence all his descendants are in their image.[93] And this would explain the rather abrupt reappearance of the two archons. They were associated with the four elements/evil substances, and so it is natural that they are mentioned here as set by Ialdabaoth over the (four?) elements (*archai*) to control the tomb of the human body.[94]

(f) The descent of the Mother's spirit and its saving activity

With this reference to the installation of the two archons over the human body, the *Apocryphon*'s description of the present character of that body, composed of evil material elements, sexually divided with the male superior to the female, expelled from Paradise, subject to the forces of reproduction and the constraints of an inferior moral order derived from the archontic offspring of Ialdabaoth, is completed. But that is not the whole story: at once we hear of a new initiative further developing – indeed climaxing – the Genesis reinterpretation, namely the birth of Seth and its implications. Once again LR seems to represent a theological expansion of SR based on the 'Sethian' reinterpretation. Thus whereas SR simply talks of Adam knowing his own substance and begetting Seth (cf. Gen 4:25) in the manner of aeonic generation (*genea*),[95] LR relates how, when Adam recognized the likeness of his foreknowledge (*prognōsis*), he begot the likeness of the Son of Man and called him 'Seth' in the manner of begetting among the aeons.[96] LR has been led to develop the parallel with heavenly Adam(as) and Seth: earthly Adam recognizes the image of heavenly Man/Adamas (produced, it will be recalled, from the aeon First Thought/*prognōsis*),[97] and begets Seth in that image and with that figure's name.

Here the ambiguity over where exactly the phrase about the similarity to heavenly generation belongs, whether to Seth's production, as in III and LR, or to the following passage about the Mother sending her spirit, as in B,[98] might suggest the secondary character of this section with its further signs of the effects of Valentinian and 'Sethian' reinterpretation. Thus while B has the Mother, in accordance with the heavenly race in the aeons, sending what is hers, i.e. her spirit, III has the Mother being sent her own spirit.[99] Who is this Mother? Janssens argues on the basis of the mention of the heavenly race that she must be the Pronoia and not Sophia,[1] but LR appears to assume that 'the Mother' refers to Sophia. Thus it reads: 'so (*homoiōs*) the *other* Mother (i.e. Barbelo/Pronoia) sent down her spirit which is like her'.[2] SR then has the spirit descend to (or for) her to raise up the substance (*ousia*) which resembles him, after the pattern (*typos*) of the perfection, to rouse them from the oblivion and wickedness of the grave,[3] while LR diverges, referring to the Mother sending down the spirit as the antitype (*antitypos*) of those in perfection (*plērōma*), since she intended to prepare a dwelling for the aeons who were to come down.[4]

Now the descent motif and the awkward 'to her' of B do recall the previous mission of Sophia's consort to correct her deficiencies.[5] LR and III have seen the awkwardness of B's version and tried to emend, the former by suggesting that 'the Mother' is Barbelo, not Sophia, the latter making Sophia the object, both insisting on her essentially passive role. The version in B would thus seem more original,[6] but itself a clumsy attempt to reconcile two different traditions, the earlier that of the redeemer Sophia restoring the divine element to Seth and his descendants after Adam and Eve had lost it, as in the 'Ophite' system,[7] the later the Valentinian and 'Sethian' influenced tradition of the consort/ spirit who descends from the Pleroma first to the passive Sophia and then to her spiritual descendants, the race of Seth, to correct the deficiency.

The continuation, unique to LR, which has him (i.e. the spirit, although the previous subject had been the Mother), cause them to drink water of oblivion from the First Archon to make them ignorant of where they had come from,[8] is obviously the work of LR's redactor, perhaps in an effort to give what he interprets as Barbelo's spirit an appropriate role, at the same time explaining why the race of Seth was not entirely saved at that point. Since Barbelo has already sent her spirit/Epinoia/Zoe to help Adam, perfect creation and correct Sophia's deficiency,[9] it cannot simply do the same here (i.e. awaken those akin to it from their earthly oblivion, work on the seed, etc. as in SR). Instead it is given the roles of preparing earthly dwellings for those divine beings (souls?) to be sent down later, and ensuring that the Sethians forget their origin, hence the need for a final divine intervention.

The secondary character of LR at this point is also evident from the sequel: whereas SR has the seed as the object of the spirit's activity, in LR the seed is the subject, left dangling with no apparent object.[10] And comparison with earlier and later passages dealing with the Epinoia's mission suggests that LR has misunderstood or reinterpreted the basic soteriological pattern which SR reflects better.[11] Just as the Epinoia, the good spirit, was sent out to help Adam, work at the created order, etc., so too the Mother's own spirit has the task of awakening from oblivion those of Adam's descendants consubstantial with it, the elect seed of Seth, and preparing them for the final redemptive descent of the Holy Spirit (in the rite of the five seals?).

Finally it is worth noting how the whole pattern and terminology of this saving event[13] both recall the descriptions of the mission of the consort to Sophia,[14] the Epinoia to Adam,[15] and Sophia to her seed,[16] on the one hand and echo Valentinian and 'Sethian' language and conceptions on the other. Yet it is surely first worth noting once again the underlying similarity to the 'Ophite' system: the *Apocryphon*'s pattern of four redemptive missions can be reduced to involve only two figures, Sophia's consort and herself, as with the 'Ophites',[17] the major difference being that whereas the latter highlights Sophia's redemptive role and only alludes to her need for redemption in passing,[18] the *Apocryphon* does the reverse. Sophia appears predominantly in need of redemption and only faint traces remain of her redeeming role.[19] Nevertheless both texts, as Schottroff has persuasively argued,[20] have the identical aim of exonerating Sophia from blame for the present state of the cosmos, but achieve it by diametrically opposed solutions. For our *Apocryphon* Sophia is deficient, therefore she cannot redeem; for the 'Ophites' Sophia is entirely free from blemish, therefore she does redeem.

Yet if there is an underlying similarity of structure here between the *Apocryphon* and the 'Ophites', the influence of Valentinian and 'Sethian' ideas on the former is even more unmistakable. As regards the first, Sophia's original request for salvation, the consent of the Pleroma and the dispatch of her consort to correct her deficiency unmistakably recall the pattern in certain Valentinian texts which know of one fallen Sophia.[21] Then there is the concatenation of concepts occurring without explanation such as awakening, oblivion, the seed, raising up or correcting, deficiency and perfection, employed in a manner reminiscent of their – virtually technical – usage in Valentinianism.[22] And as regards the second, we have frequently drawn attention to the 'Sethian' character of features found here such as the seed and the centrality of (heavenly) Seth.

Conclusion

With the reference to Seth, the 'other seed' of Gen 4:25, the *Apocryphon* concludes its reinterpretation of the primal history, Genesis 1–4. Although this is the major soteriological component of the *Apocryphon*, there still remain the section on the destiny of souls, the further Genesis reinterpretation and the Pronoia hymn, to be dealt with in the following chapter. Thus any conclusions at this point can only be preliminary.

First, it is undoubtedly the case that the Genesis reinterpretation is fundamental to the *Apocryphon*, as well as to the 'Ophite' system and the related *Hypostasis of the Archons* and *On the Origin of the World*, and is also implied, we suggested, by Irenaeus' (incomplete) summary of the Barbelognostic myth. It is used to explain our present condition, enslaved in an evil material body, exiled from Paradise, subject to the passions, sexual division and the reproductive process, under the control of alien rulers and their dubious morality, a battleground of two opposed spirits, one divine, the other counterfeit. On the other hand John's questions and the Saviour's responses and interjections are undoubtedly a later addition.

Second, Genesis is obviously reinterpreted in our texts in accordance with an existing Gnostic myth or myths, in a plastic and varied way, so that different interpretations occur of the same events, as we have seen. However, behind that variety one can detect in each text a fundamental concern (or concerns) which tends to determine the interpretation. In the case of the *Apocryphon* we can detect not only the original Barbelognostic (and 'Ophite') concern with the paradoxical figure of Sophia, obedient higher and disobedient lower Wisdom, both creator and redeemer, whose experience is paradigmatic for the Gnostic him- or herself, but also the frame story and dialogue reworking with its Pronoia–Epinoia scheme, playing down Sophia's redeeming role and replacing it with the Epinoia and the triple descent of Pronoia, and the 'Sethian' reinterpretation with its periodization of salvation history involving heavenly Seth and his descendants. Yet all three reflect in their varying emphases the central paradox of the Gnostic experience of salvation: the possession on the one hand of the possibility of salvation (often expressed as a continuing process of revelation), yet the need on the other for a final saving revelation from heaven. This explains the otherwise baffling and apparently inconsistent process of salvation history charted in Genesis: Adam is continually saved by heavenly interventions yet keeps on forfeiting that salvation through further archontic stratagems. Salvation/revelation is not simply original and continuous, but must be decisive and eschatological. Conversely, the Gnostic *Heilsgeschichte* implies that salvation is not a permanent possession but a gift of grace, which requires constant effort to retain.

Third, this paradox can help us to a provisional answer to our opening questions about salvation. On (1) the understanding of salvation present, we can say that the Gnostic needs not only the possibility of salvation (the demiurgic power which all possess) but the saving descent of the Spirit (in a rite of initiation). As with the famous Valentinian formula with which we began, both rite and saving knowledge are required. On (2) the subject or object of salvation, this would seem to be not the whole person or species but only an element illuminated by or united with the divine, whether soul, spark, power, substance, seed or race. Adam himself is able to lose his divine power. On (3) whether salvation is by nature or grace, the *Apocryphon*'s Genesis reinterpretation suggests that is a false dichotomy: both are intimately involved, the possibility of salvation (nature) and the Spirit's saving descent (grace). On (4) the saviour figure, the *Apocryphon* is less clear because of the effects of the Valentinian and 'Sethian' reworkings. Thus we have a series of saviour figures, the Saviour of the frame story, the Mother/Barbelo/Pronoia, the Epinoia and the Holy Spirit, but again the logic of the experience of salvation suggests that they only make sense in the light of a decisive eschatological revelation/salvation, that of and in Christ. They explain how the possibility of salvation was always there, but only realized now in and through the Holy Spirit of Christ in the rite of Gnostic initiation. This in turn suggests an answer to (5), the time of salvation. Although the possibility was always there, only from now on, in the light of the Christ event and the descent of the Holy Spirit, can there be decisive, final salvation. We shall have to see how far the section on the destiny of various souls confirms this analysis.

Finally as regards the question of the priority of the versions, although there are again some exceptions, in the main the short recension seems closer to the original, the long recension being more prone to spiritualize, to attempt to reduce apparent inconsistencies, and to reveal the influence of Valentinian and 'Sethian' interpretations.

Notes

[1] Iren. 1.21.4.

[2] 18.4–11; cf. 24.28ff. and 16.31–17.4.

[3] CH 1.18.

[4] 21.

[5] Cf. the comments of Isidore, Basilides' son in Clem. Alex. *Strom.* 6.6.53.4.

[6] Cf. e.g. Filoramo, *History* 38–46.

[7] 21f.

[8] Cf. *Gnosis 1*, 2ff.; Rudolph, *TRu* 36, 8; MacRae, 'Sleep' 496–507.

[9] Cf. *Gos. Truth* 22.2–20.

[10] Quispel, 'Anthropos' 234; Colpe, RGG^3 2 1657. On this, see Schenke, 'Die neutestamentliche Christologie und der gnostische Erlöser' in Tröger, *Gnosis und Neues Testament* 208.

[11] 'La conception de l'homme dans la gnose valentinienne', *Gnostic Studies 1* 37–57, esp. 50, citing Tert. *Adv. Val.* 29: 'spiritalem ex Seth de

obvenientia superducunt, iam non naturalem sed indulgentiam, ut quos Achamoth de superioribus in animas bonas depluat.'

[12] On *physei sōzomenos* (the force of the participle has not always been observed) in the heresiologists, cf. Iren. 1.6.2f.; *Exc. ex Theod.* 56.3; Clem. Alex. *Strom.* 2.10.2; 115.1; 4.89.4; 5.33; Orig. *Princ.* 3.4.4f.; *Comm. in Joh.* 2.14; Epiph. *Pan.* 31.7.6–11. See also Basilides in Clem. Alex. *Strom.* 5.3.2–3. On this idea in Bultmann, cf. *Das Evangelium des Johannes* (Göttingen, 1941, 1962²), 21–4, 96f., 114, 240 (ET 28–31, 64ff., 135, n. 4, 250f.); *Theology of the New Testament 1* (London: SCM, 1952), 168, 181–3. See also J. Zandee, 'Gnostic Ideas on the Fall and Salvation', *Numen* 11 (1964), 13–74, esp. 18, 41, 43, 46; W. Schmithals, *Gnosticism in Corinth*, tr. J. E. Steely (Nashville: Abingdon, 1971), 28; H.-M. Schenke in *Umwelt des Urchristentums* 1 (Berlin, 1971³), 379.

[13] 'Animae' 65–97, arguing on the basis of the *Apocalypse of Adam* and Valentinian evidence. On this, see Rudolph, *TRu* 37 (1971), 12f.

[14] Cf. 119.16ff.

[15] 'Valentinian Claim', *passim*.

[16] See ch. 5, p. 168f.

[17] Cf. e.g. Iren. 1.6.1; 7.5.

[18] For a balanced summary of this, see e.g. Rudolph, *Gnosis* 117f.

[19] 127.16f.

[20] So e.g. Quispel, 'Anthropos' 234; Colpe, *Schule* 30, 198; Schmithals, *Gnosticism* 30, n. 12; see further Filoramo, *History* 103, n. 11. But, cf. Colpe's revised view in 'New Testament and Gnostic Christology' in *Religions in Antiquity* (Essays in Memory of E. R. Goodenough) ed. J. Neusner (Leiden: Brill, 1968), 227–43, esp. 242.

[21] 'Erlöser' 208.

[22] *Gnosis* 118–47.

[23] *History* 104f.

[24] On this, see esp. Bousset, *Hauptprobleme* ch. 6, 238–76; Reitzenstein, *Erlösungsmysterium*; Colpe, *Schule* and Rudolph, *Tru* 36, 11f.; *Gnosis* 121ff.

[25] Cf. *Gnosis* 121, 131f.

[26] Arai, 'Zur Christologie des Apokryphons des Johannes', *NTS* 15 (1968/69), 318; Schottroff, *Glaubende* 99. But for her the *Apocryphon* is non- rather than pre-Christian.

[27] 'Erlöser' 214.

[28] *Glaubende* 10.

[29] 'Erlöser' 211f. On this theme of primal and continuous revelation, see Rudolph, *Gnosis* 132–4.

[30] 217. Cf. Rudolph, *Gnosis* 148f.

[31] *Gnosis* 149–52.

[32] Cf. *1 Apol.* 5f., 46; *2 Apol.* 8, 10, 13; *Dial.* 56ff.

[33] Cf. e.g. the views of Epiphanius' Sethians, *Pan.* 39.3.5.

[34] Cf. e.g. *AJ* II 15.1–5/IV 23.14–20; *HA* 87.30–88.3. *OW* 112.25–113.5 develops the latter conception: Adam is created in the image of light-Adam to trap the latter and avert his threat to destroy the archons.

[35] Cf. e.g. Iren. 1.30.6.

[36] Cf. e.g. *OW* 113.5–10; *SJC* III 106.24–107.11/B 103.10–104.7; *TP* 40.22–9. *Treat. Seth* 51.20–56.20 presents a christological version of the motif.

[37] Iren. 1.30.6.

[38] II 19.15–18/IV 29.24–7. Cf. II 14.18–24/IV 22.23–23.2.

[39] Cf. B 51.1–7/III 23.19–24.1 and B 47.20–48.5/III 21.21–4. In *HA* 92.32–93.2, Norea cries out to a male figure, the Holy One, the God of the All, and in *Norea* 27.11–22; 28.26–30, Norea cries out to various male figures including the Father of the All (Adamas).

[40] Father: cf. B 30.6/III 9.17 and II 6.16; B 48.2 and II 14.19; B 51.5/III 23.22 and II 19.17/IV 29.27; B 52.18/III 24.25 and II 20.9f.; Mother: cf. B 71.6 and II 27.33f. But B 75.11/III 39.11f. have 'Mother–Father' where LR omits it!

[41] Cf. B 71.6f. and II 27.33f./IV 43.9f. (Mother–Father). III 36.19f. is lacunous and unclear.

[42] Iren. 1.30.12.

[43] Mother–Father/Pronoia: cf. II 19.17ff.; 20.9ff.; 25.2–16 ('the other Mother'!); 27.33ff. (glossing the Epinoia as 'of the Pronoia of light'); Holy Spirit/Zoe/Mother of living: cf. B 38.9–13 and par; 53.4–54.4 and par (identified with the Epinoia); II 21.13–16 and par (SR has Ennoia); Epinoia: cf. B 59.21–60.2 and par; B 71.5–14 and par (identified with Holy Spirit); Christ *passim*; Sophia: cf. B 47.11–14 and par; 54.18–55.4/III 25.17–23 (Sophia to correct her deficiency through the Epinoia: LR again emends to stress Sophia's passivity: II 20.24–8/IV 31.24–7); II 23.20–4 (LR here revealingly has Sophia as active, identified with Zoe etc.); B 76.1–5/III 39.18–21 (the Mother raising up her seed – perhaps an allusion to Barbelo, but its omission by LR suggests its redactor thought Sophia was the subject).

[44] *Muséon* 84, 412f. She appeals to B 38.7–13 and par where the Holy Spirit who alone sees Sophia's abortion is identified as 'Zoe, the Mother of all living' (Gen 3:21 LXX), and who for Janssens is Sophia herself; to B 44.19ff. where Sophia moving to and fro is the Holy Spirit of Gen 1:2; and to B 53.4–10 which identifies the good, merciful spirit with the Epinoia and Zoe. (LR seems to obscure that association by having the helper sent through the good spirit: II 20.14–19). Tardieu, *Écrits* 319, rightly sees the origin of the figures of the Spirit, Zoe Mother of all living, and the Epinoia of light, in all their fluidity yet ultimate identity, in speculations based on Gen 2:7b, 2:18 and 3:20.

[45] Cf. the mission of the Epinoia, named 'Zoe', to instruct creation and help correct Sophia's deficiency in B 52.17–54.4 and par; Adam's recognition of the Epinoia (identified as the Mother's consort) as

'Mother of the living' (Gen 3:20) in B 59.20–60.16 and par. In the latter LR (II 23.5–24/IV 35.26–36.17) revealingly insists that it was Sophia who descended to correct her deficiency, identifying her as 'Zoe', despite its earlier identifications of the Holy Spirit and the Epinoia with the latter (in II 10.17f. and par and 20.17–19 respectively). There is also the odd phrase earlier in II 9.25: 'the Sophia of the Epinoia', suggesting a close connection. Tardieu's claim, *Écrits* 274, that the last phrase is a trace of a supposed title for this whole section 'The revelation of the Epinoia' is pure speculation, but he is right to point to the character of Epinoia as 'anti-Sophia par excellence'.

[46] 39.13–40.19. Cf. the very similar formula describing Sophia in her redemptive descent in *AJ* II 23.20–4.

[47] Cf. *HA* 88.11–15 (the descent of the spirit, an echo of Gen 2:7b and 2:18); 89.11–17 (the spiritual woman, 'mother of the living' of Gen 3:20); 89.31–90.12 (the spiritual woman enters the snake of Gen 3); 95.5–96.3 (Zoe, daughter of Sophia as redeemer and consort of the righteous Sabaoth).

[48] In *Norea* 27.11–28.12 the Epinoia (perhaps even associated with light in the lacuna in 27.11) is evidently a heavenly soteriological figure, the abode of Norea, whose resemblance to Sophia as her archetype we have already noted (see ch. 2, p. 45f.).

[49] The 'Ophite' system too, however, has traces of redeeming entities alongside Sophia, e.g. the tree of knowledge (1.30.7) and trace of light reintroduced into Adam and Eve (1.30.9).

[50] B 51.1–7/III 23.19–24.1. The reading of III 23.21 'in a *prouniko[s]*', is perhaps preferable to B 51.3f. which applies it to the archon, in light of a supposed contrast with her present innocent state. Thus the *ḥn oumntatkakia* of B 51.4f. is an antithesis to the *ḥn ouprouniko* of III 23.21. However, the earlier reference in B 37.10f. (the *phrourikon* of III 15.3 is an obvious emendation) to the birth (?) of Ialdabaoth through her *prounikos* might support either interpretation. *TP* 39.26–32 refers only to the innocence of Epinoia/Sophia from whom Ialdabaoth took power, while *Treat. Seth* 50.25–30 talks of 'our sister Sophia (cf. *AJ* B 36.16/III 14.9f.) who is a *prounikos*' (although again in the context of innocence: *mntatkakia*). See ch. 4, p. 123f.

[51] Cf. II 19.15–18/IV 29.24–7 and II 9.35–10.1 which refers to Sophia's 'invincible power'. In the light of the continuation, her production of an incomplete abortion, this scarcely suggests such power! Such omission by LR of a term with apparent sexual connotations is further evidence of its spiritualizing tendency.

[52] The key to the confusion seems to lie in the phrases 'and the light-God' of B 51.7 and 'the five lights' of III 23.23. These must represent misunderstandings of the original reading preserved in LR in which the five illuminators were the object of the verb, not attached to the subject. Till's rejection (142) of 'the five lights' of III 23.23 since there

were only four and suggestion that the redactor of III must have read *ptou* as *pt* (an abbreviation of *pnoute*), following B, is unjustified, since (*a*) Giversen, *Apocryphon* 225, points out that five lights have already been mentioned, namely Christ and the four; (*b*) such a misreading by the redactor of III is unlikely – he is perfectly familiar with the abbreviation *pt* for *pnoute* which he actually uses in the passage on the origin of the illuminators (III 11.16; cf. 12.19, 21, 25), and more importantly, (*c*) it alone can explain the confusion. Conversely the 'light-God' of B 51.7 is a more likely misunderstanding of *ptou*; Till admits that the conjunction *mn* cannot have its normal meaning here, distinguishing him from the Father. The reference to the Autogenes and the four may have been a marginal gloss to supply the missing object of the verb, III omitting the Autogenes.

[53] Arai's argument, 'Christologie' 305f., that the Autogenes of B 51.10 is an addition to the original four lights of III 24.2f., which II and IV have emended to five to avoid inconsistency, is not convincing. He fails to see the significance of the 'five lights' of III 23.23, and of the possessive prefix in III 24.2, 'with *his* four lights'. The four illuminators are always closely associated with the Autogenes in the Nag Hammadi texts (cf. *GE* III 62.24ff./IV 74.9ff.; *TP* 38.16–39.13; *Zost.* 127.14–128.7) and the five appear to be key figures in the five seals rite.

[54] II 19.20f./IV 30.2f.

[55] B 51.10–12 (*smot*)/III 24.3f. (*typos*): see Tardieu, *Écrits* 317. On the descent in disguise motif, cf. *TP* 42.17f. (*smot*); 49.6f. (?*smot*); 49.15–17 (*eine*); *Treat. Seth* 56.21–7 (*eine*). Arguments in favour of the latter might include the question why a mention of angels rather than simply Ialdabaoth (for which a possible solution will be offered below); the need for such a disguise in order to persuade a Ialdabaoth ignorant of any superior being; *typos* perhaps representing a *lectio difficilior* than *topos*, and the fact that in the next saving action no mention is made of a descent.

[56] B 51.12–52.11/III 24.4–20; II 19.21–20.5/IV 30.3–26.

[57] Thus the Demiurge is advised to breathe into Adam's face (the *ḥo* of B 51.15 and par is the *prosōpon* of Gen 2:7 LXX).

[58] Cf. the play on *prouniko* and *ergon/argon* in B 37.10–13 and par with B 50.11–52.1 and par. To consider the *ḥōb* of SR as a translation of *ergon* (Crum, *Dictionary* 653a) and part of a continuing wordplay is surely preferable to Tardieu's strained suggestion, *Écrits* 318, of *ḥōtb* from a supposed original *ptōma*, emended into *sōma* by LR (II 19.25), although he is very conscious of the wordplay on *a-ergon*, and its basis in Genesis 2 (despite overlooking the obvious reference in Gen 2:2 LXX to God's ceasing from his *erga*).

[59] II 19.27f.

[60] II 19.27–32.

[61] Cf. the related (or original?) concept in Saturninus (Iren. 1.24.1).

[62] Iren. 1.30.6.

[63] Cf. Iren. 1.5.5–6; *Exc. ex Theod.* 50.2–3 (retaining the *pnoē zōēs* of Gen 2:7 LXX); 53.2–5.

[64] Cf. B 67.1–14/III 34.3–15. LR (II 26.10–19/IV 40.25–41.6) is clearly confused. This distinction finds an exact parallel in that of Tatian between the human soul and the divine spirit (*Or. ad Graec.* 12–15).

[65] Iren. 1.30.6–8.

[66] 30.9, 14.

[67] See n. 63 above.

[68] Fragment 1 in Clem. Alex. *Strom.* 2.8.36.2. It is not clear whether Valentinus envisaged the deposition of the seed via the Demiurge. The attempt of C. Markschies, *Valentinus Gnosticus? Untersuchungen zur valentinianischen Gnosis mit einem Kommentar zu den Fragmenten Valentins* (WUNT 65) (Tübingen: J. C. B. Mohr (Paul Siebeck), 1992), to interpret Valentinus solely in terms of the fragments, which in this case (13–53) leads to a rejection of any intermediate Demiurge figure or Gnostic myth such as found in Iren. 1.29 or the *Apocryphon,* is unconvincing. The fragment cannot be properly understood without such a myth which here would involve the Demiurge urging the creation of man, his angels doing the work and the Logos (so rightly Markschies, 32, 50) sowing the seed. An echo of this can perhaps be found in Heracleon's interpretation of sowing in fragments 35 and 36, where mention is made of the heavenly Son of Man who sows (i.e. the Logos?) and of the angels of the dispensation (i.e. the psychic angels of the Demiurge) as mediators of that sowing.

[69] Cf. *Exc. ex Theod.* 53.3f.; Iren. 1.5.6; Heracleon frags 35–6 (also *Exc. ex Theod.* 2.1; 35.2–4).

[70] Cf. *Exc. ex Theod.* 50.2; 53.2; Heracleon frag. 36.

[71] Schottroff's argument, *Glaubende* 10, 68, that each episode represents a complete act of salvation and that hence one should not interpret the narrative as a *Heilsgeschichte* but only as a variety of ways of describing the Gnostic's existential situation, does not take this into account. As Rudolph suggests, *TRu* 36, 29, she may be too influenced by Johannine (i.e. Bultmannian!) lines of interpretation.

[72] Cf. Janssens, *Muséon* 84, 411.

[73] We have already noted the title of Armoges, the first Barbelo-gnostic illuminator in Iren. 1.29.2: '*Soter*', suggesting his role in their missing views on redemption, and the creative and revelatory functions of the fourth, Eleleth (cf. *AJ* B 34.2–7 and par; *TP* 39.13–40.4; *GE* III 56.22–57.1/IV 68.5–10; *HA* 94.2–97.21). In *Norea* 28.24–29.5, the four holy helpers who intercede for her are obviously the four illuminators.

[74] See ch. 2, p. 31f. Cf. the passages on the final saving descent of the spirit, e.g. B 64.3–13 and par; 65.3–66.13 and par; 67.1–14 and par, and

parallels involving Autogenes/Christ, the four, the Holy Spirit and saving initiation in *GE* III 62.24–64.9 and par; *HA* 96.17–97.9; *TP* 47.28–48.35; 49.20–36; *AA* 85.22–31.

⁷⁵ B 51.20–52.1/III 24.12–14.

⁷⁶ II 19.32f./IV 30.17f. The latter is fragmentary but appears to agree word for word.

⁷⁷ Cf. B 49.6–9/III 22.15–18; II 15.3–5, 11–13/IV 23.16–20, 29–24.2. The long recension, linking power with light, is preferable. See ch. 5, p. 184f.

⁷⁸ B 52.9f., 13–15/III 24.18f., 21–3 (Adam as wiser and having entered the light).

⁷⁹ Cf. *GE* III 66.22–67.4 and par; *TP* 45.12–20; 48.12–35; 49.28–32.

⁸⁰ B 52.1–11/III 24.14–20, 26–8; II 19.34–20.5/IV 30.19–26. On humans as *phronimōteroi* than the evil powers through their understanding of the true Son of God, cf. Zos. *Omega* 16 (Scott–Ferguson, *Hermetica* 4.108.21ff.). LR omits the reference in SR to Adam's having the souls of the seven powers and their authorities, consistent with its earlier failure to mention the seven and 360 of B 50.16–51.1 and par. Cf. the Jewish mythologoumenon of the jealousy of the first angel and his cohorts towards Adam because of his glory and God's command to them to worship him (*Vit. Adae* 12–16; *Schatzhöhle*, ed. Bezold 4; Cyp. , *Zel. et liv.* 4 (CSEL 3.1; Hartel 421.8ff.); Aug., *Gen. ad lit.* 11.2.140). On the theme of envy in the Paradise account, see W. C. van Unnik, 'Der Neid in der Paradiesgeschichte nach einigen gnostischen Texten' in M. Krause ed., *Essays on the Nag Hammadi Texts in Honour of Alexander Böhlig* (NHS 3) (Leiden: Brill, 1972), 120–32; B. A. Pearson, 'Jewish Haggadic Traditions in the *Testimony of Truth* from Nag Hammadi' in *Ex Orbe Religionum 1* (Supplements to *Numen* 21) (Leiden: Brill, 1972), 457–70 (= *Gnosticism* 39–51).

⁸¹ B 52.11–15 and III 24.20–2 derive the first two from the last. II 20.5–7 and IV 31.27–31.1 may be preferable in correlating all three and repeating that the man shone rather than that he entered his light. Sophia is associated with intelligence (*phronēsis*) in B 33.7 and 34.7 and par, and with innocence in *TP* 39.29; 40.15. On the ideas of light-Adam and his innocence, cf. also Zos., *Omega* 12 (Scott–Ferguson 4.107.11–14).

⁸² B 52.15–17/III 24.23f.; II 20.7–9/IV 31.1–3. This is best seen, as Giversen, *Apocryphon* 257, suggests, as a preparation for being clothed in matter.

⁸³ B 52.17–53.10/III 24.25–25.11; II 20.9–19/IV 31.3–8, 15f. LR omits the description in SR of Adam as 'the first to come down, who was called', probably because the first part recurs as a concluding statement in B 55.13f./III 26.25f.; II 21.13f.

⁸⁴ B 53.10–18/III 25.12–17; II 20.19–24/IV 31.16–23. SR is perhaps to be preferred in that it preserves the Valentinian contrast *plērōma*-

hysterēma, which a redactor of the Greek version of LR has failed to spot, misreading *sperma* for *plērōma*, under the influence of the 'Sethian' redaction. This latter may then have suggested the phrase about the identity of Gnostic ascent and descent as found in *Steles Seth* 127.20f.

85 B 53.18–54.4/III 25.17–23; II 20.25–8/IV 31.24–7. We have already noted the way LR tends to play down or even exclude any trace of Sophia's positive saving role, or her identification with us as the paradigm of the Gnostic experience of salvation, the *salvator salvandus*. Thus it makes her the object of salvation here and again omits the reference in SR to 'our sister Sophia, who is like us', as at B 36.16 and par. Paradoxically, it adds just such a reference combining Sophia as redeemer and sister where SR omits it, at II 23.20–2!

86 B 54.5–9/III 25.23–26.3; II 20.28–31/IV 31.27–32.5. Tardieu, *Écrits* 320, is probably right to see 'shadow' (*aposkiasma*) as a mistake for 'particle' (*apospasma*) and certainly right in preferring the *rouein* of SR to the *ouonh ebol* of LR on the grounds of a mistaken understanding of an original Greek *ephanē*. Janssens, *Muséon* 84, 413, sees this episode as a simple recollection of B 52.8ff. and par, but B and III omit the original reference to man shining (could it have been because of this doublet?) and the cause here is different: the presence of the Epinoia rather than of the Mother's power. But the repetition suggests an attempt to introduce and justify a further stage or element in man's history or make-up, viz. his material body.

87 B 54.9–11/III 26.3–6; II 20.32f./IV 32.5–7. III 26.4f. adds 'the entire archonship of the powers' probably to make sense of the singular verb. Tardieu's rendering of it as 'leant towards [him]' is not convincing. The *kataneue* of SR is evidently a confusion of the original Coptic *eiōrm* of LR, meaning 'stare, look intently' (Crum, *Dictionary* 84b) with *jōrm*, 'make a sign, nod agreement' (Crum 785b, note the Sahidic form *eiōrm*). Such confusion is common (cf. R. Kasser, *Compléments au dictionnaire coptique de Crum* (Cairo, 1964), 109) and the frequency in the text of the Greek loan-word *kataneuein* in similar contexts may have abetted the error. The reference in LR to the superiority of Adam's thought (II 20.33/IV 31.7) seems secondary in the context, an echo of the previous comment.

88 B 54.14–55.1/III 26.8–13; II 20.35–21.4. SR adds flame (*krōm*) as a fourth element and the mixture with the winds as a separate event. Since II 20.35–21.2 uses the same word (*sate*) for fire and fiery winds, this may suggest an attempt to correct SR by omitting the fourth element and telescoping events. Giversen, *Apocryphon* 258, points to the striking correspondence between the four elements and the origin of the four bodily demons in II 18.2–6: heat, cold, damp, dryness. Here we pass from the psychic demons and their composition to the creation of material, perishable elements.

[89] B 55.2–9/III 26.13–19; II 21.4–9/IV 32.16–22. The elements are now given in their more usual order from heaviest to lightest. The identification of matter with the darkness of ignorance in II 21.7f. appears secondary, and its adjectival form *etshbbiaeit* according to Crum, *Dictionary* 552b, can mean either 'variegated' (*poikilos*) or 'different, alien' (*diaphoros, xenos*), but surely not the 'opposed' of Krause's translation (166). LR, perhaps misunderstanding *antimimos*, consistently replaces it with *etshbbiaeit* (II 21.9; 24.31f.; 26.20) or *etshēs* (II 26.27, 36; 27.32f.; 29.24). See A. Böhlig, 'Zum Antimimon Pneuma in den koptischen Texten' in *Mysterion* 162–74. Janssens, *Muséon* 84, 414, argues persuasively for the *antikeimenon* of B 55.8f. as the antithesis of the good spirit. The *antimimos* of III 26.19 is probably by assimilation to the distinct later figure of III 34.16 and par. *PS* seems to be aware of this figure as both internal element and external power, even suggesting in ch. 132 a possible origin of the form *etshbbiaeit*. Cf. Book 1, ch. 39 (Schmidt–MacDermot 63.21f.); 3 chs 111–17 (Schmidt–MacDermot 280–301); ch. 132 (Schmidt–MacDermot 332f.: the soul drinks a cup of forgetfulness filled with every various (*etshōbe*) desire, which becomes the body of the soul and like it, and is called the *antimimon pneuma*).

[90] B 55.9–13/III 26.20–3; II 21.9–12. The 'fetter of oblivion' (*lēthē*: III 26.23; *bshe* II 21.12) is preferable to the 'bond of matter' of B 55.12f. despite Till's note (p. 302 of his edition). Cf. e.g. *SJC* B 103.17/III 107.5f. It is our whole situation, subject to ignorance, passion and mortality, not just our materiality which is summed up thus.

[91] B 55.13–15/III 26.23–27.1; II 21.12–14. B omits the first point. As noted, the second point occurs only here in II and may have been omitted at 20.17f. to tidy the text. The third point may reflect Adam's dual nature; heavenly soul on the one hand, tomb of the body on the other. See Till's ed. 151n. Schenke's attempt, 'Erlöser' 216, to see here and in B 53.6f. and par traces of Adam the Primal Man descending to save his members, is vitiated by his obvious confusion of heavenly Adamas with earthly Adam.

[92] II 21.14–16/IV 33.1. This despite the earlier assertion in II 20.25 that she is already in him.

[93] B 55.15–18/III 27.2–4. As Till suggests (150), the *protos* of B 55.16 is a likely musunderstanding of the *proontos* of III 27.2.

[94] Cf. B 27.4–19/III 7.12–23.

[95] Thus Janssens, *Muséon* 84, 413, may be correct to see this and the earlier mention of the Epinoia's general saving work as anticipatory.

[96] B 55.18–57.19/III 27.4–28.16; II 21.16–22.9/IV 33.1–34.9.

[97] B 55.18–56.3/III 27.4–8. *tēs tryphēs* in Gen 2:15 does occur in Jer. *Quaest. in lib. Gen.* 2, 15 (CC 72.4), as well as in Gen 3:23f. LXX and Sahidic.

[98] II 21.16–19/IV 33.1–5. In *HA* 88.24–32 it is the archons who put Adam in the garden and command him to eat, but its author is much more faithful to the text of Genesis. Cf. *OW* 115.27–9.

[99] *Écrits* 321. Cf. the *trophē* of III 27.9f. for the *tryphē* of B 56.3f., 5.

[1] B 56.3–10/III 27.9–14; II 21.19–24/IV 33.5–14.

[2] B 56.10–17/III 27.14–21; II 21.24–9/IV 33.14–21. See n. 89 above on the tendency of LR to misunderstand, paraphrase or avoid the term *antimimon pneuma*. Cf. the role of the counterfeit demon in Zos. *Omega* 16 (Scott–Ferguson, *Hermetica* 4.108.21f.), seeking to mislead (*planēsai*) Adam.

[3] B 56.17–57.8/III 27.21–28.6; II 21.29–22.2/IV 33.21–34.5. A summary of a confused passage. SR seems to make more sense over the branches, leaves and sap than LR with its awkward 'deaths', 'shadow', 'blossom' and darkness as a place of rest, but LR's linking desire to the seed may be preferable.

[4] B 57.8–19/III 28.6–16; II 22.3–9/IV 34.5–9. Cf. the 'Tree/Knowledge' figure of the original Barbelognostic scheme (Iren. 1.29.3).

[5] On the one hand it has already had the archons' command 'Eat!', and on the other the archons are not supposed to know about the present or future existence of the Epinoia in man. Although Janssens' insistence, *Muséon* 84, 415f., that the Epinoia is no more to be identified with the tree of knowledge than the counterfeit spirit with the tree of life is defensible, her appeal to B 60.16ff. as evidence of such a distinction in the former case is not convincing since the parallel in LR does not support this.

[6] B 57.20–58.7/III 28.16–23; II 22.9–15/IV 34.15–21. The snake here may represent the Devil and thus correspond to the snake-like son of the 'Ophite' Ialdabaoth in Iren. 1.30.5.

[7] It is part of the later frame story and internally inconsistent, referring in B 57.20/II 22.9 to 'them', although Eve has not yet appeared! The redactor of III 28.16f. has seen and corrected this.

[8] So too Janssens, *Muséon* 84, 417. The integral role of the snake is suggested by the virtual recapitulation of his role in B 63.2–6 and par, attributed to the First Archon, of whom the snake is a manifestation.

[9] Cf. B 60.16–61.4/III 30.14–19.

[10] II 23.24–35/IV 36.17–37.4.

[11] Janssens, *Muséon* 84, 416, is probably right to insist on the distinction between the Epinoia who instructs, and the Saviour who raises up (B 57.20/III 28.16f.; II 22.9. Cf. B 64.6–13 and par; 76.1–5/III 39.18–21; II 31.12–14/IV 48.14–18). That, as she admits, it is not always easy to determine which figure, Pronoia (i.e. Saviour) or Epinoia is at work, is due to the fluidity and ambivalence of the redeemer figures noted above: The Pronoia of redaction (a^2) frequently acts through the Epinoia who is an emanation from her and the second main mode of her activity.

[12] But an obvious Gnostic interpretation of the 'coat of skin' of Gen 3:21, cf. the Valentinian view in Iren. 1.5.5; *Exc. ex Theod.* 55.1f. And there are traces of a similar idea of humanity's original superior state and fall into mortality and ignorance in e.g. the 'Ophite' system of Iren. 1.30.9 and *AA* 64.14–65.25.

[13] Particularly the tree of life as in fact ignorance and death; the interpretation of the tree of knowledge as salvific is quite common, cf. e.g. *HA* 88.26–89.3; 89.31–90.10; *OW* 118.24–119.19 (the latter parallels *AJ* in having Zoe/Eve enter the tree of knowledge, 116.25–9).

[14] Cf. the role of the snake-like son of Ialdabaoth produced from the dregs of matter who is the origin of (evil?) spirit, oblivion, wickedness, etc. in Iren. 1.30.5. The doctrine of the two spirits may well originate from Jewish sectarian ideas such as those found in the Qumran scrolls. Cf. W.-D. Hauschild, *Gottes Geist und der Mensch* (Munich: Kaiser, 1972), 255f.

[15] B 58.8–10/III 28.23–5; II 22.15–18. B 58.8 has Eve as the object and a future tense over against the past tenses of III 28.24 and II 22.15f. As Tardieu suggests, *Écrits* 323, its redactor has succumbed to the influence of the text of Genesis: Eve has not yet appeared! Neither subject nor object is entirely clear from the pronouns; the former appears to be Adam rather than either the previous subject, the snake, whom Eve heeds, or the First Archon, as B (and the similar formulation at B 61.7f. and par?) might suggest, and the latter the First Archon and not the snake. This ambiguity has evidently been partly caused by the Saviour's interjection, further proof of its later character.

[16] II 22.16–18. Its use of 'the light of the Epinoia' instead of the more usual 'Epinoia of light' may have been prompted by the redactor's awareness that the Epinoia is later said to enter Adam (II 22.28ff. and par).

[17] B 58.10–12/III 28.25–29.1; II 22.18–20/IV 34.26–8.

[18] Cf. B 58.10–12 and par; 59.7–9 and par; 59.12–16/III 29.18–21. B's parallel is more exact than that of III.

[19] II 22.32–23.2/IV 35.14–22.

[20] B 59.17–19/III 29.21–24; II 23.3f.

[21] Cf. Iren. 1.24.1; *HA* 87.11–88.3. But SR, bald as it is, may imply the 'Ophite' version: Ialdabaoth actually takes Adam's power to form Eve.

[22] Cf. Iren. 1.30.7. Baur's emendation: *de eius* (i.e. Adam's) *Enthymesi* for the *de sua* of the text, is perhaps preferable here, *pace* Harvey, *Irenaeus* 1, 233, n. 2, because of the parallelism with *AJ*'s LR.

[23] Cf. *HA* 89.17–31; *OW* 116.8–117.15. There is a trace of it in Iren. 1.30.7 after Eve's creation. Cf. also *AJ* B 62.3ff. and par.

[24] Cf. 1.30.6–7. However, the figure and activity of the 'Ophite' Sophia we have argued underlies *AJ*'s Epinoia.

[25] Cf. passages involving the Epinoia (B 53.4–54.4; 55.15–18; 57.8–19 and par) which use terms like 'correction', 'perfection' (*plērōma*),

'deficiency' (*hysterēma*), 'instruction', 'awakening' and 'formlessness', and passages concerning the power (B 51.8–52.15; 54.5–9; 58.8–12 and par).

[26] B 58.12–14 (*bshe*)/III 29.1f. (*ekstasis*); II 22.20f./IV 34.28f.(*bshe*). See Crum, *Dictionary* 519ab s.v. *obsh*, which is given as rendering *hypnos, lēthē*, but not the *ekstasis* of III and Gen 2:21 LXX. However as Bullard notes, *Hypostasis* 74, a Sahidic version of Gen 2:21 does read *bshe*.

[27] B 58.14–59.6/III 29.2–12; II 22.21–8/IV 34.29–35.7. LR pedantically adds a reference to Moses' first book, and SR expands the allusion to oblivion, citing the verb from Isa 6:10 as a lead-in to the quotation which it gives in the form 'ears of their hearts'. For the Coptic of Isa 6:10, see R. Kasser, 'Citations des grands prophètes bibliques dans les textes gnostiques coptes' in Krause, *Essays* 59. On a similar interpretation of the sleep as ignorance, cf. *HA* 89.3–7.

[28] Cf. II 22.16f. See n. 19, p. 250.

[29] B 59.6–9/III 29.12–15; II 22.28–30.

[30] B 59.9–12/III 29.15–17; II 22.31f. Cf. the variants of this theme of the archontic rape of spiritual/earthly Eve in *HA* 89.18–31; *OW* 116.8–33.

[31] 89.3–31.

[32] 115.31–117.15.

[33] 89.3–15.

[34] 89.17–31.

[35] 115.31–116.25.

[36] 116.25–117.15.

[37] Iren. 1.30.7. Here too the archontic rape fails since Sophia empties Eve of her power beforehand.

[38] Cf. B 60.3f.: Adam recognized his own *ousia*. Here III 30.3f. (Adam recognized his *synousia* which is like him) appears to be a compromise between B and II 23.9 (he recognized his likeness (*eine*)).

[39] Cf. B 59.20–60.16/III 30.1–14; II 23.4–26.

[40] Cf. B 60.12–16/III 30.10–14 and II 23.18–24 where LR has been misled by the evident gloss on the consort of Gen 2:24 to refer the title 'Zoe, the Mother . . .' to Sophia rather than to the Epinoia. Janssens' attempt, *Muséon* 84, 418f., to show the propriety of the title in the case of earthly Eve as repository of the Epinoia/Sophia (cf. Giversen, *Apocryphon* 263) is not convincing: it is not at all clear that the Epinoia is present in earthly Eve at this point. Earlier (cf. B 38.10–13/III 15.19–21; II 10.17f.) the title '(Zoe), the Mother of (all) living' had been applied to the Holy Spirit, a likely synonym for the Epinoia, and at II 24.11 the Epinoia is qualified as 'life'. And the secondary character of the Epinoia material is also implied by the fact that in SR Adam becomes sober *before* the Epinoia removes the veil and he sees his consort (cf. B 59.20f. and par).

[41] B 60.3–16/III 30.3–14; II 23.9–24/IV 36.1ff.

[42] Giversen, *Apocryphon* 263, insists that the *eros* of II 23.23 must refer to Adam's wife, despite the fact that the text clearly has Sophia as subject. Its understanding of her as Adam's consort has led it to a further reference to Gen 2:24 and the harassed copyist of II 23.17ff. to repeat an entire sentence. Tardieu's ingenious interpretation, *Écrits* 325, in terms of Adam and Eve's union reversing Sophia's failure to unite with her consort, is undermined by the secondary character of Sophia's consort, as demonstrated above.

[43] Even if LR's attempt to reconcile the two traditions, that of the power and the later one of the Epinoia, be adjudged secondary, it has developed a suggestive concept: as Adam was created in the image of heavenly Man to gain something of his light and power, so Eve was created in the image of the Mother of all living (i.e. the Holy Spirit/Epinoia/offspring of Pronoia–Barbelo), in order to gain control of her.

[44] Cf. B 57.20–58.10 and par.

[45] B 60.16–19/III 30.14–17; II 23.24–6/IV 36.17ff. LR differs somewhat here: II 23.24–6 has Adam and Eve taste the perfect knowledge through the Pronoia (character or attribute?) of the heavenly authority (*authentia*) and through her (the Epinoia?), while the fragmentary parallel in IV inserts a phrase after 'authority' which in Krause's reconstruction (p. 236) speaks of the revelation and of her (the Epinoia?) giving Adam knowledge. This is close to B 60.18f., perhaps omitted by II either accidentally through homoeoteleuton, or deliberately, to remove the awkward reference to the Epinoia and reconcile this with the Saviour's previous assertion.

[46] B 60.18–61.4/III 30.16–19. On the eagle as a supernatural messenger and possible representation of Christ, see Janssens, *Muséon* 84, 419f. and Tardieu, *Écrits* 326, with reference to Lampe, *PGL* s.v. *aetos*. On the syncretistic background and likely contrast between snake and eagle implied here, see MacRae, 'Sleep' 500.

[47] II 23.24–31/IV 36.17–29.

[48] *Écrits* 325f.

[49] King, 'Sophia' 168f., would see in this, the earlier passage of Christ's interjection (II 22.3–10) and the Pronoia hymn, the tendency of LR to replace an original Epinoia or Pronoia by Christ.

[50] Note the similarities of expression and terminology in the three episodes: the emphatic 'I' and the verb *seḥō* in II 22.9 and 31.12f.; the raising (*toounos*) from sleep (*ḥinēb*) of 23.30f. and 31.5f. Again in 23.28f. the Epinoia is from the Pronoia of pure light, while in 31.11f. the Saviour identifies himself as the Pronoia of the pure light. MacRae, 'Sleep' 496–507, in arguing for the centrality of the Pronoia hymn and its three descents scheme, finds evidence for the first (unsuccessful) mission of the Saviour in the awakening of Adam and Eve here; although the Epinoia is the subject in SR, he finds traces of the Saviour's activity in it, e.g. B 57.8–58.1.

[51] B 60.18–61.5/III 30.16–20. Here LR tries to echo the Genesis account in referring to 'them' (II 23.30f.), and III 30.18f., although lacunous, seems aware of this by its plural 'their perfection'. Certainly B 61.5f. goes on to talk of the fault of both.

[52] II 23.31–3/IV 36.29–37.1; B 61.5–7/III 30.20–2.

[53] II 23.33–35/IV 37.1–4. The verbs are precisely those just employed to describe the Saviour's redemptive activity!

[54] B 61.7–9/III 30.22f.; II 23.35f./IV 37.4–6. The similarity to B 58.8f. and par might suggest that Ialdabaoth was the subject in the latter too, *pace* Tardieu (see n. 15, p. 250). *HA* 90.13–29 and *OW* 119.19–120.3 remain much more faithful to Gen 3:7–13, using the passage to cast further light on the ignorance of the archons.

[55] Iren. 1.30.7. The only difference is that the 'Ophites', like the *HA* and *OW*, give the snake a major revelatory role and treat the tree of knowledge motif literally.

[56] Cf. II 23.37/IV 37.6 and B 61.9f./III 30.23.

[57] Cf. *OW* 120.7f. Tardieu, *Écrits* 326, also sees here the wordplay *adam/adamah*. The reading could also further represent its spiritualizing tendency: as the 'Ophite' Sophia removes the trace of light from Adam and Eve to avoid the divine principle sharing in the curse (1.30.8), so LR has Ialdabaoth curse Adam's earth.

[58] II 23.37–24.4/IV 37.7–11. The subject of 'he was lord' is evidently Ialdabaoth rather than Adam, as in Gen 3:16.

[59] B 61.10–15/III 30.24–31.2. III has direct speech, perhaps under the influence of Gen 3:16.

[60] *Écrits* 327.

[61] So Giversen, *Apocryphon* 264. Cf. B 51.1–14 and par. Janssens, *Muséon* 84, 420f., sees it as that of Gnostic marriage, the 'great mystery' of *Gos. Phil.*: Ialdabaoth did not know of the secret power hidden in Eve to allow Sophia to correct her deficiency.

[62] II 21.26–9 and par.

[63] Cf. King, 'Sophia' 170, on the heavenly plan as involving the equality of male and female.

[64] B 61.16–19/III 31.2–4; II 24.4–6. The *saḥou* ('curse') of B 61.16 is an excusable error for the *saḥō-* of III 31.2, and B 61.18f. is probably mistaken in connecting the angels with the next episode. The version in LR, which has Ialdabaoth revealing his ignorance independently and without clear motivation (II 24.4–6) is evidently secondary, the redactor having misread the infinitive form.

[65] B 61.19–62.3/III 31.4–6; II 24.6–8/IV 37.15–17. In *HA* 91.3–5 and *OW* 121.4f. the archons cast them out. Cf. *AA* 66.23–5, where darkness comes over their eyes. This may be a Gnostic reinterpretation of the rabbinic understanding of the 'coats of skin' of Gen 3:21 (see Tardieu, *Écrits* 327), but may also echo the Jewish legend of the natural darkness which overtakes and terrifies Adam and Eve after their expulsion from

Paradise (cf. *'Abot R. Nat.* 176; *Gen. Rab.* 11.2; 12.6; *'Abod. Zar.* 8b; Ginzberg, *Legends* 1, 86; 5, 112f., 116.

[66] Cf. King, 'Sophia' 164ff.

[67] Iren. 1.30.7.

[68] 1.30.8.

[69] Cf. *HA* 89.17–31; *OW* 116.8–117.15.

[70] 89.21. Cf. Iren. 1.30.7 (*concupiscentes*).

[71] 116.13–25. Cf. the Audians of Theodore bar Konai, *Schol.* 11. See on this H.-C. Puech, 'Fragments retrouvés de l'Apocalypse de l'Allogène', *Mélanges Franz Cumont 2* 946f. (= *En quête de la gnose 1* 280f.); Bullard, *Hypostasis* 84.

[72] *OW* 117.15ff.

[73] Bullard, *Hypostasis* 84; Janssens, 'Thème' 488–94, esp. 490f.; Stroumsa, *Seed, passim.*

[74] *Origini* 495.

[75] Cf. *Tg. Ps. J.* on Gen 1; *Pirqe R. El.* 21; Ginzberg, *Legends* 1, 105; 5, 133f.; the Archontics of Epiph. *Pan.* 40.5.3. In Justin's *Baruch* (Hipp. *Ref.* 5.26.22f.), Naas, Eden's third angel, seduces both Adam and Eve and is thus responsible for both adultery and pederasty.

[76] B 62.3–8/III 31.6–9. The *mñtathēt* ('folly') of B 62.6, while appropriate in the context (cf. *HA* 89.24f.: the spiritual woman laughing at the senselessness (*mñtathet*) of the archontic attempted rape), is probably due to a misreading of the Greek *agnoia* underlying the other three versions as *anoia*.

[77] II 24.8–13/IV 37.17–23. Cf. II 22.16–18/IV 34.20f., and II 23.33–5/ IV 37.1–4 where the parallels in SR make no mention of Epinoia.

[78] II 24.13–15/IV 37.23–6.

[79] Iren. 1.30.8. Cf. II 20.14–19; 23.24–6, 37; 24.13ff.

[80] B 62.8–10/III 31.10–12; II 24.15–17/IV 37.27–9. LR has to specify the subject, the First Archon, because of its addition of the Pronoia.

[81] II 24.18f./IV 38.1–3. Cf. Orig. *C. Cels.* 6.30; *PS* Book 3, ch. 126 (Schmidt–MacDermot 318.3f., 17).

[82] B 62.10f./III 31.12f. (Jave bear-faced, Eloim cat-faced).

[83] IV 38.4–6 (II 24.19f. has omitted the identification through homoeoteleuton); B 62.13–15/III 31.14–16.

[84] B 62.15–18/III 31.16–19; II 24.20–4/IV 38.6–10. The slight differences in III from B are probably stylistic: its favoured term *krōm* (cf. 15.12; 16.5; 18.6, 13; 26.10) to the *kōht* of B 62.16; its order 'earth and water' influenced perhaps by the earlier enumeration of elements at III 26.16. The latter passage may also explain why B 62.16f./III 31.18[?] prefer *pneuma* to the 'wind' (*tēy*) of II 24.22/IV 38.8.

[85] Cf. B 62.18–63.2/III 31.19–21 and II 24.24–7/IV 38.10–14. The order 'Abel and Cain' of III 31.20f. may be the redactor's attempt to match names with characteristics: righteous Abel and unrighteous Cain.

[86] B 63.9–12/III 32.3–6; II 24.32–4/IV 38.21–4. Giversen, *Apocryphon* 264, notes the distinct agreement between this passage and the earlier one (II 21.6ff. and par) dealing with the creation of the material body. Eloim and Jave govern the bodies of later generations because they govern the elements of which human bodies are composed.

[87] Cf. Iren. 1.30.9; *HA* 91.11–14. Giversen, *Apocryphon* 264, is clearly wrong to call them Adam's sons. On the righteous/unrighteous syndrome, cf. Ptolemy's *Ep. ad Floram* in Epiph. *Pan.* 33.7.7 (the intermediate, righteous Demiurge produced a twofold power (i.e. righteous/unrighteous?), but he himself is the image of the superior (Good) power), and the respective roles of (unrighteous) Ialdabaoth and (righteous) Sabaoth in *HA*.

[88] It might have changed the order of archontic names because it knew Elohim came (Gen 1:1) before Yahweh occurs (Gen 2:4b). And we have noted its tendency to stress the negative character and ignorance of Ialdabaoth (e.g. in II 19.27f.; 22.34–23.2; 24.4f. and par).

[89] Cf. B 58.4–7 and par. For the similarity of language, see following note.

[90] B 63.2–6 (*ñouepithymia ñspora*)/III 31.21–32.1 (*ñouspora ñepithymia*); II 24.26–9 (*ñouspora ñepithymia*). The verb of B 63.2 'began' (*afshōpe*) may have been corrected to 'continued' (*so*) in III 31.22 and II 24.26/ IV 38.14 because of the earlier passage about the snake's role in this (cf. B 58.4–7 and par). II 24.27 has perhaps omitted the reference to marriage in B 63.3/III 31.22 because *synousia* was thought to imply it. And the form *ta adam* of II 24.29/IV 38.17 is obviously a corrective by the redactors of LR – Eve is made responsible! See King, 'Sophia' 170f.

[91] B 53.6–9/III 32.1–3; II 24.29–32/IV 38.17–21. III 32.1–3: 'so that through it (f.), namely this substance (*ousia*), it (f.; i.e. the desire?) produced their image through the counterfeit (*antimimon*) spirit (*pneuma*)', seems preferable to B 63.6–9: 'so that it is through this substance (*ousia*) which produces an image from their counterfeit (*antimimon*)'. II 24.29–32/IV 38.17–21 is rather different. It reads: 'Now he produced (*tounous*, an echo of Gen 4:25 LXX *exanestēse*/Coptic *tounes*? Cf. C. Wessely, *Studien zur Palaeographie und Papyruskunde* 15 (Griechische u. koptische Texte theologischen Inhalts 4) (Leipzig, 1914), 35, cited inaccurately by Bullard, *Hypostasis* 93) through the intercourse (*synousia*) the begetting of the image of the bodies and provided (*chōrēgein*) for them from his varying spirit'.

[92] *ousia* occurs in SR to refer to the identity of substance of Adam and Eve, as in B 60.3f., where III 30.3f. reads *synousia*, showing how easy is the shift we suggest LR has made. In B 63.12f. and par, where Adam begets Seth after recognizing his own *ousia*, LR once again avoids and paraphrases the term. See n. 96 below.

[93] Cf. the language of B 55.3–13 and par, with its precise echo of the different adjectives applied to the spirit here: *antimimon* in SR, *etshbbiaeit* in LR.

[94] B 63.9–12/III 32.3–6 (*spēlaion*); II 24.32–4/IV 38.21–4 (*spēlaion*). Cf. the striking similarities of language with the passages on the four elements forming the 'tomb' (*spēlaion*) of the body (B 54.11–55.13 and par), and on the two archons set over the four (B 62.15–18 and par). On the term *archai* for the four elements, cf. Plato, *Tim.* 48B, etc.

[95] B 63.12–16/III 32.6–9. Could the 'his own lawlessness' (*anomia*) of III 32.6f. derive from a misreading of the original capitalized Greek, e.g. *tēn ousian homoian aytōi*? The term *genea*, although unfortunately ambiguous, seems to refer here to the process of generation rather than the race (see following note). Despite B 63.14f., which obviously assigns the last phrase to the following passage on the Mother sending her spirit (cf. traces of this in the *homoiōs* of III 32.9 and II 25.2f.), it makes more sense to relate it to Seth's begetting as a spiritual, non-sexual process.

[96] II 24.34–25.2/IV 38.24–30. The translation of *genea* by the Coptic *jpo* in II 25.2/IV 38.29, suggests that the translators of LR certainly understood the Greek term to refer to the process, as we argued above. Note once again the way LR appears to avoid or paraphrase the term *ousia*.

[97] Cf. II 8.28f.

[98] Cf. III 32.6–10; II 24.34–25.3/IV 38.24–31 and B 63.12–18. See n. 95 on this page.

[99] B 63.14–18/III 32.8–10.

[1] *Muséon* 84, 421. This is of course with reference to B only. Cf. the role of Protennoia in *TP* 45.29ff.

[2] II 25.2–4/IV 38.30–2. The form *ke* could be interpreted as 'also' here (see Crum, *Dictionary* 91 s.v. *ke* IIe and IVa), but in any case the unqualified term 'the Mother' always seems to refer to Sophia in *AJ*. Cf. B 37.17 and par; 38.17 and par; 42.17f. and par; 43.2 and par; 44.19f. and par; 46.1, 9 and par; 51.2, 14, 19 and par, etc. The parallel to B 76.1 in III 39.19 does read 'this Mother' with apparent reference to Barbelo, but this may be because the redactors of III, as here, refuse to admit Sophia could have acted as redeemer.

[3] B 63.18–64.3/III 32.10–14. III omits the descent, the term *ousia* (although its version may paraphrase the term *homoousios* or *homoiousios*), and has the Greek loan-words *plērōma*, *lēthē* and *spēlaion*.

[4] II 25.2–7/IV 38.30–39.4. Cf. the roles of Sophia in Iren. 1.30.11f., the Glory in *AA* 77.9–12 and Seth in *GE* III 63.10–18 and par.

[5] Cf. B 46.18ff. and par; here the form *nas* does not appear to be an ethic dative, as Giversen, *Apocryphon* 265, argues it is in B 63.18, against Till who sees the latter as corrupt (166).

[6] So too Schottroff, *Glaubende* 62–4.

⁷ Iren. 1.30.9. Cf. the similar theme in *AA* 64.6–66.8.

⁸ II 25.7–9/IV 39.4–7.

⁹ Cf. B 52.17–54.3 and par.

¹⁰ Cf. B 64.3–5/III 32.14f. and II 25.9–11/IV 39.7–9. All use the Greek *hypourgein*, cf. the activity of the Epinoia in II 20.19f.

¹¹ On the Epinoia, cf. II 20.14–24/IV 27.34–28.4. The introduction of the new interpretation of the spirit's role has meant a loss of continuity and lack of a subject. That the previous subject was also neuter (the spirit) might have led a Greek redactor to interpret the neuter accusative (*to sperma*) as a nominative.

¹² Janssens, *Muséon* 84, 422, suggests this figure can only be the Pronoia, the 'blessed Father–Mother'.

¹³ The Spirit's descent, the awakening (*tounos*) of the substance (*ousia*) after the heavenly archetype from oblivion (*bshe/lēthē*) and evil, the mention of the seed (*sperma*), of the Holy Spirit raising up (*taḥo erat-/sōḥe erat-*) from deficiency (*shta/hysterēma*) to perfection (*plērōma*).

¹⁴ B 47.1–13/III 21.4–13; II 14.5–13/IV 22.5–15 (*pneuma, plērōma, taḥo erat-/sōḥe, sht.* Cf. B 60.12–14/III 30.11f. (*taḥo erat-, hysterēma*).

¹⁵ B 53.4–17/III 25.6–17; II 20.14–24 (*pneuma, r̄ḥōb/hypourgein, taḥo erat-/sōḥe, jōk/plērōma, shta/hysterēma, tounos*); B 71.5–13/III 36.20–5; II 27.33–28.5 (*pneuma, (shp) hise, sperma, tounos*).

¹⁶ B 76.1–5/III 39.19–21 (*taḥo erat-, sperma, hysterēma*). Cf. *Exc. ex Theod.* 35.2.

¹⁷ Cf. 1.30.6–12. See Schenke, 'Nag-Hamadi-Studien III' 356–61.

¹⁸ Cf. 1.30.12.

¹⁹ Cf. e.g. B 47.13f. and par; 54.2–4 and par; II 23.20–2; B 76.1–5/III 39.19–21.

²⁰ *Glaubende* 44ff., 72ff., 79.

²¹ Cf. B 47.1–13 and par and e.g. *Tri. Trac.* 86.8–87.17; *Exc. ex Theod.* 23.1f.; Iren. 1.14.5. See also Hipp. *Ref.* 6.32.2–5.

²² On awakening/raising up (*tounos*), cf. *Gos. Truth* 30.14–23; on oblivion, cf. *Gos. Truth* 17.24, 33, 36; 18.1, 6, 8, 11, 18; 20.38; 21.36; *Tri. Trac.* 77.23; 98.3; on the seed, cf. e.g. Iren. 1.5.6; 6.4; 7.1f., etc.; *Exc. ex Theod.* 1.1–3; 2.1; 21.1f.; 26.1–3; Heracleon frags 16 and 36; Marcus in Iren. 1.15.3; Valentinus frag. 1, etc.; on raising up and correcting (*diorthōsis/epanorthōsis*, cf. *taḥo erat-* in Crum, *Dictionary* 456b and *sooḥe* ibid., 380b), cf. Hipp. *Ref.* 6.32.4f.; *Exc. ex Theod.* 30.2; 35.2, etc.; Iren. 1.13.1; 14.5; on deficiency and perfection, cf. e.g. Hipp. *Ref.* 6.31.5f.; *Gos. Truth* 21.14–23; 24.25–33; 24.37–25.3; 35.8–36.3; *Treat. Res.* (C I,3) 48.38–49.6; *Tri. Trac.* 86.19–23; 87.1–4, etc. See Zandee, 'Gnostic Ideas' 35–9; 41–3; 59–61.

7

Gnostic Soteriology 2:
The Destinies of Souls

There now follows in the *Apocryphon* what appears to be a digression in which John asks the Saviour six questions about the destinies of various types of souls,[1] followed by a seventh about the origin of the counterfeit spirit.[2] Points in favour of it as a later interpolation would include both formal and material ones: formally, its character as a digression, part of the later dialogue, a self-contained piece which Giversen describes as catechetic, a didactic account which could have stood by itself without the question and answer framework,[3] and the fact that what follows this section corresponds quite well with what precedes it;[4] materially, its abrupt reference to souls as soteriological factors, only previously paralleled in the 'Sethian' passage on the illuminators as abodes of various souls.[5] In the anthropogony the soul was an archontic product, the divine element being the Mother's light-power which Ialdabaoth did not share with his offspring but himself inbreathed into Adam.[6] And along with the light-power motif we noted that of the Epinoia or Holy Spirit descending and working on humanity to ensure its eventual salvation.

Now both of these concepts do appear to occur in the dialogue although, as we shall see, there is some confusion in our texts as to their precise relationship. Thus we hear of the descent of the Spirit of life and its union with the power, which is necessary for full salvation.[7] But there seems virtually no awareness of, let alone attempt to accommodate, the earlier 'Sethian' passage about the various classes of souls as respectively the seed of Seth, the souls of the saints in the third aeon and those late repenting souls in the fourth. Nor, conversely, does the earlier passage hint at a doctrine of reincarnation such as is referred to in the dialogue section.[8] On the other hand, elements in the dialogue section such as the references to 'pure light' as the goal of the elect souls and of their worthiness of 'the great lights', do tie in with earlier passages.[9]

It is true that the independent existence of just such a form of soteriological dialogue is attested elsewhere, notably by *Pistis Sophia*, much of which is taken up with the Saviour's answers to the questions of his disciples about who will be saved and what will befall various types of sinners. In fact *Pistis Sophia* offers the closest parallel to this section of the *Apocryphon*. Thus Philip asks Jesus if he has turned upside down the bondage of the archons and their Heimarmene for the sake of the salvation of the world and he replies that he has for the salvation of all souls.[10] More significantly, chapters 111, 112 and 131, which deal with what compels a man to sin, present a clear and systematized doctrine of the three elements in humanity found in the *Apocryphon*: the power (which is from above and enables man to stand), the soul, and the counterfeit spirit (which derives from the archons of Heimarmene and compels men to sin).[11] Finally chapters 147 and 148 deal with the questions of John about the fate of a man who has committed no sin but who has not discovered the Saviour's mysteries, and of a man who has sinned but has discovered them.[12]

However, comparison of the two seems to suggest that the redactor of *Pistis Sophia* has made use of material that goes back to the *Apocryphon*.[13] Indeed Böhlig himself considers that the counterfeit spirit passages in *Pistis Sophia* may represent a later addition.[14] He does highlight certain significant differences between the two accounts: *Pistis Sophia* is not concerned with salvation history as is the *Apocryphon*; it focuses on the fate of the individual after death or before life. The two also differ in anthropology: *Pistis Sophia* has a fixed scheme whereby the power and the counterfeit spirit are in man from the beginning and there is no mention of the spirit of life, while the *Apocryphon* is less systematic. But Böhlig's conclusion that the redactor of the former has detemporalized and dehistoricized the tradition of the counterfeit spirit common to both would further support the suggestion that *Pistis Sophia* is later and dependent. Finally, the ultimate difference between them: that *Pistis Sophia* presents salvation in terms of knowledge of and initiation into mysteries, while the *Apocryphon* presents it in terms of the descent and presence in humanity of the spirit or Epinoia, is only superficially true and readily explicable in terms of the different respective concerns of each.[15] More interestingly, if *Pistis Sophia* did know this passage of the *Apocryphon*, then it clearly knew it in its present dialogue form.

The *Sophia of Jesus Christ* also seems dependent on the *Apocryphon*, not only as regards its dialogue form, basic hierarchy (Father/Spirit/Son), use of the Sophia myth and designation of the Gnostic elect as 'the immovable race' (*genea*),[16] but also in its eschatological concern. In answer to a final question from Mary about the origin and ultimate destination of the disciples, the Saviour, after allusion to the Sophia myth of the *Apocryphon* and mention of his plan to unite heavenly Spirit and demiurgic breath, delineates the different grades and resting places of believers in relation to Father, Spirit and Son, according to their degrees of knowledge of these and possession of the appropriate token.[17] Moreover, although other examples of the Saviour replying to eschatological questions of the disciples suggest the existence of a developed genre,[18] Giversen's point about the unity of the piece minus the dialogue frame and, more significantly, Tardieu's about this passage as reflecting the necessary third (future) part of the myth, indicate its integral character, whether or not it was originally in the form of a dialogue.[19]

This primarily eschatological passage is placed here and not at the end of the *Heilsgeschichte*, as in the *Sophia of Jesus Christ*, for example,[20] because it arises naturally from the mention of the work of the Mother's spirit on the seed and the eschatological descent of the Spirit. And the reference in John's question to the pure light, as already indicated, explicitly harks back to the opening description of the realm of the supreme beings, establishing the continuity of this section with what has gone before.[21] According to this and the preceding passage, then, it would seem to be the seed of the Mother, consubstantial with her spirit, and implicitly identified in John's question with (some of) the souls of men, which is the object of salvation. But the Saviour further qualifies redeeming knowledge: it is hard to reveal to anyone other than those of the immovable (or unshakeable) race (*genea*).[22] Now such a designation is a hallmark of Schenke's 'Sethian' Gnostics.[23] Where it does appear in the *Apocryphon* it seems to be secondary and form part of the 'Sethian' reworking.[24] Thus the reference to 'souls' as the primary vehicles of salvation in the *Apocryphon* at this point no longer needs to be interpreted as an interpolation, but as perhaps reflecting an earlier – if not the original – understanding.[25]

1 The types of souls and their salvation

In this section salvation appears to involve two elements: (*a*) the descent of the Spirit of life into the soul after its birth[26] (which can also apparently be designated as having the saving knowledge),[27] and (*b*) the presence of the power of the Mother in every soul, with which the Spirit must unite[28] and without which no human can stand.[29] As already indicated, this does correspond to a fundamental theme of the main body of the *Apocryphon*, that salvation involves the combination of the power of the Mother, i.e. the capacity for salvation (symbolically represented in Adam's raising), and the Spirit of life from the Father. The former has been taken over by *Pistis Sophia*. But whereas its systematization of the traditions in the *Apocryphon* has led it to stress the presence of the counterfeit spirit in humanity from the beginning and omit direct mention of the Spirit of life,[30] the *Apocryphon* represents the fate of our human souls as dependent on which spirit comes to them, the Spirit of life or the counterfeit spirit.[31] This fundamental soteriological pattern suggests that the long recension, which at one point has the Spirit of life increase and the power come to the soul,[32] is less preferable than the short, according to which the Spirit is brought to the soul after birth (i.e. at Gnostic baptism?), to strengthen it.[33] This suggests that neither spirit is present in all the souls,[34] and appears to contradict the earlier passage where the counterfeit spirit was one of the four elements making up material man.[35] Later on we gather that the counterfeit spirit's origin postdates the Flood![36]

The most likely explanation of this last apparent contradiction is, as Tardieu has shown in his analysis of the *Apocryphon*, the addition by a later editor of the reinterpretation of Genesis 5–9 to complete the story, introduced – not very skilfully as we shall see – by John's final question about the origin of the counterfeit spirit.[37] We might explain the prior contradiction in terms of a – not always explicit – distinction between a good or evil spirit within humanity (i.e. a capacity for salvation or damnation) and the Holy Spirit and his demonic counterpart who work from the outside.[38] As the Holy Spirit (or Epinoia) descends to save the Mother's power (or seed), so the counterfeit spirit leads astray humanity, of whose material bodies (counterfeit) spirit is a constituent part and who reproduce by it. The body and sex are the means by which the evil counterfeit spirit gained entry into us and whereby we remain enslaved.[39]

Salvation therefore depends primarily on the descent and presence of the Spirit of life (or of the saving knowledge), but also on the human response. Thus the passage is led to distinguish various types within humanity (*a*) by which of the two spirits prevails and (*b*) by the human response. The first type or class of souls, on whom the Spirit of life descends and unites with the power, responds by ascetic combat of or freedom from the passions, and use of the body as a mere, temporary instrument, as they await reception into and purification in the great illuminators and the final goal of eternal life.[40]

However, that it is the Spirit's presence which is fundamental for salvation and makes it apparently automatic, is evident from the description of the second class of souls, those who have not performed the good work of ascetic combat. All they need is the presence of the Spirit after their birth and its union with the Mother's power, to strengthen the soul and free it from evil.[41] The reference to the fact that they will 'in any case (*pantē pantōs*) live' precisely echoes both what Irenaeus quotes certain Valentinians as claiming and a passage in the Valentinian *Tripartite Tractate*: they, the pneumatics, will be saved not by certain actions but because they are spiritual by nature.[42] Further, the idea that the soul is saved or led into evil depending on which spirit inhabits it is reminiscent of the view of Valentinus himself, echoed in Hippolytus' account of the Valentinians.[43] According to Valentinus the heart is like an inn inhabited by evil spirits, or, when cleansed, by the Father, while in Hippolytus it is a matter of the soul as an inn being occupied by demons or heavenly Logoi.

But there are some striking differences, if also a concealed similarity. First, unlike Valentinianism, souls are not saved by nature, only by the descent of the Spirit after birth: all have the capacity (the Mother's power), not all have the Spirit. Second, it is a matter not of plural good and evil spirits but of the Holy Spirit versus its demonic counterpart, the counterfeit spirit.[44] Conversely, as with Valentinianism, salvation should not be understood as an entirely automatic process. As we shall see, some souls with saving knowledge (i.e. those initiates on whom the Spirit has descended?) can yet reject it and turn away.[45] And the whole Valentinian scheme depends on the value of this present world as the necessary sphere for the formation, education and perfection of the pneumatic seed, just as the first class of souls in the *Apocryphon* reaches perfection through ascetic effort.[46]

If then in the *Apocryphon* the power of the Mother is the indispensable precondition of life and salvation, and the presence of the Holy Spirit of life the effecter of ultimate redemption, which is not an assured possession or automatic process but seems to follow birth (i.e. spiritual and sacramental rebirth), what role does knowledge play? Theodotus' classic definition of Gnostic salvation insists that it is not just baptism but the unique Gnostic knowledge which saves.[47] Now the term does crop up in the context of the third class of souls, those who have not come to complete knowledge. The reason given for this situation is the activity of the counterfeit spirit. Those ignorant souls led astray by it will be fettered once more (in matter or bodies?) until they are saved from forgetfulness and acquire knowledge. In this way they will become perfect and saved.[48] We have already suggested that the motifs of the descent of the Spirit and acquiring saving knowledge are similarly described and thus in effect equivalent.[49] This is strengthened by comparing the activities of the two spirits: the role of the counterfeit spirit leading souls into ignorance and evil is balanced by the descent of the Holy Spirit leading elect souls into knowledge and perfection, as already reflected in the mythologoumenon of the two trees of Paradise, the counterfeit spirit and the Epinoia.[50]

The reference to the third class of souls is preceded by a rather garbled passage describing the saved souls' departure from the flesh and evil and safeguarded ascent to the repose of the aeons (or eternal rest),[51] which once again fails to suggest any differentiation along the lines suggested in the earlier 'Sethian' passage, confirming its character as a later interpolation and interpretation. The allusions to the flesh and evil lead naturally to the question of the ignorant souls (the third class) overcome by the counterfeit spirit, and their fate; after being drawn to evil and forgetfulness they are apparently stripped of their bodies (at death?), but are once more cast by the First Archon's authorities into chains until finally liberated. Does this imply reincarnation, as hinted above? Tardieu argues no, such souls are trapped in the planetary sphere until finally liberated.[52]

However, Tardieu's arguments are not entirely persuasive. One has to consider the process, the language and the parallels, particularly in *Pistis Sophia*. Just as the archetypal man Adam (or rather his soul) was finally trapped in a material body as a fetter of oblivion, so too are the souls of his ignorant successors.[53] And since the process of salvation (being saved from forgetfulness, acquiring knowledge), namely baptism and chrismation promising spiritual rebirth and the descent of the Spirit, requires a human body, this implies reincarnation. This is surely how one must understand the passage underlying John's question about how souls can possibly re-enter their mother's womb, as also the later remark about how by following Gnostics such souls are saved and do not enter another flesh.[54] The language of authorities consorting with and Gnostics accompanying such souls does not necessarily imply a disembodied sojourn in the planetary spheres, and the parallel passages in *Pistis Sophia* (which I have argued are dependent on the *Apocryphon* and its traditions) do clearly teach reincarnation in another body for wicked and ignorant souls.[55]

It is important to note here how closely John's question about how souls can become small enough to re-enter the womb (*physis*) of the mother or into the man is bound up with the prior passage dealing with ignorant souls who, after the death of the body, are cast into another until saved. The Saviour does not reject John's question but supplies a solution of a sort: such souls are given to elect souls as their guardians and reach salvation and knowledge by accompanying and obeying them (i.e. by being initiated through them?).[56] This means their freedom from their existing body and no *further* reincarnations, not no process of reincarnation at all! Once again there is no hint that such souls are inferior, as the earlier 'Sethian' passage on the destinies of souls indicated, a further sign of its later character.

The final class of souls comprises those who did have knowledge but apostatized. They will be taken to the place of the angels of poverty and finally tortured with eternal punishment along with all who have blasphemed the Holy Spirit.[57] Such an equation of rejection of saving knowledge with blasphemy of the Holy Spirit is further confirmation of the hypothesis outlined above that saving knowledge and the descent of the Spirit in Gnostic initiation are synonymous. The blasphemy against the Spirit can only involve the rejection of the claim that through Gnostic initiation the Holy Spirit has descended to indwell and save them.

Thus, in conclusion, the conflicting nature of the Gnostic experience of salvation, of the reality in some of the sense of election, the need nevertheless for ascetic denial of the world, the facts of ignorance on the part of others and of inexplicable rejection by still others who did have the saving knowledge, is well reflected in this dialogue passage. The *Apocryphon* attempts to do justice and reconcile this conflict by its governing theme:

the descent of the Father's Holy Spirit as the effecter of salvation and the presence of the Mother's light-power as its indispensable precondition. Salvation is thus possible for all, but not automatic: it depends on the divine initiative (the saving descent of the Spirit in Gnostic initiation) and on the correct human response (ascetic freedom from the passions, or at least acceptance of the initiative).[58] It is not a matter of nature (unlike the Valentinian threefold scheme), or gender, or of merit and reward (unlike a Judaeo–Christian view) and does not necessarily imply different eras, stages or degrees of salvation (unlike the later 'Sethian' reinterpretation or the Valentinian view).

Moreover, it attempts to combine elements of the three understandings of salvation found in unresolved tension in Saturninus' scheme, as noted in previous chapters: salvation as 'by nature', as a permanent possession by grace and as a gift, capable of being lost or rejected. Thus the soul which has united with the Spirit will certainly be saved without the need for works; it can later be described in terms of belonging to the 'seed' or the 'immovable race', a concept approaching that of 'nature'. The priority of the gracious divine initiative is also stressed, but room is found for the possibility of loss or rejection of the divine gift. That this passage seems to concentrate on the soul as the essential vehicle of salvation, and not the Mother's power, as previously, need not imply that the dialogue is an interpolation;[59] what is fundamental is the final saving descent of the Spirit. The Mother's light-power represents not a provisional salvation, as earlier passages might suggest, but the *capacity* for salvation.

2 Further archontic measures and counter-measures: the counterfeit spirit, Fate, the Flood

The narrative of the Gnostic salvation history, dealing with Genesis 5–9, is resumed after John's seventh question, about the origin of the counterfeit spirit.[60] The question evidently acts as a bridge, and an artificial harmonizing one at that, since the answer comes much later and there are contradictions and awkwardnesses in the content. Tardieu has persuasively argued for this passage dealing with Genesis 5–9 as a later editorial insertion (his (n^1)), which I would argue is part of the 'Sethian' reinterpretation (my (a^3)), since it involves characteristic concepts such as 'the seed' and 'the immovable race'. Thus the text refers at once to the Holy Spirit identified as the Epinoia with her seed (*sperma*), working with us and awakening the thought (or seed) of the perfect immovable race of the man of light,[61] which picks up the passage directly before the dialogue, which spoke of the Mother or her spirit working on the seed until the descent of the Holy Spirit.[62] We have already called attention to the 'Sethian' character of such passages,[63] and the confused state of the text here – no principal verb, the peculiar form of III, the lack of connection with what follows – is further evidence of interpolation and redaction.

As we have already argued, the 'Mother' of SR must be understood from her activity and attributes as Barbelo, the 'Mother–Father' of LR, originally the higher Sophia, the consort of the supreme being, although of course the term 'Mother' also applies sometimes to the lower, fallen Sophia. Indeed, traces of Sophia's original status and her redeeming activity have survived all attempts to distance her from Barbelo and from any kind of redemptive role, and these relics at times contribute to the disarray of our texts. Yet the main obvious source of that confusion here is the further application of the Pronoia–Epinoia scheme. Thus what is being described appears to be a further – or a résumé of a previous – redemptive activity of the Spirit/Epinoia in close conjunction with the Mother–Father, i.e. Barbelo. That LR describes her as 'the Epinoia of the forethought (*pronoia*) of light',[64] could be seen as part of this process as well as an attempt to harmonize more with the closing Pronoia hymn,[65] as is its qualification of the spirit as 'in every form':[66] both strikingly recall the triple descent of the thought (*meeue*, i.e. *epinoia*) of the Pronoia of that hymn.[67] Perhaps not surprisingly, MacRae claims to find in this passage the second descent of the redeemer figure of the hymn,[68] but there is little evidence of this in the text and little real correlation; indeed whereas the Epinoia here successfully wakens the elect and provokes an archontic counter-reaction, in her second advent in the hymn the Pronoia (or Epinoia) is depicted rather as provoking an anticipation of the End.[69]

The confusion in B and LR, which has the Holy Spirit/Epinoia raise up or awaken the seed (*sperma*) of the elect rather than their thinking,[70] is, as I suggested above, evidently a further sign of the effect of the 'Sethian' reworking, with its themes of the seed and the immovable, perfect race. Certainly the version in III makes more sense, recalling as it does the earlier passage about the Ennoia awakening the thinking of Adam.[71] But the idea of raising up seed at once recalls Eve's words about Seth in the LXX of Gen 4:25; behind the confusion in our texts may lie a deliberate

'Sethian' wordplay involving both the raising up of the Gnostic race of (heavenly) Seth and the awakening of its thought.[72] The version in III is thus justified in interpreting the garbled language of B and LR about the identity of the men or race involved: it is the immovable race of the perfect Man of light (Adamas and hence also Seth?).[73]

Aware that humans (or the elect) surpass him in the elevation of their wisdom, the First Archon wants to take control of their thinking, ignorant of their superior intelligence.[74] The last phrase is further evidence of the secondary nature of this passage in that the First Archon and even his minions had previously not been ignorant but all too aware of the intellectual superiority of Adam (and hence of his offspring)![75] Fate (*heimarmenē*) is then produced by the First Archon and his authorities, LR adding that this resulted from their adultery with each other's Sophia (or wisdom),[76] and continuing with a digression, virtually unparalleled in SR, describing the evil nature of Fate and its universal dominion.[77] A similar negative evaluation of Heimarmene occurs in Zosimus' *On the Letter Omega* in which 'Hermes' and Zoroaster are said to have asserted that the race of philosophers was superior to Fate,[78] and in which is related the 'Hebrew' and Hermetic myth of the enslavement of the spiritual light-man in the earthly Adam, the product of Heimarmene,[79] and his liberation from the body and Heimarmene through the advent and continuing activity of the Son of God.[80] Here too we find the protological and eschatological figure of the counterfeit demon (*antimimos daimōn*), leading men astray by his false claim to be Son of God and associated with Heimarmene which traps those who possess merely corporeal over against intellectual (*noeros*) perception (*akoē*).[81]

More relevant perhaps is the picture presented in *On the Origin of the World*, where Heimarmene is seen as the fellow-worker with seven archons, who were thrown down upon the earth and produced demons who led humanity astray by teaching them magic and idolatry. She originated from the agreement of the gods of justice and injustice, and as a result the cosmos was thrown into confusion and error, ignorance and oblivion (*bshe*). Humanity served the demons from creation to the consummation and advent of the true Man.[82] This last passage appears to bear some relation to the digression in LR. In it Heimarmene is begotten by the First Archon and his powers (surely including the righteous and unrighteous rulers of the material body, Jave and Eloim) as the last of the variable bonds, stronger than that which unites gods, angels, demons and men, the source of all evil, forgetfulness (*bshe*) and ignorance, binding humanity through time.[83]

There is of course no exact parallel in *On the Origin of the World* to the long recension of the *Apocryphon*'s conception of the powers' adultery with each other's wisdom (or Sophia) as the origin of Heimarmene. But there are traces of both of these ideas/figures in it. Thus we hear of a Sophia (of Ialdabaoth!) in the sixth heaven responsible for the creation of the heavenly constellations and thus for time and order in the cosmos, i.e. the Jewish creative Wisdom figure,[84] while at the final revelation of the truth in the archons' realm it is said that all their wisdoms are put to shame and their Heimarmene found to be under condemnation.[85] This juxtaposition suggests that both are making use of a tradition which traced the origin of Heimarmene to the wisdom of the archons (perhaps envisaged more mythologically in terms of the archons' intercourse with the figure of creative Wisdom), and linked the evils and ignorance in the world with Fate.

The two recensions then concur in summarizing the effect of the creation of Fate. Everything is bound by time since Fate is lord over everything.[86] Thus although there is little trace in SR of LR's conception of Heimarmene's origin and responsibility for evil in the world, its negative view of Fate and of the archontic plan may have stimulated LR to develop its presentation, relying on other traditions about Heimarmene.

Having thus described the final determinant of human existence, Fate and its instrument, time, the 'Sethian' redactor is free to develop the concept of history, the genuine *Heilsgeschichte* of the Gnostics as the earthly race of the heavenly Seth, by further appeal to Genesis. The earlier reinterpretation, while active in reworking the Cain and Abel traditions, made very little of the birth of earthly Seth. But this addition, in order to depict the further counter-measures of the archons in human history as part of its schematization of world history in terms of a continuing battle between the heavenly Sethians and the evil powers (and of a triple descent scheme of the Saviour), makes use of the Jewish mythologoumenon based on Gen 6:2–4 of the intercourse of angels with the daughters of men,[87] and of details of the Flood narrative in Genesis 6 and 7. However, it reverses the order, ignoring the biblical sequence and logic: the Flood is not the consequence of the (fallen) angels' misconduct with the daughters of men. Rather, first the Flood, allegorized as darkness, then the angelic seduction are successive – unsuccessful – attempts of the

First Archon to destroy humanity, which find their climax in the creation of the counterfeit spirit. The angels are not fallen, nor do they generate giants as in the Jewish interpretation; they are deliberately sent to produce human offspring for their pleasure as creatures in the power of the First Archon. Once again we encounter the Gnostic freedom of reinterpretation of scripture, particularly Genesis and its contemporary Jewish interpretation, to accommodate and illustrate their own theology.

Echoing Gen 6:6 and 6:17, the First Archon repents of all that had come into existence through him and decides to bring a flood over the whole human creation.[88] But once again a divine redeemer/revealer comes to the rescue; the greatness of Pronoia, i.e. the Epinoia (of light) according to SR, or the greatness of the light of the Pronoia according to LR, instructed Noah.[89] Although SR may have added the gloss about the Epinoia in an attempt to harmonize with the main body of the *Apocryphon*, it seems more likely that LR, which normally tends to add references to the Epinoia, omitted it by mistake or deliberately.[90] On the other hand, the expression in LR, 'greatness of the light of Pronoia' also recalls some of the self-designations of the Pronoia revealer/redeemer of the closing hymn, and thus may represent another attempt by LR to integrate this passage more thoroughly.[91]

Noah, the text continues, tried unsuccessfully to warn humanity,[92] and there follows a further 'correction' of Genesis: not, as 'Moses' said, 'he hid himself' (B) or 'they hid themselves (III, II, IV) in an ark', but 'he hid himself' (B) or 'they hid themselves (III, II, IV) in a place'.[93] No such form of words, of course, occurs in Genesis 7: verse 7 has Noah enter the ark and verse 15 speaks of them (Noah and family) going in. However, in *1 Enoch* 10.2 an angel says to Noah: 'Hide yourself!' and the *Apocryphon*'s redactor may be echoing this kind of pseudepigraphical tradition, or a blend of it and Genesis 7.[94] It adds a further correction: not only Noah but also other men (cf. Gen 7:23 LXX) of the immovable race went into a place and covered themselves with a cloud of light.[95] This is evidently part of the 'Sethian' reinterpretation, as is the understanding of Noah as one of the immovable race, since in texts such as the *Hypostasis* and the *Apocalypse of Adam* (which do not have the classic 'Sethian' self-designation 'immovable race'), Noah is an ambivalent figure associated with the evil Demiurge or his son the righteous Sabaoth.[96]

Noah recognizes his heavenly authority, along with those with him, through the light which shines upon them, because darkness covers everything on earth.[97] As Tardieu notes, the redactor completely recasts the Genesis account, turning the Flood into the darkness with which the small portion of light must battle, while, as we suggested, he also reinterprets Noah as a Gnostic and not the reluctant servant of the Demiurge.[98]

Then follows the motif of the angelic seduction of men based on Gen 6:2–4 and its interpretation in Jewish and Jewish–Christian circles. But instead of the angels being cast down on the earth for their wickedness, seducing the daughters of men and producing the giants out of hostility to God, as in the customary Jewish and Christian interpretation,[99] the *Apocryphon* makes their action a result of the First Archon's joint plan with them. Since the 'Flood' failed and the Gnostic Noah escaped, the descent of the angels is developed as a further counter-measure and explanation of how humanity after Noah was enslaved: the angels are sent to the daughters of men to produce offspring for their (the angels') enjoyment. But this too is given a twist: their scheme failed at first.[1] As a result they finally decide to create a counterfeit (or despicable) spirit like the Spirit which had come down.[2] But which Spirit is involved here? Is it the Holy Spirit, the Epinoia who wakened Adam, or the spirit of Sophia, the Mother, sent to Adam's descendants?[3] The former seems ruled out since in that episode the Epinoia is concealed from the archons[4] and since it is precisely the latter episode which is picked up as the connecting link for the further Genesis reinterpretation.[5]

The answer to Janssens' question how, if the counterfeit spirit was only created after the 'Flood', could it have been involved in the creation of material man,[6] is, of course, that we are dealing with two separate sources. The original source had the counterfeit spirit produced as an element in the archontic creation of the material body in response to the descent and concealment of the Holy Spirit in the psychic Adam,[7] while this later version has it created in imitation of the Holy Spirit as a final archontic device to divert humanity from salvation.[8] Here one could fruitfully compare the account in Zosimus in which the conflict similarly takes place on and reflects two levels, one within and one outside humanity. There is the struggle between the inner spiritual man and the external Adam, created by the archons and Fate and enslaved in a primal event. Then there is the opposition between the continuous redemptive activity of the Son of God in human history and the hostile endeavours of his counterpart, the counterfeit demon, who appears later on the scene and claims to be the Son of God.[9] In both cases it is not the power or inner spiritual man, which belongs to us by nature, which ensures our redemption but the presence and activity of the Spirit or Son of God awakening the power, freeing the enslaved inner man. Salvation is essentially something which comes to us and is thus a matter of grace. It can be lost.

The *Apocryphon* then returns to the mythologoumenon of the angelic seduction: the angels transformed their appearance into the likeness of the husbands of the daughters of men, a motif found in Jewish and Jewish–Christian circles.[10] However, the Gnostic interpretation again intervenes: this was to fill them with the spirit of evil.[11] The Enochic motif is further developed: the angels brought precious metals to humans and led them into distractions.[12] SR adds the reason, 'so that they should not think of their immovable forethought (*pronoia*)',[13] omitted by LR perhaps because of its different view of Pronoia as the second highest heavenly figure with the key role in redemption.[14] LR then has a passage expanding the description of human seduction into distraction and ignorance which is evidently an addition.[15] It mentions people being led astray into many errors, growing old and not finding rest, dying without having discovered truth or the true God (cf. Heb 3:8–11, quoting Ps 95(94):7–11), so that the whole creation (*ktisis*) became enslaved forever from the foundation (*katabolē*) of the world (*kosmos*) until now (cf. Dan 12:1/Matt 24:21).[16]

The *Apocryphon* then recounts how the angelic initiative finally succeeds: the angels took women and begot children from the darkness through the counterfeit spirit.[17] They closed their hearts and became hardened through the hardness of the counterfeit spirit until now.[18] In this deliberate echo of biblical language the *Apocryphon* supplies the final characteristic of human existence, the problem of human blindness and the rejection of the saving message and of the divine revealer/redeemer, the Holy Spirit.[19] It is the work of his rival, the counterfeit spirit, who, according to the text, is thus responsible both for humans reproducing and for their lack of spiritual perception.[20] Such a reference also neatly links in with the opening dialogue: it was not the Saviour who led people astray and hardened their hearts, as the Pharisee, Arimanius, had insinuated to John, but the demonic counterfeit spirit, the creation of the archons.[21]

3 The closing Pronoia hymn and epilogue

The last statement would appear to mark the conclusion of the *Heilsgeschichte* and this seems to be confirmed by the marked divergence of the two recensions at this point. SR, apparently continuing the soteriological exposition, abruptly asserts that the blessed Mother–Father who is rich in mercy takes form (*morphē*) in her seed (*sperma*).[22] This is followed by the Saviour's pronouncement that at first he ascended to the perfect aeon.[23] Thereupon the epilogue proper begins, echoing the prologue, with both recensions in general agreement that, as is customary in Gnostic gospels, the Saviour gives instructions to John about the transmission in writing of what he has said to his fellow spirits (*homopneuma*), namely the mystery of the immovable race.[24] But SR interrupts the epilogue at this point with the Saviour's statement, which as Puech points out properly belongs to the dogmatic exposition,[25] that the Mother came another time before him and what she did in the cosmos was to correct her deficiency (*hysterēma*).[26] SR then adds the Saviour's promise, actually unfulfilled, but echoing the prologue: 'I will teach you (plural, i.e. the disciples?) what will happen.'[27] The two recensions then concur in their version of the Saviour's closing instructions to John (in the first person in SR, but in the third in LR) to preserve his teaching in writing and keep it safe; his curse upon any who traffic in it for material gain; his commission to John (in the third person in both recensions) of the mystery and his disappearance, whereupon John proceeds to proclaim the message to his fellow disciples.[28] LR adds the phrase: 'Jesus the Christ. Amen.'[29]

LR's version of the epilogue is not broken up like that of SR, but follows neatly from the hymnic *ego eimi* revelation discourse of the Saviour, identified as the perfect Pronoia of the All, who relates her three saving descents in disguise to this world (as Hades), in the third of which she enters a human body to awaken and initiate the imprisoned Gnostic (the five seals rite), to free him from the power of death.[30] LR thus begins the hymn in the first person right after the mention of the counterfeit spirit's activity until now, making no mention of the Mother–Father taking form or the Mother's previous visitation and saving action, and starting the epilogue (still in the first person) with the Saviour's assertion of his future ascent (not past, as in SR) to the perfect aeon.[31]

What is the precise relation between the two recensions, particularly as regards the Pronoia hymn? Is it a late addition to LR, either as composed by its redactor(s) or as an earlier autonomous piece? As we shall see, the striking similarities to *Trimorphic Protennoia* might suggest the latter. Was it therefore omitted by the redactor(s) of SR as a later, not properly integrated insertion? Conversely, is it original, supplying the fundamental structure of the *Apocryphon*? Again, is it Christian or non- and pre-Christian, a form of Jewish Wisdom hymn? Finally, as we shall argue, is it not perhaps best interpreted as part of the Johannine framework of redaction (a²), the triple descent of the Saviour/Pronoia as Father, Mother and Son (Logos), which follows on naturally from the dialogue on the souls?

Doresse, perhaps the first to discuss the relation of the recensions, refuses to commit himself: he suggests the possible secondary character of the passage, noting its hymn-like quality, but at once speculates whether its archaic style might not imply it was original and omitted by SR, whose text is confused here.[32] Giversen points to the special character of the passage in relation to LR and also suggests that SR omitted it for (unspecified) editorial reasons.[33] Schottroff agrees with Giversen, arguing that the statements of SR must be understood as redemptive and that the redeemer's discourse must already have been present in the tradition underlying SR. However, she does attempt to offer the more satisfactory reason for its omission, that it was felt to be a doublet of Jesus' appearance to John.[34] MacRae claims to find the three revelatory descents in the text itself (the Saviour's message to John being the third),[35] and thus denies Jonas' characterization of the hymn as an 'Iranian' insertion into an essentially 'Syrian' type of Gnosticism. The best way to account for it, says MacRae, is as 'a Gnostic liturgical fragment probably recited at a ceremony of initiation much in the manner of a Christian baptismal homily or hymn'.[36] While MacRae in the later discussion admits the secondary character in time and nature of this part of the long recension, his overall conclusion points to the antiquity of the hymn and its pre- and non-Christian character.[37] Finally, he alludes to the striking similarities in content, structure and form between the hymn and *Trimorphic Protennoia*.[38]

Turner, in his edition of the latter, accepts MacRae's analysis, arguing that, in light of the likely priority of SR, the absence of the Pronoia hymn from it suggests that the hymn may have existed separately from the *Apocryphon*. He goes on to posit that *Trimorphic Protennoia* is an expansion of an earlier version of that non-Christian 'aretalogical, sapiental Pronoia hymn' found in the long recension of the *Apocryphon*.[39] He claims to find the threefold descent of Protennoia echoing the three descents of Pronoia in the main body of the latter, but his identification of the first two differs from MacRae's.[40] Moreover neither MacRae nor Turner explore the question of the precise relation between this supposed pre-Christian Pronoia hymn and our *Apocryphon*, whether, for example, the former underlies the latter: they seem to accept it as an ancient literary unit added later, yet also assume a necessary correlation between the three descents of the hymn and saving events in the main text. The failure to find or agree on a convincing correlation between the hymn and the rest of the *Apocryphon* is highly significant for any attempt to answer our question of the relation between the recensions as regards the hymn.

Arai also argues that the revelation discourse (or hymn) of the Pronoia figure is a later addition, but he understands it as a *Christian* interpretation of III 39.11–13 (the Mother–Father taking form in her offspring).[41] The Mother–Father is Sophia and her taking form is to be seen in terms of the Valentinian understanding of the formation of shapeless and ignorant Achamoth and thus also of the pneumatics.[42] This eschatological formation and perfection of Sophia with her offspring has been transmuted by LR into the triple descent of Christ, with the deliberate omission of any reference to the saving action of Sophia (B 76.1–5/III 39.19–21). But he also questions the originality of SR's epilogue in its present form: the dislocations and abrupt changes of subject mark an attempt to interpolate and stress the role of Christ as redeemer alongside the original view of Sophia alone as such.[43] However, his interpretation is a little strained and far-fetched and is undermined by Tardieu's persuasive demonstration that SR still retains traces of the Pronoia hymn.[44]

Tardieu's own solution is also to posit the Christian character (and Jewish Wisdom roots) of the Pronoia hymn, but as the original basis of the *Apocryphon*, a pastiche of the Johannine Prologue by a dissident member of the Johannine circle, replacing the creative Word by Providence (Pronoia) who eventually becomes not flesh but Word. This hymn was so well-known that it was omitted by the original redactor (n) but added by a later (n[1]), only to be omitted by the redactor of SR (o).[45] Indeed Tardieu claims to find evidence of the existence and use of the hymn in two other sources; the Naassene hymn in Hippolytus and the three 'calls' of Mani's myth in his *Pragmateia*.[46] This may be so, and his relating of the hymn to the Johannine Prologue illuminating, but his reconstruction and explanation of the redactional process of omission, addition, omission is rather fanciful.

Indeed, all such attempts to argue for the antiquity and autonomy of the Pronoia hymn stumble on the awkward fact that it makes little or no sense on its own, unless interpreted against the light of an existing myth, since the purpose of the first two descents is far from clear. How Turner's hypothetical earlier version could have made enough sense to form the basis of *Trimorphic Protennoia* is even more unclear. On the other hand it does seem to have been excluded by SR, and the latter's evident unhappiness with the term and figure 'Mother–Father', associated with the attributes 'rich in mercy' and 'as a first Man', as well as what I will argue is its implied rejection of the idea that the supreme female figure could have descended, may supply a better explanation of the provenance of the hymn and the reason for its omission. Here Turner, although unconvincing over the relation of the Pronoia hymn to *Trimorphic Protennoia*, has rightly suggested that the three descents in the main body of the *Apocryphon* are 'essentially those to be found in *On the Origin of the World* (II,5), *Hypostasis of the Archons* (II,4) and Irenaeus' 'Ophite' account (*Haer.* I.30.6–12)'.[47] Thus he sees them as a major feature of Sethian gnostic mythology, with the *Apocryphon* as seemingly a combination of the Sethian–Barbeloite cosmogony and Sophia myth of Irenaeus 1.29 and the 'Ophite' anthropogony and soteriology of Irenaeus 1.30.

If one removes the Sethian label, Turner's analysis concurs very much with mine, and his pointer to the pattern of three descents in *On the Origin*, the *Hypostasis* and Irenaeus 1.30.6–12 is extremely suggestive, if not spelled out in detail. I would propose the following analysis of how the descent scheme and Pronoia hymn evolved, following Turner's suggestion. The key lies in the changing role of Sophia. In the original soteriological section of the Christian myth underlying the *Apocryphon*, not included in Irenaeus' summary, Sophia, as Arai rightly surmises, was the major figure in salvation as well as cosmology, playing the kind of role she does in the related 'Ophite' myth, reflecting a Christian–Gnostic interpretation of Jewish speculations on Wisdom and her descents to the world. Thus her first saving action or descent in my view was her rebuke to the First Archon and appearance as heavenly Man/Adamas, the first stage in the divine plan to recover the lost light-power.

In the 'Ophite' version Sophia merely supplies a mental picture of man and does not actually descend.[48] In the elaborate, reduplicated and clearly secondary versions in the *Hypostasis* and *On the Origin*, either she, as Pistis (to distinguish her from her daughter Sophia Zoe), rebukes Ialdabaoth for his boast, inserts light into matter and descends before returning,[49] or, as Incorruptibility, looks down revealing her (man-like) image to the creator archons,[50] or she rebukes Ialdabaoth, informing him of the existence of an immortal light-man who will appear in his creations and destroy them, reveals her likeness and withdraws above.[51] These are evident doublets of what I would argue is the more original version underlying our present *Apocryphon*, in which Sophia rebukes Ialdabaoth for his boast of being the only god by referring to the existence of heavenly Man, descends (or lets her image descend) disguised as him, then reascends. It is to this, not, as Turner claims, to the descent of Autogenes and the illuminators to engineer Ialdabaoth's inbreathing,[52] that the first descent of the Saviour in the Pronoia hymn corresponds.[53]

Turner is then correct to identify the second descent of the Pronoia (originally the second descent of Sophia herself as Zoe, awakening Adam by her call) with the dispatch of the Epinoia/Zoe by the merciful Mother–Father to instruct Adam and thereby put right Sophia's deficiency,[54] and the third with her (male) manifestation as Christ, which, as he points out, coincides in SR with the appearance of the Saviour in the Christian dialogical frame story itself, and in LR with the Pronoia hymn.[55] Now the 'Ophite' system, if not explicitly teaching a first or second descent of Sophia, retains a trace of Sophia's third descent when, united with her consort Christ, she enters Jesus.[56] Prior to that, like the Epinoia/Zoe of the *Apocryphon*, she had worked continuously at saving the divine dew of light and proclaimed the existence of the true First Man and imminent descent of Christ, causing terror to the archons.[57] Moreover both the *Hypostasis* and *On the Origin* do have a second descent in the person of Sophia's daughter, Zoe, as well as a final one in the person of the True Man or Word, i.e. Christ.[58] Thus in these last, evidently transitional texts, we can observe the process whereby Sophia is no longer the predominant saving figure who descends or intervenes three times, but is being supplemented or replaced by offshoots (Zoe, Eve), with Christ as the culminating Saviour.

Now what we have observed in the *Apocryphon* is precisely the final replacement of Sophia as Saviour by the Pronoia (Barbelo/

merciful Mother–Father) and the Epinoia figures, the former
particularly identified with the Saviour in the prologue and
Pronoia hymn. The essential unity of the two is worth noting, since
I would contend that the Pronoia hymn is part of redaction (a^2),
showing the influence of Johannine (as well as 'Ophite' and
Valentinian) material.[59] The Johannine Saviour or Word (himself
based on Sophia/Wisdom) has been identified with the supreme
female figure, Barbelo (originally higher Sophia), as the Father's
providence or Pronoia, in her three forms or modalities of Father,
Mother and Son (the original Gnostic triad).[60] The three initiatives
or descents of Sophia, first anthropogonic (through her voice
proclaiming heavenly Man and her heavenly Adam image), then
eschatological (through her voice awakening Adam and proclaiming his future ascent and her heavenly Eve/Zoe image) and
finally soteriological (through her voice proclaiming the Word
or Son through the prophets and the Baptist and her union with
the Son, Christ in the human body), supplied the basis for the
construction of the Pronoia hymn with its three descents of the
Saviour/Pronoia, first as Father (First Man),[61] then as Mother
(Zoe, Mother of all living) and finally as Son, saving the elect
through illumination and the five seals initiation rite.[62] Indeed
the – overlooked – links between the passage on the destiny of
souls and the Pronoia hymn[63] would support both my view of the
hymn being integral to the *Apocryphon* as part of redaction (a^2),
and of the intervening reinterpretation of Genesis 5–9 as part of
the 'Sethian' reworking of redaction (a^3).

However, the difficulties presented by a male Saviour identified
with a female (Pronoia) or androgynous (Mother–Father) figure,
added perhaps to the present awkwardness of correlating the three
descents with the main body of the text (vividly illustrated by
the disagreements among modern commentators!), might well
account for the omission of the Pronoia hymn by SR, as it does
for its tendency to play down references to Pronoia and its general
conversion of 'Mother–Father' into either 'Father' or 'Mother'.[64]
Indeed, SR's later acknowledgement that the Mother (i.e. Sophia)
did come another time before the Saviour, and that what she did
in the cosmos was to put right her deficiency,[65] could well be
interpreted as its 'correction' of the claim that the supreme female
being, Pronoia/Barbelo, had descended into this evil realm to
instruct and save the elect, particularly finally in the guise of the
Saviour: this may be the decisive reason why SR omitted the
hymn.[66] With the omission of the hymn the Saviour's allusion to

his future ascent was also changed by SR to refer to a past ascent to the perfect aeon.[67]

The remarkable similarities to *Trimorphic Protennoia* can best be explained, not in terms of the latter originating from the Pronoia hymn as an ancient autonomous fragment expanded by aretalogical passages of uncertain provenance, with the mythological material (essentially the Barbeloite cosmogony) being added later, as Turner argues, but rather in terms of the latter being influenced by redaction (a²) as a whole, developing even further the triadic structure of anthropogonic Voice and image of Man, eschatological Voice and Zoe, soteriological Word and Son, suggested in the main text and summarized in the Pronoia hymn.[68] The influence of the Johannine material evident in redaction (a²) of the *Apocryphon* is more clear-cut, appropriately enough, in the third section of *Trimorphic Protennoia*, producing the 'stupendous parallels' of Colpe. On the other hand, the apparent parallels with Seth and his threefold parousias in *The Gospel of the Egyptians* and the triple descent of the Illuminator of the *Apocalypse of Adam* are best interpreted in terms of a 'Sethian' adaptation of the Saviour/Pronoia scheme to fit its characteristic periodization of history. Pressed to avoid the charge of novelty, early third-century Gnostics developed the theme of heavenly Seth and his 'immovable race', identifying the Saviour as Seth or the Illuminator, who descends three times to save his seed from flood, fire and the schemes of the archons, the third time putting on or appearing in a body explicitly or implicitly that of Jesus, in the context of initiation.[69]

For, as already indicated, the interest in heavenly Seth as redeemer and progenitor of the elect race of Gnostics only seems to emerge alongside and, as I have argued, in reaction to 'orthodox' interest in Seth, at the beginning of the third century. Thus it is Epiphanius' *Christian*–Gnostic Sethians who interpret Christ as descending from Seth's race, and indeed as 'Seth himself, who both now and then visits (*epiphoitan*) the human race', sent down by the supreme female deity.[70]

If then, as I have argued, Sophia was the original saving figure, descending or intervening at three decisive points in world history, on the last occasion in union with (or replaced by) Christ, where does this idea come from? Is it based on supposed pre-Christian Jewish–Gnostic Wisdom speculations, as e.g. MacRae would argue,[71] or is it merely a Gnostic interpretation of a much older, widespread pagan myth of an interfering female, as Culianu has suggested,[72] or can it only be understood in terms of a Christian understanding of Christ as bringing decisive revelation and salvation, as I would claim? Again the function and interpretation of the figure and myth of Sophia are fundamental. In the basic Gnostic myth (as in Valentinianism), Sophia is the paradigm of the Gnostic's own experience, responsible for the present plight of the Gnostic, fallen into matter and oblivion; awakened by the divine 'call' of Christ, the saving revelation which is sealed and confirmed by the descent of the Holy Spirit; working in this world to enlighten Gnostics until the decisive eschatological descent of Christ, her ultimate consort. Without that element of decisive revelation as salvation brought by Christ and appropriated through initiation, schemes involving prior descents of figures such as the Pronoia or Seth do not seem to make much sense. What is involved in such prior descents is more the *capacity* for final salvation in term of primal and continuous revelation, or revelation at decisive points (anthropogony, eschatological role of Eve/Zoe as 'Mother of all living'). One has to ask the question of this group of 'Sethian' texts: Was salvation really final before the third descent of Christ/ the Pronoia/heavenly Seth?

That the Jewish figure of Wisdom should underlie and have decisively influenced the Gnostic myths of Sophia, as MacRae has shown, is not surprising: the parallels are striking, particularly with regard to the Hellenistic–Jewish Wisdom books, Ecclesiasticus and Wisdom of Solomon. Thus Janssens and Schenke have rightly drawn attention to the way the figure of Wisdom underlies not only Sophia herself, but also Barbelo/Pronoia and Epinoia in the *Apocryphon* and related works: they are projections of Sophia herself, the consort and agent of the Father in creation, revelation and redemption.[73] But the earliest myths of Sophia – those of Irenaeus' Gnostics (and of the Valentinians) – are *Christian–Gnostic*, the argument of this book. They have not undergone later Christianization, since the anointing, perfection and elevation of the heavenly Son, Christ, is, as I have argued above, the fundamental paradigm of Gnostic initiation and salvation: the rite of baptism (in the name of Father, Mother and Son) does seem to culminate in chrismation (the five seals), associated with the presence of the Holy Spirit.[74] Here the parallels with the complex more 'orthodox' Christian initiation rite of baptism, chrism and sealing with the Holy Spirit are striking, and the likelihood of Gnostic influence on the latter two is, as Lampe has argued, very plausible.

However, even the earliest versions of the myth, both Gnostic and Valentinian, show the essential ambivalence of Sophia and the incipient tendency to split her into two, the supreme Mother who is always *salvator*, and the lower Sophia (the Valentinian Achamoth and 'Ophite' Prunicus), who, if *salvator*, is yet originally and ultimately *salvandus*. The later redactions of the *Apocryphon* finally eliminate virtually all traces of Sophia as redeemer, replacing her with Barbelo/Pronoia and Epinoia, while the 'Sethian' reinterpretation and texts neglect or down-play Sophia and develop the saving role of heavenly Seth. Thus Schenke's understanding of Christ in the 'Ophite' system, the *Apocryphon* and *Trimorphic Protennoia* as the result of a Christianization of a non-Christian Jewish-based (Sethian) Gnostic myth seems a reversal of the truth.[75]

Schenke himself claims to find the classic form of an archetype of the Gnostic redeemer myth in the second of the *Three Steles of Seth* (Sophia as Mother rescuing her children), since it clarifies what is obscure in other texts, that Sophia is Barbelo, the heavenly consort. This he thinks influences the details of *Thunder*, which itself he sees as the classic form of the Gnosticizing of the Jewish Sophia concept. In the *Apocryphon*, he argues, Pronoia is just another name for Sophia and the 'Ophite' system of Irenaeus 1.30 combines a pre-Christian section with Sophia as redeemer (3–11a) with a Christian–Gnostic (11b–14) in which Sophia and Christ together redeem humanity. But in the Jewish Wisdom tradition, Sophia's role is much more that of co-creator and inspirer than redeemer – and she certainly does not 'fall';[76] why figures like Barbelo, Pronoia and Thunder should be considered primary expressions of Sophia rather than she herself is not explained, and the *Three Steles of Seth* seems to fit better as a late 'Sethian' text dependent on *Allogenes* and its more metaphysical speculations. In the *Apocryphon* Sophia is clearly distinct from Barbelo/Pronoia, and to divide the 'Ophite' text into two halves, one pre-Christian, the other Christian, without adequate support in the text, seems arbitrary. In any case, as argued above, neither Sophia nor her replacements seem to offer decisive salvation until the final descent into a human body. What they offer is the *capacity* for that salvation via primal revelation (the creation of Adam in the divine image) and continuous or eschatological revelation (Zoe's awakening Adam and instructing him and his offspring about the future). For decisive revelation as salvation, the actual coming of the Saviour and the subsequent Gnostic rite of initiation are vital.

Conclusion

Analysis of the later soteriological passages of the *Apocryphon*, namely the dialogue on the souls, the archontic counter-measures and the closing Pronoia hymn of the long recension, has tended to confirm our provisional conclusions in the last chapter. They have revealed, first, that if one removes the dialogue (part of redaction (a^2)), the passage on the souls was indeed integral to the original *Apocryphon*, echoing the basic soteriological pattern of the Mother's light-power as the *capacity* for salvation which needs the descent of the Father's Holy Spirit (in the rite of sealing/perfection) for completion. Salvation depends on which spirit dominates; the Holy Spirit or its demonic counterpart, the counterfeit spirit. Further, it involves both divine initiative and human response: it can be rejected. Thus, second, the earlier passage with a different soteriology, assigning souls to the four aeons of Adam and Seth corresponding to their varied responses, we diagnosed as part of the 'Sethian' reinterpretation, as also the further treatment of Genesis 5–9, involving Fate, the Flood and the origin of the counterfeit spirit. This does not quite harmonize with the rest and reflects typical 'Sethian' concerns such as the 'immovable seed' of heavenly Seth and the periodization of history in terms of flood, conflagration and judgement.

Third, we were led to conclude that the Pronoia hymn of the long recension was not an autonomous piece either basic to the *Apocryphon* or tacked on later, but part of redaction (a^2), the Johannine framework of prologue, dialogue and epilogue with its Pronoia/Epinoia scheme, which in turn profoundly influenced *Trimorphic Protennoia* and other related texts. Thus, fourth, the figure of the Saviour is not part of a Christianization of a non- and pre-Christian Jewish–Gnostic original, but integral: redaction (a^2) transferred Sophia's original saving descents to Barbelo, now identified as Pronoia, with a triple mode of being as Father/Mother/Son, instead of her original status as Mother in the primal Gnostic triad, with the Son or Saviour, Christ, as the third mode of Pronoia's triple descent. Such a triple descent scheme, with its 'Sethian' parallel, only makes sense in the light of a Christian understanding of salvation, involving a decisive saving act by Christ in a human body, appropriated by the elect through a rite of initiation; otherwise the two prior descents appear incomplete and meaningless. Understood in this Christian–Gnostic context, they can be seen in terms of a scheme of primal, continuous and decisive revelation, an attempt to resolve the classic dilemma faced by more 'orthodox' Christians: how to present salvation before Christ as a genuine and continuing possibility, as a reality now in the light of the decisive Christ event, yet not complete till the consummation.[77] The 'Sethian' reinterpretation attempted to bolster the Christian–Gnostic claims to antiquity, truth and continuity by developing the concept of heavenly Seth, his seed, the 'immovable race' of the elect and, in the *Apocalypse of Adam* and *Gospel of the Egyptians*, his three parousias, in place of the earlier triple descent scheme of Sophia/Pronoia in the *Apocryphon*.

Fifth, although Jewish Wisdom speculations are central to the Gnostic Sophia myth, the myth itself is essentially Christian, a Christian–Gnostic understanding, parallel to but distinct from more 'orthodox' contemporary Logos and Wisdom speculations about the origin, nature and redeeming function of Christ. It expounds the primal begetting, anointing and elevation of the Son, Christ, and the primal fall and redemption of heavenly Wisdom, as distinct figures and paradigms of the Gnostic experience. Thus while the more 'orthodox' tendency was to unite the Logos and Wisdom speculations to refer to the one figure of the incarnate Son, the Gnostic tendency, so characteristic of their mentality and mythology, was increasingly to split and multiply the redeemer figures to avoid any idea of a heavenly 'fall' or actual incarnation of the divine. Hence the later redactions of the *Apocryphon* and 'Sethianized' texts dependent on it successively relieve Sophia of all trace of her original active role in revelation and redemption, and replace her with other figures, primarily a modalist trinity based on the Mother–Father, Barbelo.[78]

Finally, as regards the relations between the two recensions, SR has clearly misunderstood the integral character of the Pronoia hymn and omitted it, in a laudable attempt to deny that the supreme female deity could have descended into this world, although in other respects it tends to remain more faithful to the original. LR again shows a tendency to creative interpretation and 'correction', feeling the need to emphasize the role of the Pronoia character and integrate the hymn more successfully. It also tends to stress the more negative aspects of Ialdabaoth and his regime.

Notes

[1] B 64.13–71.2/III 32.22–36.15; II 25.16–27.31/IV 39.16–43.6.

[2] B 71.2–5/III 36.15–17; II 27.31–33/IV 43.6–8.

[3] *Apocryphon* 266.

[4] Thus the reference to labour on the seeds in the expectation of the Spirit's future descent (B 64.3–13 and par) is picked up by the reference to the Spirit/Epinoia labouring and elevating the seed, leading to Ialdabaoth's further countermove (B 71.5–72.2 and par). Indeed, the reference to Ialdabaoth seems a more appropriate link than the garbled passage on the seed.

[5] Cf. B 36.2–15 and par.

[6] Cf. B 42.15–43.4 and par.; 48.16–50.6 and par; 51.1–52.8 and par.

[7] Cf. B 65.3–6/III 33.4–6; II 25.23–5/IV 39.25–8.

[8] Cf. B 68.13–70.8/III 35.2–36.4; II 26.32–27.21.

[9] On the 'pure (*eilikrinēs*) light' as the realm of the supreme Father, cf. B 26.18f./III 7.5 (omitted by LR); B 29.18f./III 9.10–12; II 6.10f./IV 9.11–13; B 30.8/III 9.19; II 6.18/IV 9.22f. On 'the great lights' as the four illuminators, cf. B 33.1f./III 11.17; IV 11.5f. (the lacuna seems to require 'great', which II 7.32f. has omitted. Cf. *GE* IV 64.15–23/III 52.20–53.1 (where the 'great light' of the latter does not simply imply the original Greek *phōstēr*, as is clear from the former, despite the annoying lacunae); IV 74.11; IV 77.7f./III 65.12; *TP* 48.28f.). B's reading (65.7f.), 'worthy to enter these great lights' may be an expansion of III 33.6f., 'worthy of these . . .' LR's reading 'greatnesses', i.e. *megethos* (cf. Crum, *Dictionary* 251a), may show awareness of the lack of harmony with the earlier 'Sethian' passage. Further, *megethos* is a Valentinian technical term meaning (*a*) an attribute and title of the supreme being (cf. e.g. Iren. 1.1.1; 2.1; 2.2; 19.2; 21.4; *Gos. Truth* 42.14; *Tri. Trac.* 52.26; 53.1; 54.20) and (*b*) angel (cf. Iren. 1.13.3; 13.6; 14.5. See on this Sagnard, *La gnose valentinienne*, index s.v. *megethos*). However, the term does occur in non-Valentinian texts referring to heavenly beings, cf. *Eug* V 3.6/III 73.5 (*SJC* B 86.11f./III 95.23f.); 6.23/III 77.17 (*SJC* B 95.14/III 102.5); III 86.5f. (*SJC* B 109.16); III 88.10f. (*SJC* B 113.18/III 112.10f.); *GE* III 54.19f./IV 66.7 (plural); *OW* 103.30; *HA* 95.1.

[10] *PS* Book 1, chs 22–3 (Schmidt–MacDermot 32.14–23).

[11] Book 3, chs 111–12 (Schmidt–MacDermot 281–91); 131 (332–7). Cf. Böhlig, *Mysterion* 167–74.

[12] Book 4, chs 147–8 (Schmidt–MacDermot 381.21–384.23).

[13] Thus besides the three elements, power, soul, counterfeit spirit, there is mention of the receivers (*paralēmptōr*) (ch. 112, Schmidt–MacDermot 288.21f., cf. *AJ* B 65.4–6 and par); of the soul as made pure (*eilikrinēs*) light (ch. 131, Schmidt–MacDermot 337.16f., cf. *AJ* B 64.14–16 and par); of the power in the soul that enables people to stand (ch. 131, Schmidt–MacDermot 336.21–337.1; 340.19–21, cf. *AJ* B 67.4–7 and par).

[14] *Mysterion* 168f.

[15] Thus *AJ* does appear to hint at an underlying rite of initiation or mystery (the five seals; cf. II 31.23–5) while *PS* (Book 4, ch. 143, Schmidt–MacDermot 372.15–373.3) speaks of the baptisms of fire and Holy Spirit and spiritual anointing as the supreme mystery which takes souls to the Treasury of Light.

[16] See on this Tardieu, *Écrits* 62–4.

[17] Cf. *SJC* B 117.12–124.9/III 114.8–118.3.

[18] Cf. e.g. *Ep. Pet. Phil.* (C VIII,*2*) 134.18–138.3; *1 Apoc. Jas* (C V,*3*) 28.29–30.13; *Ep. Apost.* 11–51.

[19] See Giversen, *Apocryphon* 266, and Tardieu, *Écrits* 35. Hauschild's description, *Geist* 234f., of this passage as based on a Jewish catechesis in terms of the two spirits such as that found at Qumran, overlooks its fundamental dualism, its Gnostic parallels and its Gnostic concept of the divine power present in humanity as the precondition of salvation which requires union with the divine spirit.

[20] B 121.13–127.2. Cf. *HA* 96.15–97.21.

[21] See n. 9 above.

[22] B 64.16–65.3/III 32.25–33.3 (*asaleuton*); II 25.18–23/IV 39.19–25.

[23] Cf. *TLZ* 100 (1975), col. 97; 'Phenomenon', 591. The 'immovable race' (*genea ñatkim*) occurs in *GE* III 51.8f./IV 63.2f.; III 59.13–15; 61.19f./IV 73.3f.; *Steles Seth* 118.12f. and possibly *Zost.* 6.27; 51.15f. See on this theme, M. A. Williams, *The Immovable Race: A Gnostic Designation and the Theme of Stability in Late Antiquity* (NHS 29) (Leiden: Brill, 1985).

[24] E.g. it occurs in the Saviour's address to John in B 22.15f.;II 2.24f./IV 3.20f., here and at B 75.20ff./III 39.18; II 31.31f./IV 49.12f., or as an addition as in III 36.24f., where B and LR omit it, or in B 73.8–10/III 38.2f.; II 29.9f./IV 45.6f. where Noah and men of the immovable race hide in a place (cf. *AA* 69.19–25). Its occurrence in *SJC* B 88.8f./III 97.8f. (see n. 16 above) suggests that it depends on *AJ* in its 'Sethian' version.

[25] Cf. the 'Ophite' system in Iren. 1.30.14 where it is the holy souls with knowledge (= trace of light) which are saved.

[26] B 65.3f./III 33.4f.; II 25.23f./IV 39.25–27; B 66.14–67.2/III 33.25–34.5; II 26.8ff./IV 40.21–6; B 67.7–13/III 34.9–14; II 26.15–17/IV 40.32–41.4. Janssens, *Muséon* 84, 423, is surely correct to identify the Spirit of life with the Holy Spirit. Although Hauschild, *Geist* 255, is right to suggest the Jewish tradition of the two spirits as found e.g. in 1QS iii.13–iv.26, as the background, more significant is surely the echo of the descent of the Spirit on Christ at his baptism (cf. Matt 3:16; Mark 1:10; Luke 3:22; John 1:32f.; Acts 1:8).

[27] Cf. B 68.13–16/III 35.2–5; II 26.32–5/IV 41.21–4 and B 69.12f.; II 27.9–11, where having the knowledge is related to becoming perfect and saved, as with having the Spirit descend. See below.

²⁸ B 65.4f./III 33.5; II 25.24/IV 39.27. Cf. the association of *dynamis* with the descent of the Holy Spirit in Acts 1:8.

²⁹ B 67.4–7/III 34.7–9; II 26.12–14/IV 40.29–32. Cf. B 51.14–52.1 and par. R. McL. Wilson, 'The Spirit in Gnostic Literature', in B. Lindars, S. Smalley eds., *Christ and the Spirit in the New Testament* (Moule FS) (Cambridge, 1973), 350, appears to identify the spirit as the biological principle and the power as the spiritual, failing to note the identification of B 51.14–52.1 and par.

³⁰ See Book 3, ch. 131 (Schmidt–MacDermot 332–7). But, cf. Book 4, ch. 141 with its references to the Holy Spirit descending on Jesus and saving souls (Schmidt–MacDermot 368). Conversely, *AJ* preserves a trace of the idea that the counterfeit spirit constituted a basic element in our human make-up (cf. B 55.2–13 and par).

³¹ Cf. B 67.14–18/III 34.15–18; II 26.20–2/IV 41.6–10.

³² II 26.15–18/IV 40.32–41.4.

³³ B 67.7–13/III 34.9–14.

³⁴ This would weaken Hauschild's argument, *Geist* 234f., about the influence on *AJ* of the Qumran doctrine of two spirits in humanity, present in equal measure from the beginning.

³⁵ Cf. B 55.3–11 and par and B 63.5–9 and par. In the latter the counterfeit spirit is the agent of human procreation. See Janssens, *Muséon* 84, 423f.

³⁶ Cf. B 74.6–10/III 38.16–20; II 29.21–6.

³⁷ See *Écrits* 41–2, 334ff. Cf. B 71.2ff. and par, where the continuation about the Mother and her Epinoia is linked rather clumsily to mention of the First Archon.

³⁸ This kind of distinction might underlie the Qumranic teaching. Cf. 1QS iii.18–iv.18 on the two angels or spirits and the two spirits in us. See W. D. Davies, 'Paul on Flesh and Spirit' in K. Stendahl ed., *The Scrolls and the New Testament* (London, 1958), 172f.

³⁹ Cf. Böhlig, *Mysterion* 171. Thus in *AJ* B 65.11–66.1 and par, the elect souls are free from passions and desire and use the flesh as an instrument only. Although Böhlig, ibid., and Hauschild, ibid., rightly suggest the likely influence of Jewish sectarian ideas about the two spirits in humanity on this complex conception, in *AJ* it is thoroughly Gnostic and dualist – the supreme God is not responsible for the evil spirit. *PS* sees the counterfeit spirit as burdening the soul with human desires and passions so that it sins (e.g. Book 3, ch. 111). Cf. also the picture in Zos., *Omega* 16 (Scott–Ferguson, *Hermetica* 4.108.21ff.), of the counterfeit demon, jealous of the Son of God who is disguised in various forms, divine and human, to save the elect, imitating him and leading men astray as before.

⁴⁰ B 65.3–66.13/III 33.4–23; II 25.23–26.7/IV 39.25–40.20. Note not only the New Testament echoes which Tardieu, *Écrits* 331, alludes to: 2 Tim 2:10; Matt 19:21; Mark 10:17; Luke 10:25; 18:18, but also *PS* Book 4, ch. 147 (Schmidt–MacDermot 383.10f.). The version in III 33.4f., with

the Spirit uniting with the power, seems preferable to the more confused versions in B 65.3ff. and II 25.23ff./IV 39.25ff. LR's preference for 'greatnesses' in II 25.26/IV 39.30 instead of the 'the great lights' of B 65.8f./III 33.7 may represent an attempt to remove the evident lack of agreement with the earlier passage on the illuminators as abodes of various souls (B 35.20–36.15 and par). The 'fear' (*hote*, i.e. *phobos*) of B 65.15, against the *phthonos* of the rest, may derive from a misreading in a Greek version. The *agathon* of II 26.6 is clearly an error for the original *athlon* attested by IV 40.19.

[41] B 66.13–67.14/III 33.23–34.15; II 26.7–19/IV 40.20–41.6. The redactor of II has omitted the end of John's question and the Saviour's reply through homoeoteleuton. LR evidently breaks the pattern of the Spirit coming, uniting with the power (already present) and strengthening the soul, and the mention in III 34.10f. of the Spirit being brought to the counterfeit spirits is probably a mistaken marginal gloss to supply an object.

[42] Cf. Iren. 1.6.2/Epiph. *Pan.* 31.20.7, cf. 7.8 (*pantē te kai pantos*); *Exc. ex Theod.* 56.3; Heracleon frag. 46; *Tri. Trac.* 119.16–18. Cf. 119.33 where it is said of the psychic race that they will be saved entirely (*pantōs*).

[43] Cf. frag. 2 in Clem. Alex. *Strom.* 2.20.114.3–6; *Gos. Phil.* 65.1–66.4 and Hipp. *Ref.* 6.34.6.

[44] Correspondingly, while the Valentinian concern about evil spirits probably led them to pioneer pre-baptismal exorcism (see on this Elizabeth A. Leeper, 'From Alexandria to Rome: The Valentinian Connection to the Incorporation of Exorcism as a Prebaptismal Rite', *VC* 44 (1990), 6–24), the Gnostic concern with the pre-temporal anointing of Christ and the eschatological descent of the Spirit probably led them to introduce chrism and insignation.

[45] Cf. B 70.8–71.2 and par.

[46] Cf. Iren. 1.6.1; 6.4; 7.1; 7.5; *Exc. ex Theod.* 57; 67f.; 79. That *AJ*'s underlying scheme has not been influenced by Valentinianism is suggested both by the absence of the characteristic threefold division, and by the application of the term 'the calling' (i.e. *klēsis*) and the idea of salvation by ascetic works, to the first elect group. They are evidently not to be equated with the intermediate 'psychics' of Valentinianism of whom these two ideas are characteristic (cf. e.g. *Exc. ex Theod.* 56.3–58.2; Heracleon frags. 13 and 27).

[47] *Exc. ex Theod.* 78.1–2.

[48] B 68.13–69.13/III 35.2–18; II 26.32–27.11/IV 41.21–42.10. Cf. B 67.14–17 and par.

[49] See n. 27 above.

[50] Cf. the opposing roles of the spirit of the Archon and the Holy Spirit according to the libertine Gnostics of Epiph. *Pan.* 26.6.1–4.

[51] B 67.19–68.13/III 34.18–35.2; II 26.22–32/IV 41.10–20.

[52] *Écrits* 332f. His arguments are: (*a*) the verb used of the authorities circling round with (*kōte ñ-*) rules out any idea of reincarnation; (*b*) the redactor of LR (his n[2]) has misunderstood *AJ*'s point with its *shteko* of the bodily prison (II 27.8), because (*c*) as John's following question, which in its echo of Nicodemus' question in John 3:4 is intended to rule out any immediate appeal to reincarnation, attests, reincarnation is admitted in the belief in time as a term for the process of expiation, as parallel passages of *PS* suggest.

[53] Cf. the similarities of language in the earlier passage, B 55.2–13 and par.

[54] B 69.14–70.8/III 35.18–36.4; II 27.11–21/IV 42.11–23. Janssens, *Muséon* 84, 424, certainly allows the possibility of reincarnation here, appealing to B 55 and the similarity with John 3:4; whereas in the latter the Saviour reproaches Nicodemus for his ignorance, here he congratulates John for his percipience (*parakolouthēsis*), in a typical Gnostic reverse interpretation. But like Giversen, *Apocryphon* 266f. and Tardieu, she is misled by the final phrase into denying reincarnation. *PS*, which does clearly teach reincarnation in an expansion of the hints in *AJ*, in earlier passages (Book 3, chs. 111: Schmidt–MacDermot 281.21–282.1 and 132: Schmidt–MacDermot 341.13–18; 345.8–13) relates respectively the growth of the soul and its salvation from the body and its original assignation to the woman and man for whom it is destined.

[55] Note in *PS* Book 4, ch. 147 (Schmidt–MacDermot 381.17–383.11) the case of the ignorant, righteous soul reincarnate until it finds the mysteries of the light (i.e. an initiation rite like the five seals?). The 'Ophite' system also seems to teach a cyclic process of souls being inserted in bodies by the Demiurge until all the holy souls are saved and he only has his own psychic souls to insert (Iren. 1.30.14), and the libertine Gnostics of Epiphanius, whose system seems based on the myth of *AJ*, have ignorant souls reincarnated by the chief Archon in animal bodies (*Pan.* 26.10.8).

[56] Cf. *Gos. Phil.* 77.7–78.12 which seems to reflect a similar situation: initiated, anointed Gnostics with the Holy Spirit and knowledge serve those uninitiated who remain unfree and ignorant.

[57] B 70.8–71.2/III 36.4–15; II 27.21–31/IV 42.24–43.6. Cf. Matt 12:31 and par. Tardieu, *Écrits* 334, claims a contrast with the similar Judaeo-Christian belief (Ps. Clem. *Hom.* 3.6.1, 4f.; *PS* Book 4, ch. 147: Schmidt–MacDermot 380.10–15) whereby a continual blasphemer is ultimately annihilated. But he fails to note *Apoc. Pet.* (Ethiopic) 6f.; 10 (= Greek frag. 22, 34) which does teach the eternal punishment of blasphemers and apostates.

[58] Cf. *PS* Book 3, ch. 104 (Schmidt–MacDermot 264.8–13): even a righteous, sinless man cannot be saved without initiation into the mysteries of the kingdom of light.

⁵⁹ Although Giversen, *Apocryphon* 267f., points to awareness of the discrepancy by *AJ* in that it equates the soul with the power (his example from II 26.26 is based on a misunderstanding; B 67.12f./III 34.13f. is a better one), he appeals to the different context as requiring different terminology, and accepts that ultimately the dialogue 'can very well be understood as an integrated part of AJ's account of the teaching'.

⁶⁰ B 71.2–5/III 36.15–17; II 27.31–3/IV 43.6–8 (*pña etshēs*).

⁶¹ B 71.5–14; II 27.33–28.5/IV 43.8–17. III 36.18–37.1 begins with a passage unparalleled in the others, unfortunately very fragmentary. It has the Saviour speaking of a vision by [Holy?] Spirit into the one (f.) rich in mercy. Here LR has its characteristic 'Metropator' (II 27.33f./IV 43.9) this time to the 'Mother' of SR (B 71.6), rather than the more usual 'Father' in such a context (cf. B 51.5f./III 23.22f. and II 19.17f./IV 29.2f.; B 52.17f./III 24.25–25.1 and II 20.9f./IV 31.3–5). III 32.9f. has the Mother as object, perhaps aware of the ambiguity. The long also wrongly identifies the Mother–Father with the holy spirit, the Epinoia.

⁶² B 63.14–64.13/III 32.8–22; II 25.2–16/IV 38.29–39.15. The same verbs (*r̄hōb/hypourgein*) are used in B 53.11/III 25.12; II 20.19 and the present passage (II 27.34–28.3) confirms that at II 25.9–11/IV 39.7–9 LR is wrong to make the seed the subject.

⁶³ See ch. 6, p. 237, nn. 13ff. (p. 257).

⁶⁴ II 28.1f.

⁶⁵ Cf. its addition of Pronoia in e.g. II 23.24, 29 (plus light); 24.13.

⁶⁶ II 27.35.

⁶⁷ Cf. II 30.11–15/IV.46.23–9 (the Pronoia transformed herself in her seed (*sperma*) and went on every road); 30.24 (she is the remembrance of the Pronoia); 31.11/IV 48.14–17 (she is the Pronoia of pure light, the thought (*meeue*) of the virgin spirit). Cf. also *TP* 35.11–18 (the Protennoia dwells in every creature); 45.21f. (she hid and revealed herself in everyone); 47.13–17 (the third time she wore everyone's garment); 49.6f. (she was dwelling in them [in the form *smot*! of each] one), etc.

⁶⁸ 'Sleep' 501.

⁶⁹ Cf. II 28.1–11/IV 43.12–24 and 30.21–32/IV 47.8–22. The allusiveness of the latter is expanded in *TP* 42.17–45.2. See below for my suggestion as to how the Pronoia hymn developed from and is related to the main text.

⁷⁰ B 71.7–14; II 27.33–28.5. Cf. III 36.18–37.1.

⁷¹ Cf. III 36.23f. and B 55.15–18/III 27.2–4. However, III's different version at this point may represent an attempt to clarify the confusion in the text. II 28.4, perhaps to avoid the awkwardness of the expression 'seed in the thinking', tacks the thinking on to the seed.

[72] The same verb (*tounos* with *sperma*) occurs of Ialdabaoth's vain attempt at rape, B 62.4/III 31.9 (not in LR). It is used to represent *exanistanai* in the Sahidic of Gen 4:25.

[73] III 36.23–37.1. II 28.3f. applies 'perfect' to the race rather than the man (as in e.g. II 8.32; B 35.3/III 13.lf. of Adamas), and has lost the connection of the race with the man. B 71.13f. with its addition of 'eternal' may be more original (cf. the eternal light man in *OW* 103.19. In *Melch.* 6.5f. and *AnonBru* ch. 13 (Schmidt–MacDermot 252.9f.) Adamas is the light-Man). A copyist of a Greek version of III may have misread 'eternal light' (*phōs aiōnion*) as 'luminous' (*phōteinos*).

[74] B 71.14–72.2/III 37.1–6; II 28.5–10/IV 43.17–24. LR's version, which has them exalted above him in the height (II 28.6f.), is evidently an addition, part of its spiritualizing interpretation, further distancing the Demiurge from the spiritual world.

[75] Cf. e.g. B 52.8–15/ III 24.17–23; II 20.3–7 (the three Coptic expressions seem to render the Greek *phronēsis*); B 54.7–11/III 26.2–6; II 20.30–3/IV 32.3–7. Tardieu, *Écrits* 335, makes the same point and rightly sees in LR, which omits the clause 'since he was ignorant' and makes the reference to the Archon's ignorance apply to his future inability to control them (II 28.9–11), both the clumsy work of the original redactor adding the whole section and that of LR, attempting to soften the awkwardness. As a corollary, however, this passage may well have been formed on the lines of the two referred to above, especially the second, with its references to height and wisdom.

[76] B 72.2–4/III 37.6f.; II 28.11–16/IV 43.24–30. This translation, in line with Giversen, *Apocryphon* 101, seems better than their committing adultery together with Sophia (i.e. the fallen aeon), as in Tardieu, Krause and Wisse (in *NHLE*). For reasons, see below.

[77] II 28.15–30/IV 43.29–44.17. On the archons of Heimarmene as responsible for human sin and wickedness, cf. *PS* Book 3, ch. 111 (Schmidt–MacDermot 283.4–7). The mention of gods, angels, demons and every [human] race being united (with a fetter, i.e. time? but since the object is feminine and fetter masculine in Greek, perhaps something like destiny, *moira*, is more likely; cf. again *PS* Book 3, ch. 111: Schmidt–MacDermot 284.4f.), has a parallel in B 72.6–10/III 37.9–12, which refer to the archon(s) binding gods, angels, demons, men with time to entrap them in the fetter of Fate. Since LR has already dealt with this in its digression it omits it here.

[78] 5 (Scott–Ferguson, *Hermetica* 4.105.10f.).

[79] 12 (107.11–15).

[80] 8 (106.6–12); 14f. (107.25–108.12).

[81] 16–18 (108.21–109.19). Note the comparative of *phronimos* (l.23), recalling the *phronēsis* we suggested (n. 75 above) underlies *AJ* B 52.8f. and par; 54.7f. and par. Zosimus' version, however, which Edwards, 'Neglected' 45ff., would rather fancifully describe as 'a digest of the

whole creed', is evidently influenced by a rather different rendering of the mythologoumenon, with its male Son of God instead of female Epinoia/Holy Spirit, but it may attest the originality of the male redeemer. Could his source have been a – or the – 'Book of Zoroaster' of *AJ* and Porphyry (*Vit. Plot.* 16)?

[82] *OW* 123.4–25. Cf. 125.28f. where the Heimarmene of the seven archons is condemned through the appearance of the Gnostics, although in 121.13–20 its fixed nature prevents the archons reducing human lifetimes. In *Poimandres* too Heimarmene is ambivalent: in 1.9, 15 and 16 it appears beneficent, yet in 24–6 the powers of the harmony or fate are stripped off as the souls ascend.

[83] II 28.11–31/IV 43.24–44.19. Cf. *PS* Book 1, ch. 22 (Schmidt–MacDermot 32.14–20), where Philip asks the Lord whether he has turned the bondage of the archons and their Heimarmene and confused them to save the world, and Book 3, ch. 111 (284.4–7), which speaks of destiny (*moira*) guiding a man to death via the archons and their bonds with which Heimarmene binds them.

[84] 102.26, 35–103.4; 112.1–10. Cf. Prov 3:19; 8:22–31; Wis 7:21–30; 9:1–3.

[85] 125.23–30. Böhlig (104 of his edition) cites 1 Cor 2:6ff.; the contrast of the wisdom of this aeon with the secret wisdom of God. Cf. Wis 7:7.

[86] B 72.4–12/III 37.8–14; II 28.30–2/IV 44.18–20. We have attempted to show why LR omits the mention of gods, etc. in B 72.6–8. The continuation in B 72.8–10/III 37.11f. about all being in Fate's fetter would no longer make sense with its subject removed, nor would the gloss in B 72.11f./III 37.13f. ('a wicked and perverse idea') with the change from final to circumstantial clause. On the gloss, cf. Tatian, *Or. ad Graec.* 8.1.

[87] Cf. *Tg. Yer. 1* on Gen 6:4; *1 Enoch* 6–7; 64.1f.; *Jub.* 5.1; *T. Reub.* 5.6–7; Justin, *2 Apol.* 5, etc.

[88] B 72.12–17/III 37.14–18; II 28.32–29.1/IV 44.20–5. The Sahidic of Gen 6:6 has the same verb (*r̄ḥēt*) as B 72.12f. and par, and appears to be a free rendering of the LXX influenced perhaps by Gen 6:8. Gen 6:17 in Sahidic has the same verb (*eine*) as II 28.35. The *anastēma tēr̄f* of B 72.16f./III 37.17f. is an exact echo of Gen 7:4 and 23 LXX (*pan to anastēma*), as Tardieu, *Écrits* 336, has noticed and duly translated, unlike Till (185/320 of his edition) and Krause (103/282 of his).

[89] B 72.17–73.2/III 37.18–21; II 29.1–3/IV 44.25f. All four attest *m̄tnoč*, evidently a rendering of *megethos*, commonly a term for the supreme being in Valentinianism but here associated with Pronoia and identified with the chief revealer/redeemer of the main body of *AJ* in SR. Cf. the role of Wisdom in Wis 10:4 and the description of her in 7:26.

[90] This last is all the more likely in the light of the fact that the version in III 37.19f. which has the Pronoia form a thought, i.e. the Epinoia, may represent an awareness that the two are originally distinct, hence

the omission by LR. Cf. II 23.28/IV 36.24–6 where the Epinoia is from the Pronoia, i.e. distinct.

[91] Cf. II 30.15f. ('I am the richness of the light, the remembrance of the Pleroma'); 30.24 ('I am the remembrance of the Pronoia'); 30.33f. ('I am the light which exists in the light . . .'); 31.11f. ('I am the Pronoia of the pure light').

[92] B 73.2–4./III 37.21f.; II 29.3–6/IV 44.27–45.1. LR adds detail: Noah told the whole race (*sperma*); it was those alien to him who did not listen, i.e. Noah is one of the true Gnostics, the seed of Seth, the 'Alien'. On the motif, cf. 2 Pet 2:5; *1 Clem.* 7.6; Josephus, *Ant.* 1.3.1; *b. Sanh.* 108ab; *Gen. Rab.* 30.7; *Tanh. Noah* 5, etc. See Ginzberg, *Legends*, 1, 153; 5, 174f.

[93] B 73.4–7/III 37.22–38.1; II 29.6–8/IV 45.1–5. The plural in the latter three may be due to the influence of Gen 7:15 and 23, or to assimilation to the following phrase: 'not only Noah but men of the immovable race'.

[94] Cf. *HA* 92.11 where the ruler of the forces tells Noah to hide (*ḥōp*) in the ark.

[95] B 73.7–12/III 38.1–5; II 29.8–12/IV 45.5–9. The idea of a light cloud as place of concealment is a common Gnostic *topos*, cf. *AJ* B 38.6–13 and par; *AA* 69.19–25; 75.17–76.7. In *T. Abr.* 9.8–10.1 it is the vehicle of Abraham's heavenly journey.

[96] Cf. *HA* 92.4–14 (Sabaoth as Noah's ally versus the archons responsible for the Flood); *AA* 70.10–71.8 (the Creator God's protection of Noah and his race). The latter may represent an early stage of 'Sethian' reinterpretation, however, since it alludes to the race or seed of Seth (65.5–9). See ch. 2.

[97] B 73.12–18/III 38.5–10; II 29.12–15. The reading in B with Noah as subject is perhaps preferable as an echo of Gen 7:23; 'Noah . . . and those with him in the ark' (cf. the Sahidic: m̄n̄ netñm̄maf n̄ḥoun ñtkibōtos and B 73.14f.: m̄n̄ netñm̄maf ḥm̄pouein and Iren. 1.30.10: 'eos . . . qui circa Noe erant in arca'). III 38.5–8 with its plural 'they' destroys the sense of 'those with him' and weakens any allusion to Gen 7:23 by turning the relative clause into a circumstantial while LR introduces an allusion to a female light-figure with Noah who shines on them (II 29.13f.). This is probably the work of its redactor, either alluding to Norea (so Tardieu, *Écrits* 337, alluding to *HA* 92.4–18 and Epiph. *Pan.* 26.1.7–9), or to the Epinoia (cf. B 60.17–19 and par, which refer to the authority (*authentia*) by which she instructs Adam). Its continuation implying that the First Archon is the subject, not Noah, may betray the influence of Gen 7:4 and 10.

[98] *Écrits* 337.

[99] Cf. *1 Enoch* 6.2 in R. H. Charles, *Apocrypha* 2 191; Janssens, 'Thème' 488–94. On the use of *1 Enoch* and the Pseudo-Clementine myth (Ps. Clem. *Hom.* 12–13), etc., see Tardieu, *Écrits* 162, 338f., and on the theme as a key to Gnostic theology and mythology, cf. G. Stroumsa, *Seed, passim.*

¹ B 73.18–74.6/III 38.10–16; II 29.16–21/IV 45.14–21. The clumsiness of SR (B 74.1f. has the archon's angels send their angels; III 38.11f. has him plan with his angels then send them) has perhaps led LR (II 29.16f.) to have the archon plan with his powers then send his angels.

² B 74.6–10/III 38.16–20; II 29.21–6/IV 45.21–7. B has accidentally omitted the clause 'when they realized they had been unsuccessful'. The addition by LR of the reason, to pollute the souls (II 29.25f./IV 45.26f.), is clearly secondary. The 'despicable' of II 29.24/IV 45.25 (also II 26.27/IV 41.15f.; II 26.36/IV 41.25f.; II 27.32f./IV 43.8; II 30.11/IV 46.22) may derive from a misreading of *antimimon* as *atimon* (cf. Crum, *Dictionary* 375b s.v. *sōsh*, and Böhlig, *Mysterion* 164), a more likely explanation than Giversen's qualitative of *shōsh*, to make equal (*Apocryphon* 268). Böhlig, ibid., n. 5, refers to the Sahidic of 1 Cor 12:23 where *atimos* is translated by *sesh*.

³ For the former, cf. B 53.4–17 and par; for the latter B 63.16–64.3 and par. Cf. II 25.3ff./IV 38.29ff. which apparently interpret the spirit there sent down as the Holy Spirit/Epinoia, resolving the dilemma.

⁴ Cf. B 53.18–20 and par.

⁵ Cf. B 63.14–64.13 and par and B 71.5–72.2 and par.

⁶ *Muséon* 84, 427.

⁷ B 52.17–55.18 and par. Cf. the role of the counterfeit spirit in *PS* Book 3, ch. 111 (Schmidt–MacDermot 280–6) as an element in humans distinct from but bound to the soul, which grows with it and seeks to control it.

⁸ The figure of the counterfeit spirit in this version very much recalls that of the eschatological Antichrist, first alluded to in 1 John 2:18, 22; 4:3 and 2 John 7 (cf. also 2 Thess 2 and Rev 13:11f.), but very much developed at the end of the second and beginning of the third centuries (cf. e.g. Hippolytus' commentary *De Christo et Antichristo*, MPG 10, 725ff.), the likely period of this addition to *AJ*.

⁹ *Omega* 8, 11f., 14f., 16–18. Cf. 2 Thess 2:1–4.

¹⁰ B 74.11–13/III 38.20–2; II 29.26–8/IV 45.27–9. B 74.12f. wrongly has the singular and misses the reference to the likeness. On the motif, cf. *Tg. Ps.-J* on Gen 6:2; *T. Reub.* 5.6f.; Ps. Clem. *Hom.* 8.12.2–13.1f. The attempt of Perkins, *Gnosticism* 15f., 24f., following Stroumsa and Pearson, to derive the basic Gnostic mythemes from Gen 6:1–4 and *1 Enoch* 6:2–8:4 as interpreted in such circles, fails if – as I contend – this section of *AJ* is a late addition (redaction (a³)).

¹¹ This is the sense: the versions diverge on the details. B 74.13–16 misunderstands the phrase as a causal clause and reads 'tormented' (*moukh*) for 'filled' (*mouh*). III 38.22–4 is marred by lacunae, as is IV 45.30–46.2, but both seem to agree with II 29.28–30 in having the angels fill the women with the spirit of darkness. LR adds 'which they had mixed for them' then echoes III in tacking on the reference to evil.

¹² B 73. 16–75.1/III 38.25–39.3; II 29.30–4/IV 46.2–10. Cf. *1 Enoch* 8:1; 65:6–8; Ps. Clem. *Hom.* 8.14.1–3. The *perispasmos* of III 39.3 may be a misreading of the *peirasmos* of B 75.1: the two are interchanged in the MSS tradition of Ecclesiastes LXX, e.g. at 3:10, 4:8 and 8:16 where A has *p[e]irasmos* to the *perispasmos* of ℵ and B, and at 5:13 where ℵ has *p[e]irasmos* to the *perispasmos* of A and B.

¹³ B 75.1–3/III 39.4f. Cf. the 'eternal pronoia' of Wis 17:2.

¹⁴ Cf. e.g. II 6.5; 7.22/IV 11.14; II 14.20/IV 22.25; II 23.24/IV 36.17; II 24.13f./IV 37.24f.; II 28.2; 30.12, etc.

¹⁵ II 29.33–30.7.

¹⁶ Tardieu, *Écrits* 162, 339, while noting the Dan 12:1/Matt 24:21 echo, fails to register the Psalm 95/Hebrews 3 allusion, which is far more obvious than his reference to Ecclus 40:1–10. There may also be a faint echo of Rom 8:19–22 in the last phrase.

¹⁷ B 75.3–7/III 39.5–8: II 30.7–9. LR again qualifies the spirit as 'despicable' (*etshēs*), and its reading: 'after (*kata*) the likeness (*eine*) of their spirit (*pneuma*)', may be due either to its awareness that the text had just mentioned the angels filling the women with the spirit (cf. II 29.26–30), or to its view of demiurgic generation as always after the image of heavenly (cf. e.g. II 12.34–13.5; 19.28–32; 22.32–6).

¹⁸ B 75.7–10/III 39.8–11; II 30.9–11/IV 46.19–23, cf. B 20.1 and par. Since *tom* can stand for either *pōroun* or *typhloun* (cf. Crum, *Dictionary* 421b), the 'he hardened' of B 75.7 may be an echo of 2 Cor 4:4: 'the god of this aeon blinded (*etyphlōsen*) the minds . . .') or John 12:40: 'he hardened (*epōrōsen*) their hearts' (Sahidic *tōm ñhēt*: Crum, *Dictionary* 412b, a citation of Isa 6:10).

¹⁹ For biblical parallels, cf. e.g. Exod 8:15, 32; 9:7 (LXX *barynein tēn kardian*); 4:21 (Sah *ti + nshot*); 9:34; 10:1 (LXX *sklerynein tēn kardian*); Isa 6:10 (LXX *hē kardia pachynesthai* = Sah *nousht*: Crum, *Dictionary* 237a, cf. Sah of Matt 13:15; Acts 28:27); Ps 95 [94]:8 (LXX *sklērynein tēn kardian* = Sah *ti + nshot*: Crum, *Dictionary* 238a; cf. Sah of Heb 3:8); Deut 9:27 (LXX *sklērotēs* = Sah *nshot*: Crum, ibid.); John 12:40 (see previous note); Rom 9:18 (*sklērynein* = Sah *nshot*: Crum, *Dictionary* 237a).

²⁰ The secondary character of this passage is perhaps further suggested by the difference between the representations of the role of the counterfeit spirit here and in the dialogue on the fate of souls: in the former there is no reference to his hardening activity and errant souls can come to salvation. Certainly this section presents a more negative view of the Demiurge and the counterfeit spirit.

²¹ Cf. B 19.6–20.3/III 1.4–15; II 1.5–17.

²² B 75.10–13/III 39.11–13. That SR here finally refers to the merciful Mother–Father, whom it had earlier identified either as Father (cf. B 30.6/III 9.17; B 48.1; B 51.5f./III 23.22f.; B 52.18f./III 24.25–25.1) or Mother (cf. B 71.5f./III 36.18ff.), might suggest the originality of the

title, misunderstood by its redactors. See above chs 5, p.183; 6, p. 217f., and below n. 64.

[23] B 75.14f./III 39.13f. The phrase *n̄shrp* could be a version either of 'at first' (*prōton*) or 'from the beginning' (*ap' archēs*) (see Crum, *Dictionary* 587b). The former would fit this sentence better; the latter might go better with the previous sentence. 'The perfect aeon' is a designation of Barbelo in B 27.14f./III 7.19. Cf. Eph 4:8–10.

[24] B 75.15–76.1/III 39.14–18; II 31.27–32/IV 49.8–13. Cf. B 22.10–16; II 2.20–5.

[25] Hennecke–Schneemelcher–Wilson, *NTA* 1 327.

[26] B 76.1–5/III 39.18–21. Comparison with B 54.1–3/III 25.20–2 suggests both that the *sperma* of B 76.4f. is a misreading of the *hysterēma* of III 39.21, rather than vice versa, and that the reference here is to Sophia and her original 'fall'. Cf. B 47.4–14 and par.

[27] B 76.5f./III 39.21f. Cf. B 22.2–6; II 2.16–18.

[28] B 76.7–77.5/III 39.22–40.9; II 31.32–32.6/IV 49.13–26. LR has the third person since it does not include the previous passage. In the light of the opening reference in II 1.1f., SR's version, which has the mystery as object entrusted, may be preferable to LR, which has the secrets presented in a mystery.

[29] II 32.6/IV 49.26.

[30] II 30.11–31.25/IV 46.23–49.6. Puech, in Hennecke–Schneemelcher–Wilson, *NTA* 1 327, compares Ecclus 24:32 in the Latin translation and the *descensus ad inferos* motif. Bousset, *Hauptprobleme* ch. 6, esp. 242, 255–60, would see the latter as an independent Gnostic theologoumenon influencing the Christian motif. For an alternative view, seeing it and the triple descent scheme as Christian–Gnostic adaptations of e.g. 1 Pet 3:18 and the Johannine Prologue, see below.

[31] II 31.25–7/IV 49.6–8. Cf. B 75.14f./III 39.14. Although there is no mention of the Mother–Father, the common attribute of this figure, 'the merciful one', does occur (cf. II 31.16/IV 48.22 and II 20.10/IV 31.5; II 27.35).

[32] *Secret Books* 209–11.

[33] *Apocryphon* 270–3. He suggests that the Pronoia's third appearance is to John.

[34] *Glaubende* 108f.

[35] 'Sleep' 498–501; the first Adam's awakening by the Epinoia (B 55.15–18), the second the reference to the Epinoia's soteriological activity sparked by the question about the origin of the counterfeit spirit (II 27.33–28.5), and the third the Saviour's present revelation to John.

[36] 502. He compares the reconstruction by P. Pokorny of a Gnostic mystery initiation from the Naassene Preaching and CH I and XIII ('Epheserbrief und gnostische Mysterien', *ZNW* 53 (1962), 160–94, esp. 178–80).

[37] 507 and *passim*.

[38] 502; 'The Ego-Proclamation in Gnostic Sources', in E. Bammel ed., *The Trial of Jesus: Cambridge Studies in honour of C. F. D. Moule* (SBT second series) (London: SCM, 1970), 132; 'Jewish Background' 91 n.3. Cf. Janssens, 'Le Codex XIII de Nag Hammadi', *Muséon* 87 (1974), 342, 351–2.

[39] John D. Turner, 'NHC XIII, *1*' in Hedrick, *Nag Hammadi Codices XI, XII, XIII* 384f., 396–401. His analysis of the compositional history has four stages; first the *Grundform* of the non-Christian Pronoia hymn, then the aretalogical expansions, then the accommodation to the developed, Christianized Sethian–Barbeloite cosmogony of *AJ*, etc. and finally the polemical Christian–Sethian material of the third tractate. See below.

[40] Thus, following Janssens ('Le Codex XIII', 348–51), he finds (389f.) the first descent of the Pronoia as 'Merciful Father' (or Metropator) in B 51.1–52.3 and par (the descent of the Autogenes and the four illuminators), the second in the figure of the Epinoia hiding in Adam in B 52.17–54.9 and par, agreeing with MacRae over the last.

[41] 'Christologie' 311–14.

[42] 309–11. He misunderstands the Coptic form of Mother–Father as 'fatherly Mother'. He associates this formation both with the prior passage about the eschatological descent of the spirit to the seed (B 63.16–64.13/III 32.8–22) and the later passage describing the Mother's correcting her deficiency (B 71.1–5/III 39.19–21).

[43] 315. Cf. King, 'Sophia' 168ff., who finds in Codex II Christ taking a larger role than figures like the Epinoia and Sophia and 'a distinct devaluation of the feminine and of women' (171).

[44] *Écrits* 42, 163, 340. In fact Arai's identification of the Mother–Father with Sophia is questionable since the former, often qualified as 'rich in mercy', is evidently Barbelo/Pronoia (cf. II 5.5f.; 6.16f.; 14.19ff.; 19.17f.; 20.9f.; 27.33f. and par in IV). Cf. II 31.16 describing the Pronoia/Saviour as 'the merciful one'.

[45] *Écrits* 40–3, 339–44.

[46] 43f.

[47] 'Codex XIII' 390.

[48] Cf. Iren. 1.30.6.

[49] Cf. *HA* 94.19–33.

[50] Cf. *HA* 87.11–33.

[51] Cf. *OW* 103.2–32. Later she sheds light on Sabaoth, Ialdabaoth's obedient son (104.3–6), and later still, in response to Ialdabaoth's boast that he is the only god, and demand to see any prior deity, a light descends in which is a man-like image, i.e. light-Adam(as) (107.17–108.25).

[52] 'Codex XIII' 390.

[53] This is surely strengthened by the reference to the confusion caused by the heavenly voice in Iren. 1.30.6, *AJ* II 14.24–30; 30.16–20 and *TP* 40.19–22. The creation of Adam in the image of heavenly Man, not his

inbreathing, is surely the first soteriological step. Besides, there is no allusion to Pronoia *descending* or the foundations of chaos shaking in the inbreathing episode.

[54] 'Codex XIII' 390, referring to B 52.17–54.9; 59.6–61.7 (not 21.7!) = II 20.9–31; 22.28–23.36. The allusion in the Pronoia hymn to her 'plan' (*oikonomia*: II 30.27/IV 47.15, cf. Eph 1:10; 3:9; Ign. *Eph.* 18.1; 20.2; *SJC* III 91.4/B 78.4f., etc.) could refer to this general saving activity. Although *AJ* has no allusion to the upheaval caused by the second descent, traces of it remain in *OW* 115.30–116.10: the consternation caused to the archons by Sophia's daughter, Zoe, calling Adam to awaken (cf. *HA* 89.11–20). Note also the allusion to the voice sent from Incorruptibility to help (*boēthia*, cf. *AJ* B 53.6 and par) Adam in 88.17–19, and Sophia's second call rebuking Ialdabaoth and Eve, reminding them of First Man and Woman in Iren. 1.30.7. This will be important when we come to the development of *TP*.

[55] 'Codex XIII' ibid.

[56] Iren. 1.30.12.

[57] Cf. Iren. 1.30.8–12.

[58] Cf. *HA* 88.11–19 (the descent of the spirit to animate Adam, linked to the voice from Incorruptibility); 89.11–17 (the coming of the spiritual woman as Zoe, the mother of the living, calling Adam awake); 96.33–97.4 (the appearance of the True Man in creaturely form to teach and anoint); *OW* 115.11–116.33 (Sophia Zoe sends her breath, then her daughter Eve to awaken Adam); 123.31–125.32 (about the perfect Man and the coming of the Logos to destroy the archons' work).

[59] Note e.g. the parallel *ego eimi* statements in the prologue (B 21.18–22.9; II 2.12–20) and the hymn (II 30.11–16, 24, 33–35; 31.11–16). Aspects of the Saviour's appearance in the prologue (light and the world trembling: B 20.20–21.2.; II 1.31–3) find an echo in the hymn (cf. II 30.15–31.2).

[60] Cf. the opening vision, B 20.19–22.9; II 1.30–2.20, where the Saviour appears in light, causing the cosmos to shake (cf. the Pronoia hymn), and in three male forms (corresponding to Barbelo's designation as triple-male, cf. B 27.21 and par?), proclaiming 'I am the Father, I am the Mother, I am the Son', offering to teach about past, present and future and about the perfect Man. On the Johannine parallels and echoes, see Tardieu, *Écrits* 340–4.

[61] Hence the otherwise rather baffling stress on Barbelo/Pronoia as the first man, the first to appear (cf. B 27.19f.; II 5.7; B 29.10–12; II 6.3–5; II 14.18–24).

[62] That elements of the final descent strikingly recall Acts 16:23–34 (imprisonment, darkness, foundations shaking, fetters falling off, light, message of salvation through Jesus, baptism), might further confirm the Christian character of the hymn.

[63] Thus the angels of poverty appear in both, cf. II 27.25/IV 42.29 and II 31.18/IV 48.24f., both describe our condition in this world similarly (chains, forgetfulness and sleep, cf. II 26.3f., 7/IV 41.29–42.1, 5 and II 31.5f., 10, 20f./IV 48.6f., 13, 28f.), and both allude to the initiation rite involving receivers and seals (cf. II 25.36–26.3/IV 40.11–16 and II 31.22–5/IV 49.1–6 and *TP* 47.34–48.35; *GE* III 65.26–66.8/IV 78.1–10).

[64] See n. 22, p. 294. SR's mention of 'the merciful Mother–Father' (taking form in her offspring (*sperma*)) only and precisely here where LR has no mention of it (cf B 75.10–13/III 39.11–13; II 30.11–13), is admittedly awkward for my hypothesis of SR's suppression of the title: the reference to the Pronoia (i.e. Barbelo, the merciful Mother–Father of LR) transforming herself into her offspring in the original may have triggered it, or previous garbled passage about the merciful Mother (+ Father in LR) with her offspring (*sperma*: B 71.5–10/III 36.18–23).

[65] B 76.1–5/III 39.18–21.

[66] This explanation would also resolve the otherwise awkward problem of several saving comings of heavenly beings in *AJ*: Sophia's consort, the Autogenes and illuminators and the Epinoia.

[67] This probably refers to the Ascension, cf. B 19.15f./III 1.9; II 1.11f. and B 20.12–19; II 1.27–29. SR might reflect continuing Valentinian influence here: to the striking parallels to its version of the Mother–Father taking form in her seed noted by Arai ('Christologie', 309–11), one could add the title 'Mother–Father/*mētropatōr*' (used of the Demiurge controlled by Achamoth: Iren. 1.5.1), Sophia correcting her deficiency (cf. Hipp. *Ref.* 6.32.4f.; *Exc. ex Theod.* 35.2), and the Saviour's original ascent as 'first-born son' according to Valentinus and those closest to him (cf. *Exc. ex Theod.* 32.3–33.4; Iren. 1.11.1; *Tri. Trac.* 77.37–78.8; *Val. Exp.* 33.35ff.).

[68] The aretalogical passages can then be very satisfactorily explained as expansions of the 'I am' statements in the prologue and Pronoia hymn (and the added attributes of Barbelo in the main text) of redaction (a²) of *AJ* (cf. also *OW* 114.7–15). Similarly the Naassene Preaching makes most sense in the light of the Johannine and Valentinian influenced redaction (a²) of *AJ* as an extended meditation on the three elements in the universe and the Man/Adamas figure as found in pagan mythological traditions, addressed as Father–Mother, the uncharacterized prototype of Christ, the Logos, who in the hymn descends to inform the Gnostics and impart saving knowledge via an initiation ceremony involving seals.

[69] Cf. *GE* III 62.24–64.3/IV 74.9–75.17 and *AA* 76.8–77.18 and the similar speculations of the Sethians in Epiph. *Pan.* 39.2.4–3.5. Note the traces of a female Sophia/Pronoia redeemer figure in the Metanoia of *GE* III 59.9–60.2/IV 70?-71.11, and the way Seth is added to the

Autogenes and the four illuminators, as sent by them to undergo three saving parousias in *GE* III 62.24–64.9/IV 74.9–75.24.

[70] *Pan.* 39.3.5; cf. 1.3.

[71] 'Jewish Background', 86–101, esp. 88–94.

[72] I. P. Culianu, 'Feminine versus Masculine. The Sophia Myth and the Origins of Feminism' in H. G. Kippenberg, H. J. W. Drijvers eds, *Struggles of the Gods: Papers of the Groningen Work Group for the Study of the History of Religions* (Berlin/New York/Amsterdam: Y. Kuiper, 1984), 65–98, esp. 94f.

[73] Cf. Janssens, *Muséon* 84, 416; Schenke, 'Nag-Hamadi–Studien III' 356–61.

[74] Cf. *HA* 96.33–97.5 (True Man, Spirit, chrism/*chrisma*); *GE* III 67.15–68.1 (incense/*stoei* (= *myron*, cf. Crum, *Dictionary* 363a) mixed with water, cf. Marcosians of Iren. 1.21.3f./Epiph. *Pan.* 34.20.7f.); Hipp. *Ref.* 5.9.22 (Naassenes as only true Christians, anointed with unutterable ointment/*chrisma*); *Gos. Phil.* 74.12–22. See ch. 2.

[75] 'Erlöser' 213f. Cf. MacRae, 'Discourses' 112.

[76] In Wisdom 10f. she does save, but only those within the Jewish heritage and in this-worldly terms.

[77] Cf. a similar phenomenon in contemporary more 'orthodox' Christians like Justin in their use of the Logos scheme to suggest primal revelation (the Logos in creation), continuous revelation (the Logos/Spirit sowing seeds of truth in all and inspiring the Old Testament prophets) and decisive revelation (the Logos incarnate). The ambiguity in Justin and his contemporaries about the distinct role of the Spirit over against the Logos/Son and the precise identity of the figure of Wisdom equally reveals how similar were their concerns and speculations to those of the Gnostics.

[78] Cf. again the contemporary modalist Monarchian speculations of more 'orthodox' Christians, combatted by Hippolytus, Tertullian and Origen. Conversely, against the argument of King, 'Sophia', Christ does not replace Sophia in the later forms of *AJ* – he was always the Saviour!

8

Gnostic Eschatology

Introduction

Can one speak of Gnostic eschatology in the strict sense of a doctrine of the last things?[1] Zandee claims that the Gnostic is not primarily interested in eschatology, in the development of history, but rather in his own inner awakening to true knowledge.[2] Peel sums up the traditional view of Gnostic eschatology as being that the Gnostic 'knower', by receiving the saving 'gnosis' of who he is, whence he has come and whither he returns (a conscious echo of the famous formula of Theodotus), has already obtained in his earthly life the essentials of his eschatological hope.[3] Schweizer asserts that Gnosis does recognize an 'eschatology', but not in the sense of a single all-decisive, all-perfecting action of God: rather it is determined through the self-discovery of the Gnostic. 'Eschatological' means chiefly the release of spirit from matter.[4] The Gnostic thus experiences a kind of 'instant' or 'realized' eschatology: with his or her response to the 'call' he/she experiences awakening, resurrection, rebirth. This kind of realized eschatology is expressed in most pregnant form by the statement in the *Gospel of Truth*: 'Since the deficiency came into being because the Father was not known, therefore when the Father is known, from that moment on the deficiency will no longer exist.'[5] Or as Irenaeus reports of the Gnostics: 'They . . . affirm that the resurrection from the dead is no other than the recognition of their so-called truth.'[6]

For his part Filoramo stresses both the syncretistic character of Gnostic eschatology, borrowing contemporary elements of varying provenance, but equally what is new in it: the role of the descending and ascending Saviour as paradigmatic of the Gnostic experience of redemption as well as the typical tension in its individual eschatology between the 'already' and the 'not yet', and the consequent necessary role of this world, time and history:

301

'Only with the end of the world, therefore, can the drama of Gnostic salvation be fulfilled.'[7] A realized eschatology must be balanced by a futurist, an individualist involving the heavenly journey of the soul or self by a collective involving the Gnostic 'Church'.

Peel isolates four facets of what he calls the traditional view of Gnostic eschatology.[8] First, he alludes to the evident close connection in some Gnostic texts between the reception of baptism and the present realization of future hopes.[9] Second, he refers to the idea in some texts that, through his reception of the 'saving knowledge', the 'knower' comes to full realization of his divine nature in the present.[10] The third facet Peel refers to is the conviction in some texts that the spiritual man, illuminated with 'gnosis', has already been transferred to the realm of light.[11] A final facet is the view in some texts that the eschaton is felt to have arrived in the present for the Gnostic.[12]

The other major aspect of the traditional view of Gnostic eschatology which Peel notes is the idea that death marks the point of departure of the 'pneuma-self' from the body. He gives detailed evidence of this view in Gnostic sources, without, however, referring at this point to its presence in modern interpreters.[13] But, as he himself goes on to suggest, there must be some final end-goal of the ascent of this self; apparently the reabsorption of the light-self into its original or into the Godhead. So even on this view of 'present' or 'realized' eschatology involving the individual self, there is, implicit or explicit, a universalist, futurist perspective.[14]

Indeed this is admitted by those such as Jonas and Bultmann who most stress the 'realized' nature of Gnostic eschatology and sharpen that stress by their existentialist interpretation of Gnostic mythology.[15] For Jonas, as Schottroff points out, the saving 'call' contains the promise of redemption as a presupposition of final redemption. The Gnostic world-view is essentially directed to the future, the absolute future, that is, it is eschatological.[16] Bultmann too is aware of the futurist aspect. 'Gnosticism,' he says 'tends to produce an individualistic type of mysticism, in which the redemption, the ascent of the Self, is anticipated in meditation and ecstasy.'[17] Anticipation, that is, implies a future consummation.

For if there is undoubtedly much support in the Gnostic texts for an eschatology which is seen as present and realized, and which involves the individual 'pneuma-self' and its post-mortem ascent, there is also, as Peel has convincingly demonstrated, equally a considerable body of evidence for a futurist eschatology which is universalist, i.e. involving the whole cosmos and the ultimate restoration of the various mixed elements to their original condition.[18] Peel gives a detailed survey of *Endzeit* speculation,[19] but we might cite examples relevant to our discussion of the *Apocryphon*. Thus the 'Ophites' of Irenaeus describe the consummation as occurring when the entire trace of the spirit of light is gathered together and taken up into the Aeon of Incorruptibility.[20] The Valentinian school of Ptolemy refer to the consummation taking place when the whole spiritual element, the spiritual men who have perfect knowledge, is shaped and perfected in knowledge and enters the Pleroma or bridal chamber.[21] This process is called the restoration (*apokatastasis*) and the goal pictured as eternal (or 'aeonian') rest.[22]

But the question then arises: Is this process to be understood as basically atemporal and cyclical, so that the end-time coincides with the primal time, as Zandee argues?[23] Or should we with Haardt, Peel, Foerster, Rudolph, Filoramo and others, stress the importance of the end-goal of the soteriological process and see this not as cyclical but as unrepeatable, and always related to a concluding eschaton?[24] Or can we find aspects of both views to some extent combined? Thus there is evidence that some Gnostics believed in the transmigration of souls,[25] a view we found echoed in the *Apocryphon*,[26] and the 'Ophites' of Irenaeus seem to believe in a continuous process of souls descending, ascending and redescending into bodies. The holy souls, i.e. those with the trace of light or with knowledge of Christ, are rescued from this cycle by Jesus.[27] This also raises the question posed by John in the *Apocryphon*: Will all the souls be saved, or to the same degree and destination, or are there different types and degrees of salvation?

Finally there is the question mark set by Schottroff against any kind of futurist eschatology, even as espoused by Jonas and Bultmann in terms of the post-mortem survival and ascent of the individual soul, or of the ecstatic anticipation of that liberation and ultimate restoration to the heavenly world.[28] She is seeking to answer the question touched on in the previous chapter: When is the time of salvation? Her question applies primarily to the Fourth Gospel, but she finds in Gnosis the closest similarity to and also the basis for the Johannine view that the time of redemption is the time of revelation. Sacramental or eschatological forms of Gnosis may have existed, but they are to be explained as peripheral phenomena.[29] Her Gnostic evidence for this claim is primarily the Pronoia hymn of the *Apocryphon*, which, as we have indicated, she considers to be independent of the main body and not at all influenced by Christian traditions, although post-Christian.[30] However, her only concern is with the time of redemption as it relates to Gnosis, and this narrowing down, as we shall see, may well have distorted her view of the Gnostic understanding of redemption and led her to play down or ignore the integral nature of the Pronoia hymn and the futurist eschatological element in Gnostic theology. Thus Rudolph argues that Schottroff has gone too far in explaining sacramental or eschatological Gnosis as peripheral phenomena and suggests that she is too much under the spell of the Johannine view.[31]

In our analysis of the eschatological ideas of the 'classic Gnostic myth' presented in the *Apocryphon* and related texts we shall therefore have to consider to what extent the eschatology is predominantly 'realized' or 'futurist' or a blend of both; to what extent it is individualist, in terms of the separation of the soul or pneuma-self from the body and its post-mortem ascent, or universalist, in terms of the involvement of the entire cosmos in the restoration process; whether the ultimate redemption involves everyone and to the same degree or destination; and finally whether the process is cyclical or linear or one utilizing both approaches.

Perhaps one of the most striking features about the *Apocryphon*, when compared with the 'Ophite' or Valentinian myths and systems described by Irenaeus or other related works from Nag Hammadi such as *On the Origin of the World*, is the apparent paucity of eschatological features and ideas, apart from the dialogue on the destinies of souls and the Pronoia hymn. We find no mention of the theme of resurrection, or of the syzygy concept of the Gnostic and his/her angel and their heavenly marriage, so central to Valentinianism. Of the geography of heaven and hell or the apocalyptic-eschatological timetable of cosmic catastrophe and universal restitution we only have passing hints. What we do get are various concepts linked to the various stages of redaction, with some attempt to harmonize them. Thus the best procedure in this chapter, unlike the previous ones, would appear to be to analyse the eschatological concepts according to my proposed reconstruction of sources and redactions. Therefore we will look first at the concepts of the original myth underlying the central exposition, then at those in the frame story and Pronoia hymn, and finally at the 'Sethian' material.

1 The eschatology of the main narrative

Despite the fact that the frame story and dialogue are later additions, the threefold structure of the underlying myth, a myth of past, present and future, is still discernible in that the original form of the *Apocryphon* reconstructed by us consisted of theogony and cosmogony ('What was': the primal revelation of Father, Mother and Son and the fall of Sophia), anthropogony ('What is': the origin and history of humankind in the image of heavenly Adamas) and soteriology ('What is to come': the advent of the eschatological Spirit, cosmic catastrophe, restoration of Sophia's 'deficiency' by means of the final gathering of all the saved souls into the perfect aeon). Apart from the passage on the destinies of souls, the events of the last section are either merely hinted at or only found in later strata, the Pronoia hymn in particular. But comparison with related texts and systems such as the 'Ophites' of Irenaeus, the *Hypostasis, On the Origin of the World* and *Trimorphic Protennoia* suggests the plausibility of such a scheme: in contrast to their fascination with apocalyptic and the details of the end, the *Apocryphon* is primarily concerned with the history of spirit from its origin in the great invisible Spirit to its destiny in human souls as its ultimate avatars. Thus the passage on the destinies of human souls marks the fitting (and original) climax of the work. We could profitably compare the climax of the Valentinian myth of Ptolemy's school in Irenaeus' 'Great Notice': the centre of interest lies in the relative destinies of the spiritual and psychic beings.[32]

Thus the centre of eschatological interest in the main narrative must be the passage on the destinies of souls, but there are other eschatological allusions and motifs which must first be dealt with. There is, for example, the deficiency/perfection theme related to Sophia and her offspring already discussed in previous chapters, which, although fundamental to the myth, seems to evince Valentinian influence. The correction of Sophia's (or Adam's, i.e. humanity's) deficiency by various figures as an event with cosmic and eschatological significance is a recurring motif in the text.[33] The Epinoia is sent out to set humanity up in its perfection (*plērōma*), teach it about the descent of its defect (*hysterēma*) and about its own ascent.[34] The archontic prohibition concerning the tree of knowledge is an attempt to prevent Adam from looking up to his perfection.[35] Again, Adam is taught to eat the knowledge so as to remember his perfection, the result being spatial separation from Ialdabaoth.[36] 'Perfection' would appear to refer to the original state of humanity to which it is eventually to be restored, and is thus a term, as in Valentinianism, with collective and futurist connotations.

Then, second, there is the garbled episode of the descent of the Mother's spirit with the purpose, according to SR (whose version we argued was more original),[37] of awakening the substance akin to it after the type of the perfection (*plērōma*), and working for the seed in anticipation of the eschatological descent of the Spirit to free it from defect.[38] We suggested that the confusion in this passage was originally due to the influence of 'Sethian' reinterpretation which attracted further redactoral activity; B represented the more original state of affairs, a combination of the earlier tradition of Sophia as redeemer restoring the divine element to earthly Seth and his descendants with the Valentinian and 'Sethian' tradition of the consort/spirit who descends to the passive Sophia and then to her spiritual offspring, the seed of Seth, to correct her deficiency. The spirit's activity with the seed parallels on the human level that of the Mother's consort at a prior stage and higher level, and anticipates the eschatological gift of the Spirit in the initiation ceremony inaugurated by the Saviour (the five seals). The Spirit's restoration and perfection of the heavenly aeon, which thus depends on the individual Gnostics, both reflects a universal–futurist dimension and (not surprisingly) leads the redactor of LR to speak in Valentinian fashion of the whole Pleroma thereby becoming holy and faultless.[39]

Certainly we can understand the passage as an obvious bridge, attempting to explain how the Gnostic elect survived the demi-urgic assaults on it up to the present revelatory and saving descent of the Saviour and the eschatological descent of the Holy Spirit. Although every event of this sort involving divine revelation and activity would seem to mark a complete act of redemption, as Schottroff would argue,[40] we must realize the decisive character of the Saviour's descent and revelation and the preliminary character of previous revelatory events; what the latter manifest is a capacity for or interim degree of revelation and salvation, which only becomes realized or perfected with the coming of the Saviour, and his inauguration of the initiation rite involving the eschatological descent and activity of the Holy Spirit.[41]

Thus it is no accident that this passage on the spirit's descent anticipating the eschatological coming of the Holy Spirit should lead immediately into the passage on the destinies of various souls, the most overt treatment of eschatology in our text. Since we have discussed the passage in detail in our previous chapter, it will be sufficient here to highlight the eschatological implications in terms of our questions. First it is clear that not all souls will be saved; it all depends on which spirit descends on the soul and unites with it, the Spirit of life or the counterfeit spirit, and on whether the soul accepts or rejects the saving knowledge.[42] Those who turn away will suffer eternal punishment, thus implying that there will be no ultimate restoration of all things to their original state, or separation off into their respective elements or types as, e.g. in the 'Ophite' and Valentinian schemes.[43]

Salvation for those souls united with the Spirit seems to be undifferentiated and immediate on death; they enter the great illuminators, ascending to the dignity of eternal imperishable life, the calling and rest.[44] But the very terminology of their reception after laying aside the flesh, by its repeated echoes of New Testament eschatological language (calling, endurance, completion of the contest, inheritance of eternal life)[45] might suggest a futurist perspective. This is certainly the case with the prior mention of the eschatological Spirit's activity in perfecting the Gnostics to establish the aeon (or Pleroma) as free of deficiency.[46] And the collective character of this process is expressed by the reference to saved souls devoting themselves ascetically to the incorruptible (*aphthartos*) assembly.[47] This strikingly recalls the 'Ophite' concepts of the incorruptible aeon and the heavenly Church, the archetype and ultimate goal of the earthly body of the elect.[48]

We even have a kind of Gnostic Purgatory: the texts refer to enlightened souls who are worthy to enter the great illuminators as being purified from evil 'there'.[49] This would appear to refer to the illuminators, but they are not a kind of intermediate purification stage, like the Valentinian 'Middle', the Harmony of *Poimandres* or the realm of sun and moon in Manichaeism, but represent the final destination of the elect.[50] Thus after death the saved souls escape from wickedness and through the incorruptible oversight (*episcopē*: SR) are brought to the repose (*anapausis*) of the aeons.[51] Again this might refer to the immediate post-mortem state of the elect soul, but the term 'repose' often has a universal eschatological connotation.[52]

Such is the destiny of those souls who have united with the Holy Spirit and possess the saving knowledge. But even for those souls who have been dominated by the counterfeit spirit and remain in ignorance, there is still a chance of salvation via the process of reincarnation. We have defended this interpretation of the text in the previous chapter; suffice it to recall that such a process is attested in the 'Ophite' system, *Pistis Sophia* and the speculations of Epiphanius' libertine Gnostics, all of which we have argued are related to the *Apocryphon*.[53] And as we argued, such reincarnate souls are given to elect souls who act as their guardians, enabling them to reach knowledge and be initiated and thus escape further reincarnations. This mirrors the situation of the elect souls who come to knowledge and are initiated through their guardian angels, the illuminators, as e.g. Norea is by Eleleth in the *Hypostasis*.[54]

The final category, already discussed in the last chapter, is that of those souls who possessed the saving knowledge but apostatized. As saved souls ascend to a particular location, the incorruptible aeon, so apostate souls go to the place to which the angels of poverty will withdraw, for whom (SR) or where (LR) there is no repentance.[55] They will be kept for the day (of judgement?) when all those who have blasphemed the Holy Spirit will suffer eternal punishment.[56] The divergence between the versions may be caused by unclarity over the status of these angels of poverty: are they the angels of punishment characteristic of apocalyptic as LR seems to imply,[57] or are they apostate angels who are also to be punished, as SR might suggest?[58] That all four versions continue with a plural conjunctive ('and they will guard them'),[59] and that the angels of poverty recur in the Pronoia hymn as to be avoided in their role of ensnaring ignorant souls, might support the originality of LR here.[60] In any case, the text seems to teach what is essentially a twofold scheme of salvation/damnation; salvation is assured for those souls on whom the Holy Spirit descends at once (or after a period of being deluded by the counterfeit spirit and of reincarnation) and who respond positively, whereas those souls with the knowledge who yet deny the presence of the Holy Spirit and turn away will suffer eternal punishment.

Although this scheme, from its relative simplicity, might seem early, it is rather sophisticated, avoiding the crude dualism of the two types of humanity in Saturninus, and the sophisticated double predestinationism suggested by the Valentinian threefold division of the created order.[61] Moreover it is demonstrably Christian, echoing New Testament eschatological texts and strikingly akin to mainstream Christian ideas involving the post-mortem fate of souls. According to the latter, of course, it was only the souls of martyrs that went straight to heaven; all the rest went to an intermediate realm to await the judgement which, in the case of sinners, would involve eternal punishment.[63] Of course, in the case of the Gnostics only the souls of apostates would be punished; salvation is denied to the flesh, which inevitably narrows the possibilities of punishment and the graphic detail beloved of apocalyptic.

The passage on the destiny of souls thus does seem to combine individual and realized elements (elect souls on leaving the body at death go straight to heaven) with a collective futurist perspective (allusion to the incorruptible gathering and aeon, and to 'rest' for elect souls), which, however, is not universalist (apostate souls are eternally punished). The very qualified belief in reincarnation (only for ignorant souls) suggests the irreversible character of the process. On the other hand determinism is excluded: the subtle balance between divine initiative and human response is maintained. Finally, the references to the Holy Spirit mark the essential link with the initiation rite; *pace* Schottroff, sacraments are fundamental to these Gnostics. The comparative simplicity, optimism and distinctiveness of their scheme again suggests the independence of the Gnostic myth in its original form from Valentinian and other influence.

2 The eschatology of the frame story and Pronoia hymn

The eschatology of the frame story and Pronoia hymn generally corresponds to and confirms that of the main narrative. The treatise on theogony, cosmogony, anthropogony and soteriology, on past, present and future, becomes a revelation dialogue between the Saviour and John culminating in a hymn relating the former's three decisive revelatory descents in relation to past, future and present. The eschatological atmosphere is established at once by the Pharisee's question: 'Where is your master . . . ?' and John's reply: 'He has returned to the place from which he came.'[64] Not only is this permeated by Johannine allusions,[65] but 'the place' (*topos*) appears as the final location of the Gnostics both in the dialogue on the souls[66] and the Pronoia hymn.[67] John's

series of questions culminates in the eschatological: 'Of what
sort is that aeon to which we shall go?'; the Saviour having revealed
to them that that aeon was of the type (*typos*) of the incorruptible
aeon, but not what it was like.[68] Now in the main narrative the
Father's aeon is described as 'incorruptible'[69] and the same term
is used of the supreme heavenly realm and goal of the elect souls
in the 'Ophite' system of Irenaeus.[70]

Moreover, details of the Saviour's epiphany and proclamation
have eschatological overtones as well as fitting in with the structure
of the main narrative. As in certain of the apocryphal Acts, Christ
appears simultaneously as one yet three: as child, old man and
youth.[71] As Puech notes, underlying this is the theme of the *aiōn*
(representing past, present and future simultaneously), but more
relevant perhaps is the triple-male category of redaction (a²).[72]
Further, his message has an eschatological orientation in that he
proclaims 'I am with you (plural) always' (cf. Matt 28:20 and John
14:16), and asserts that he has come to teach John about past,
present and future and about the perfect Man.[73] The repetition
by the Saviour in the epilogue of SR of his promise to teach about
the future,[74] a promise which remains unfulfilled, may be its
attempt to make up for omitting the Pronoia hymn, which does
at least give some eschatological hints, as we shall see.

In any case, the reference to the perfect Man as a protological
and eschatological figure is central to the myth of the *Apocryphon*
and related texts. The original, protological, true Man after whose
image we were made, we have argued, is Adamas, although
ultimately he may be seen as a projection or facet of the Son,
Christ, who is the eschatological Adam, the perfect Man.[75] The
entire Naassene Preaching centres on the fall into matter and
spiritual regeneration of us creatures of the perfect Man, Adamas,
while the *Hypostasis* and *On the Origin of the World* relate the coming
of the true Man (i.e. Christ) as the climax of the redemption of
the elect and the judgement of the archons. In redaction (a²) of
the *Apocryphon* we have contended that Sophia and her redeeming
role were replaced by Barbelo/Pronoia as Father–Mother–Son,
who thus appears both as first Man to the archons and as the
Saviour/Pronoia figure of the final hymn.

As part of the Johannine frame story, the eschatological passage
on the destiny of souls, the original climax of the work, was recast
as a dialogue between the Saviour and John, in which John asks
six questions. The last of these (on apostate souls) was then
followed by the Pronoia hymn with its Johannine echoes and triple

descent scheme based on key events in the central myth, as we have suggested in the previous chapter. Eschatological features include the Saviour's description of her/himself as 'the remembrance of the Pleroma' (*plērōma*,[76] a Valentinian term with collective futurist connotations), the perfection that is the goal of the Gnostics,[77] her/his concern on the second descent with a plan (*oikonomia*), and reascent lest the (under)world be destroyed before the time.[78] Both *plērōma* and *oikonomia* suggest progress towards a final goal, the salvation of the elect and destruction of the cosmos. Indeed we identified this second descent with the Epinoia's instruction of Adam about his ascent. Again in the third descent we hear of the Saviour filling her/his face with the light of 'the completion (*synteleia*) of their aeon', an obscure phrase but one which must have some cosmic–eschatological reference.[79]

The honoured place to which the Saviour raises the awakened Gnostic is clearly the spatially-conceived eschatological goal found elsewhere in the *Apocryphon*,[80] although Schottroff argues that this is not tied to some temporal future or distinguished from the Gnostic's hearing the call.[81] That the Gnostic is further urged to protect her/himself from the angels of poverty and demons of chaos and is sealed with the five seals to prevent death having power over her/him any longer, also has a final ring about it.[82] Again Schottroff argues that these concepts, change of location and victory over death, are mythological, intended to enlarge or expand the existential act of hearing which is the essence of redemption for this passage.[83] That such an existential interpretation is required is shown, according to her, by the fact that the two concepts cannot logically be united into a common mythological scheme.[84]

However, Schottroff's treatment of the Pronoia hymn as an independent unit we have shown to be questionable: the evident links with the main narrative and dependent character of the hymn demand that we take seriously the hints of a future-eschatological perspective in it. Further, the concepts of change of place and victory over death need not be incompatible. The latter does not rule out a future-eschatological perspective and the former positively invites it. A similar reply might be given to Peel, who interprets the five seals as an example of sacramentally realized eschatology.[85] Comparison with the parallel (and dependent) passages in *Trimorphic Protennoia* and the *Gospel of the Egyptians* is essential here. The initiatory rituals in the former do

seem prima facie to suggest a present experience of salvation as a
result of the ceremony, although the agents involved are clearly
heavenly beings.[86] The picture in the latter also suggests this-
worldly experience, if with a more evident future orientation 'they
will by no means taste death'.[87] But comparison with the
Apocryphon, which we have argued has decisively influenced both
texts, suggests the necessity of a futurist-eschatological perspective.
Souls which have the Spirit (i.e. via the five seals rite) remain in
the body until death and then ascend to the aeon to be purified
there. Hence Sophia's 'deficiency' will not be removed until the
consummation, when all the elect souls are gathered in.[88]

3 The eschatology of the 'Sethian' reinterpretation

As we have shown, the eschatologies of the main narrative and of
the frame story and Pronoia hymn of redaction (a^2), are consistent,
teaching an undifferentiated salvation for saved souls to the
incorruptible aeon, the realm of the four illuminators, and
damnation only for apostates. However, this is plainly contradicted
by the passage on Adamas and Seth in relation to the four
illuminators.[89] Unlike the picture of these in other related
Barbelognostic texts as angelic revealers and guardians, they now
appear as hierarchically ranked spatial entities, aeons, to which
are assigned respectively heavenly Adamas, his son Seth, the elect
seed of Seth and souls who had the saving knowledge but only
repented later. These aeons appear to mark the eternal resting
places of the souls, hence final distinctions remain, as in the
Valentinian scheme of Ptolemy.[90]

Such a scheme also recurs in uncontestably 'Sethian' works from
Nag Hammadi, such as the *Gospel of the Egyptians*[91] and *Zostrianos*,
where it has the form of a ladder of perfection.[92] As we have
argued, this scheme is part of a 'Sethianizing' interpretation of
the original Barbelognostic myth which, in reaction to mainstream
Christian criticism of novelty, seeks to trace the elect back to
heavenly Seth as spiritual progenitor of his 'seed', 'the immovable
race'.[93] This does establish a continuity in the history of salvation
which, in dependence on Jewish legends about earthly Seth, is
structured in terms of three parousias of Seth in response to
attempts by the archons to destroy his seed through flood and
fire, but it does import an element of predestination not present
in the original. Not all souls who are initiated and respond
appropriately to the Spirit's presence will be saved, but only the

'immovable' seed of Seth, whose salvation has been guaranteed throughout history, and who only require the rubber stamp of the five seals rite.[94] Other souls who eventually repent may be saved, but only to an inferior aeon.

Conclusion

Thus in answer to the questions we posed at the beginning: although there are passages in the *Apocryphon* which suggest a realized eschatology in mystical or sacramental or even existentialist terms, they are balanced by those with a futurist–universal perspective. Sophia's 'deficiency' will not be corrected until all the elect souls (those not only in the divine image and with the divine power, but who are sealed and thereby united with the Spirit and who respond in faith) are saved. Again, an individualist stress on the soul and its destiny is balanced by the collective concepts of the spatio-temporal heavenly aeon, or Church, and of the heavenly Man. But any tendency to predestinationism and automatic salvation is effectively countered by the subtle balance of divine initiative and human response charted in the passage on the destinies of souls. Thus while it is the soul that is the object of salvation, not all will be saved. Yet the outlook is optimistic: meritorious action is not necessary and reincarnation holds out the possibility of finally acquiring saving knowledge; damnation is retained only for the category of apostates. Finally, the cyclic tendency implied in reincarnation is a necessary and congruent element in an irreversible movement towards an ultimate salvation and separation expressed in and mediated through the five seals sacrament.

This subtle and sophisticated picture, in line with the 'Ophite' system yet strikingly independent of Valentinianism as of the apocalyptic speculations of related or dependent works like *On the Origin of the World*, *Trimorphic Protennoia* and *Pistis Sophia*, underwent Valentinian and 'Sethian' reworkings which introduced elements of predestinationism (the 'seed', the 'immovable race', etc.) and weakened the tension and paradox of this essentially Christian system. This is summed up in the paradigmatic figures and experiences of Sophia and of the Son, Christ: salvation means coming to realize who one really is through exile and repentance and self-begetting, as with Sophia, and then of anointing and elevation to perfection, as with the Son. It tries to do justice to the Gnostic assurance of salvation as somehow already present through the decisive revelation/intervention of the Saviour and the initiation rite introduced by him, as well as to their awareness that salvation remained provisional, dependent on their faithful response, which would make an essential contribution to the final consummation.

Notes

[1] On Gnostic eschatology, see M. L. Peel, 'Gnostic Eschatology and the New Testament', *NovT* 12 (1970), 141–65; Jonas, *Religion* 44–6; J. Zandee, 'Gnostische Eschatologie', *X Internationaler Kongress für Religionsgeschichte 11–17 September 1960 in Marburg* (Marburg, 1961), 94f.; Rudolph, *Gnosis* 171–204; MacRae, 'Apocalyptic Eschatology in Gnosticism' in D. Hellholm ed., *Apocalypticism in the Mediterranean World and the Near East: Proceedings of the International Colloquium on Apocalypticism, Uppsala, August 12–17, 1979* (Tübingen: J. C. B. Mohr (Paul Siebeck), 1983), 317–25; Pétrement, *Separate* 160–70; Filoramo, *History* 128–41.

[2] 'Eschatologie' 94.

[3] 'Eschatology' 143. Cf. Pétrement, *Separate* 160ff. ('Gnosticism has a preference for realized eschatology'). Theodotus' formula (*Exc. ex Theod.* 78) implies that liberation occurs through a combination of initiation rite (baptism) and saving knowledge.

[4] E. Schweizer, 'Gegenwart des Geistes und eschatologische Hoffnung bei Zarathustra, spätjüdischen Gruppen, Gnostikern und den Zeugen des neuen Testaments', *The Background of the New Testament and its Eschatology* (Studies in Honour of C. H. Dodd) (Cambridge, 1956), 500f.

[5] *Gos. Truth* 24.28–32. Cf. the similar Marcosian formulation in Iren. 1.15.2.

[6] 2.31.2.

[7] *History* 129–33.

[8] 'Eschatology' 150–3.

[9] Illustrated from Menander, the Pronoia hymn of *AJ*, the Marcosian baptismal formula, the Hermetica, the Naassene Preaching and the *Epistle to Rheginus*.

[10] Illustrated from the *Gospel of Truth*, *Poimandres* and the *Apocryphon of James* as well as other Nag Hammadi texts such as the *Authoritative Teaching* (C VI,3) and the *Teachings of Silvanus* (C VII,4) whose Gnostic character has been questioned (see on the former R. van den Broek, 'The Authentikos Logos: A New Document of Christian Platonism', *VC* 33 (1979), 260–86; on the latter the introduction by M. L. Peel and J. Zandee in *NHLE*).

[11] Illustrated from the *Epistle to Rheginus*, the Hermetica and the *Authoritative Teaching*.

[12] Illustrated from the *Gospel of Thomas*, the *Gospel of Truth* and the *Dialogue of the Saviour* (C III,5).

[13] 'Eschatology' 153–5. For modern support, cf. e.g. R. Bultmann, *Primitive Christianity in its Contemporary Setting* (London: Collins, 1962), 200f.

[14] Cf. MacRae, 'Apocalyptic' 318, who suggests that a future-orientated apocalyptic perspective may be fundamental to the Gnostic world-view.

[15] Peel, 'Eschatology' 145.

[16] L. Schottroff, 'Heil als innerweltliche Entweltlichung: Der gnostische Hintergrund der johanneischen Vorstellung vom Zeitpunkt der Erlösung', *NovT* 11 (1969), 294–317, esp. 311f. (referring to Jonas, *Gnosis* 1, 127; 2, 11).

[17] *Primitive* 203.

[18] 'Eschatology' 155–62.

[19] 'Eschatology' 155–9.

[20] 1.30.14.

[21] Iren. 1.6.1; 7.1; *Exc. ex Theod.* 62.2–65.2.

[22] On *apokatastasis*, cf. Iren. 1.8.4; 14.1; 21.3; Heracleon frag. 34; *Treat. Res.* 44.31; *Tri. Trac.* 123.19, 21, 27; 133.7; *Gos. Phil.* 67.18. Cf. Basilides in Hipp. *Ref.* 7.26.2; 27.4,11, etc. On 'rest' as an eschatological phenomenon, cf. *AJB* 36.7ff. and par; 68.12ff. and par; Heracleon frags 12, 32–4, 42; *Gos. Truth* 40.30–41.14; *Gos. Phil.* 66.19; *Book of Thomas* (C II,7) 145.13, etc.

[23] 'Eschatologie' 95: 'Die Endzeit fällt zusammen mit der Urzeit'. Zandee quotes (without identifying) *Tri. Trac.* 127.23–5 ('that the end should be as the beginning').

[24] So Peel, citing R. Haardt, 'Das universaleschatologische Vorstellungsgut in der Gnosis' in K. Schubert ed., *Vom Messias zum Christos: Die Fülle der Zeit in religionsgeschichtlicher und theologischer Sicht* (Vienna, 1964), 331; W. Foerster, *Gnosis 1* 7; Rudolph, *TRu* 36, 28f., *Gnosis* 202f.; Filoramo, *History* 134f., etc.

[25] So Peel, 'Eschatology' 155, with reference to the Carpocratians of Iren. 1.25.4; *Apoc. Paul* (C V,2) 20.20–3; 21.17–21; and Celsus on the Ophites in Orig. *C. Cels.* 6.24–38, esp. 33–6 (*not* Iren. *Adv. haer.* 1.6.24–38 as in Peel).

[26] See our treatment of B 68.13–70.8/III 35.2–36.3; II 26.32–27.21/IV 41.10–42.23 in ch. 7.

[27] Iren. 1.30.14: 'ut *rursus* [the Demiurge] demittat eas (the holy souls) in saeculum, tantum eas quae sunt ex substantia eius.'

[28] 'Heil', esp. 303, 311, 315f.

[29] 'Heil' 315ff.

[30] 304.

[31] *TRu* 36, 29.

[32] Cf. Iren. 1.7.1, 5.

[33] On her awareness of her deficiency and its future effects, cf. B 44.19–45.19 and par; on the attempt to have her correct her deficiency, cf. B 46.9–47.14 and par; on the Epinoia's role to help Sophia correct her deficiency (and Adam his), cf. B 53.18–54.4 and par; B 60.13–61.5 and par; on Sophia's descent to correct her deficiency, cf. II 23.20–4 (and III 39.18–21); on the cosmic saving role of the eschatological Spirit, cf. B 64.3–13 and par.

[34] B 53.4–18 and par.

[35] B 57.8–19 and par. II 22.7 reads *plērōma*. Cf. B 56.10–17 and par. This may be a reference to Adam's perfect heavenly archetype, but one cannot rule out a future reference, implicit in the archetype.

[36] B 61.2–9 and par. III 30.20 reads *plērōma*.

[37] See ch. 6, section 3f.

[38] B 63.14–64.13/III 32.8–22; II 25.2–16.

[39] II 25.14–16/IV 39.13–15.

[40] *Glaubende* 9f., 97–9.

[41] Cf. the very similar contemporary solution of Justin Martyr: those before Christ who lived 'with *logos*' had something of the truth, but Christians now have the whole *Logos* incarnate in Christ (*1 Apol.* 46; *2 Apol.* 13, etc.).

[42] See ch. 7, section 1.

[43] Cf. Iren. 1.30.14 and 1.7.1, 5.

[44] Cf. B 64.3–8 and par; 65.20–66.12 and par; 67.18–68.13 and par.

[45] Cf. respectively 2 Thess 1:11; 1 Cor 13:7; 2 Tim 2:10, 4:7; Matt 19:29 par, etc.

[46] Cf. B 64.3–13 and par.

[47] B 65.8–19/III 33.7–15 (*souḥ = ekklēsia*, cf. Crum, *Dictionary* 373b). LR (II 25.30/IV 40.4) has missed the reference to the assembly.

[48] Iren. 1 30.2 (the incorruptible (*aphtharton*) aeon, the true, holy Church (*ekklēsia*) ... the calling (*appellatio*) ...). This would further confirm the originality of this material. Cf. Orig. *C. Cels.* 6.35 and the similar Valentinian concept, Iren. 1.5.6; *Tri. Trac.* 97.5–9. *GE* III 55.2–6/IV 66.14–19 (the incorruptible (*aphthartos*) spiritual (*pneumatikos*) Church (*ekklēsia*) in the four illuminators of the Autogenes) has expanded *AJ*'s picture.

[49] B 65.3–11/III 33.4–9; II 25.23–9/IV 39.25–40.3.

[50] Cf. Orig. *C. Cels.* 6.35 where Origen interprets Celsus' allusions to an earthly Church and circumcision as references to the belief of some (Ophites?) in a heavenly Church and the circumcision in it as purification. However in *PS* Book 2, ch. 100 (Schmidt–MacDermot 249.20–252.12) purification of souls appears to take place in this world.

[51] B 67.18–68.13/III 34.18–35.2; II 26.22–32/IV 41.10–20.

[52] Cf. e.g. the index to Foerster, *Gnosis 2* s.v. rest, repose; *OW* 125.8f.; *GE* III 65.4. See on this P. Vielhauer, '*ANAPAUSIS*: zum gnostischen Hintergrund des Thomasevangeliums', *Apophoreta* (BZNW 30) (Berlin:

Töpelmann, 1964), 281–99. Further support for a universal-eschatological interpretation might come from the term *episcopē*, which in the case of 1 Pet 2:12 and of 1QS iii.18; iv.6, 12, 18–23, where according to M. Black, *The Scrolls and Christian Origins* (London: Nelson, 1961), 135, its exact parallel *pequddah* occurs, refers, in Black's view, to the Last Visitation of God.

[53] See ch. 7, n. 55, p. 288. It was also apparently taught by the Carpocratians (Iren. 1.25.1–4); Basilides (frag. 4 in Clem. Alex. *Strom.* 4.12.83.1; frag. 5 in Orig. *In Rom.* 5.1) and the Manichees (*Acta Archelai* 10.1–8).

[54] Cf. the role of the angels of light in Celsus' Ophite diagram, Orig. *C. Cels.* 6.27.

[55] B 70.8–15/III 36.4–10; II 27.21–7/IV 42.24–43.1.

[56] B 70.16–71.2/III 36.10–15; II 27.27–31/IV 43.2–6.

[57] Cf. e.g. *1 Enoch* 56.1; 62.11f.; 63.1f.; 64; 66–7; *2 Enoch* 10; *Apoc. Zeph.* 4.1–7; *T. Levi* 3.2f.; *T. Abr.* 12; *Apoc. Paul* 22.1–10, etc.

[58] In *1 Enoch* 53.3; 54.6 we find both types of angels side by side.

[59] B 70.16/III 36.10; II 27.28/IV 43.2. The form does not necessarily imply a passive, as most translators assume.

[60] Cf. II 31.18f./IV 48.24f. The possibility of repentance is surely more applicable to the souls than to angels whose status and role is not evidently evil. In *OW* 'poverty' (*mn̄t̲h̲ēkē*) seems to be an attribute of this world (cf. 110.12f.; 112.13, 21f.; 118.1).

[61] Cf. Rudolph, *Gnosis* 186f.

[62] Esp. Matt 12:31 and par, and Matt 25:41,46. On eternal punishment of the apostates, etc. cf. Rev 20:10; Mark 9:48; Jude 7.

[63] On the martyrs' immediate ascent, cf. e.g. Iren. 4.33.9; Tert. *Anima* 55–8; *C. Marc.* 4.34; on the intermediate realm, cf. e.g. *1 Clem.* 5.4–7; 6.1; 50.3; Justin, *Dial.* 5.3; Iren. 5.31.1f.; Ps. Hipp. *C. Graec.* 1f. (MPG 10.796A–800A); on eternal punishment, cf. e.g. Ign. *Eph.* 16.2; Hermas, *Sim.* 9.18.2; *2 Clem.* 17.5–7; Justin, *1 Apol.* 8, 28; *2 Apol.* 7–9; Ps. Hipp. *C. Graec.* 1 (797A); 3 (801A).

[64] B 19.10–16/III 1.4–10; II 1.8–11.

[65] Cf. e.g. John 7:33f.; 13:3; 16:5, 28; 20:17.

[66] Cf. B 67.18–68.13. However, the term only occurs in B.

[67] Cf. II 31.13f./IV 48.17f.

[68] B 20.12–19; II 1.24–9.

[69] B 26.6–9/III 6.19–21 (*aphthartos*); II 4.10–13/IV 6.10–13. Cf. the 'perfect aeon' of B 75.14f./III 39.13f.; II 31.25–7/IV 49.6–8.

[70] 1.30.2, 11, 13, 14.

[71] B 21.3–13; II 2.1–9. Cf. *Acta Petri* 20f.; *Acta Johannis* 73, 88; *Acta Pauli* Hamburg papyrus p. 3; *Acta Andreae et Matthaiae* 18. See on this Puech in Hennecke–Schneemelcher–Wilson *NTA* 1 321, n. 1. In *PS* Book 1, ch. 4 (Schmidt–MacDermot 7.13–8.2) Christ appears in three light forms.

[72] Puech refers to E. Peterson, 'Einige Bemerkungen zum Hamburger Papyrus-fragment der Acta Pauli', *VC* 3 (1949), 149–59. Peterson (158) explains the motif in the apocryphal Acts from Tatian's treatment of time in *Or. ad Graec.* 26.1: men believe time has three forms, past, present and future, but in reality there is only the *aiōn hestōs*.

[73] The first phrase recalls Rev 1:1, 4, 9, 19; 4:1; 22:6f.

[74] B 76.5f./III 39.21f. The plural reference, 'to you', of B 76.6, is probably a mistake since the following 'to you' is singular. A copyist of B may have misread the *tēnou on* of III 39.22 as *tēytn̄*.

[75] See ch. 5, section 1.

[76] C II 30.16/IV 47.1f.

[77] Cf. the presentation and role of the Valentinian Jesus, star and fruit of the Pleroma in Iren. 1.2.6; Hipp. *Ref.* 6.32.1f.; *Tri. Trac.* 86.23–87.23.

[78] II 30.21–32/IV 47.8–22 (*oyeish*). In Eph 1:10, 3:2 and 3:9, *oikonomia* has an evident soterio-eschatological connotation and 1:10 refers to the *oikonomia* of the *plērōma* of the *kairos* (on *oyeish* as a Coptic equivalent of *kairos*, see Crum, *Dictionary* 499b–500a). On *pro kairou*, cf. Matt 8:29; 1 Cor 4:5.

[79] II 31.1f./IV 47.29–48.2. Cf. its use in *OW* 110.13; 114.24; 121.26f.; 122.6–8, 33; 123.30f.; 125.32f.; *GE* III 61.3/IV 72.12; III 62.21; *TP* 44.33f. The phrase could be an allusion to John 1:5.

[80] II 31.13f./IV 48.17f. Cf. B 68.4f.

[81] 'Heil' 308.

[82] II 31.16–25/IV 48.22–49.6.

[83] 'Heil' 309, 313.

[84] 313.

[85] 'Eschatology' 150.

[86] 48.12–35; cf. 49.28–38.

[87] *GE* III 65.26–66.8/IV 78.1–10.

[88] Note the futurist allusions in the post-initiation invocation in *GE* (III 66.22–68.1/IV 79.3–80.15): 'the man in whom thou wilt purify me into thy life . . .' (III 67.19–21); 'that I may live with thee in the peace of the saints' (III 67.25f.).

[89] B 35.20–36.15/III 13.17–14.9; II 9.11–24.

[90] The attempts of Schenke ('System' 166f.) and Tardieu (see *Écrits* 272, etc.) to see in the four illuminators/aeons a periodization of history or of world ages seems artificial and unconvincing, particularly over the difficulties of interpreting the last class of souls. If they represent the historical Sethians why do they need to repent and why are they so late in repenting?

[91] *GE* III 65.12–22/IV 77.7–19 clearly echoes *AJ* B 35.20–36.15, but assigns the sons of Seth to the third illuminator and their souls to the fourth, in more explicit dependence on the Valentinian distinction.

[92] Cf. 6.7–7.22; 29.1–20. Here the four illuminators are set over four aeons as ascending stages in a process of purificatory baptism and

illumination. For a classic summary of the 'Sethian' understanding of mystical ascent, cf. *Steles Seth* 127.20f.: 'The way of ascent is the way of descent.'

[93] See ch. 1, sections 3 and 4, ch. 3, section 2d, etc.

[94] Cf. *AA* 82.19–83.23; *GE* III 60.2–66.8/IV 71.11–78.10.

Bibliography

A Primary literature

Adam, A. *Texte zum Manichäismus* (Kleine Texte für Vorlesungen und Übungen 175) (Berlin, 1969²).

Barc, B., *L'Hypostase des Archontes: Traité gnostique sur l'origine de l'homme, du monde et des archontes NH II,4* (BCNH, Section 'Textes' 5) (Québec: Université Laval/Louvain: Peeters, 1980).

Baynes, C. A., *A Coptic Gnostic Treatise contained in the Codex Brucianus* (Bruce MS. 96, Bod. Lib. Oxford) (Cambridge, 1933).

Bethge, H.-G. et al., ' "Nebront": Die zweite Schrift aus Nag-Hammadi Codex VI: Eingeleitet und übersetzt vom Berliner Arbeitskreis für koptisch-gnostisch Schriften' *TLZ* 98 (1973), 97–104.

Bezold, C., *Die Schatzhöhle* (Leipzig: Hinrichs, 1883).

Böhlig, A. and Labib, P., *Koptisch-gnostische Apokalypsen aus Codex V von Nag Hammadi im Koptischen Museum zu Alt-Kairo* (Wissenschaftliche Zeitschrift der Martin-Luther-Universität, Halle-Wittenberg, Sonderband) (Halle, 1963).

Böhlig, A. and Labib, P., *Die koptisch-gnostische Schrift ohne Titel aus Codex II von Nag Hammadi im Koptischen Museum zu Alt-Kairo* (Deutsche Akademie der Wissenschaften zu Berlin, Institut für Orientforschung, 58) (Berlin: Akademie, 1962).

Böhlig, A., Polotsky, H. J. and Schmidt., C., *Kephalaia 1.1* (Manichäische Handschriften der staatlicher Museen Berlin 1) (Stuttgart: Kohlhammer, 1940).

Böhlig, A. and Wisse, F., *Nag Hammadi Codices III,2 and IV,2: The Gospel of the Egyptians* (NHS 4) (Leiden: Brill, 1975).

Bullard, R. A., *The Hypostasis of the Archons* (PTS 10) (Berlin: De Gruyter, 1970).

Charles, R. H., *The Apocrypha and Pseudepigrapha of the Old Testament in English* (2 vols, Oxford: Clarendon, 1913).

Clement of Alexandria, *Extraits de Théodote*, ed. F. Sagnard (SC 23) (Paris: Editions du Cerf, 1970).

Clement of Alexandria, *Stromateis 1–6*, ed. O. Stählin, rev. U. Treu (GCS 52) (Berlin: Akademie, 1985).

Clement of Alexandria, *Stromateis 7–8*, ed. O Stählin, rev. L. Fruchtel/U. Treu (GCS 17²) (Berlin: Akademie 1970).

Doresse, J., '"Le livre sacré du grand Esprit invisible" ou "L'Evangile des Egyptiens"', *JA* 254 (1966), 316–435; 256 (1968), 289–386.

Epiphanius of Salamis, *Panarion (haer. 1–33)*, ed. K. Holl (GCS 25) (Leipzig: Hinrichs, 1915).

Epiphanius of Salamis, *Panarion (haer. 34–64)*, ed. K. Holl, rev. J. Dümmer (GCS 31) (Berlin: Akademie, 1980).

Evangelium veritatis, eds M. Malinine, H.-C. Puech, G. Quispel (Zürich/Stuttgart: Francke, 1956); *Supplementum* id. and W. C. Till (Zürich: Francke, 1961).

The Facsimile Edition of the Nag Hammadi Codices (Leiden: Brill, 1972–7).

Filaster of Brescia, *Diversarum haereseon liber*, ed. F. Marx (CSEL 38) (Prague/Vienna/Leipzig: Tempsky, 1898).

Foerster W., ed., *Die Gnosis 1 & 2* (Zürich: Artemis, 1971; ET *Gnosis 1 & 2* ed. R. McL. Wilson, Oxford: Clarendon, 1972, 1974).

George Syncellus, *Chronographia*, ed. G. Dindorf (CSHB) (Bonn: Weber, 1829).

Gibson, M. D., 'The Book of the Rolls', *Apocrypha Arabica* (Studia Sinaitica 8).

Giversen, S., *Apocryphon Johannis: The Coptic Text of the Apocryphon Johannis in the Nag Hammadi Codex II with Translation, Introduction and Commentary* (Acta Theologica Danica V) (Copenhagen: Munksgaard, 1963).

Haardt, R., *Gnosis, Character and Testimony*, tr. J. F. Hendry (Leiden: Brill, 1971).

Hedrick, C. W. ed., *Nag Hammadi Codices XI, XII, and XIII* (NHS 28) (Leiden: Brill, 1990).

Hegemonius, *Acta Archelai*, ed. C.H. Beeson (GCS 16) (Leipzig: Hinrichs, 1906).

Hennecke, E. and Schneemelcher, W. (ET ed. R. McL. Wilson), *New Testament Apocrypha* (2 vols, London: SCM 1963–5).

Henrichs, A. and Koenen, L., 'Der Kölner Mani-Codex (P. Coln. inv. nr. 4780)', *ZPE* 19 (1975), 1–85; 32 (1978), 87–199; 44 (1981), 201–318; 48 (1982), 1–59.

Hippolytus of Rome, *Refutatio omnium haeresium*, ed. P. Wendland (GCS 26) (Leipzig: Hinrichs, 1916).

Ibn al Nadim, *Fihrist: Mani: Seine Lehre und seine Schriften*, ed. G. Flügel (Leipzig: Brockhaus, 1862).

Irenaeus of Lyons, *Libros quinque adversus haereses*, ed. W. W. Harvey (2 vols, Cambridge, 1857).

Irenaeus of Lyons, *Contre les hérésies 1*, ed. A. Rousseau and L. Doutreleau (SC 263–4) (Paris: Editions du Cerf, 1979).

Janssens, Y., 'L'Apocryphon de Jean', *Le Muséon* 83 (1970), 157–65; 84 (1971), 43–64, 403–32.

Janssens, Y., 'Le Codex XIII de Nag Hammadi', *Le Muséon* 87 (1974), 341–413.

Janssens, Y., *La protennoia trimorphe (NH XIII,1)* (BCNH, Section 'Textes' 4) (Québec: Université Laval, 1978).

Kasser, R., 'Bibliothèque gnostique V: l'Apocalypse d'Adam', *RThPh* 17 (1967), 316–33.

Kasser, R., 'Bibliothèque gnostique I: le livre secret de Jean = *Apokryphon Ioannou*', *RThPh* 14 (1964), 140–50.

Koenen, L. and Römer, C., *Der Kölner Mani Codex* (Papyrologica Coloniensia 14) (Opladen: Westdeutscher, 1988).

Krause, M. and Labib, P., *Die drei Versionen des Apokryphon des Johannes im koptischen Museum zu Alt-Kairo* (ADAIK Koptische Reihe 1) (Wiesbaden: Harrassowitz, 1962).

Krause, M. and Labib, P., *Gnostische und hermetische Schriften aus Codex II und Codex VI* (Glückstadt: Augustin, 1971).

Kropp, A., *Ausgewählte koptische Zaubertexte* (3 vols, Brussels, 1930–1).

Layton, B., *The Gnostic Scriptures* (Garden City: Doubleday, 1987).

Layton, B., 'The Hypostasis of the Archons or the Reality of the Rulers', *HTR* 67 (1974), 351–426; 69 (1976), 31–102.

Leisegang, H., *Die Gnosis* (Stuttgart: Kroner, 1955[4]).

Lipsius, R. A. and Bonnet, M, *Acta Apostolorum Apocrypha* (Darmstadt, 1959).

Ménard, J. E., *L'Évangile selon Philippe* (Strasbourg/Paris: Letouzey & Ane, 1967).

Nagel, P., *Das Wesen der Archonten aus Codex II der gnostischen Bibliothek von Nag Hammadi* (Wissenschaftliche Beiträge der Martin-Luther-Universität Halle-Wittenberg) (Halle, 1970).

Origen of Alexandria, *Contra Celsum*, ed. P. Koetschau (GCS 3) (Leipzig: Hinrichs, 1899).

Origen of Alexandria, *Contra Celsum*, ed. H. Chadwick (Oxford, 1953, 1979).

Parrott, D. M. ed., *Nag Hammadi Codices V,2–5 and VI* (NHS 11) (Leiden: Brill, 1979).

Parrott, D. M. ed., *Nag Hammadi Codices III,3–4 and V,1* (NHS 27) (Leiden: Brill, 1987).

Pearson, B. A. ed., *Nag Hammadi Codices IX and X* (NHS 15) (Leiden: Brill, 1981).

Plato, *Timaeus* in *Plato*, vol. 7, trans. R. G. Bury (LCL) (London/Cambridge, Mass: Heinemann/Harvard University Press, 1961).

Plotinus, *Enneads* in *Plotinus*, vol. 2, trans. A. H. Armstrong (LCL) (London/Cambridge, Mass: Heinemann/Harvard University Press, 1966).

Poimandres of Hermes Trismegistus, *Corpus Hermeticum 1*, ed. A. D. Nock, tr. A. J. Festugière (Paris: Budé, 1945).

Porphyry, *Vita Plotini* in *Plotinus*, vol. 1, trans. A. H. Armstrong (LCL) (London/Cambridge, Mass: Heinemann/Harvard University Press, 1966).

Preuschen, E., 'Die apokryphen gnostischen Adamschriften aus dem Armenischen übersetzt und untersucht' in *Festgruss Bernhard Stade* (Giessen: Ricker, 1900), 163–252.

Pseudo-Tertullian, *Adversus omnes haereses*, ed. A. Kroymann (CSEL 47) (Vienna/Leipzig: Tempsky, 1906).

Robinson, J. M., *The Nag Hammadi Library in English* (Leiden: Brill, 1988³).

Schenke, G., '"Die dreigestaltige Protennoia": Eine gnostische Offenbarungsrede in koptischer Sprache aus dem Funde von Nag Hammadi eingeleitet und übersetzt vom Berliner Arbeitskreis für koptisch-gnostische Schriften', *TLZ* 99 (1974), 731–46.

Schenke, H.-M., 'Das Ägypter-Evangelium aus Nag-Hammadi-Codex III', *NTS* 16 (1969/70), 196–208.

Schmidt, C., *Koptisch-gnostische Schriften 1*, 4th ed. H.-M. Schenke (GCS 45(13)) (Berlin: Akademie, 1981).

Schmidt, C. and MacDermot, V., *Pistis Sophia* (NHS 9) (Leiden: Brill, 1978).

Schmidt, C. and MacDermot, V., *The Books of Jeu and the Untitled Text in the Bruce Codex* (NHS 13) (Leiden: Brill, 1978).

Scott, W. and Ferguson, A. S., *Hermetica* (4 vols, Oxford: Clarendon, 1924–36).

Tardieu, M., *Écrits Gnostiques. Codex de Berlin* (Sources gnostiques et manichéennes 1) (Paris: Editions du Cerf, 1984).

Tertullian of Carthage, *Adversus Valentinianos*, ed. A. Kroymann in *Tertulliani Opera 2* (CCSL 2) (Turnhout: Brepols, 1954).

Theodore bar Konai, *Liber Scholiorum*, ed. A. Scher (CSCO 69) (Louvain, 1960); ed. and trans. H. Pognon, *Inscriptions mandaites des coupes de Khouabir* (Paris: Welter, 1899).

Theodoret of Cyrrhus, *Haereticarum fabularum compendio*, ed. J. P. Migne, Patrologia Graeca 83.

Till, W. C., *Die gnostischen Schriften des koptischen Papyrus Berolinensis 8502* (TU 60, rev. ed. H.-M. Schenke) (Berlin: Akademie, 1972).

Völker, W., *Quellen zur Geschichte der christlichen Gnosis* (Sammlung ausgewählter kirchen- und dogmengeschichtlicher Quellenschriften, Neue Folge 5) (Tübingen, 1932).

Wilson, R. McL., *The Gospel of Philip* (London: Mowbray, 1962).

Zosimus of Panopolis, *On the Letter Omega*, ed. W. Scott and A. S. Ferguson, *Hermetica 4: Testimonia*.

B Secondary literature

Aland, B. ed., *GNOSIS: Festschrift für Hans Jonas* (Göttingen: Vandenhoeck & Ruprecht, 1978).

Arai, S., 'Zur Christologie des Apokryphons des Johannes', *NTS* 15 (1968/69), 302–18.

Barc, B. ed., *Colloque international sur les textes de Nag Hammadi, Québec 22–25 août 1978* (BCNH Section 'Etudes' 1) (Québec: Université Laval/Louvain: Peeters, 1981).

Barc, B., 'Samaël–Saklas–Yaldabaôth: Recherche sur la genèse d'un mythe gnostique' in *Colloque international sur les textes de Nag Hammadi*, ed. Barc, 123–50.

Beltz, W., 'Bemerkungen zur Adamapokalypse aus Nag-Hammadi Codex V' in *Studia Coptica*, ed. Nagel 159–63.

Benko, S., 'The Libertine Gnostic Sect of the Phibionites according to Epiphanius', *VC* 21 (1967), 103–19.

Bergmeier, R., *Glaube als Gabe nach Johannes* (BWANT 112) (Stuttgart/Berlin/Köln/Mainz, 1980).

Bergmeier, R., 'Königlosigkeit als nachvalentinianisch Heilsprädikat', *NovT* 24 (1982), 316–39.

Bianchi, U. ed., *Le origini dello gnosticismo: Colloquio de Messina 13–18 Aprile 1966* (SHR/Supplements to *Numen* 12) (Leiden: Brill, 1967).

Black, M., 'An Aramaic Etymology for Jaldabaoth?' in *The New Testament and Gnosis*, ed. Logan and Wedderburn, 69–72.

326 *Bibliography*

Black, M., *The Scrolls and Christian Origins* (London: Nelson, 1961).
Blackstone, W. J., 'A Short Note on the "Apocryphon Johannis"', *VC* 19 (1965), 163.
Böhlig, A., 'Die Adamapokalypse aus Codex V von Nag Hammadi als Zeugnis jüdisch-iranischen Gnosis', *OC* 48 (1964), 44–9.
Böhlig, A., 'Zum Antimimon Pneuma in den koptisch-gnostischen Texten' in *Mysterion und Wahrheit* 162–74.
Böhlig, A., 'Die himmlische Welt nach dem Ägypterevangelium von Nag Hammadi', *Le Muséon* 80 (1967), 5–25.
Böhlig, A., 'Der jüdische und judenchristliche Hintergrund in gnostischen Texten von Nag Hammadi' in *Le origini dello gnosticismo*, ed. Bianchi, 109–40.
Böhlig, A., *Mysterion und Wahrheit* (AGSJU 6) (Leiden: Brill, 1968).
Böhlig, A., 'Zum "Pluralismus" in den Schriften von Nag Hammadi: die Behandlung des Adamas in den Drei Stelen des Seth und in Ägypterevangelium"', in *Essays on the Nag Hammadi Texts in Honour of Pahor Labib*, ed. Krause (NHS 6) (Leiden: Brill, 1975), 19–34.
Böhlig, A., Review of Giversen, *Apocryphon Johannis, BO* 24 (1967), 175–7.
Böhlig, A., 'Triade und Trinität in den Schriften von Nag Hammadi' in *The Rediscovery of Gnosticism* 2, ed. Layton, 617–34.
Bonner, C., 'An Amulet of the Ophite Gnostics' in *Commemorative Studies in Honor of Leslie Shear* (Hesperia Supplement 8) (Athens, 1949), 43–6.
Bonner, C., *Studies in Magical Amulets* (University of Michigan Studies, Humanistic Series vol. 49) (Ann Arbor, 1950).
Borsch, F. H., *The Christian and Gnostic Son of Man* (SBT second series 14) (London: SCM, 1970).
Bousset, W., *Hauptprobleme der Gnosis* (FRLANT 10) (Göttingen: Vandenhoeck & Ruprecht, 1907).
Bradshaw, P., *The Search for the Origins of Christian Worship* (London: SPCK, 1992).
Broek, R. van den, 'The Authentikos Logos: A New Document of Christian Platonism', *VC* 33 (1979), 260–86.
Broek, R. van den, 'Autogenes and Adamas: The Mythological Structure of the Apocryphon of John' in *Gnosis and Gnosticism*, ed. Krause (NHS 17), 16–25.
Broek, R. van den, 'The Creation of Adam's Psychic Body in the *Apocryphon of John*' in *Studies in Gnosticism and Hellenistic Religions*, ed. van den Broek and Vermaseren, 38–57.

Broek, R. van den, 'Jewish and Platonic Speculations in Early Alexandrian Theology: Eugnostus, Philo, Valentinus and Origen' in *The Roots of Egyptian Christianity*, ed. Pearson and Goehring, 190–203.

Broek, R. van den, 'The Present State of Gnostic Studies', *VC* 37 (1983), 41–71.

Broek, R. van den and Vermaseren, M. J. eds, *Studies in Gnosticism and Hellenistic Religions Presented to Gilles Quispel on the Occasion of his 65th Birthday* (EPRO 91) (Leiden: Brill, 1981).

Brox, N., '*Gnostikoi* als häresiologischer Terminus', *ZNW* 57 (1966), 105–14.

Bultmann, R., *Das Evangelium des Johannes* (Göttingen, 1941, 1962²; ET *The Gospel of John*, tr. G. R. Beasley-Murray, R. W. N. Hoare, J. K. Riches, Oxford: Blackwell, 1971).

Bultmann, R., *Primitive Christianity in its Contemporary Setting* (London: Collins, 1962).

Bultmann, R., *Theology of the New Testament*, 2 vols, tr. K. Grobel (London: SCM, 1952–5).

Burkitt, F. C., *Church and Gnosis* (Cambridge, 1932).

Carroll, S. T., 'The *Apocalypse of Adam* and Pre-Christian Gnosticism', *VC* 44 (1990), 263–79.

Casey, R. P., 'Naassenes and Ophites', *JTS* 27 (1926), 374–87.

Casey, R. P., 'The Study of Gnosticism', *JTS* 36 (1935), 45–60.

Colpe, C., 'Heidnische, jüdische und christliche Über-lieferung in den Schriften aus Nag Hammadi II' JbAC 16 (1973), 106–26; III 17 (1974), 109–25; IV 18 (1975), 144–65; V 19 (1976), 120–38; VI 20 (1977), 149–70; IX 23 (1980), 108–27.

Colpe, C., 'New Testament and Gnostic Christology' in *Religions in Antiquity* (Essays in Memory of E. R. Goodenough), ed. J. Neusner (Leiden: Brill, 1968), 227–43.

Colpe, C., *Die religionsgeschichtliche Schule: Darstellung und Kritik ihres Bildes vom gnostischen Erlösermythus* (FRLANT 60) (Göttingen: Vandenhoeck & Ruprecht, 1961).

Culianu, I. P., 'Feminine versus Masculine. The Sophia Myth and the Origins of Feminism: Struggles of the Gods' in *Papers of the Groningen Work Group for the Study of the History of Religions*, ed. H. G. Kippenberg and H. J. W. Drijvers (Berlin/New York/Amsterdam: Y. Kuiper, 1984), 65–98.

Culianu, I. P., 'La femme céleste et son ombre: Contribution à l'étude d'un mythologème gnostique', *Numen* 23 (1976), 191–209.

Dahl, N. A., 'The Arrogant Archon and the Lewd Sophia: Jewish Traditions in Gnostic Revolt' in *The Rediscovery of Gnosticism 2*, ed. Layton, 689–712.

Daniélou, J., *Théologie du judéochristianisme* (Tournai: Desclée, 1958; ET *The Theology of Jewish Christianity*, tr. J. A. Baker, London: Darton, Longman & Todd, 1964).

Davies, W. D., 'Paul on Flesh and Spirit' in *The Scrolls and the New Testament*, ed. K. Stendahl (London: SCM, 1958), 157–82.

Dix, G., 'Confirmation, or the Laying on of Hands?' (*Theology* Occasional Paper no. 5) (London: SPCK, 1936).

Doresse, J., 'Les Apocalypses de Zoroastre, de Zostrien, de Nicothée . . . (Porphyre, Vie de Plotin, 16)' in *Coptic Studies in Honor of W. E. Crum* (Boston, 1950), 255–63.

Doresse, J., 'Nouveaux textes gnostiques coptes découverts en Haut-Egypte: La bibliothèque de Chenoboskion', *VC* 3 (1949), 130–41.

Doresse, J., *The Secret Books of the Egyptian Gnostics* (London: Hollis and Carter, 1960).

Doresse, J., 'Trois livres gnostiques inédits: Évangile des Egyptiens – Épitre d'Eugnoste – Sagesse de Jésus Christ', *VC* 2 (1948), 137–60.

Drijvers, H. J. W., 'The Origins of Gnosticism as a Religious and Historical Problem', *NedTTs* 22 (1968), 321–51.

Edwards, M. J., 'Gnostics and Valentinians in the Church Fathers', *JTS* n.s. 40 (1989), 26–47.

Edwards, M. J., 'Neglected Texts in the Study of Gnosticism', *JTS* n.s. 41 (1990), 26–50.

Eltester, W. ed., *Christentum und Gnosis* (BZNW 37) (Berlin: Töpelmann, 1969).

Fallon, F. T., *The Enthronement of Sabaoth: Jewish Elements in Gnostic Creation Myths* (NHS 10) (Leiden: Brill, 1978).

Fallon, F. T., 'The Gnostics: The Undominated Race', *NovT* 21 (1979), 271–88.

Fauth, W., 'Seth-Typhon, Onoel und der eselsköpfige Sabaoth: Zur Theriomorphie der ophitisch-barbelognostischen Archonten', *OC* 57 (1973), 79–120.

Filoramo, G., *A History of Gnosticism* (Oxford: Blackwell, 1990).

Fischer-Mueller, E. A., 'Yaldabaoth: The Gnostic Female Principle in its Fallenness', *NovT* 32 (1990), 79–95.

Foerster, W., 'Das Apocryphon des Johannes' in *Gott und die Götter: Festgabe für Erich Fascher zum 60 Geburtstag* (Berlin: Evangelische Verlagsanstalt, 1958), 134–41.

Foerster, W., 'Das System des Basilides', *NTS* 9 (1962/3), 233–55.

Foerster, W., *Von Valentin zu Heracleon* (BZNW 7) (Giessen, 1928).

Frickel, J., 'Naassener oder Valentinianer?' in *Gnosis and Gnosticism*, ed. Krause (NHS 17), 95–119.

Ginzberg, L., 'Die Haggada bei den Kirchenvätern', *MGWJ* (1899/1900), 1–131.

Ginzberg, L., *The Legends of the Jews* (7 vols, Philadelphia, 1909–38).

Giversen, S., 'The Apocryphon of John and Genesis', *ST* 17 (1963), 60–76.

Goehring, J. E., 'A Classical Influence on the Gnostic Sophia Myth', *VC* 35 (1981), 16–23.

Good, D. J., 'Sophia in Valentinianism', *Second Century* 4 (1984), 193–201.

Grant, R. M., 'The Earliest Christian Gnosticism', *CH* 22 (1953), 88–90.

Grant, R. M., *The Early Christian Doctrine of God* (Charlottesville, 1966).

Grant, R. M., *Gnosticism and Early Christianity* (New York: Harper and Row, 1966²).

Grant, R. M., *Gnosticism, An Anthology* (London: Collins, 1961).

Greer, R. A., 'The dog and the mushrooms: Irenaeus' view of the Valentinians reassessed' in *The Rediscovery of Gnosticism 1*, ed. Layton, 146–71.

Haardt, R., 'Das universaleschatologische Vorstellungsgut in der Gnosis' in *Vom Messias zum Christos: Die Fülle der Zeit in religionsgeschichtlicher und theologischer Sicht*, ed. K. Schubert (Vienna, 1964), 315–36.

Haenchen, E., 'Aufbau und Theologie des Poimandres', *ZTK* 53 (1956), 170–91.

Haenchen, E., 'Gab es eine vorchristliche Gnosis?', *ZTK* 49 (1952), 316–49.

Harnack, A von, *Lehrbuch der Dogmengeschichte 1* (Freiburg/Leipzig, 1894³; ET *History of Dogma*, tr. N. Buchanan, London: Williams and Norgate, 1905).

Hauschild, W.-D., *Gottes Geist und der Mensch* (Munich: Kaiser, 1972).

Hedrick, C.W., 'The Apocalypse of Adam: A Literary and Source Analysis' in *SBL 1972 Proceedings* vol. 2, ed. L. C. McGaughy (Los Angeles: SBL, 1972), 581–90.

Hedrick, C. W., 'Christian Motifs in the *Gospel of the Egyptians*; Method and Motive', *NovT* 23 (1981), 242–60.

Hedrick, C. W. and Hodgson, R. eds, *Nag Hammadi, Gnosticism and Early Christianity* (Peabody, Mass.: Hendrickson, 1986).

Helmbold, A. K., 'The Apocryphon of John', *JNES* 25 (1966), 259–72.

Helmbold, A. K., 'The *Apocryphon of John*: A Case Study in Literary Criticism', *JETS* 13 (1970), 173–9.

Hilgenfeld, A., *Die Ketzergeschichte des Urchristentums* (Leipzig: Fues, 1884).

Hyatt, J. P. ed., *The Bible in Modern Scholarship* (Nashville: Abingdon, 1965).

Jackson, H. M., 'Geradamas, the Celestial Stranger', *NTS* 27 (1980/1), 385–94.

Jackson, H. M., 'The Origin in Ancient Incantatory *Voces Magicae* of Some of the Names in the Sethian Gnostic System', *VC* 43 (1989), 69–79.

Janssens, Y., 'Le thème de la fornication des anges' in *Le origini dello gnosticismo*, ed. Bianchi, 488–94.

Jervell, J., *Imago Dei: Gen. 1:26 in Spätjudentum, in der Gnosis und in den paulinischen Briefen* (FRLANT 76) (Göttingen: Vandenhoeck & Ruprecht, 1960).

Jonas, H., *Gnosis und spätantiker Geist I & II* (FRLANT 159) (Göttingen: Vandenhoeck & Ruprecht, 1993).

Jonas, H., *The Gnostic Religion* (rev. ed., Boston: Beacon, 1963; 1970³).

Jonas, H., 'The Secret Books of the Egyptian Gnostics', *JR* 42 (1962), 262–73.

Kasser, R., 'Citations des grands prophètes bibliques dans les textes gnostiques coptes' in *Essays on the Nag Hammadi Texts in Honour of Pahor Labib* (NHS 6), ed. M. Krause (Leiden: Brill, 1975), 59–66.

Kasser, R., 'Le "livre secret de Jean" dans ses différentes formes textuelles coptes', *Le Muséon* 77 (1964), 5–16.

Kasser, R., 'Textes gnostiques: Remarques à propos des Éditions récentes du livre secret de Jean et des Apocalypses de Paul, Jacques et Adam', *Le Muséon* 78 (1965), 91–8.

Kelly, J. N. D., *Early Christian Doctrines* (5th ed., London: A & C Black, 1977).

King, K. L. ed., *Images of the Feminine in Gnosticism* (SAC 4) (Philadelphia: Fortress, 1985).

King, K. L., 'Sophia and Christ in the *Apocryphon of John*' in *Images of the Feminine in Gnosticism*, ed. King, 158–76.

Klijn, A. F. J., *Seth in Jewish, Christian and Gnostic Literature* (Supplements to *NovT* 46) (Leiden: Brill, 1977).

Kragerud, A., 'Apocryphon Johannis: En formanalyse', *NorTT* 66 (1965), 15–38.

Krause, M. ed., *Gnosis and Gnosticism* (NHS 8) (Leiden: Brill, 1977).

Krause, M. ed., *Gnosis and Gnosticism* (NHS 17) (Leiden: Brill, 1981).

Krause, M., 'Das literarische Verhältnis des Eugnostosbriefes zur Sophia Jesu Christi: zur Auseinandersetzung der Gnosis mit dem Christentum' in *Mullus: Festschrift Theodor Klauser* (JbAC Ergänzungsband 1) (Münster: Aschendorff, 1964), 215–23.

Krause,. M., 'Der Stand der Veröffentlichung der Nag Hammadi-Texte' in *Le origini dello gnosticismo*, ed. Bianchi, 61–89.

Lampe, G. W. H., *The Seal of the Spirit* (London: SPCK, 1967[2]).

Layton, B., *The Rediscovery of Gnosticism: Proceedings of the International Conference at Yale, New Haven, Connecticut March 28–31, 1978* vol. 1, *The School of Valentinus*; vol. 2, *Sethian Gnosticism* (SHR 41) (Leiden: Brill, 1980–1).

Leeper, E. A., 'From Alexandria to Rome: The Valentinian Connection to the Incorporation of Exorcism as a Pre-baptismal Rite', *VC* 44 (1990), 6–24.

Leipoldt, J. and Gressmann, W. eds, *Umwelt des Urchristentums I* (Berlin, 1971[3]).

Lipsius, R. A., *Der Gnosticismus, sein Wesen, Ursprung und Entwickelungsgang* (Leipzig, 1860).

Lipsius, R. A., *Die Quellen der aeltesten Ketzergeschichte neu untersucht* (Leipzig, 1875).

Lipsius, R. A., *Zur Quellenkritik des Epiphanios* (Leipzig, 1865).

Logan, A. H. B., 'The Epistle of Eugnostos and Valentinianism' in *Gnosis and Gnosticism*, ed. Krause (NHS 17), 66–75.

Logan, A. H. B., 'The Jealousy of God: Exod 20:5 in Gnostic and Rabbinic Theology' in *Studia Biblica 1978*, 1: Papers on Old Testament and Related Themes (*JSOT* Supplement Series 11) (Sheffield: Sheffield Academic Press, 1979), 197–203.

Logan, A. H. B., 'John and the Gnostics: The Significance of the Apocryphon John for the Debate about the Origins of the Johannine Literature', *JSNT* 43 (1991), 41–69.

Logan, A. H. B. and Wedderburn, A. J. M. eds, *The New Testament and Gnosis: Essays in Honour of Robert McL. Wilson* (Edinburgh: T & T Clark, 1983).

Longenecker, R. M. and Tenney, M. C. eds, *New Dimensions in New Testament Study* (Grand Rapids: Eerdmans, 1974).

MacRae, G. W., 'The Apocalypse of Adam Reconsidered' in *SBL 1972 Proceedings: Seminar Papers* (Missoula, Mont.: Scholars Press, 1972), 573–7.

MacRae, G. W., 'Apocalyptic Eschatology in Gnosticism' in *Apocalypticism in the Mediterranean World and the Near East: Proceedings of the International Colloquium on Apocalypticism, Uppsala, August 12–17, 1979*, ed. D. Hellholm (Tübingen: J. C. B. Mohr (Paul Siebeck), 1983), 317–25.

MacRae, G. W., 'The Coptic Gnostic Apocalypse of Adam', *The Heythrop Journal* 6 (1965), 27–35.

MacRae, G. W., 'Discourses of the Gnostic Revealer' in *Proceedings of the International Colloquium on Gnosticism, Stockholm, August 20–25 1973*, ed. G. Widengren (Stockholm: Almqvist and Wiksell/Leiden: Brill, 1977), 111–24.

MacRae, G. W., 'The Ego Proclamation in Gnostic Sources' in *The Trial of Jesus: Cambridge Studies in Honour of C. F. D. Moule*, ed. E. Bammel (SBT second series 13) (London: SCM, 1970), 129–34.

MacRae, G. W., 'The Jewish Background of the Gnostic Sophia Myth', *NovT* 12 (1970), 86–101.

MacRae, G. W., 'Seth in Gnostic Texts and Traditions' in *SBL 1977 Seminar Papers*, ed. P. J. Achtemeier (Missoula, Mont.: Scholars Press, 1977), 17–24.

MacRae, G. W., 'Sleep and Awakening in Gnostic Texts' in *Le origini dello gnosticismo*, ed. Bianchi, 496–507.

McGuire, A., 'Virginity and Subversion: Norea Against the Powers in the *Hypostasis of the Archons*' in *Images of the Feminine in Gnosticism*, ed. King, 239–58.

Markschies, C., *Valentinus Gnosticus? Untersuchungen zur valentinianischen Gnosis mit einem Kommentar zu den Fragmenten Valentins* (WUNT 65) (Tübingen: Mohr/Siebeck, 1992).

Ménard, J. E. ed., *Les textes de Nag Hammadi. Colloque du Centre d'Histoire des Religions, Strasburg, 23–25 octobre 1974* (NHS 7) (Leiden: Brill, 1975).

Meyer, M. W., 'A Response to Prouneikos' in *Images of the Feminine in Gnosticism*, ed. King, 67–70.

Mina, T., 'Le papyrus gnostique du Musée Copte', *VC* 2 (1948), 129–36.

Mitchell, L. L., *Baptismal Anointing* (Alcuin Club Collections no. 48) (London: SPCK, 1966).

Morard, F., 'L'Apocalypse d'Adam du Codex V de Nag Hammadi et sa polémique anti-baptismale', *RevScRel* 51 (1977), 214–33.

Nagel, P. ed., *Studia Coptica* (BBA 45) (Berlin: Akademie, 1974).

Nilsson, M. P., 'Sophia-Prunikos', *Eranos* (APS) 45 (1947), 169–72.

Orbe, A., *Hacia la Primera Theologia de la Procesión del Verbo: Estudianos Valentinianos 1* (AG 99) (Rome, 1958).

Orbe, A., 'Sophia Soror' in *Mélanges d'histoire des religions offerts à H.-Ch. Puech* (Paris: Presses Universitaires de France, 1974), 355–63.

Orbe, A., *La Unción del Verbo: Estudianos Valentinianos 3* (AG 113) (Rome, 1961).

Pagels, E., 'Conflicting Versions of Valentinian Eschatology: Irenaeus' Treatises vs. the Excerpts from Theodotus', *HTR* 67 (1974), 35–53.

Pagels, E., 'The Valentinian Claim to Esoteric Exegesis of Romans as Basis for Anthropological Theory', *VC* 26 (1972), 241–58.

Parrott, D. M., 'The Thirteen Kingdoms of the Apocalypse of Adam: Origin, Meaning and Significance', *NovT* 31 (1989), 67–87.

Pasquier, A., 'Prouneikos. A Colorful Expression to Designate Wisdom in Gnostic Texts' in *Images of the Feminine in Gnosticism*, ed. King, 47–66.

Pearson, B. A., 'Egyptian Seth and Gnostic Seth' in *SBL 1977 Seminar Papers*, ed. Achtemeier, 25–43.

Pearson, B. A., 'The Figure of Seth in Gnostic Literature' in *Gnosticism, Judaism, and Egyptian Christianity*, ed. Pearson, 52–83.

Pearson, B. A., 'Gnosticism as Platonism' in *Gnosticism, Judaism, and Egyptian Christianity*, ed. Pearson, 148–64.

Pearson, B. A., *Gnosticism, Judaism, and Egyptian Christianity* (SAC 5) (Minneapolis: Fortress, 1990).

Pearson, B. A., 'Jewish Haggadic Traditions in the Testimony of Truth from Nag Hammadi' in *Ex Orbe Religionum 1* (SHR 21) (Leiden: Brill, 1972), 457–70.

Pearson, B. A., 'Revisiting Norea' in *Images of the Feminine in Gnosticism*, ed. King, 265–75.

Pearson, B.A., '"She Became a Tree" – A Note to CG II,4:89, 25–6', *HTR* 69 (1976), 413–15.

Pearson, B. A., 'The Tractate Marsanes (NHC X) and the Platonic Tradition' in *GNOSIS*, ed. Aland, 373–84.

Pearson, B. A. and Goehring, J. E. eds, *The Roots of Egyptian Christianity* (SAC 1) (Philadelphia: Fortress, 1986).

Peel, M. L., 'Gnostic Eschatology and the New Testament', *NovT* 12 (1970), 141–65.

Perkins, P., 'Apocalypse of Adam: Genre and Function of a Gnostic Apocalypse', *CBQ* 39 (1977), 382–95.

Perkins, P., 'Apocalyptic Schematization in the Apocalypse of Adam and the Gospel of the Egyptians' in *SBL 1972 Proceedings: Seminar Papers* vol. 2 (Missoula, Mont.: Scholars Press, 1972), 591–5.

Perkins, P., 'Gnostic Christologies and the New Testament', *CBQ* 43 (1981), 590–606.

Perkins, P., *Gnosticism and the New Testament* (Minneapolis: Fortress, 1993).

Perkins, P., 'Ireneus and the Gnostics', *VC* 30 (1976), 193–200.

Perkins, P., 'Logos Christologies in the Nag Hammadi Codices', *VC* 35 (1981), 379–96.

Perkins, P., 'On the Origin of the World (CG II,5): A Gnostic Physics', *VC* 34 (1980), 36–46.

Perkins, P., 'Sophia as Goddess in the Nag Hammadi Codices' in *Images of the Feminine in Gnosticism*, ed. King, 96–112.

Peterson, E., 'Einige Bemerkungen zum Hamburger Papyrusfragment der Acta Pauli', *VC* 3 (1949), 149–59.

Pétrement, S., *Le Dieu séparé: les origines du gnosticisme* (Paris: Editions du Cerf, 1984; ET *A Separate God*, tr. C. Harrison, London: Darton, Longman & Todd, 1991).

Pétrement, S., *Le dualisme chez Platon, les gnostiques et les manichéens* (Paris, 1947).

Pétrement, S., 'Les quatre illuminateurs. Sur le sens de l'origine d'un thème gnostique', *REA* 27 (1981), 3–23.

Poirier, P.-H. and Tardieu, M., 'Catégories du temps dans les écrits gnostiques non-valentiniens', *LTP* 37 (1981), 3–13.

Pokorny, P., 'Epheserbrief und gnostische Mysterien', *ZNW* 53 (1962), 160–94.

Prigent, P., *Justin et l'Ancien Testament* (Paris: Gabalda, 1964).

Puech, H.-C., *En quête de la gnose 1: La gnose et le temps* (Paris: Gallimard, 1978).

Puech, H.-C., 'Fragments retrouvées de l'Apocalypse d'Allogène' in *Mélanges Franz Cumont 2* (Brussels, 1936), 938–62 (= *En quête 1* 271–300).

Puech, H.-C., 'Les nouveaux écrits gnostiques découverts en Haut-Egypte' in *Coptic Studies in Honor of W. E. Crum* (Bulletin of the Byzantine Institute 2) (Boston, 1950), 91–134.

Quispel, G., 'La conception de l'homme dans la gnose valentinienne', *Eranos Jahrbuch* 15 (1947), 249–86 (= *Gnostic Studies 1* 37–57).

Quispel, G., 'L'inscription de Flavia Sophe' in *Mélanges Joseph Ghellinck, S.J.* (Museum Lessianum-Section Historique 13), 201–14 (= *Gnostic Studies 1* 58–69).

Quispel, G., 'The Demiurge in the Apocryphon of John' in *Nag Hammadi and Gnosis*, ed. R. McL. Wilson (NHS 14) (Leiden: Brill, 1978), 1–33.

Quispel, G., 'Ezekiel 1:26 in Jewish Mysticism and Gnosis', *VC* 34 (1980), 1–13.

Quispel, G., *Gnosis als Weltreligion* (Zürich, 1972²).

Quispel, G., *Gnostic Studies*, 2 vols (Istanbul, 1974–5).

Quispel, G., 'Der gnostische Anthropos und die jüdische Tradition', *Eranos Jahrbuch* 22 (1953) (Zürich, 1954), 195–234 (= *Gnostic Studies 1* 173–95).

Quispel, G., 'Origen and the Valentinian Gnosis', *VC* 28 (1974), 29–42.

Quispel, G., 'The Original Doctrine of Valentine', *VC* 1 (1947), 43–73.

Reitzenstein, R., *Das iranische Erlösungsmysterium* (Bonn, 1921).

Reitzenstein, R., *Poimandres* (Leipzig: Teubner, 1904).

Robinson, J. M. 'The Coptic Gnostic Library Today', *NTS* 14 (1967/8), 365–401.

Robinson, J. M., 'The discovery of the Nag Hammadi codices', *BA* 42 (1979), 206–24.

Robinson. J. M., 'From Cliff to Cairo' in *Colloque international sur les textes de Nag Hammadi*, ed. Barc, 21–58.

Robinson, J. M., 'The Three Steles of Seth and the Gnostics of Plotinus' in *Proceedings of the International Colloquium on Gnosticism*, ed.Widengren, 132–42.

Robinson, J. M. and Koester, H., *Trajectories through Early Christianity* (Philadelphia: Fortress, 1971).

Rudolph, K., 'Gnosis und Gnostizismus, eine Forschungsbericht', *TRu* 34 (1969), 121–75; 181–231; 358–61; 36 (1971), 1–61.

Rudolph, K., *Die Gnosis: Wesen und Geschichte einer spätantike Religion* (Leipzig: Koehler and Amelang, 1977; ET *Gnosis*, tr. R. McL. Wilson et al., Edinburgh: T & T Clark, 1984).

Rudolph, K., 'Der gnostische 'Dialog' als literarisches Genus' in *Probleme der koptischen Literatur*, ed. P. Nagel (Wissenschaftliche Beiträge der Martin-Luther-Universität Halle-Wittenberg 1) (Halle, 1968), 85–107.

Rudolph, K., 'Ein Grundtyp gnostischer Urmensch Spekulation', *ZRGG* 9 (1957), 1–20.

Sagnard, F.-M.-M., *La gnose valentinienne et le témoignage de S. Irénée* (Paris, 1947).

Schenke, H.-M., *Der Gott 'Mensch' in der Gnosis: Ein religionsgeschichtlicher Beitrag zur Diskussion über die paulinische Anschauung von der Kirche als Leib Christi* (Göttingen: Vandenhoeck & Ruprecht, 1962).

Schenke, H.-M., 'Nag-Hamadi-Studien I: Das literarische Problem des Apokryphon Johannis', *ZRGG* 14 (1962), 57–63; 'Nag-Hamadi-Studien II: Das System der Sophia Jesu Christi', ib., 263–78; 'Nag-Hamadi-Studien III: Die Spitze des dem Apokryphon Johannis und der Sophia Jesu Christi zugrundeliegenden gnostischen Systems', ib., 352–61.

Schenke, H.-M., 'Die neutestamentliche Christologie und der gnostische Erlöser' in *Gnosis und Neues Testament*, ed. Tröger, 205–25.

Schenke, H.-M., 'Das sethianische System nach Nag-Hammadi Schriften' in *Studia Coptica*, ed. Nagel, 165–73.

Schenke, H.-M., 'The Phenomenon and Significance of Gnostic Sethianism' in *The Rediscovery of Gnosticism 2*, ed. Layton, 588–616.

Schmidt, C., 'Irenäus und seine Quelle in adv. haer. I 29' in *Philotesia. Paul Kleinert zum 70 Geburtstag dargebracht*, ed. A. Harnack et al. (Berlin: Trowzisch, 1907), 317–36.

Schmidt, C., *Plotins Stellung zum Gnostizismus und kirchlichen Christentum* (TU 20) (Leipzig: Hinrichs, 1901).

Schmidt, C., 'Ein vorirenäisches gnostisches Originalwerk in koptischen Sprache', Sitzungsberichte der kgl. preussischen Akademie der Wissenschaften (Berlin, 1896), 839–47.

Schmithals, W., *Gnosticism in Corinth*, tr. J. E. Steely (Nashville: Abingdon, 1971).

Scholem, G., 'Jaldabaoth Reconsidered' in *Mélanges d'histoire des religions offerts à H.-Ch. Puech*, ed. A. Guillaumont and E.-M. Laperrousaz (Paris: Presses Universitaires de France, 1974), 405–21.

Scholem, G., 'Die Vorstellung von Golem in ihrem tellurischen und magischen Beziehungen', *Eranos Jahrbuch* 22 (1953) (Zürich, 1954), 237–43.

Scholer, D. M., *Nag Hammadi Bibliography 1948–1969* (NHS 1) (Leiden: Brill, 1971).

Scholten, C., *Martyrium und Sophiamythos im Gnostizismus nach den Texten von Nag Hammadi* (JbAC Ergänzungsband 14) (Münster: Aschendorff, 1987).

Schottroff, L., 'Animae naturaliter salvandae: zum Problem der himmlischen Herkunft des Gnostikers' in *Christentum und Gnosis*, ed. Eltester, 65–97.

Schottroff, L., *Der Glaubende und die feindliche Welt* (WMANT 37) (Neukirchen-Vluyn: Neukirchner Verlag, 1970).

Schottroff, L., 'Heil als innerweltliche Entweltlichung: Der gnostische Hintergrund der johanneischen Vorstellung vom Zeitpunkt der Erlösung', *NovT* 11 (1969), 294–317.

Schweizer, E., 'Gegenwart des Geistes und eschatologische Hoffnung bei Zarathustra, spätjudischen Gruppen, Gnostikern und den Zeugen des neuen Testaments' in *The Background to the New Testament and its Eschatology* (Studies in honour of C. H. Dodd) (Cambridge, 1956), 482–508.

Scopello, M., 'The Apocalypse of Zostrianos (NH VIII,1) and the Book of the Secrets of Enoch' *VC* 34 (1980), 376–85.

Scopello, M., 'Le mythe de la chute de anges dans l'Apocryphon de Jean (II,¹) de Nag Hammadi', *RevScRel* 54 (1980), 220–30.

Scopello, M., 'Youel et Barbelo dans le traité de l'*Allogène*' in *Colloque international sur les textes de Nag Hammadi*, ed. Barc, 374–82.

Segal, A. F., *Two Powers in Heaven: Early Rabbinic Reports about Christianity and Gnosticism* (SJLA 25) (Leiden: Brill, 1978).

Segelberg, E. 'The Baptismal Rite according to Some of the Coptic–Gnostic Texts of Nag Hammadi' in *Studia Patristica* 5, ed. F. L. Cross (Berlin: Akademie, 1962), 117–28.

Sevrin, J.-M., *Le dossier baptismal Séthien: Études sur la sacramentaire gnostique* (BCNH Section 'Études' 2) (Québec: Université Laval, 1986).

Shellrude, G. M., 'The Apocalypse of Adam: Evidence for a Christian Gnostic Provenance' in *Gnosis and Gnosticism*, ed. Krause (NHS 17), 82–91.

Sieber, J. H., 'An Introduction to the Tractate Zostrianos from Nag Hammadi', *NovT* 15 (1973), 235–40.

Smith, M., 'The History of the term Gnostikos' in *The Rediscovery of Gnosticism 2*, ed. Layton, 796–807.

Stead, G. C., 'The Valentinian Myth of Sophia', *JTS* n.s. 20 (1969), 75–104.

Stroumsa, G. A. G., *Another Seed: Studies in Gnostic Mythology* (NHS 24) (Leiden: Brill, 1984).

Stroumsa, G. A. G., 'Form(s) of God: Some Notes on Metatron and Christ', *HTR* 76 (1983), 269–88.

Stroumsa, G. A. G., 'Polymorphie divine et transformation d'un mythologème: l'*Apocryphon de Jean* et ses sources', *VC* 35 (1981), 412–34.

Tardieu, M., 'Les livres mis sous le nom de Seth et les Séthiens de l'hérésiologie' in *Gnosis and Gnosticism*, ed. Krause (NHS 8), 204–10.

Tardieu, M., '*Psychaios spinther*. Histoire d'une métaphore dans la tradition platonicienne jusqu'à Eckhart', *REA* 21 (1975), 225–55.

Tardieu, M., *Trois mythes gnostiques: Adam, Eros et les animaux d'Égypte dans un écrit de Nag Hammadi (II,5)* (Paris: Études Augustiniennes, 1974).

Tardieu, M., 'Les trois stèles de Seth: un écrit gnostique retrouvé à Nag Hammadi', *RSPT* 57 (1973), 545–75.

Tardieu, M. and Dubois, J.-D., *Introduction à la littérature Gnostique 1* (Paris: Editions du Cerf/Editions du CNRS, 1986).

Thornton, L. S., *Confirmation: its place in the baptismal mystery* (London: Dacre, 1954).

Till, W. C., 'Die Gnosis in Ägypten', *PP* 12 (1949), 233–8.

Till, W. C., 'The Gnostic Apocryphon of John', *JEH* 3 (1952), 14–22.

Tripp, D. H., 'The Sacramental System of the Gospel of Philip' in *Studia Patristica* 17/1, ed. E. A. Livingstone (Oxford: Pergamon, 1982), 251–60.

Tröger, K.-W. ed., *Altes Testament – Frühjudentum – Gnosis: Neue Studien zu 'Gnosis und Bibel'* (Berlin: Evangelische Verlagsanstalt, 1980).

Tröger, K.-W. ed., *Gnosis und Neues Testament: Studien aus Religionswissenschaft und Theologie* (Berlin: Evangelische Verlagsanstalt, 1973).

Turner, J. D., 'The Gnostic Threefold Path to Enlightenment: The Ascent of Mind and the Descent of Wisdom', *NovT* 22 (1980), 324–51.

Turner, J. D., 'Sethian Gnosticism: A Literary History' in *Nag Hammadi, Gnosticism and Early Christianity*, ed. Hedrick and Hodgson, 55–86.

Unnik, W. C. van, 'Die "geöffneten Himmel" in der Offenbarungsvision des Apokryphons des Johannes' in *Apophoreta: Festschrift Ernst Haenchen* (BZNW 30) (Berlin: Töpelmann, 1964), 269–80.

Unnik, W. C. van, 'Gnosis und Judentum' in *GNOSIS*, ed. Aland, 65–86.

Unnik, W. C. van, 'Die Gotteslehre bei Aristides und in gnostischen Schriften', *TZ* 17 (1961), 166–74.

Unnik, W. C. van, 'Der Neid in der Paradiesgeschichte nach einigen gnostischen Texten' in *Essays on the Nag Hammadi Texts in Honour of Alexander Böhlig*, ed. M. Krause (NHS 3) (Leiden: Brill, 1972), 120–32.

Unnik, W. C. van, *Newly Discovered Gnostic Writings* (SBT 30) (London: SCM, 1960).

Vielhauer, P., '*ANAPAUSIS*: zum gnostischen Hintergrund des Thomasevangeliums' in *Apophoreta: Festschrift Ernst Haenchen* (BZNW 30) (Berlin: Töpelmann, 1964), 281–99.

Wedderburn, A. J. M., 'Philo's Heavenly Man', *NovT* 15 (1973), 301–26.

Welburn, A. J., 'The Identity of the Archons in the "Apocryphon Johannis"', *VC* 32 (1978), 241–54.

Welburn, A. J., 'Reconstructing the Ophite Diagram', *NovT* 23 (1981), 261–87.

Werner A., 'Bemerkungen zu einer Synopse der vier Versionen des Apokryphon des Johannes' in *Studia Coptica*, ed. Nagel, 137–46.

Whittaker, J., 'Self-Generating Principles in Second Century Gnostic Systems' in *The Rediscovery of Gnosticism 1*, ed. Layton, 176–89.

Widengren, G. ed., *Proceedings of the International Colloquium on Gnosticism, Stockholm, August 20–25, 1973* (Stockholm: Almqvist & Wiksell, 1977).

Williams, M. A., *The Immovable Race: A Gnostic Designation and the Theme of Stability in Late Antiquity* (NHS 29) (Leiden: Brill, 1985).

Williams, M. A., 'Stability as a Soteriological Theme in Gnosticism' in *The Rediscovery of Gnosticism 2*, ed. Layton, 819–29.

Wilson, R. McL., 'The Early History of the Exegesis of Gen. 1:26' in *Studia Patristica* 1, ed. K. Aland and F. L. Cross (TU 63) (Berlin: Akademie, 1957), 420–37.

Wilson, R. McL., *Gnosis and the New Testament* (Oxford, 1968).

Wilson, R. McL., *The Gnostic Problem* (London: Mowbray, 1958).

Wilson, R. McL., 'The Spirit in Gnostic Literature' in *Christ and the Spirit in the New Testament*, ed. B. Lindars and S. Smalley (Cambridge, 1973), 345–55.

Wilson, R. McL., 'The Trials of a Translator: Some Translation Problems in the Nag Hammadi Texts' in *Les textes de Nag Hammadi*, ed. Ménard (NHS 7) (Leiden: Brill, 1975), 32–40.

Wilson, R. McL., 'The *Trimorphic Protennoia*' in *Gnosis and Gnosticism*, ed. Krause (NHS 8), 50–4.

Wilson, R. McL., 'Twenty Years After' in *Colloque international sur les textes de Nag Hammadi*, ed. Barc, 59–67.

Wintermute, O., 'A Study of Gnostic Exegesis of the Old Testament' in *The Use of the Old Testament in the New and Other Essays. Studies in Honor of William Franklin Stinespring*, ed. J. M. Efird (Durham: Duke University Press, 1972), 241–70.

Wisse, F., 'The Nag Hammadi Library and the Heresiologists', *VC* 25 (1971), 205–23.

Wisse, F., 'The Redeemer Figure in the Paraphrase of Shem', *NovT* 12 (1970), 130–40.

Wisse, F., 'The Sethians and the Nag Hammadi Library', in *SBL 1972 Proceedings: Seminar Papers* (Missoula, Mont.: Scholars Press, 1972), 601–7.

Wisse, F., 'Stalking Those Elusive Sethians' in *The Rediscovery of Gnosticism 2*, ed. Layton, 563–76.

Yamauchi, E. M., 'Jewish Gnosticism? The Prologue of John, Mandaean Parallels, and the Trimorphic Protennoia' in *Studies in Gnosticism and Hellenistic Religions*, ed. van den Broek and Vermaseren, 467–97.

Yamauchi, E. M., *Pre-Christian Gnosticism: A Survey of the Proposed Evidence* (London: Tyndale Press, 1973).

Yamauchi, E. M., 'Pre-Christian Gnosticism in the Nag Hammadi Texts', *CH* 48 (1979), 129–41.

Yamauchi, E. M., 'Some Alleged Evidences for Pre-Christian Gnosticism' in *New Dimensions in New Testament Study*, ed. Longenecker and Tenney, 46–70.

Zaehner, R. C. *Zurvan: A Zoroastrian Dilemma* (Oxford, 1955).

Zandee, J., 'Gnostic Ideas on the Fall and Salvation' *Numen* 11 (1964), 13–74.

Zandee, J., 'Gnostische Eschatologie' in *X Internationaler Kongress für Religionsgeschichte 11–17 September 1960 in Marburg* (Marburg, 1961), 94–5.

Index of Names

Modern Authors

341

Ancient Authors

Index of Ancient Sources

Biblical Books (with Apocrypha)